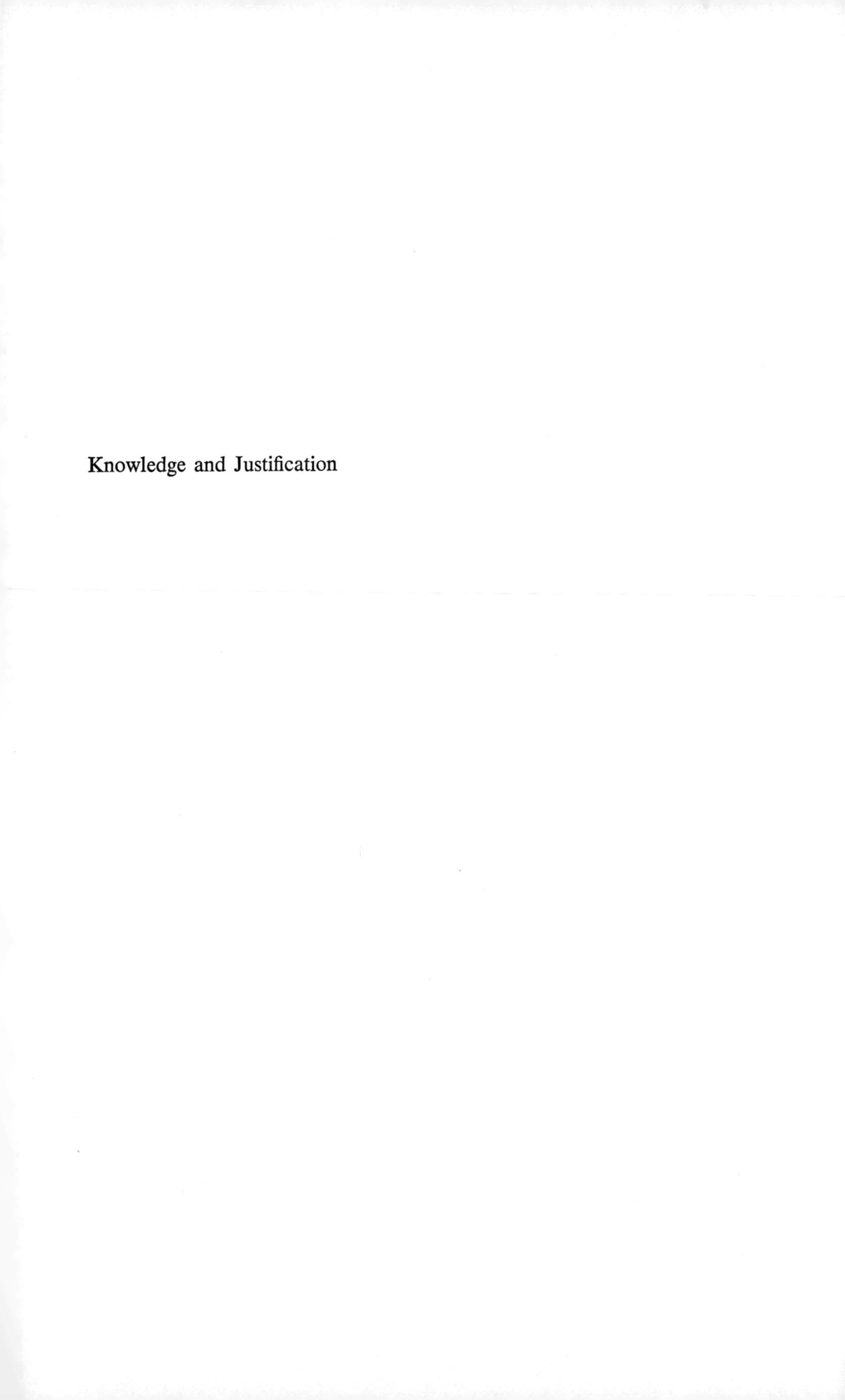

Knowledge and Justification

Knowledge and Justification

John L. Pollock

Princeton University Press PRINCETON, NEW JERSEY

Published by Princeton University Press
Princeton and London

Library of Congress Cataloging in Publication Data
will be found on the last printed page of this book

Printed in the UNITED STATES OF AMERICA by
Princeton University Press, Princeton, New Jersey

To

HERBERT FEIGL

who introduced me
to philosophy

Preface

ONE of the most firmly entrenched beliefs of contemporary philosophy is that the only way to analyze a concept is to state its truth conditions. In epistemology this has led to the search for reductive analyses. These are analyses that state the truth conditions of concepts in terms of the grounds we employ in ascribing the concepts to things. Thus we are led to phenomenalism and behaviorism, and their analogues in other areas of knowledge. But these attempts at reductive analysis have invariably failed, leaving epistemology shipwrecked on the shoals of a barren theory of conceptual analysis. The purpose of this book is to defend an alternative theory of conceptual analysis according to which concepts can be analyzed in terms of their justification conditions rather than their truth conditions. The first two chapters provide a theoretical justification for this alternative scheme of analysis, but the strongest possible argument in its favor must consist of actually carrying out the proposed analyses. Accordingly, the remaining chapters attempt to provide the analyses for a number of epistemologically problematic concepts, and in so doing solve a number of traditional epistemological problems. Only the reader can judge how successful this attempt has been.

The epistemological theory I am concerned to defend has historical antecedents, although they are surprisingly meager. The one area in which it has been pursued vigorously is the philosophy of mind. In that area it is represented by the "criteriological theory" apparently stemming from Wittgenstein and further developed by Malcolm, Strawson, Shoemaker, and others. My position is also suggested by some of Carnap's remarks on the logical concept of probability, although the connection is rather tenuous. The only philosopher who has seriously defended this sort of view across a wide spectrum of philosophical problems is Roderick Chisholm, and I am probably closer to him than to any other philosopher.

A terminological matter should be raised here. Being an unrepentant Platonist, I make free use of the terms "concept" and "proposition". I also tend to use the term "statement" interchangeably with "proposition". Some philosophers may be put off by this Platonistic terminology. However, in the first nine chapters of the book, that is all it is—terminology. A philosopher who prefers words and sentences to concepts and propositions can translate my proclamations into his terminology without loss. It is only in the final chapter that the Platonistic terminology gains substance. In that chapter I argue explicitly for a Platonistic view of concepts and propositions and argue that, contrary to popular opinion, conceptual analysis is not about language. The contemporary view that all we are doing in philosophy is analyzing language is a myth.

Many parts of this book have grown out of journal articles. The entire book can be regarded as growing out of my article "Criteria and Our Knowledge of the Material World". Chapter 1 is a minor revision of "What Is an Epistemological Problem?". Chapter 2 contains material from "Perceptual Knowledge" and greatly revised material from "The Structure of Epistemic Justification". Chapters 3 and 4 are taken, with minor revision, from "Perceptual Knowledge". Some of the material in chapter 8 comes from "The Logic of Projectibility". Part of chapter 10 grows out of "Mathematical Proof".

I am indebted to The Research Foundation of the State of New York for three summer fellowships which helped considerably in the early stages of writing this book, and to The American Council of Learned Societies for a fellowship for the spring and summer of 1972 which allowed me to bring the book to completion. I am also indebted more than I can say to my colleagues, friends, and students for helpful comments and criticism along the way. I am particularly indebted to Rolf Eberle, Keith Lehrer, and John Turk Saunders.

JOHN L. POLLOCK

Rochester, New York
November 1972

Contents

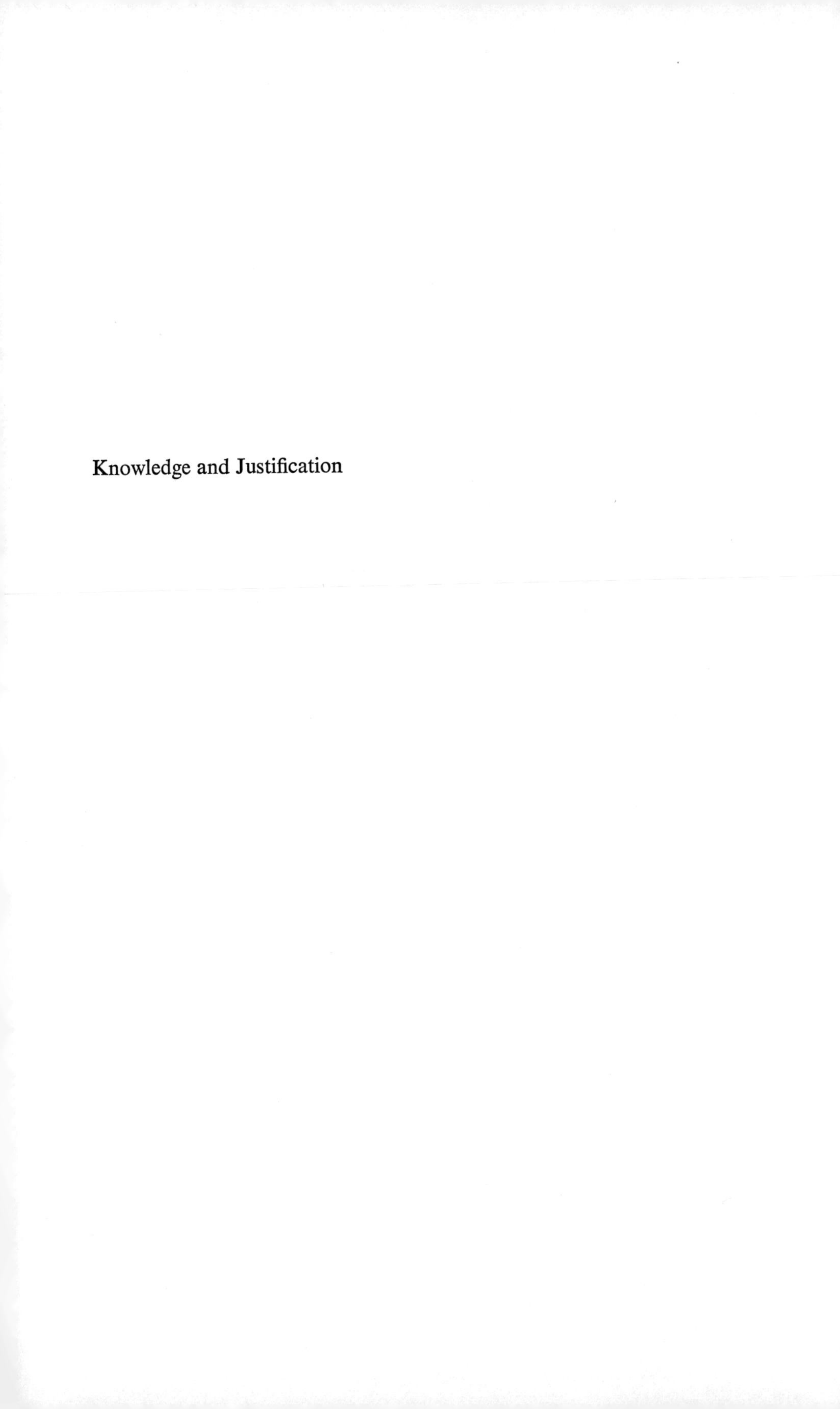

Knowledge and Justification

Chapter One

What Is an Epistemological Problem?

1. The Fundamental Problem of Epistemology

LET us begin by looking at an example of a classical epistemological problem:

There is a book sitting on my desk in front of me. But, now, suppose I ask myself how I know that there is, or more generally, how I know that there is anything there at all (regardless of whether it is a book). A sensible answer to this question would be, "Because I see it." We know that there are material objects around us because we see them, feel them, hear them, etc. And the statement that we see something, or feel it, or hear it, logically entails that it is there to be seen, or felt, or heard. But now, I *say* that I see something (a book) there before me on my desk, but how do I *know* that I do? Mightn't I be hallucinating, or seeing an after-image, or witnessing some sort of cleverly constructed optical illusion? My experience might be exactly the same as when I really am seeing a book, and yet there might not be any book there, because I am hallucinating. Generalizing this, how do we know we *ever* perceive the things we think we do? Mightn't we always be hallucinating?

As it has sometimes been denied that it is even meaningful to suppose we might *always* be hallucinating, let us make this possibility more concrete. Suppose that a group of psychologists, biophysicists, and neurologists have constructed an adequate explanation of the neurophysiology of perception, and to test their explanation they take a subject from birth and wire him into a computer which directly stimulates his brain in such a way as to give a coherent, but completely false, sequence of sensations. In the subject's own mind he would seem to live out a completely normal life, growing up, making friends, going to school, getting a job, marrying and raising a family, etc. And yet all those years he was really sealed into an experimental apparatus in which he was fed intravenously and never had any contact with the outside world. It is true that in the present state of neurophysiology this could not be done, but it is certainly a meaningful hypothesis and a logical possibility.

Now, how do I know that I am not in the position of the subject of the above experiment? Perhaps a group of scientists have me hooked into such a computer, and all of the experiences that I think I have had since birth are really figments of the computer. How can I possibly know that this is not the case? It seems that any reason I can have for thinking that I am not hooked into such a computer must be either a reason for thinking that such a hypothesis is logically impossible, or else an empirical reason, arrived at inductively, for thinking that it is false as a matter of fact. But it is hard to see how this skeptical hypothesis can be logically impossible (it seems to make perfectly good sense—we know what it would be like for someone to be wired into a computer), and it seems that in order to have inductive evidence for an empirical reason I would already have to be able to rely upon some of my perceptions—which I cannot do without simply begging the question against the skeptical hypothesis. How then can I know that the skeptical hypothesis is false?

Faced with this sort of argument, one might be tempted to conclude that the skeptic is right—we really don't know the things we think we know. But such a conclusion flies in the face of common sense. There are many things that I know: I know that there is a desk before me, that I am holding a pen and writing on a piece of paper. I know that the walls of my study are lined with books, and that it is raining outside. All of these things I am certain about. It would be ridiculous to conclude that it is in principle impossible for me to know them.

That an argument "$P_1, \ldots, P_n$; therefore $\sim Q$" is valid does not establish that its conclusion is true. It merely establishes that *if* the premises are true *then* the conclusion is true. Or better, it establishes that at least one of the propositions $P_1, \ldots, P_n, Q$ is false. The argument does not by itself determine which is false. A skeptical argument proceeds from prima facie reasonable premises to the conclusion that we do not know things that we are quite certain we do know. But all that such an argument establishes is that *either* one of the premises $P_1, \ldots, P_n$ is false *or* that proposition Q (that we do have the sort of knowledge we think we do) is false. In deciding which of these propositions to reject, all we can do is seize upon the one we are least certain about. But we will never be as certain about the premises of a skeptical argument as we are that we do have knowledge. So it will always be more reasonable to reject one of the premises than to accept the skeptical conclusion. A skeptical argument can only be construed as a *reductio ad absurdum* of its premises. There must be something wrong with any skeptical argument. Presented with such an argument, what we must decide is which premise to reject.

Skeptical arguments generate epistemological problems. Apparently reasonable assumptions lead to the conclusion that knowledge of a certain sort (e.g., knowledge of the physical world, or knowledge of other minds) is impossible. Faced with such an argument, our task is to explain how knowledge is possible. The problem is not to show *that* knowledge is possible; that much we can take for granted. What we must do is find the hole in the skeptical argument that makes it possible for us to have the knowledge we do. The problems of epistemology are problems of how we can possibly know certain kinds of things that we claim to know or customarily think we know. In general, given a statement *P*, we can ask, "How do you know that *P*?" This is the general form of an epistemological problem. The question "How do you know that *P*?" is a challenge—a demand for justification. The task of the epistemologist is to explain how it is possible for us to know that *P*, i.e., to explain what justifies us in believing the things we do.[1]

Returning for a moment to the skeptical argument with which this chapter began, we can be confident that it proceeds from a false premise. Its conclusion, which is that knowledge of the physical world is impossible, is certainly mistaken. The task of the epistemologist is to find the false premise. This is not a task that can be undertaken at this point. Preliminary groundwork is

[1] To forestall misunderstanding, let me hasten to say that the task I am undertaking is not that of investigating knowledge per se but merely that of investigating epistemic justification. Gettier [1963] has made it painfully obvious that knowledge requires more than justified true belief, but in this book I will not try to say what more is required. The task I have set myself is not to determine when we have knowledge but is the more fundamental one of determining when our beliefs are justified.

necessary. We will return to this skeptical argument in Chapter Two, at which time it will be possible to pinpoint the error.

2. Reductive Analyses

Now let us turn to a second skeptical argument, around which the contents of this book will be organized. The development of this argument is rather involved, occupying this entire section. At the end of the section, the argument will be summarized.

Our knowledge can be separated into areas according to subject matter. These areas will include knowledge of the physical world, knowledge of the past, knowledge of contingent general truths, knowledge of other minds, a priori knowledge, and possibly knowledge of moral truths. The significance of these areas is that each has associated with it a characteristic *source* of knowledge. For example, the source of our knowledge of the physical world is perception. This is not to say that the only way to know that a physical object has a certain property is by perceiving the object. There are other ways, e.g., we may remember that it does, or we may be told that it does. But these other ways are all parasitic on perception. If we could not acquire knowledge of the physical world through perception, we could not acquire it in any of these other ways either. Analogously, the source of our knowledge of the past is memory; the source of our knowledge of contingent general truths is induction; the source of our knowledge of other minds is the behavior of other bodies. It is not clear just what are sources of knowledge either of a priori truths or of moral truths.

Given a statement *P*, let us call the conditions under which one would be justified in believing-that-*P* the *justification conditions* of the statment *P*. We can distinguish between two problems. The first is to *state* the justification conditions for the propositions in each of our areas of knowledge, and the second is to *prove* that those are the justification conditions. These two problems are not unrelated, but they are distinct problems. The second has generally interested epistemologists more than the first. Epistemologists have usually been content to give only a very rough description of the justification conditions of statements, and then have gone ahead to try to prove that those are the justification conditions. For example, the classical Problem of Induction is one of justifying induction as a way of learning the truth of universal generalizations. Although they've never been very clear about just what those grounds are, few philosophers doubt that we do base knowledge claims on inductive grounds. But what is demanded is a proof that we are justified in doing so. And similarly, the Problem of Perception is the problem of explaining how we can justify basing knowledge claims about physical objects on sense perception. It is not doubted that we do in fact base them *somehow* on sense perception, but what is wanted is a proof that we are justified in doing so.

The fundamental problem of epistemology is to explain what it is that justifies us in making the kinds of knowledge claims that we do customarily make. This problem has traditionally been construed as requiring a justification for our basing knowledge claims on the grounds on which we do in fact base them (a *proof* that what we suppose to be the justification conditions really are the justification conditions). In other words, it has been identified with the second of the above two problems. On the face of it, there seems to be a very good reason why we should, in principle, be able to give a proof of the sort desired. If we cannot establish any connection between one state of affairs and another, then we cannot be justified in making claims about the one state of affairs on the basis of the other. Thus if we cannot justify our customary grounds for knowledge claims, then we cannot take them as justifying our claims to knowledge. But if we cannot take them as justifying those claims, then they do not justify those claims, and so they are not really good grounds at all. Therefore, unless we can, in principle, give a proof of the sort desired, we are led to skepticism.

How might we set about justifying our basing knowledge claims on some particular source (such as perception)? It seems that there can be only two ways in which this might be done. We could either justify it inductively, showing that it does in fact tend to lead to true knowledge claims, or else we could justify it logically, showing that there is some sort of logical connection between the source and the knowledge of which it is a source. But an inductive justification is impossible. We could only inductively justify a source of knowledge if we had independent access to both the source and the knowledge of which it is a source, and then could compare them and see that there is a correlation. But we do not have independent access to the knowledge that these sources are supposed to provide. They constitute *the* sources of this knowledge. For example, we do not have access to the physical world except *through* perception, and so there is no way to compare the physical world with perception to see that perception is a reliable guide unless we beg the question and assume in the beginning that it is.

It seems then that the only way to justify a source of knowledge is by establishing some sort of logical connection between the source and the knowledge it is supposed to give us. A logical connection must arise from the meanings of the concepts or statements involved in the knowledge claims. And (and *here* is the step which I shall deny) it has traditionally been supposed that the only way to analyze the meaning of a statement or concept is to give its truth conditions—to say what conditions must be satisfied in order for the statement to be true or for the concept to be correctly ascribable to an object.[2] Furthermore, not just any statement of truth conditions will suffice. Starting from the truth conditions of a statement, we could never establish a logical connection between that statement and the source of knowledge which is supposed to yield the statement unless those truth conditions were stated in terms of the same concepts as are used in describing the source. Thus, for example, we could never establish a logical connection between perception and statements about the material world unless we could state the truth conditions of the latter in terms of the concepts used in describing perception.

An analysis of the truth conditions of a statement in terms of the concepts used in describing the source of our knowledge of that kind of statement is what philosophers have called a *reductive analysis*. Since Descartes, epistemologists have been concerned almost exclusively with giving reductive analyses of statements, and we now see why. Given assumptions that philosophers have traditionally accepted, it follows that the only way to prove that the purported justification conditions of a statement really are the justification conditions is by giving a reductive analysis of the statement in which the truth conditions are stated in terms of the same concepts as the justification conditions.

Philosophers have commonly supposed that they know more or less how we are justified in making the kinds of knowledge claims

[2] We have inherited this assumption most recently from logical atomism and logical positivism, but it is not new. It is really the same sort of thing that Locke, Berkeley, and Hume, and for that matter Socrates, were doing.

we do. Although they have not generally been able to state the justification conditions precisely, they felt that they could at least pick out the general sources of our knowledge in different areas. For example, our knowledge of the physical world comes from sense perception. And our knowledge of other minds comes from people's behavior. And our knowledge of right and wrong (if we can properly speak of "knowledge" here) comes from nonmoral states of affairs in the world. Thus if we are to justify these sources of knowledge, it seems we must seek reductive analyses of these statements in terms of these sources. Working within this traditional framework, phenomenalism becomes the only possible theory of our knowledge of the material world, behaviorism becomes the only possible theory of our knowledge of other minds,[3] and some form of naturalistic ethics becomes the only possible theory of our knowledge of moral truth.

It seems that in order to justify sources of knowledge we are driven inexorably to reductive analyses. This appears to be the only way to derive the justification conditions of statements from the meanings of those statements. And it seems that if the justification conditions are not derivable from the meanings of the statements—if there really is no logical connection between them—then they cannot be the justification conditions, because if we cannot justify our sources of knowledge, then they do not justify our claims to knowledge and so are not really sources of knowledge at all. We seem forced to conclude that we must have either reductive analyses or skepticism. They are the only two possibilities.

Let us ask then whether reductive analyses are always possible. Unfortunately, the answer seems to be "No". For example, consider our knowledge of the physical world. A reductive analysis there would take the form of phenomenalism. I think the strongest argument against phenomenalism is that from "perceptual relativity". According to phenomenalism a statement about physical objects is to be analyzed as a (perhaps infinite) conjunction of

[3] This is oversimplifying a bit in the case of behaviorism, because the possibility of an inductive justification of our source of knowledge has been maintained by the supporters of the argument from analogy. But if we can agree with those who maintain that the argument from analogy will not work, and thus that an inductive justification is impossible, then it seems to follow that behaviorism is the only possible theory.

statements about experience. Then the physical object statement must entail each of those statements about experience. But a physical object statement cannot entail any statement about experience: given any physical object statement and any statement about experience, we can imagine circumstances in which the physical object statement is true, and yet due to malfunction of certain organs, or hallucination, the statement about experience is false. For example, we can recall the example of the man who is wired into a computer that directly stimulates his brain. This is done in such a way that his experience is entirely independent of what is actually going on around him, so that his experience is always delusive. Given any proposed entailment between a material object statement and a statement about his experience, we can always program the computer in such a way as to make the latter statement false even when the former is true. Consequently there is no entailment.

Thus it seems that the search for reductive analyses that will solve the problem of our knowledge of the physical world is stymied. Nor is this the only place in which the attempt to find reductive analyses seems to have failed. Consider our knowledge of other minds. Here the reductive analysts are the behaviorists who try to reduce statements about persons to statements about material objects. But behaviorism does not seem to work,[4] and so reductive analyses do not offer a solution to the problem. Consider the philosophy of logic. Quine and his followers have argued, in effect, that no reductive analyses can be given of such logical concepts as analyticity, implication, and logical necessity, and on this basis they have actually been led to embrace a kind of logical skepticism wherein they deny the very existence of these concepts. We have a corresponding problem in ethics. Reductive analyses in ethics take the form of naturalistic ethical theories in which the meaning of an ethical statement is analyzed in terms of statements about the physical world. But the apparent existence of the Naturalistic Fallacy vitiates such analyses. In all of these areas the search for reductive analyses has been fruitless.

Thus the traditional epistemologist finds himself forced to the conclusion that either reductive analyses can be given in the various areas of knowledge or else skepticism is true. And he cannot find any reductive analyses.

[4] See Chapter Nine.

The above skeptical argument has been rather long and involved, so let me lay it out explicitly step by step:

1. If we cannot establish a connection between one state of affairs and another, then we cannot be justified in making claims about the one state of affairs on the basis of the other.
2. Thus if we cannot establish a connection between our customary sources of knowledge and the states of affairs of which they are supposed to yield knowledge, then they are not sources of knowledge after all.
3. It is impossible to establish such a connection inductively without begging the question.
4. Thus the only way to justify a source of knowledge is to establish a logical connection between it and the states of affairs of which it is supposed to yield knowledge.
5. A logical connection must arise out of the meanings of the knowledge claims.
6. The only way to analyze the meaning of a statement is to give its truth conditions.
7. Thus the only way to justify a source of knowledge is to analyze the truth conditions of the knowledge claim in terms of the concepts used in describing the source of knowledge, i.e., to give a reductive analysis.
8. It is impossible to give reductive analyses.
9. Therefore our sources of knowledge cannot be justified and hence are not sources of knowledge at all.

The conclusion of this argument is certainly false, so one of the steps of the argument must fail. The philosopher's problem is to discover which.

3. A Theory of Meaning

The solution to our skeptical dilemma is to deny that the meaning of a statement must always be given by stating its truth conditions, i.e., to deny step 6 of the above argument. It will be argued that often the meaning of a statement can be given in another way—by stating its justification conditions. Or more precisely, often the meaning of a statement is uniquely determined by the justification conditions of it and its denial. The more I think about this, the more obvious it seems to me and the less in need of argument.

Despite the exhaustive search for truth condition analyses which has occupied philosophy for many years, such analyses are distinguished by their rarity. It is the truly exceptional statement or concept for which truth condition analyses have actually been found. Stop and think how many even simple concepts can literally be "defined". To learn the meaning of a concept is certainly not to learn its "definition". It is to learn how to use it, which is to learn how to make justifiable assertions involving it. Thus it seems to me inescapable that the meaning of a concept is determined by its justification conditions. This seems to me obvious, but I realize it does not seem obvious to those steeped in the tradition of analytic philosophy, so I will now endeavor to give a detailed argument to establish what I think is really obvious.

My initial thesis is that often, as a matter of logic, the meaning of a statement is uniquely determined by the justification conditions of it and its denial. This thesis will be defended in two steps. First it will be shown that it holds for statements of the simple form "x is a φ", and then it will be concluded from this that the thesis holds in general.

3.1 *The Analysis of Concepts*

Rather than talk directly about the statement "x is a φ", it proves convenient to talk about "the concept of a φ". By "the justification conditions of the concept of a φ" will be meant the justification conditions of the statement "x is a φ", i.e., the conditions under which one could justifiably ascribe the concept of a φ to something. It will be argued that, at least for many concepts, what it means to say that something is an instance of that concept is uniquely determined by the justification conditions of that concept.

Let us say that a person *has* the concept of a φ if he knows what it means to say of something that it is a φ. Given any concept, there is a set of conditions C which must be satisfied before a person can be said to have acquired that concept. As different things are required in order for a person to have acquired different concepts, the conditions C will differ for each concept. Thus a concept is uniquely determined by the set C of conditions which must be satisfied in order for a person to be said to have acquired that concept. It will now be argued that, for many concepts, the conditions C are in turn uniquely determined by the justification conditions of the concept, and thus those latter conditions also uniquely determine the concept.

Just what is necessary before we can truly say of a person that he has learned the concept of a certain kind of thing, such as "red thing" or "bird"? We frequently talk about a person "knowing what a bird is" rather than about his having the concept of a bird. But we must be careful with the locution "*S* knows what a bird is", because it can be used to mean two quite different things. There is a clear sense in which an ornithologist knows more about what a bird is than does a layman, e.g., he knows that birds are warm blooded, that they have livers, etc. But this sort of knowledge about birds cannot be part of having the concept of a bird. All that we can require of a person in order for him to have a concept is "conceptual knowledge"—knowledge of things that are in some sense constitutive of the concept itself—and not knowledge of contingent facts. Someone must already have had the concept of a bird before these contingent facts could have been discovered. For example, if the naturalist who first discovered that birds are warm blooded had not already known what a bird was, he could not have told that it was a bird that he was examining.

It is the sense of "*S* knows what a bird is" in which the naturalist had to already know what a bird was that is equivalent to "*S* has the concept of a bird". This just means "*S* knows a bird when he sees one".[5] If *S* does not know a bird when he sees one, then he does not know what a bird is, regardless of the amount of theoretical knowledge he may have about birds. On the other hand, if *S* does know a bird when he sees one, even though he may not be able to tell us much about birds, then he knows what a bird is—he has the concept of a bird.

To say that *S* knows a bird when he sees one is just to say that he can pick birds out from among other things—he can identify birds. Thus to acquire the concept of a bird is to learn how to identify birds. But this is still not as clear as we might desire. What is necessary in order for a person to know how to identify birds? There is perhaps a temptation to say that one must know what would count as making "*x* is a bird" true—one must know the truth conditions for "*x* is a bird". But it does not take much reflection to see that this is not the case. Although a philosopher or a

[5] This is not a literal use of "sees".

lexicographer *might* (although I doubt it) be able to construct a definition of "bird" that would give us such a set of truth conditions, very few ordinary speakers of English would be able to do that, and we could not by any stretch of the imagination maintain that those ordinary speakers do not have the concept of a bird.

A person may very well have the concept of a bird without being able to give a definition or state truth conditions for "x is a bird". But one might suppose instead that in order for a person to know how to identify birds, although he need not be able to say what makes something a bird, he must nevertheless "do the identifying"—ascribe the concept "bird" to things—just when the truth conditions are satisfied.

But if this is understood as requiring that the person never make a mistake, then clearly it is too stringent a requirement. Suppose we are teaching a child what a bird is. The simple fact that the child makes a mistake, thinking perhaps that a very cleverly constructed duck hunter's decoy is a bird, is not sufficient to show that the child has not learned what a bird is or learned how to identify birds. The reason this would not count as showing that the child has not learned what a bird is is that he might have been perfectly justified in thinking that the decoy was a bird, because it looked so much like one that anyone would have been justified in taking it to be one. If his ascription of the concept were thus justified, even though false, this would excuse his mistake from showing that he had not learned what a bird is.

Suppose then that the child ascribed the concept "bird" to things in cases where his ascription could not possibly be justified on grounds like the above. Would this count as showing that he has not acquired the concept? No, because the child might know better than to ascribe the concept on such flimsy grounds but do it anyway. He might not have been paying attention. Perhaps he was just careless. The simple fact that the child occasionally ascribes the concept "bird" to things unjustifiably would not in itself show that he has not acquired the concept.

But if in fact the child did not *know how* to ascribe the concept and its complement justifiably (i.e., he did not know how to justifiably determine whether something was a bird),[6] this would show

[6] By "the complement of the concept of a φ" I mean the concept of a non-φ.

that he had not learned how to identify birds and so does not have the concept.

Conversely, when the child has learned to judge justifiably whether a thing is a bird (i.e., he has learned to ascribe the concept and its complement to things justifiably), we are satisfied that he knows how to identify birds and so has got the concept right—he knows what a bird is.

Of course, when we say that the child must "know how" to ascribe the concept to things justifiably, this is knowledge in the sense of practical knowledge, rather than theoretical knowledge. The child must *know how* to ascribe the concept to things justifiably, but he need not *know what* is required for his ascription of it to be justifiable. Few people would be able to articulate the grounds on which they justifiably judge that something is a bird.

Thus far I have concerned myself only with the concept "bird", and I have concluded that to learn the concept "bird" is to learn how to justifiably ascribe that concept and its complement to things. The question that arises now concerns the extent to which this conclusion can be generalized to apply to other concepts. It seems clear that the conclusion can be generalized immediately to cover many concepts of *kinds* of things, such as the concept of a red thing, the concept of a four-legged thing, the concept of a cat, etc. It can also be generalized to cover the concepts of many relations between things, such as "brother of" or "taller than", because those can be thought of as concepts of kinds of ordered pairs (or more generally, ordered *n*-tuples). Frequently, when we have a concept that can be thought of as the concept of a kind of thing, then we can say that the meaning or identity of that concept is uniquely determined by the conditions under which we would be justified in ascribing it or its complement to something.

It would be nice if the above result held for all concepts of kinds of things, but it is doubtful that it does. There are essentially two ways of explaining a new concept to a person. You can give a verbal definition or an ostensive definition. When you use an ostensive definition to teach a person a concept, what you are teaching him is how to judge whether something is an instance of that concept. Thus the above account applies immediately to all concepts that can be introduced by ostensive definitions. Let us call such concepts *ostensive concepts*. On the other hand, when you use a verbal definition to teach a person a concept, you characterize the concept in terms of other concepts the person already has. At first it may seem that this is simply another way of specifying the justfication conditions of the concept. For example, if a θ is defined to be anything that is both a φ and a ψ, then we have in effect said that one is justified in taking something to be a θ iff he is justified in taking it to be both a φ and a ψ. Unfortunately, some definitions are more complex than this. For example, suppose we define a θ to be anything that is a φ but which nobody knows to be a φ. Then to know that something is a θ one would have to know both that it is a φ and that nobody knows that it is a φ, which is impossible. Consequently, there are no conditions under which one would be justified in thinking of something that it is a θ. The justification conditions of the concept of a θ constitute the null class. Under these circumstances, it would not be true that to know what a θ is is to know how to determine whether something is a θ. It seems that in this case, to know what a θ is would be something like knowing the definition of a θ and having the concepts involved in the definition. Thus we cannot conclude that the concept of a θ is uniquely determined by the justification conditions of it and its complement.

One concept may be defined verbally in terms of some other concepts, and those concepts in turn defined in terms of some further concepts, and so on, but this cannot go on indefinitely. We cannot define *all* concepts verbally without going around in a circle. Our sequence of verbal definitions must eventually terminate with some concepts that can be defined ostensively. Furthermore, if the concept of a φ is defined verbally in terms of some concepts $\psi_1, \ldots, \psi_n$, which are in turn defined verbally in terms of some ostensive concepts $\gamma_1, \ldots, \gamma_m$, then by putting all of the definitions together we can obtain a definition of φ in terms of $\gamma_1, \ldots, \gamma_m$. Consequently, if a concept φ can be defined by means of a sequence of verbal definitions which terminate ultimately with ostensive concepts, then φ can be defined directly in terms of ostensive concepts. This means that there are in general only two kinds of concepts—those that can be defined ostensively, and those that can be defined verbally in terms of others than can be defined ostensively.[7] This in turn implies:

[7] These are not exclusive. A concept might be definable in both ways.

(3.1) Given any concept, either it is characterized by the justification conditions of it and its complement, or it can be defined verbally in terms of other concepts that are so characterized.

This is a very important principle. It will be because of this principle that the skeptical argument fails.

3.2 *The Analysis of Statements*

Having discussed the meaning of concepts, and hence the meaning of statements of the simple form "x is a φ", we can now turn to the meaning of other statements. In analogy to the above principle concerning concepts, it will be shown that, given any statement, either its meaning can be characterized by the justification conditions of it and its denial, or it can be analyzed in terms of other statements whose meanings can be so characterized.

A statement states that something is the case. For example, the statement that Smith is a bachelor states that Smith is a bachelor. This is a truism. Statements are differentiated by what they state to be the case, or by the kind of state of affairs in which they would be true. For example, the statement that Smith is a bachelor would be true in any state of affairs that included Smith's being a bachelor, and so by picking out this particular kind of state of affairs we can uniquely specify the statement that Smith is a bachelor by saying that it is that statement which means that a state of affairs of this kind obtains. Thus the identity of a statement is uniquely determined by the kind of state of affairs which it states to obtain.

Kinds of things are correlative with *concepts* of kinds of things. That is, two different *concepts* of kinds of things (e.g., the concept of a blue thing and the concept of a red thing) determine two different *kinds* of things. There cannot be two different concepts which are both the concept of the same kind of thing. And conversely, given any two different kinds of things, the concepts of those two different kinds of things are distinct (e.g., the concept of a blue thing is distinct from the concept of a red thing). Therefore, as the identity of a statement is uniquely determined by the kind of state of affairs which it states to obtain, it is also uniquely determined by the *concept* of the kind of state of affairs which it states to obtain.

We have seen that a concept is either definable or characterized by the justification conditions of it and its complement. Thus in particular, the concept of a kind of state of affairs is either definable or characterized by the conditions under which we would be justified in judging that the present state of affairs is or is not of that kind. Therefore the concept of the kind of state of affairs which the statement *P* asserts to obtain is either definable or characterized by the conditions under which we would be justified in judging that the present state of affairs is or is not of that kind. The latter conditions are just the justification conditions for *P* and its denial. Furthermore, a definition of the kind of state of affairs which *P* states to obtain will be a statement of the truth conditions of *P*. Thus we find that there are just two kinds of statements: those that are characterized by the justification conditions of them and their denial (*ostensive* statements), and those for which truth condition analyses can be given. In general:

(3.2) Given any statement *P*, either the meaning of *P* is characterized by the justification conditions of *P* and $\sim P$, or else the truth conditions of *P* can be stated in terms of statements whose meanings are so characterized.

Given a statement whose meaning is characterized by its justification conditions, we can say that the justification conditions are *constitutive* of the meaning of the statement. By this is meant two things. First, the justification conditions *logically determine* the meaning of the statement. Second, when one has learned to use the justification conditions, one has *thereby* learned the meaning. There is nothing over and above the justification conditions that one must learn in order to learn the meaning. In this sense, the justification conditions are all there is to the meaning of the statement. Does this mean that the meaning can be *identified* with the justification conditions? I do not believe so, but only because of a quirk in the grammar of the word "meaning". In "The meaning of the statement that *P* is . . .", the blank can only (meaningfully) be filled with a that-clause—a paraphrase of the statement that *P*. It is not false to say that the meaning of the statement is the same thing as its justification conditions—it is meaningless to say that. The problem is that "The meaning of the statement that *P*" is not a substantive term. There is *nothing* which *is* the meaning of the statement. One might say that the word "meaning" is syncategorematical. It can only function in certain narrowly restricted contexts including "has the same meaning as", "is part of the meaning of", "is meaningless", and a few others. I do not regard this as a terribly important philosophical fact. I think it is little more than an accident of language. I can see no obstacle to philosophers extending the use of the word "meaning" artificially so as to make it a substantive term, and then it would be quite reasonable to identify meaning with justification conditions. However, without extending the use of the word "meaning", I can still express my main point by saying that for ostensive statements, although we may not be able to identify the meaning with the justification conditions, the meaning is not something over and above the justification conditions either. Once we have given the justification conditons, we have thereby given the meaning. There is nothing more we have to do to give the meaning.

Principle 3.2 is reminiscent of a verification theory of meaning. It amounts to saying that the verification theory of meaning holds for some statements (insofar as "means of verification" is understood as "justification conditions"). But this principle also allows for there to be statements for which the verification theory fails. These will be statements that are meaningful because their truth conditions can be stated in terms of other meaningful statements, even though their meaning cannot be explained by giving their justification conditions. A simple example would be "It is raining but nobody knows that it is raining". Both "it is raining" and "nobody knows that it is raining" are statements whose meanings can be explained by giving justification conditions, but there are no conditions under which one could be justified in believing the conjunction of the two statements. Consequently the meaning of the conjunction is not characterized by its justification conditions.

Notice also that principle 3.2 is only a conditional—not a biconditional. It leaves open the possibility that there may be truth condition analyses that do not determine (meaningful) statements. An example might be "There is a gremlin in the corner whose properties are such as to logically preclude anyone's ever knowing that he exists". These are the sorts of cases against which the logical positivists hoped to use their verification theory of meaning. As principle 3.2 has nothing to say about such cases, it is considerably weaker than any of the historical versions of the verification principle.

4. The Demise of Traditional Epistemology

Now let us return to our skeptical problem. In order for our customary sources of knowledge to actually be sources of knowledge, there must be a logical connection between the sources and the resulting knowledge claims. The skeptical argument seemed to show that this in turn required the existence of reductive analyses, and yet reductive analyses do not seem to be possible. However, in attempting to establish the necessity of reductive analyses, it was assumed that the only way to analyze the meaning of a statement is to give its truth conditions (step 6). Principle 3.2 shows that that assumption is incorrect. By virtue of principle 3.2 there is often a second way to analyze the meaning of a statement—by giving its justification conditions. Although in analyzing the meaning of a statement we may have to begin by stating its truth conditions in terms of simpler statements, the constituents of this truth condition analysis will be statements whose meanings can only be given (noncircularly) in terms of justification conditions.

Epistemologically problematic statements may be complex statements whose meanings are given by truth conditions. For example, "He is in pain, but happy to see his mother" is analyzable as "He is in pain, and he is happy to see his mother"; and "That is a red sphere" is analyzable as "That is red, and that is a sphere". But in this way, within any particular area of knowledge we quickly arrive at "simple" statements ("That is red", "He is in pain") that cannot be further analyzed in terms of truth conditions. The only noncircular way to give the meaning of such a simple statement is in terms of its justification conditions.

Given such a simple statement, our task is to show that there is a logical connection between it and the source of knowledge from which it arises. A logical connection must result from the meaning of the statement, which means for these particular statements that a connection must arise out of their justification conditions. But this is now trivial. Stating the justification conditions *just is* stating what is a source of knowledge for these statements. There is automatically a logical connection between the statement and the source of our knowledge of that statement because the source of knowledge is the sole determinant of the meaning of the statement. The problem dissolves.

This reply to the skeptical argument does more than just answer that argument. It changes our whole conception of the task of epistemology. The basic task of epistemology is to explain how it is possible to have knowledge in each of the various areas of knowledge. This was traditionally interpreted as involving two things—spelling out the justification conditions for statements in each area, and establishing that they are the justification conditions. The second half of this task is that of justifying sources of knowledge. But it only makes sense to talk about justifying a source of knowledge if it is possible to establish a nontrivial connection between the source and the knowledge, and there is no nontrivial connection. It was assumed that, having once spelled out the justification conditions for a statement, we would have to go on to *prove* that those are the justification conditions by deriving them from the meaning of the statement (which was identified with the truth conditions). To prove that the purported justification conditions are the justification conditions would be to derive them from something deeper. But in fact there is generally nothing deeper. The justification conditions are themselves constitutive of the meaning of the statement. We can no more *prove* that the justification conditions of "That is red" are the justification conditions than we can prove on the basis of something deeper about the meaning of "bachelor" that all bachelors are unmarried. Being unmarried constitutes part of the meaning of "bachelor" and as such cannot be derived from anything deeper about the meaning of "bachelor"; and analogously the justification conditions of "That is red" or "He is in pain" are constitutive of the meanings of those statements and hence cannot be derived from any deeper features of their meanings. There are no deeper features.

This means that our basic epistemological task cannot be split into two parts—spelling out the justification conditions, and establishing that we have got the right ones. These merge into a single task—spelling out the justification conditions and getting them right. This remains as the sole task of epistemology. Explaining how knowledge is possible amounts to nothing more than describing the justification conditions for statements in the different areas of knowledge. For example, we want to know exactly what the relationship is between perception and justified belief about physical objects. And we would like to be able to state what the connection is between a person's behavior and our right to make judgments about his mental states. Analogously we want to state exactly what counts as good inductive grounds for a contingent generalization.[8] These and similar questions make up the only proper problems for epistemology. In answering such questions we can still think of ourselves as mapping the "logical geography" of concepts, but this must be done as much in terms of justification conditions as in terms of truth conditions. The remainder of this book will be concerned with seeking such analyses.

[8] This is just what Goodman [1955] has called "The New Riddle of Induction".

Chapter Two

The Structure of Epistemic Justification

1. The Pyramidal Theory of Knowledge

THE fundamental problem of epistemology is one of answering questions of the form "How do you know that *P*?" and these are questions concerning what justifies one in believing that *P*. In order to answer these questions for each of the various areas of knowledge, it will be necessary to get clearer on the structure of epistemic justification.

Our knowledge of the world comes to us through what, for lack of a better term, we might call "modes of intuition", such as our senses of sight, touch, smell, taste, our interoceptive sense, our memory, etc. This much is at least a psychological fact. But philosophers have generally wanted to go further and say that these modes of intuition provide not only the psychological causes of our beliefs (or at least one link in the causal chain) but also the logical grounds for our beliefs. Associated with each of these modes of intuition there are supposed to be beliefs about the *content* of one's intuitions, about what one seems to intuit (i.e., seems to see, hear, feel, etc.), and it has often been supposed that one cannot be wrong when he holds such a belief—these beliefs are "incorrigible".[1] Then all other beliefs are supposed to be grounded on these incorrigible beliefs.

[1] More precisely, a proposition *P* is incorrigible for a person *S* iff *S*'s believing *P* logically entails that *P* is true. This definition has the unexpected result that if *P* is necessarily true then it is automatically incorrigible. For this reason it seems best also to build into the definition of incorrigibility that an incorrigible proposition be incorrigibly justified in the sense of section 2.2.

This generates a sort of pyramidal theory of knowledge. According to this theory, the propositions that a particular person knows to be true can be arranged into a pyramidal structure such that: (1) the propositions in the lowest tier are justifiably believed without requiring an independent reason for believing them, and hence constitute a foundation for knowledge; and (2) each proposition in the higher tiers of the pyramid is justified on the basis of propositions lower in the pyramid than it is. The propositions in the lowest tier are said to be *epistemologically basic*. They are those propositions that one can know to be true without appealing to anything else that one knows.

A number of questions must be asked regarding the pyramidal theory of knowledge. In connection with epistemologically basic propositions: Are there actually any epistemologically basic propositions? If so, must they be incorrigible? If they are not incorrigible, what other logical status might they have? How do they come to have that status? These questions will be examined in section 2 of this chapter. In connection with the upper tiers of the pyramid, we must ask what the relationship is between each proposition and those propositions below it which support it. This relationship is that of one proposition being a *reason* for believing another proposition, so we must investigate the concept of a reason for believing something. Philosophers have generally worked with a grossly oversimplified conception of reasons. They have commonly accepted a deductive model in which a reason can only be a reason by virtue of logically entailing what it is a reason for. This deductive model has been largely responsible for generating a number of traditional philosophical problems and making them appear insoluble. For example, there is no deductive connection between perception and the physical world, or behavior and mental states, or inductive grounds and the inductive conclusion. Consequently, accepting the deductive model makes it impossible to explain how we can have knowledge of the material world, other minds, or contingent generalizations. In section 3 the attempt will be made to clarify the way in which reasons actually work, showing that this is much more complicated than the deductive model would have us believe, and showing that once the true structure of epistemic justification is understood, many traditional problems appear relatively unproblematic.

2. Epistemologically Basic Propositions

2.1 *The Existence of Epistemologically Basic Propositions*

An epistemologically basic proposition is one that a person can justifiably believe without having a reason for believing it. Such a proposition is in some sense "self-justifying". Are there any propositions of this sort? The simplest way to answer this question is to examine the alternative to there being epistemologically basic propositions.

What is it that justifies a belief? Suppose someone justifiably believes some fact about the world on the basis of some other fact. Philosophers have often wanted to say that it is the second fact that justifies one's belief in the first fact. For example, consider the case of a person who believes there is a sheep in the field because he sees a dog that looks very much like a sheep—so much like a sheep that anyone would be justified in taking it to be a sheep until he examined it quite closely. One is apt to say that it is the *fact* that the dog looks like a sheep that justifies the person in thinking that there is a sheep in the field. But this is misleading. What is important in deciding whether the person is justified in his belief is not the fact itself but rather the person's belief that it is a fact. After all, if the person did not believe that the dog looked like a sheep, then his belief that there was a sheep in the field would not be justified, although it would of course still be a fact that the dog looked like a sheep. Thus we must say that what justifies a belief is always another belief.[2] It is a person's "doxastic state" which determines which of his beliefs are justified. Of course, we can still *talk* about facts, states of affairs, etc., justifying beliefs, but this must be understood in terms of beliefs justifying beliefs.

In order to justify a belief one must appeal to another belief, but the simple fact that a person believes one thing does not automatically mean that he is justified in believing something else which can be supported by the first belief. He must not only *have* the first belief—he must also be justified in having it. If a person believed, for no good reason, that the moon was shaped like half of an eggshell, so that it had no back side, this belief would not justify his believing further that the pictures that have been taken of the back

[2] This is a bit too narrow, as we will see in Chapter Three, but for the time being we will only consider reasons that are beliefs.

side of the moon are fraudulent. To justify a belief one must appeal to a further justified belief.

Now let us suppose that there are no epistemologically basic beliefs. This alternative is for knowledge to be, not a tree having its roots in epistemologically basic beliefs, but a vast nebula within which no beliefs are in any way more basic than any others and in which the process of justification just goes around and around without terminating anywhere. This is the view that knowledge does not have a foundation.[3] Let us examine this position more closely.

In order to justify a belief one must appeal to a further justified belief. This means that one of two things must be the case. Either there are some (epistemologically basic) beliefs that we can be justified in holding without being able to justify them on the basis of any other beliefs, or else for each justified belief there is an infinite regress of (potential) justification.[4] Let us call the latter the *nebula theory*. On this theory there is no rock bottom of justification. Justification just meanders in and out through our network of beliefs stopping nowhere.

Philosophers have a great fear of infinite regresses, and so when there are only two alternatives, and one of them involves an infinite regress, they generally opt for the other alternative. In this case this has led some epistemologists to conclude that the nebula theory is wrong and that there are epistemologically basic beliefs. But this is a very weak argument. *If* a person were to maintain that in order for a belief to be justified one must have *explicitly carried out* the justification—that is, consciously appealed to the further beliefs in terms of which the given belief is justified and seen that those further beliefs are themselves justified—then the infinite regress of justification would require a person to carry out infinitely many steps of reasoning before he could be justified in believing anything. And as this is impossible, it would follow that no belief

[3] I am uncertain whether anyone has ever held this view, although many philosophers have skirted dangerously close to it. Blanshard [1939], chap. 25, seems to take a position of this sort but later makes statements incompatible with it. Austin [1962] seems to be supporting such a view, but then on p. 110, in discussing Carnap, he says that such a view is "perfectly wild". Quine [1951] makes remarks that suggest this view but never actually commits himself to it. Popper is another possible candidate for the attribution of this view.

[4] I am calling either an infinite linear chain or a circular chain of justification an "infinite regress of justification".

could ever be justified. This conclusion is false, so it would follow that the nebula theory is incorrect. But instead it might be maintained that all that is required for a belief to be justified is for one to *be able* to justify it—he need not have done so antecedently. In other words, if a belief is justified one must hold some further justified belief which constitutes a good reason for holding the belief in question, but one need not have explicitly thought about the connection between the two beliefs. If this is correct, then the infinite regress would seem to cause no particular difficulty.

Let us ask then which of these two alternatives is the correct one. Can a person be justified in holding a belief when he has not consciously thought about the justification? It seems clear that he can. For example, suppose a person looks in the next room, sees what looks to him like a table, and thinks, "There's a table in the next room." If the circumstances are in no way unusual then it seems clear that his belief that it is a table is justified. But did he actually go through any process of justification? Did he consciously appeal to any other belief? It is unlikely that he did. He *might* have thought to himself, "That looks to me like a table, so it probably is", but most likely he simply formed the belief that it was a table without relating that belief to any other beliefs about what it looked like.

This suggests that an infinite regress of justification would not be as troublesome as it might first appear, and thus that the conclusion that there must exist epistemologically basic beliefs that are justified without being independently justifiable cannot be supported by the fact that the only alternative involves an infinite regress. But perhaps there is a better argument against the nebula theory. The nebula theory commits us to what is essentially a coherence theory of justification. According to the nebula theory, a person is justified in holding a belief P whenever he holds an infinite (possibly circular) sequence of beliefs $Q_1, Q_2, \ldots$ such that P is supported by some of the beliefs in the sequence and each belief in turn is supported by later beliefs in the sequence.[5]

[5] One might wish to put some further restrictions on this. For example, it might be reasonable to require that the sequence be noncircular. Also, some restrictions might be placed on the nature of the reasons involved. But no plausible restrictions will have any effect on the following argument. Whatever restrictions are employed, it must be admitted that *modus ponens* provides us with a good reason for its conclusion, and that is all that is needed for the argument.

The basic difficulty with this is that it cuts justification off from the world. A person could be justified in believing anything. All that would be required would be a sufficiently outlandish but coherent set of beliefs. For example, given an arbitrary belief *P*, *S* would be justified in holding it if he also happened to believe each of

$$Q_1, Q_1 \supset P; Q_2, Q_2 \supset Q_1, Q_2 \supset (Q_1 \supset P); Q_3, Q_3 \supset Q_2, Q_3 \supset (Q_2 \supset Q_1), Q_3 \supset [Q_2 \supset (Q_1 \supset P)]; Q_4, Q_4 \supset Q_3, Q_4 \supset (Q_3 \supset Q_2), Q_4 \supset [Q_3 \supset (Q_2 \supset Q_1)], Q_4 \supset \{Q_3 \supset [Q_2 \supset (Q_1 \supset P)]\}; Q_5, \ldots.$$

In this sequence of beliefs, each belief is supported by beliefs later in the sequence, but the beliefs are nowhere tied down in any way to the evidence of *S*'s senses. As long as a person's beliefs form such a coherent set, he could hold any beliefs at all regarding the colors, shapes, sizes, etc., of things, regardless of how they look or feel to him. That such an infinite regress could not provide justification seems to me to be immediately apparent. This can be underscored in the following way. Given such a coherence theory of justification, we could well imagine a person whose beliefs were such as to justify him in rejecting all of the evidence of his senses. For example, he might justifiably believe that whatever looks tall is really short, whatever looks red is really blue, whatever looks green is really yellow, whatever feels hot is really cold, etc. As long as his beliefs form a coherent set, there would be nothing wrong with this. The person would be justified in believing that all of his senses mislead him in a systematic way. Notice that this is not simply a matter of his rejecting all of the evidence of his senses and adopting a skeptical stance. He has positive beliefs concerning precisely how his senses mislead him. But I submit that it is impossible for him to be justified in holding such a set of beliefs. A person may well be justified in believing that some particular sense misleads him in some systematic way. For example, a color-blind person can know that he is color-blind; but he can only know that by relying upon other evidence of his senses. It is impossible for a person to be justified in believing that *all* of his senses systematically mislead him *all* of the time. And yet this sort of thing would be possible if the nebula theory were correct. Therefore, the nebula theory cannot be correct. An infinite regress of justification is at least not always possible. In at least some cases an infinite chain of reasons leads to absurdity. And if such an infinite regress of justification is not always possible, then it seems clear that it is never possible. An infinite regress of reasons would provide no stronger warrant for belief in one case than it does in any other case. All justification must eventually terminate with some epistemologically basic beliefs that do not require independent justification. And some of these beliefs must have *something* to do with the evidence of our senses.

2.2 *The Logical Status of Epistemologically Basic Propositions*

The nebula theory, according to which there are no epistemologically basic beliefs, is incorrect. It has generally been supposed that this forces us back to the traditional incorrigibility theory which maintains that there are epistemologically basic beliefs and that they are incorrigible. But this is a mistake. There is a broad but largely uncharted middle ground between the nebula theory and the incorrigibility theory.

In rejecting the nebula theory our conclusion is only that there can be no infinite chain of justification—justification must always terminate after finitely many steps. *If* it is agreed that justification must always proceed in terms of beliefs, and hence that it must terminate with beliefs, then we can conclude that there must exist epistemologically basic beliefs that one can be justified in holding without being able to supply independent justification. However, it may not be agreed that justification must always proceed in terms of beliefs. Sellars[6] has urged repeatedly that, for example, what justifies me in thinking that something is red is not my *belief* that it looks red to me but simply its looking red to me. If this is correct, there need be no epistemologically basic beliefs. Justification will not terminate with beliefs at all, but with mental states of some other sort. For now, I will simply reject this position, returning to it in the next chapter, at which point it will be evaluated more carefully.

Supposing then that there are epistemologically basic beliefs, must these beliefs be incorrigible? Our conclusion so far is only that these must be beliefs for which we do not need reasons. These beliefs somehow carry their justification with them—they are "self-

[6] See, for example, "Empiricism and the philosophy of mind" in Sellars [1963].

justifying". This does not require that these beliefs be incorrigible. It requires only that our simply *having* these beliefs is, at least in some cases, sufficient to make them justified (even though they might fail to be true).

We might suppose this to mean that our having such a belief logically entails that we are justified in having it. Let us say that the belief *P* is *incorrigibly justified* for a person *S* if, and only if, the mere fact that *S* believes *P* is logically sufficient to guarantee that his belief is justified. That is,

(2.1) "The belief-that-*P* is incorrigibly justified for *S*" means "It is necessarily true that if *S* believes (or were to believe) that *P* then *S* is (or would be) justified in believing that *P*."[7]

As a false belief may still be justified, an incorrigibly justified belief need not be incorrigibly true.[8] It might be supposed that what the argument used against the nebula theory shows is that justification must always terminate with incorrigibly justified beliefs.[9]

That argument does not prove, however, that there must be incorrigibly justified beliefs. It shows only that there are beliefs for which we do not have to have reasons. Our not having to have reasons for believing them does not mean that it may not be possible to have good reasons for disbelieving them. In other words, our epistemologically basic beliefs may be only *prima facie justified* in the sense that, necessarily, if we have such a belief, then in the absence of any other belief that constitutes a reason for rejecting it, the belief is justified. More precisely, let us define:

(2.2) "*P* is prima facie justified for *S*" means "It is necessarily true that if *S* believes (or were to believe) that *P*, and *S* has no reason for thinking that it is false that *P*, then *S* is (or would be) justified in believing that *P*."

[7] The hyphenation in phrases like "belief-that-*P*" and "statement-that-*P*" is merely intended to make the sentence easier to read and has no philosophical significance.

[8] This concept of an incorrigibly justified belief seems to be the same as Chisholm's concept of a *directly evident* statement (in Chisholm [1966]), although in places his discussion suggests that a directly evident statement must be true.

[9] This was my position in Pollock [1967].

The basic idea behind the concept of a prima facie justified belief is that there is a "logical presumption" in favor of the belief's being justified. If a belief is prima facie justified, one does not need a reason for believing it, but it may be possible to have a reason for disbelieving it. For example, one might urge that my belief that something looks green to me is prima facie justified (for me) because (1) in the absence of any reasons for thinking that it does not look green to me it would be justified, but (2) it might be possible for me to have reasons for thinking that it does not look green to me, which would make the belief unjustified. It will become clearer in a moment just what such reasons might look like.

The argument used against the nebula theory shows that we must at least have prima facie justified epistemologically basic beliefs. But it might be urged that, although that argument does not prove it, these beliefs are actually incorrigibly justified rather than merely prima facie justified. Unless we are prepared to go even further, however, and maintain that these beliefs are actually incorrigible, then we cannot reasonably maintain that they are incorrigibly justified. The reason for this turns around an argument that has frequently been employed against the incorrigibility theory. Consider some particular candidate for an epistemologically basic belief, e.g., a person's belief about what color something looks to him. Armstrong and others have argued as follows.[10] In the not too distant future it is possible that neurophysiologists will have an adequate theory of the neurophysiology of perception. We can suppose this theory to be very highly confirmed. Let us suppose that on the basis of this theory they are able to construct a "super electroencephalograph" (SEEG) with the help of which they can tell exactly what perceptual states a person is in. In particular, they can tell what color something looks to him. Suppose then that on some occasion a person thinks that something looks red to him, but the SEEG reports that it really looks green to him. Armstrong and the others have urged that if the neurophysiological theory were sufficiently well confirmed we would have a good reason for thinking that the person is wrong about how things look to him, and consequently his belief cannot be incorrigible.

As an argument against the incorrigibility theory this begs the question. If epistemologically basic beliefs are incorrigible, then

[10] See particularly Armstrong [1963] and Meehl [1966].

the use of a neurological theory to rebut such a belief is impossible; if the theory came in conflict with a person's judgment about how things appear to him this would simply refute the theory. But on the assumption that epistemologically basic beliefs are not incorrigible, this argument is telling against the thesis that they are incorrigibly justified. If a person can be wrong about how things appear to him, we could ascertain with the help of the SEEG that he is wrong on particular occasions. But then it would be quite possible for a person to believe that things appear a certain way to him but not be justified in that belief. For example, he might make a hasty judgment that something looks red to him, but at the same time have (but not pay attention to) sufficient neurological data to know that it really looks green to him. Thus epistemologically basic beliefs being incorrigibly justified is not a viable alternative to their being either incorrigible or prima facie justified.

2.3 *Conclusions*

We have concluded that there must be epistemologically basic beliefs and that at least some of them must have something to do with perception. Contrary to what has generally been supposed, epistemologically basic beliefs need not be incorrigible; they may be only prima facie justified. These, however, are the only two possibilities that have come to light regarding the logical status of epistemologically basic beliefs. The possibility of a belief being prima facie justified would be very puzzling on the traditional theory of meaning according to which the only way to give the meaning of a statement is to give its truth conditions. But we have seen that another way to give the meaning of a statement is in terms of its justification conditions, and to say that a statement is prima facie justified is merely to say something about its justification conditions. So there is really no problem about how a belief might come to be prima facie justified. That it is prima facie justified would simply be part of the meaning of the statement.

As yet we have said nothing about what particular propositions are epistemologically basic, or about which logical status they have—incorrigibility or prima facie justification. There is no particular reason to think that all epistemologically basic propositions are going to have the same logical status. Some may be incorrigible and others prima facie justified. In subsequent chapters, as we investigate different areas of knowledge, we will isolate different classes of epistemologically basic propositions, and at each point the attempt will be made to determine whether the propositions in that class are incorrigible or prima facie justified.

3. Reasons

3.1 *Some Elementary Observations*

The observation that our knowledge is based upon epistemologically basic beliefs indicates that our knowledge does constitute a pyramidal structure whose lowest tier consists of epistemologically basic beliefs. Now let us turn to the upper tiers. How do we get from a lower tier to a higher tier? Beliefs in each tier are justified on the basis of beliefs in the tiers below it. Justification proceeds in terms of reasons. When one belief justifies another, then the former is said to be a *reason* for the latter.[11] Sometimes, rather than talk about *S*'s belief-that-*P* being a reason for *S* to believe that *Q*, we say that *S*'s reason is the fact that *P*. But, for the reasons given in section 2.1, it is clearer to talk about reasons as being beliefs.

Reasons differ in what we might call "quality". One belief may be a better reason for believing something than another belief. For example, if one has tested a hypothesis in ten different cases this might be sufficient to justify him in believing the hypothesis to be true, and so would provide him with a reason, but if he had tested the hypothesis in a hundred different cases, this would surely provide him with a better reason for believing the hypothesis to be true. It seems that all reasons are susceptible to these differences in quality. Even in the case of perceptual beliefs there are differences. For example, if an object seen in broad daylight looks plainly red to me, this may justify me in being certain that it is red. But if the object is seen in a dark room where I can just barely discern colors, and it looks only vaguely red to me, this may only justify me in thinking that it is probably red.

[11] This is not intended to be a definition of "reason" but only a rather loose characterization. As will become apparent, the concept of a reason is really a family of concepts which share many family resemblances but about which little can be said in general. No attempt will be made to give a general definition of "reason", although definitions will be offered for certain important classes of reasons.

Let us say that a *good* reason is one that is sufficient to justify the belief for which it is a reason. We often have reasons both for believing something and for disbelieving it. These are all reasons, both pro and con, but they do not all justify what they are reasons for. Each one by itself, in the absence of any competing reasons to the contrary, would be a good reason for believing that for which it is a reason, but taken together with the other reasons it may no longer be a good reason. Thus reasons need not always be good reasons.

3.2 *Logical and Contingent Reasons*

There are two fundamentally different kinds of good reasons for believing things. Some beliefs are good reasons for holding other beliefs simply by virtue of their logical nature. For example, the justified belief that *that* is a sheep in the field is a good reason for one to believe that *there is* a sheep in the field, and this results simply from the meanings of the statement that that is a sheep in the field and the statement that there is a sheep in the field. Whenever the justified belief-that-*P* is a good reason for one to believe that *Q*, simply by virtue of the meanings of the statements that *P* and that *Q*, we will say that the statement-that-*P* is a *logical reason* for believing the statement-that-*Q*. The simplest examples of logical reasons are of course simply entailments, but it will be seen later that there are other logical reasons that are not entailments.

It is desirable to have a precise definition of the notion of a logical reason. The basic idea is that if *P* is a logical reason for a person *S* to believe that *Q*, then in order for the belief-that-*P* to be a good reason for *S* to believe that *Q* he does not have to have an independent reason for believing that $(P \supset Q)$. This suggests the following:

(3.1) The statement-that-*P* is a logical reason for *S* to believe the statement-that-*Q* iff it is possible for the belief-that-*P* to be a good reason for *S* to believe-that-*Q* without his having an independent reason for believing that $(P \supset Q)$.

Notice that this does not require that if *P* is a logical reason for *S* to believe that *Q* then *P* is always a good reason for *S* to believe that *Q*. For example, that two times two is four is a logical reason for one to think that two is the positive square root of four, but it may not be a good reason for Jones to think that, because Jones may not know what a square root is. In order for a logical reason for S to believe-that-Q to be a *good* reason for S to believe-that-Q, at the very least it is required that S understand the statement-that-Q. In section 3.5 it will be seen that for some kinds of logical reasons, other conditions must also be satisfied.

In order for a person to *have* a reason for believing something, it must be a good reason, and he must be justified in believing that it is true. So let us define "S has the logical reason P for believing that Q" to mean "(1) S justifiably believes that P, (2) P is a logical reason for S to believe that Q, and (3) P is a good reason for S to believe that Q."

Philosophers have always recognized the category of logical reasons. But they have often overlooked the fact that there are good reasons that are not logical reasons. For example, the belief that Smith said there is a woman in the next room may be a good reason for me to think there is a woman in the next room. But it is certainly not a logical reason. Let us say that a good reason that is not a logical reason is a *contingent reason.*

Although there are these two categories of good reasons—logical reasons and contingent reasons—they are closely related. At least often a belief is only a contingent reason for a person to believe something if the person also has a related logical reason for believing it. For example, the belief that Smith said there is a woman in the next room is only a good reason for me to think that there is a woman in the next room because I justifiably believe that Smith is telling the truth. And the conjunctive belief that Smith said there is a woman in the next room and he is telling the truth is a logical reason for me to think that there is a woman there. Thus in many cases, the belief P is only a contingent reason for S to believe-that-Q if S also justifiably believes some further statement R such that the statement-that-$(P \& R)$ is a logical reason for believing the statement-that-Q. Such a contingent reason only becomes a contingent reason when one acquires such a further justified belief.

The question arises whether all contingent reasons can be reduced to logical reasons in this way. It seems that they can. By definition, if P is a contingent reason for S to believe that Q, then S must have an independent reason for believing that $(P \supset Q)$. This is not yet to say that he must believe that $(P \supset Q)$ but only that he must have a reason which would justify him in believing it were he to do so. However, it seems clear that in fact he must believe it. A contingent reason for believing-that-Q is a proposition that is *discovered* to be a reason, and discovering it to be a reason is simply to discover that if it is true then Q is true. For example, if Smith's having told me that there is a woman in the next room is a good reason for me to believe that there is a woman in the next room, then I must justifiably believe that if Smith told me there is a woman in the next room then there is a woman in the next room. (Of course, I need not justifiably believe that *whenever* Smith tells me there is a woman in the next room then there is a woman in the next room.) Thus, if P is a contingent reason for S to believe that Q, then S must justifiably believe that $(P \supset Q)$. The conjunctive belief-that-(P and $(P \supset Q)$) is a logical reason for S to believe that Q. Consequently, although there are these two distinct classes of good reasons—logical and contingent—contingent reasons can always be reduced to logical reasons. Therefore, justification can be thought of as proceeding exclusively in terms of logical reasons.

3.3 *Conclusive and Nonconclusive Logical Reasons*

Simple entailments are logical reasons. It is tempting to suppose that *all* entailments are logical reasons. But this will not do. If we consider any fairly complex entailment, one might be justified in believing the antecedent but, not knowing that the antecedent does entail the consequent, not be justified in believing the consequent. For example, the Axiom of Choice entails Zorn's Lemma, but this is not an entailment that one could be expected to see without proof. Thus one might justifiably believe that the Axiom of Choice is true but not see that it entails Zorn's Lemma, and so not be justified in believing that Zorn's Lemma is true. In order for an entailment to provide a good reason, one must be justified in believing that there is such an entailment. In the case of simple entailments, we can see just by considering the meanings of the statements that the one entails the other, and so such entailments are always good reasons for anyone who understands the statements involved. But there are more complex entailments that can only be known as the result of giving a demonstration, and these entailments do not provide us with good reasons until we have given the requisite demonstrations. To give such a demonstration is to acquire an independent reason for believing that if the antecedent is true then the consequent is true. Hence, although after the demonstrations have been given the entailments provide good reasons, they are not logical reasons. They are only contingent reasons.

We have isolated one class of logical reasons, which we can call "conclusive" reasons. Let us say that:

(3.2) The statement-that-P is a *conclusive reason* for S to believe that Q, iff the statement-that-P entails and is a logical reason for S to believe that Q.

Conclusive reasons are logical reasons. Do conclusive reasons exhaust the class of logical reasons? It is astonishing how often philosophers have thought that they do. For example, Judith Jarvis Thompson [1965], p. 292, writes, "One thing that seems plain is that if 'This is *S*' does not imply 'This is *P*' it will always be at best a matter of fact, to be established by investigation, that the first is a reason for the second."[12] But there seem to be clear counterexamples to the supposition that all logical reasons are conclusive. Consider, for example, induction. A class of singular statements $P_1, \ldots, P_n$ can provide inductive grounds for an unrestricted generalization Q, and thus the conjunction $(P_1 \;\&\; \ldots \;\&\; P_n)$ of those singular statements is a good reason for the general statement Q. The conjunction of the singular statements clearly does not entail the generalization, and yet it constitutes a logical reason for believing it. This can be shown as follows. If $(P_1 \;\&\; \ldots \;\&\; P_n)$ constituted merely a contingent reason for believing that Q, then a person would have to have an independent reason for believing that $[(P_1 \;\&\; \ldots \;\&\; P_n) \supset Q]$ before the conjunction could be a reason for believing that Q. There are only two plausible alternatives for what such an independent reason might be. First, it might be an inductive reason. But then we could ask the same question with regard to that inductive reason. This appeal to further inductive reasons can only go on for finitely many steps (recall that an infinite regress of justification is impossible); eventually there has to be a stopping point which must be justified on some other basis in order to get the whole sequence of inductive justifications started in the first place. This stopping point will be a conditional of this same form which is justified in some other way. This brings us to

[12] See also Russell [1948].

the second alternative: this conditional might be entailed by some general principle which we might call a principle of the Uniformity of Nature. Philosophers have often looked for some such principle to justify induction. But even if such a principle could be found, which seems exceedingly unlikely, we could still ask what justifies us in believing it. Again, there are two possibilities. First, the principle might be a truth of logic. But in that case the conditional $[(P_1 \mathbin{\&} \ldots \mathbin{\&} P_n) \supset Q]$, being entailed by the general principle, would also be a truth of logic. And this would require that the conjunction of singular statements $(P_1 \mathbin{\&} \ldots \mathbin{\&} P_n)$ entail the general statement Q, which is impossible. Suppose instead that the general principle is not a truth of logic. Then we can ask what logical reasons there are for believing it. And on the supposition that all logical reasons are conclusive, this amounts to asking what justified beliefs entail it. These beliefs constitute a set Γ. The beliefs in Γ must be justified without appeal to the general principle, so they cannot include any beliefs justified inductively. Consequently, any general beliefs in Γ must be truths of logic. But if a set of statements some of which are truths of logic entails another statement, then the set of statements that results from deleting the truths of logic also entails the other statement. Consequently, any general beliefs in Γ can be omitted with the result that the remaining beliefs still entail the principle of the Uniformity of Nature. The remaining beliefs in Γ must constitute a class of singular statements $R_1, \ldots, R_m$. But then if the inductive grounds $P_1, \ldots, P_n$ together with the principle of the Uniformity of Nature entailed Q, the inductive grounds $P_1, \ldots, P_n$ together with the additional singular statements $R_1, \ldots, R_m$ would also have to entail Q (because the latter entail the principle of the Uniformity of Nature). And then again we would have a general statement being entailed by a finite conjunction of singular statements, which is impossible. Thus induction cannot be accounted for in terms of conclusive reasons, and so cannot itself be a contingent reason. But it cannot be denied that induction provides us with good reasons. It must be concluded that induction constitutes one example of a nonconclusive logical reason. And it will be argued throughout this book that there are many other important examples of such reasons.[13]

[13] This of course should not be taken as implying that induction and other nonconclusive logical reasons cannot be "reduced" to conclusive rea-

The supposition that all logical reasons are conclusive is intimately connected with the traditional hope that all epistemological problems can be solved by giving reductive analyses. Beginning with the pyramidal theory of knowledge, philosophers have been enamored of the idea that each statement in the pyramid is either epistemologically basic or else can be expressed as a logical construction of statements falling in lower tiers of the pyramid. This would provide us with reductive analyses of all statements in terms ultimately of epistemologically basic statements. On the supposition that such reductive analyses were always possible, it became plausible to suppose that all logical reasons were conclusive. One could think of the process of justifying a belief as proceeding upward through successively higher tiers of the pyramid in such a way that each statement was a logical construction of statements below it and thus entailed by them. Then ultimately a justified belief would be entailed by the epistemologically basic statements at the bottom of the pyramid. But in recent years it has come to seem quite unlikely that this enterprise of seeking reductive analyses can be successful. It will be established in subsequent chapters of this book that reductive analyses cannot generally be given. It becomes accordingly less likely that justification can always be viewed in terms of entailment. This makes it plausible to suppose that there are many logical reasons that are not conclusive. One of the principal objectives of this book will be to establish that this is indeed the case in most of the philosophically problematic areas of knowledge. It is precisely the unacknowledged presence of non-conclusive logical reasons in those areas that has made the areas philosophically problematic.

3.4 *Logically Good Reasons and Prima Facie Reasons*

Logical reasons that are not conclusive are particularly interesting because they have been largely overlooked by philosophers bent upon finding reductive analyses. In them lies the key to a number of stubborn epistemological problems. Let us call such reasons *logically good reasons.* Whereas conclusive reasons guarantee truth, logically good reasons only guarantee justification.

---

sons, utilizing the techniques of section 3.2, by conjoining them with a conditional stating that if the reason is true then the conclusion is true. But the point is that these reasons are logical reasons all by themselves without conjoining them with such a conditional.

Induction provides us with one example of a logically good reason. The inductive grounds for a conclusion do not constitute a conclusive reason for believing the conclusion, but, as was argued above, they do constitute a logical reason.

Many logically good reasons have a certain kind of structure which makes it reasonable to call them *prima facie reasons.* A prima facie reason is a logical reason that is *defeasible.* In other words, a prima facie reason is a reason that by itself would be a good reason for believing something, and would ensure justification, but may cease to be a good reason when taken together with some additional beliefs. Induction provides us with one example of a prima facie reason. An inductive reason is a logical reason, and it is clearly defeasible. An inductive reason for accepting a generalization can be defeated on at least two grounds. First, no matter how strong the initial inductive evidence for the generalization, if further investigation reveals a counterexample then the original reason ceases to be a good reason. Second, if it is discovered that the sample on which the original generalization was based was not a fair sample, this will make the initial reason no longer a good reason even though it was a good reason until this was discovered.

Another, perhaps more interesting, example concerns perceptual judgments. For now, I will consider only one instance of a perceptual judgment—a person's judgment that something is red on the basis of its looking red to him—but it seems clear that the conclusions drawn in connection with this one example have rather broad application to perceptual judgments in general. In the next chapter it will be demonstrated that "*x* looks red to *S*" is a logical (in fact, a prima facie) reason for *S* to believe that *x* is red, so let us assume for now that this is true. This should seem plausible without much argument. It seems indisputable that there must be some sort of logical connection between "*x* looks red to *S*" and "*x* is red". It is not just an accident that red things tend to look red to people. This vague intuition is fortified by the observation that to suppose otherwise would make it impossible for us to ever know that anything is red. If we were to suppose that the connection between something's looking red to us and its actually being red is only a contingent connection, then the only way we could ever establish the connection is inductively. But we could never establish inductively that things that look red to us tend to be red, because in order to do that we would have to be able to tell independently what things are red, and the only way we have of doing that is in terms of what things look red to us, which would beg the question. Therefore, if the connection were merely contingent, then knowledge of red objects would be impossible. But knowledge of red objects is possible, so the connection cannot be contingent; it must be a logical connection of some sort.[14]

It was the hope of phenomenalism that this logical connection could be explained entirely in terms of conclusive reasons. It was hoped that the meaning of "*x* is red" could be analyzed in such a way that *x*'s looking red under certain specifiable phenomenological conditions would logically entail that *x* is red. We saw in Chapter One that no such analysis can be given. Consequently this logical connection cannot be explained entirely in terms of conclusive reasons. But given that it is a *logical* connection, it must be explained in terms of some sort of logical reasons, and hence these reasons must be logically good reasons.

Can we describe the logical connection between "*x* looks red to *S*" and "*x* is red" in such a way as to elicit the structure of the logically good reasons involved? Ordinarily, when I can see an object clearly, and have no reason for supposing that there is something wrong with my eyes, or that there are strange lights playing on the object, or anything of that sort, I unhesitatingly judge that the object is red if it looks red to me. If I have no beliefs about *x* other than that it looks red to me, then I am justified in thinking that it is red, and this is so simply by virtue of the concepts "red" and "looks red". But if I do have certain other beliefs, my belief that *x* looks red to me may not justify me in believing that *x* is red. For example, I may believe that there are red lights shining on *x* and that in the daylight it looks white. If I had those beliefs, the simple fact that *x* looked red to me would not justify me in believing that *x* was red. Thus the belief that *x* looks red to me is a defeasible logically good reason for me to think that *x* is red, i.e., it is a prima facie reason.

A proposition which, when added to a prima facie reason, defeats the justification, is called a *defeater*. We can define this precisely as follows:

14 This argument will be strengthened considerably in the next chapter.

(3.3) If P is a logical reason for S to believe that Q, then R is a defeater for this reason iff the conjunction $(P \& R)$ is not a logical reason for S to believe that Q.

For example, "x is illuminated by red lights, and red lights often make an object look red when it is not" is a defeater for "x looks red to S" as a logical reason for S to believe that x is red.

A prima facie reason is simply a logical reason for which there exist defeaters:

(3.4) P is a prima facie reason for S to believe-that-Q iff (1) P is a logical reason for S to believe that Q, (2) there is a proposition R which is a defeater for P as a reason for S to believe that Q, and (3) R is consistent with P.[15]

Now let us examine more closely the nature of defeaters. To say that P is a prima facie reason for S to believe-that-Q is to say that in the absence of any other information S is justified in believing that it would not be true that P unless it were true that Q. Let us symbolize this subjunctive conditional as "$P \Rightarrow Q$". Then P is a prima facie reason for S to believe-that-Q iff S is prima facie justified (in the sense of section 2.2) in believing-that-$(P \Rightarrow Q)$. A defeater must be a reason for thinking that this conditional is false, i.e., a reason for S to believe that $\sim (P \Rightarrow Q)$.

There are two ways in which a proposition can be a reason for denying a conditional, and accordingly there are two kinds of defeaters. First, if P is a prima facie reason for S to believe that Q, then any reason for S to believe that Q is false (even though P is true) is a defeater. Such a defeater defeats the conditional truth-functionally. Let us call these *type I* defeaters. For example, "Jones told me that x is not red, and Jones is generally reliable" would be a type I defeater for "x looks red to me" as a prima facie reason for me to believe that x is red. Analogously, "That crow is not black" would be a type I defeater for an inductive reason for thinking that all crows are black.

The second kind of defeater attacks the connection between P and Q rather than attacking Q directly. For example, although the

[15] Clause 3 is required because, even in the case when P entails Q, $(P \& \sim P)$ is not a logical reason for believing Q, and hence $\sim P$ is a defeater. This sort of defeater must be ruled out, or all logical reasons would be prima facie.

belief that there are red lights shining on x is not a reason for thinking that x is not red, it is nevertheless sufficient to prevent the prima facie reason that x looks red to me from justifying the belief that x is red, and hence it is a defeater. This second kind of defeater is, roughly speaking, a reason for thinking that, under these circumstances, knowing-that-P is not a good way to find out whether Q. For example, if there are red lights shining on x, then knowing that x looks red to me is not a good way to find out whether x is red, because the red lights can make a white object look red. Let us call these *type II* defeaters. A type II defeater is any reason for believing that $\sim (P \Rightarrow Q)$ which is not also a reason for believing that $\sim Q$.

In the case of induction, a type II defeater is any reason for thinking that the inductive sample is not a fair sample. What is meant by saying that the sample is not a fair sample is that examining it does not constitute a good way of finding out whether the predicate in question is universally satisfied. For example, if one is attempting to show inductively that no automobile can attain a speed greater than eighty miles per hour, but it is subsequently discovered that all the automobiles examined were Volkswagens and Volkswagens have less power than many other automobiles, this constitutes a type II defeater for the inductive generalization.

If P is a prima facie reason for S to believe that Q, then in order for S's justified belief-that-P to justify him in believing that Q he must have no good reason for believing that $\sim (P \Rightarrow Q)$, i.e., there can be no proposition R justifiably believed by him which is a good reason for him to believe that $\sim (P \Rightarrow Q)$. But this is not enough to guarantee that P is a good reason for him to believe that Q. Not only can he not justifiably believe any such defeater, he cannot even *un*justifiably believe such a defeater. The simple fact that S believes a defeater, justifiably or not, is sufficient to prevent P from being a good reason for him to believe that Q. For example, suppose that S is trying to predict the colors of marbles drawn from an urn. Let us suppose that fifteen marbles have been drawn so far, and they have all been red. S might then conclude inductively that the next marble will also be red. If he has no reason for thinking either that the next marble will not be red or that there is something peculiar about the urn so that the inductive generalization does not provide him with a way of getting to know whether the next marble will be red, then it seems we would agree that he would be justified in believing that the next marble will be red. In other words, he has a prima facie reason for thinking that the next marble will be red. But in fact, this is not enough. Let us suppose that *S* believed, without justification, that he has ESP and that on that basis he can tell that the next marble will be black. Although his belief in this defeater is not justified, the mere fact that he does believe it would make it irrational for him to believe that the next marble will be red and so would prevent him from being justified in believing that.

Therefore, if a prima facie reason justifies *S* in believing that *Q*, then *S* must not believe any defeaters. It might also seem that, if *S* has a good reason for believing some defeater but does not do so, this is sufficient to prevent the prima facie reason from justifying the belief that *Q*. But upon reflection, I think that this is wrong. Suppose *R* is a defeater for *P* as a reason for believing *Q*, and suppose *S* has a good reason for believing *R* but does not believe *R*. This can only be because he does not realize that he has a good reason for believing *R*. But then surely it would be irrational to withhold belief in *Q* on this basis. One must proceed on the basis of whatever epistemic connections one sees—it is irrational to do anything else. Thus, under these circumstances, *S*'s belief-that-*Q* is justified. It only becomes unjustified once he realizes that he has good reason for believing a defeater, and that proposition (that he has good reason for believing a defeater) is itself a defeater. Consequently, I think that not believing any defeater is both a necessary and sufficient condition for a prima facie reason to justify:

(3.5) If *P* is a prima facie reason for *S* to believe that *Q*, and *S* justifiably believes-that-*P* and believes-that-*Q* on the basis of his belief-that-*P*, then *S* is justified in believing-that-*Q* iff he does not believe any defeaters for this prima facie reason.

To say that *P* is a prima facie reason for one to believe-that-*Q* is to say that there is a "logical presumption" in favor of believing the conditional ($P \Rightarrow Q$). This is a very important feature of prima facie reasons. Philosophers have often been puzzled about how a person can know on the basis of perception that something is red without first ascertaining that there are no colored lights shining on the object, that he is not hallucinating or under the influence of drugs, that he is not hypnotized, etc. Analogously, philosophers have been puzzled about how a person can justifiably draw an inductive conclusion without first ascertaining that the inductive sample is a fair sample, but in the last analysis there appears to be no way to do this short of ascertaining that what is true of the sample is true in general and hence that the inductive conclusion is true.

This is a general puzzlement arising out of a misunderstanding of how type II defeaters function. If P is a prima facie reason for one to believe that Q, it cannot be required that in order to employ this prima facie reason one must first establish that there is nothing which, if known, would constitute a type II defeater. To establish this would be to come to know on the basis of some independent reasons that the conditional $(P \Rightarrow Q)$ is true and thus that no type II defeaters can arise. But given that P is true, to establish the truth of $(P \Rightarrow Q)$ without relying upon the logical connection between the prima facie reason and the conclusion would be to establish the truth of Q without relying upon the prima facie reason. The requirement that this always be done would lead to skepticism because in many cases (such as induction or color judgments) the prima facie reason constitutes the only basic way of getting to know whether the conclusion is true. If we were not allowed to use the prima facie reasons connected with induction or perception without first justifying them (in which case they would be merely contingent reasons), then we would never be able to draw any contingent general conclusions or make any color judgments.

The solution to this puzzlement results from simply turning the argument on its head and regarding it as a reductio ad absurdum. If P is a prima facie reason for S to believe that Q, then S does not need a reason for thinking that $(P \Rightarrow Q)$. Evidence (concerning, e.g., hallucination, drugs, colored lights, etc.) is *only* relevant if it is evidence *against* the conditional. Evidence *for* the conditional is never required. To suppose otherwise leads to skepticism, but skepticism is false.

But in order for a person to know on the basis of its appearance that an object is red, mustn't he know that he is not hallucinating? The answer to this is "Yes". In normal perception, we do know that we are not hallucinating. But this does not imply that we must *first establish* that we are not hallucinating. As long as there is no reason for thinking that we *are* hallucinating, we automatically have a good reason for believing that we are not. This works as follows. In the absence of any defeaters, I am automatically justified in thinking that an object is the way it appears to me. To say that I am hallucinating with respect to the object entails that in some respect it is not the way it appears to me. Thus if an object *is* the way it appears to me then I am not hallucinating. Hence in the absence of any defeaters for my normal prima facie reasons for perceptual judgments, I am justified in thinking that I am not hallucinating.

Herein lies the solution to the skeptical problem with which this book began. How do I know that I am not wired into a computer that directly stimulates my brain in a manner entirely independent of what is going on in the world around me? The answer is quite simple. In the absence of any defeaters, I am automatically justified in believing that what appears to me to be going on around me really is occurring. But some of these occurrences are such as to logically preclude my being wired into a computer. Thus in the absence of any reason for thinking otherwise, I am automatically justified in thinking that I am not wired into such a computer. (Of course, all of this assumes that perception does provide me with prima facie reasons for judgments about the world, but this will be established in the next chapter.) The reason the skeptical argument seems initially persuasive is that I do have to know that I am not wired into such a computer, just as I do have to know that no other type I defeater holds; but I do not have to establish these facts *first* before I can make a perceptual judgment—instead I am automatically justified in accepting these facts when I make a perceptual judgment.

3.5 *Logical Reasons Again*

The concept of a logical reason was defined in 3.1. For most purposes that is a perfectly satisfactory definition. However, it would be desirable if we could define all of our concepts of kinds of reasons without recourse to the undefined concept of a good reason. The concept of a good reason is employed in the definition of a logical reason, and consequently gets carried on into the definitions of "conclusive reason", "logically good reason", and "prima facie reason". The attempt will now be made to purge these definitions of the concept of a good reason. Once having done so, one might hope (although the attempt will not be made here) that the concept of a good reason could ultimately be defined in terms of these other concepts.

Suppose *P* is a logical reason for *S* to believe-that-*Q*. Suppose *S* justifiably believes-that-*P*, and believes-that-*Q* on the basis of his belief-that-*P*. The only way his belief-that-*Q* can fail to be justified is if *P* is a defeasible logical reason, i.e., a prima facie reason, and *S* also believes some defeater for the reason. This possibility is ruled out if we suppose that *S* holds no beliefs except *P*, *Q*, and whatever is necessary to justify him in believing-that-*P*. Under these circumstances, *S* is justified in believing-that-*Q*.

Conversely, suppose that whenever *S* justifiably believes-that-*P*, and holds whatever beliefs are necessary to justify his belief-that-*P*, and believes-that-*Q* on the basis of his belief that *P*, and holds no other beliefs, he is justified in believing that *Q*. This means that it is possible for *P* to be a good reason for him to believe-that-*Q* without his having an independent reason for believing that $(P \supset Q)$; hence *P* is a logical reason for him to believe that *Q*. Thus we have:

(3.6) The statement-that-*P* is a logical reason for *S* to believe the statement-that-*Q* iff, necessarily, if *S* justifiably believed-that-*P* and held whatever beliefs are necessary to justify his belief-that-*P*, and believed-that-*Q* on the basis of his belief-that-*P*, and held no other beliefs, then *S* would be justified in believing-that-*Q*.

We can adopt this as a new definition of "logical reason", and treat 3.1 as being a true principle about logical reasons rather than a definition.

Unfortunately, in eliminating "good reason" from our definition of "logical reason", we have introduced a new undefined element: "believes on the basis of". This concept also played a role in principle 3.5. For what follows there is no reason why we cannot leave this concept unanalyzed. A few remarks will be made for the sake of clarity, but they will fall short of a complete analysis.

If *S* believes-that-*Q* on the basis of his belief-that-*P*, we say that *his reason* for believing-that-*Q* is that *P*. Sometimes a person's reason for believing a proposition *Q* is something to which he has consciously appealed in arriving at the belief-that-*Q*. For example, a person might hear the patter of rain on the roof, wonder what is causing it, and then conclude, "Oh, it is raining." But such explicit reasoning is the exception rather than the rule. Only rarely does a person move so explicitly from his reason for a belief to the belief. More commonly, a person familiar with the sound of rain will simply *come to believe* that it is raining when he hears the sound of rain on the roof, this without having any thoughts about the connection between the sound and the rain. Eminent philosophers, faced with this sort of case, have sought refuge in talk about "unconscious reasoning", but that is not explanatory and it is better to avoid such talk. It seems that all we can really say about these cases is that the person's reason for the belief is the cause of his holding the belief.

This suggests that "*S*'s reason for believing-that-*Q* is that *P*" is analyzable as "*S*'s believing-that-*P* is causally responsible for his believing-that-*Q*". However, we must put some restrictions on the kinds of causal connections involved here. There are extraordinary ways in which one belief may cause another belief. For example, a person who is mentally unstable, when faced with a difficult situation, might lapse into a psychotic state which is characterized in part by his believing that he is Napoleon. His belief that he is in this difficult situation would then be the cause of his believing that he is Napoleon, although we would not want to say that it is his reason for believing that he is Napoleon. Roughly speaking, reasons are not just any causes for believing something, they are "ordinary psychological" causes. Of course, the application of this phrase does little to clarify such causes. It should be possible to spell out precisely what kinds of causes are involved, but that will not be attempted here. We will, however, have occasion to refer again to these kinds of causes.

3.6 *Conclusions*

The preceding picture of epistemic justification can be summarized as follows. Justification proceeds in terms of good reasons. Good reasons can be classified as logical reasons and contingent reasons. One class of logical reasons—conclusive reasons—is quite familiar. However, these reasons do not exhaust the class of logical reasons. The more or less traditional assumption that they do has been a contributing factor in making a number of traditional epistemological problems appear insoluble. This is because the epistemic connection between such things as perception and the physical world, or inductive grounds and the inductive conclusion, or behavior and mental states, cannot be described in terms solely of conclusive reasons. We must recognize at least one additional class of logical reasons—prima facie reasons. To map out precisely what logical reasons are involved in these concepts is a difficult task, but with the help of the concept of a prima facie reason it no longer appears to be an impossible task. It will be undertaken in detail in the remainder of this book.

That the existence of prima facie reasons has not generally been recognized is probably due to the difficulty in explaining within a traditional framework how it is possible for there to be such reasons. Philosophers have traditionally thought of the meaning of a statement as being determined solely by its truth conditions. But, as we have seen, this is a mistake. The meaning of a statement is of course uniquely determined by its truth conditions, but these truth conditions can generally only be stated in a trivial way—by repeating the statement itself or by giving some rather uninteresting paraphrase of it. A more informative account of the meaning of a statement can often be given by saying under what circumstances one would be justified in thinking that the statement is true or that it is false, i.e., by saying what counts as a good reason for accepting or denying the statement. On this picture there is no difficulty in understanding how prima facie reasons are possible—they are just one kind of good reason that can be involved in making up the meaning of a statement.

Chapter Three

Theories of Perceptual Knowledge

1. Introduction

CHAPTERS One and Two have laid the groundwork for an attack on a number of traditional epistemological problems. The first of these is the problem of perception. The problem of perception is to explain how it is possible to acquire knowledge about the physical world on the basis of perception. This resolves itself into the task of giving an account of the justification conditions of statements about the physical world that shows how those statements can be based on perception. The basic tool for this task will be the concept of a prima facie reason.

Historically, philosophers have been puzzled about how there can be any conceptual connection between perception and the physical world, between appearance and reality. These seem to be two distinct realms, and there is no obvious way to bridge the gap between them. It is at this point that we must appeal to the theory of meaning elaborated in Chapter One. That there is a connection between perception and the physical world is simply part of our concept of a physical object. A physical object is, by definition, the sort of thing we perceive. Our judgments about physical objects are based on perception. Thus perception is intimately involved in the justification conditions for statements about physical objects. Those justification conditions are themselves constitutive of the concept of a physical object. This is the source of the connection. We should ask, not whether there is a connection between perception and the physical world (of course there is!), but what the connection is.

The traditional theories regarding the nature of the connection between perception and the physical world can be viewed as attempts to pinpoint the error in the following skeptical argument.[1] This argument purports to establish that knowledge of the physical world is impossible:

1. Beliefs about the physical world are not themselves epistemologically basic, and hence they must be justified by appealing to some other beliefs—presumably beliefs about the way things appear to us.
2. Beliefs about the physical world are not logically entailed by beliefs about the way things appear to us.
3. Nor can beliefs about the way things appear to us constitute an inductive reason for holding beliefs about the physical world. In order for them to constitute an inductive reason, we would have to be able to compare the way things appear to us with the way they really are and see that the former constitute a fairly reliable guide to the latter. But this is not possible because the only way we have of finding out how things really are is by way of how they appear to us, which begs the question.
4. As beliefs about the way things appear to us neither entail nor give inductive support to beliefs about the way things really are, the latter beliefs cannot be supported on the basis of the former, and consequently knowledge of the physical world is impossible.

The conclusion of this argument is false, so one of the steps must be incorrect. The traditional theories of perceptual knowledge can be regarded as different choices regarding which step to deny. Let us consider each step separately.

2. Naive Realism

Naive realism[2] denies the first step of the skeptical argument, maintaining that some beliefs about physical objects are epistemologically basic. On the common assumption that epistemologically basic beliefs must be incorrigible, naive realism is extremely

[1] See Ayer [1956], pp. 75-81.

[2] The assignment of names to the theories discussed here should be taken stipulatively. Theories historically called by these names do not always fall in the corresponding categories. For example, C. I. Lewis's phenomenalism would here be regarded as a version of scientific realism.

implausible. We can and do make mistakes in our beliefs about physical objects. Once it is recognized that epistemologically basic beliefs may be only prima facie justified, however, naive realism gains considerable plausibility.

Let us consider what sorts of beliefs about physical objects might be prima facie justified. The simplest candidate is a belief like "There is something red before me". Is this prima facie justified? Suppose I am in a dark room with my eyes closed and I have no visual sensations at all. Furthermore, I have not been told anything about the contents of the room, nor have I read anything about the contents, etc. Nevertheless, I persist in believing that there is something red before me. Surely this belief is unjustified, although I have no reason for thinking that it is false. Consequently, such a belief cannot be prima facie justified.

A better candidate is "I see something red before me". This is at least indirectly a belief about physical objects because it entails that there is something red before me. However, it still fails to be prima facie justified. This becomes evident by considering a case in which a person believes he sees something red but does not believe that what he sees looks red to him. Here it is important that the person does not believe that the object looks some other color to him—that would be a reason for thinking that he does not see something red and would spoil the example. Rather, we want the person simply to have no belief about what color it looks to him. For example, we can suppose he sees the object in silhouette on the horizon against the setting sun, but it is too far away and the light too bad to be able to tell anything about its color. Then the person has no direct visual reason for thinking that it is *not* red (although he has no such reason for thinking that it *is* red, either). In this case it seems clear that unless the person had some independent reason for thinking that the object was red, he would not be justified in thinking he saw something red. Therefore, that belief is not prima facie justified.

A final candidate which fares better than the other two is "I see that there is something red before me".[3] The counterexample that

[3] It has frequently been pointed out that "see that" has both a perceptual use and a conclusion-drawing use. To illustrate the conclusion-drawing use, I might be making my way through a heavy fog by following marks on the sidewalk and consulting a map. At some point, after examining the map, I might peer out into the fog and mutter, "I see that there is a red object

worked for the previous candidate does not work here because if what a person sees does not look red to him, that in itself is a conclusive reason for him to think that he does not see that it is red. Nor do any other counterexamples come immediately to mind. It is plausible to suppose that beliefs like this are prima facie justified, but more discussion is necessary before we can be confident that this is correct. We cannot settle this matter now but will return to it in section 9.

3. Phenomenalism

Phenomenalism attacks the skeptical argument by denying the second step and maintaining that statements about the way things appear to us may entail statements about physical objects. This basic position can be elaborated in various ways, generally taking the form that the truth conditions of statements about material objects can be expressed entirely in terms of statements about the way things appear to us. We need not go into these elaborations, however, because the basic unelaborated position can be shown to be wrong by itself. The argument is that given in Chapter One. Given any statement about the way things appear to a person and any statement about physical objects, we can imagine circumstances in which the former would be true and the latter false, thus demonstrating that the former does not entail the latter. One way of doing this is to suppose once more that we have a group of neurophysiologists who have arrived at a complete neurophysiological account of perception. To test their account, they wire a subject into a very complicated computer which directly stimulates his brain and they disconnect his sense organs from his brain. They could then arrange for things to appear any way at all to him. Given any statement *P* about the way things appear to him and any statement *Q* about the physical world, they could make *P* true

---

before me (but I can't see it)." Naive realism is only concerned with the perceptual use of "see that". In oral communication, the perceptual use is distinguished by emphasizing "see". The man in the fog might say, "I see that there is a red object before me, but I don't *see* that there is a red object before me." Some philosophers are reluctant to admit the existence of a perceptual use of "sees that". If the reader feels this inclination, he is referred to n. 18, below.

independently of the truth or falsity of *Q*, thus showing that *P* does not entail *Q*.[4]

4. Scientific Realism

The third possibility for escaping the consequences of the skeptical argument is to maintain that the gap between the way things appear to us and the way things really are can in fact be bridged inductively. It must be admitted that enumerative induction[5] will not work here, but it might be maintained that some other kind of induction will work. The natural candidate is the hypothetico-deductive method. For example, at one time, Russell maintained that we infer the existence of physical objects as the simplest explanation of why things appear to us in the way they do.[6] This position is sometimes called *scientific realism.*

I have some general misgivings about the hypothetico-deductive method. I suspect that philosophers have generally been wrong in attributing the use of what they have called the hypothetico-deductive method to scientists. I will defend this heretical view in Chapter Eight, and this constitutes what is no doubt the strongest argument against scientific realism. But this is not the only basis upon which we can attack scientific realism. According to scientific realism, we first observe certain regularities in the way things appear to us. For example, we discover that when we have the sensations that are in fact associated with walking around an object, the way we are appeared to changes in a continuous and predictable manner (which we later account for by supposing that there is a physical object there and that the way an object looks satisfies the laws of perspective).[7] After observing many such

[4] This is not *quite* true, because *Q* might be a statement about the computer. But this very limited correlation between appearance and reality is not adequate to ground phenomenalism.

[5] Enumerative induction is that form wherein (roughly) from the fact that all (or most) *observed A*'s have been *B*'s we infer that all (or most) *A*'s are *B*'s.

[6] Russell [1912], pp. 21-24.

[7] The "appeared to" terminology is used here because it is ontologically and psychologically neutral. It commits us to no theory regarding what is involved in being appeared to a certain way (e.g., redly). Accordingly, we can avoid all reference to such mysterious entities as sense data, percepts, and the like. The confused wrangling about these entities that has been so

regularities in the way things apear to us,[8] we posit the existence of physical objects to explain them. The posit is that generally the way things appear to us is determined by what physical objects are in our proximity. Subsequently, when things appear a certain way we can justifiably conclude on the basis of the above generalization that there are most likely physical objects of certain sorts around us. According to this position there are two distinct elements that go into justifying our particular beliefs about physical objects: (1) our having observed certain regularities in the way things appear to us; (2) things appearing to us in a certain way now. We might state scientific realism succinctly as the theory that the observed regularities under clause 1 together with "I am appeared to φly" constitutes a prima facie reason for me to believe that there is something φ before me (for suitable φ).

The trouble with scientific realism is that, in fact, in order for a person to make perceptual judgments about physical objects, it is not logically required that he first be aware of the regularities under clause 1, or even that he has in any sense been exposed to them. Consider a person who was born blind but at the age of thirty acquired sight through an operation. Such a person has not previously been exposed to the regularities required by the scientific realist. It follows from scientific realism that if this person were to immediately begin making judgments about the way things are on the basis of the way they look to him, his judgments would not then and there be justified. As a matter of fact, people who acquire sight in this way as mature individuals report that they do not at first "see objects" and hence do not immediately make perceptual judgments. It takes awhile before their experience takes on the character of normal perception. But although such a person may not immediately see objects, it seems we want to say that *whenever* things finally click into place and he begins to see objects he is then justified in the judgments he makes about them on the basis of the way they appear to him. If by chance a person *immediately* saw objects after his operation, his perceptual judgments would be no

---

prevalent in much of epistemology is largely irrelevant to the fundamental epistemological problems regarding perception.

[8] Throughout, I use "the way things appear to us" as a more idiomatic rendering of "the way we are appeared to"; "things" in this phrase should be taken nonreferentially, like the "it" in "it is raining".

more suspect than if he only came to see them after some time. But this directly contradicts scientific realism, so that theory cannot be regarded as giving a correct account of perceptual knowledge.[9]

One might object in some way to the above formulation of scientific realism and maintain that there is some other way of inductively bridging the gap between appearance and reality. But I take it that what characterizes *any* inductive approach to this problem is the requirement that, before one can justifiably make a perceptual judgment about the physical world, he must first have been exposed to the way things appeared to him on at least some earlier occasions. And the above example shows that even this very minimal requirement is unnecessary.

5. Descriptivism

With the possible exception of the first, it seems that none of the initial steps of the skeptical argument can be successfully attacked. This leaves only the final step. If we are to avoid the skeptical conclusion, which we must because it is clearly false, we must maintain that although statements about the way things appear to us neither entail nor give inductive support for statements about the physical world, they nevertheless give support of another kind. Ayer calls this approach *descriptivism.*[10] The principal objective of Chapters One and Two was to show that descriptivism is a feasible approach—not all logical reasons must be either conclusive or inductive.

I think we must conclude that descriptivism constitutes the correct answer to the skeptical argument. The relation between ap-

[9] In section 7 I defend a "principle of implicit reasons" which considerably weakens the requirement of scientific realism that one must be aware of regularities in the way things appear to him before he can justifiably make perceptual judgments. But even given the principle of implicit reasons, it follows from scientific realism that a person must at least have been exposed to the regularities, and the example of a person who acquires sight as a mature individual shows that even this weak implication of scientific realism is false. Thus scientific realism cannot be salvaged by appealing to the principle of implicit reasons.

[10] Ayer [1956], p. 80. Ayer uses the term "descriptivism" to refer to any theory that proceeds by attacking the final step of the skeptical argument. However, I will reserve the term for my own particular brand of descriptivism.

pearance and reality cannot be spelled out in terms of either entailment or induction. The problem is to see how it can be spelled out. The essential tool for this task is the concept of a prima facie reason. Descriptivism, as I will construe it, is simply the position that statements about the way things appear to us constitute prima facie reasons for judgments about how they are. For example, "I am appeared to redly" constitutes a prima facie reason for me to believe that there is something red before me. That this is so is simply part of the concept of something being red—this is the core of the way we discover that things are red, and hence constitutes the most important part of the conditions under which we are justified in thinking that a red object is present. Those conditions in turn (according to the theory of meaning defended in Chapter One) determine the meaning of "red". That this is correct seems almost obvious when we consider actual cases of color judgment. Ordinarily if we are appeared to redly we have no hesitation in judging that there is something red before us. We do not first try to establish that we are not hallucinating, that we are not wearing colored glasses, that we are not hypnotized, that there are no colored lights shining on the object, etc. These possibilities only become relevant if we have some concrete reason for thinking that one of them is actually the case. Then and only then is it incumbent upon us to establish that they are not the case. Indeed, this is as it must be. If in making a perceptual judgment we first had to establish that none of the things that can go wrong with perception is going wrong, we could never get off the ground, because establishing, for example, that we are not hallucinating also involves perceptual judgments. What this all means is simply that "I am appeared to φly" (for "perceptual attributes") constitutes a prima facie reason for me to think that there is something φ before me.

It seems clear that descriptivism is right as far as it goes—namely, if I am justified in believing that I am appeared to redly then, prima facie, I am justified in believing that there is something red before me. But this cannot be a *complete* account of perceptual knowledge, because it is simply false that in making perceptual judgments we generally have any beliefs at all about the way things appear to us. We simply *see things*; we are not aware of appearances. When I see a book on my desk, my thought is simply, "There is a book." I have no thought that I am appeared to bookly.

To be sure, I would unhesitatingly assent to this if asked, but in doing so I am shifting my attention and entertaining a *new* thought. Consequently, it cannot be my thinking that I am appeared to bookly which justifies my thinking that there is a book before me.

This is precisely the point that has often made naive realism seem so attractive—we do not *infer* that there is a book before us because we are appeared to bookly—we simply *see* that there is a book before us. But, unfortunately, naive realism fares no better here than any of the other theories of perceptual knowledge. We saw above that we cannot suppose statements like "There is a book" to be epistemologically basic. The only version of naive realism that is defensible is that which maintains that statements like "I see that there is a book before me" are epistemologically basic. But the above observations are equally telling against this form of naive realism as they are against descriptivism. It is simply a mistake to suppose that we first think "I see that there is a book before me" and then infer "There is a book before me". Thus the difficulty that arises for descriptivism is equally a difficulty for naive realism (and for all of the other theories of perceptual knowledge).

It might be supposed that we can escape this difficulty by distinguishing between "occurrent" and "dispositional" senses of "believe". That some such distinction is legitimate seems clear. The sense in which I now consciously believe that I am sitting at my desk typing is quite different from the sense in which, when I am not consciously thinking about mathematics, I believe that two is the positive square root of four. The clearest cases of dispositional belief are those in which we originally had an occurrent belief, and then stopped thinking about the matter. But that is not the case in perception. I did not first think "I am appeared to bookly" and on that basis now have a dispositional belief to that effect. Thus it is questionable whether this distinction can be invoked to solve our problem. Further reasons for thinking that our problem cannot be solved by appealing to dispositional beliefs will be given in section 7.

6. Direct Realism

The above difficulty suggests a modification of descriptivism. Rather than say that it is my *thinking* that I am appeared to redly which justifies me in thinking that there is something red before me, why not simply say that it is my *being* appeared to redly that constitutes the prima facie reason? This involves some rather minor revisions in the definition of "prima facie reason" so that something other than a belief can be a reason, but with those changes this becomes a rather attractive position. It is somewhat similar in flavor to naive realism, so I will call it *direct realism*.[11]

Direct realism involves rejecting our earlier conclusion (in Chapter Two) that knowledge is always based upon epistemologically basic beliefs. The argument which led to that conclusion assumed that justification always proceeds in terms of beliefs—what justifies one belief is always another belief. What does seem quite clear is that all that can be relevant in deciding whether a person is justified in holding a certain belief is his overall mental state—including his beliefs—but things other than his beliefs may be relevant too: for example, the way things appear to him. The argument by which we originally sought to establish that knowledge is based upon epistemologically basic beliefs can still be employed to show that knowledge of physical objects is based *somehow* on the way things appear to us, but perhaps not by way of *beliefs* about how things appear to us.

One thing that makes direct realism attractive is that it seems to avoid altogether the confusing issue of whether our beliefs about the way things appear to us are incorrigible; if our beliefs about physical objects are not based on the latter beliefs, then our grounds for the latter beliefs are irrelevant. Unfortunately, this is a mistake. I will argue now (1) that direct realism is only correct if beliefs about the way things appear to us are incorrigible, and (2) that if they are incorrigible then direct realism is equivalent to descriptivism.[12]

Suppose that beliefs about the way things appear to us are not incorrigible. Then one could mistakenly believe, and be justified in believing, that x looks red to him. As he is mistaken, x looks some other color to him, e.g., green. According to direct realism, he would have no reason for thinking that x is not green. His thinking that x looks red to him is not supposed to be such a reason; only x's actually looking red to him would be a reason. Thus because x looks green to him, he would be justified in think-

[11] This is the position taken by Quinton [1973].

[12] The second point is argued in section 8.

ing that *x* is green. But this is clearly wrong. As he justifiably believes that *x* looks red to him, we would take him to be justified in thinking that *x* is red, not green. It would be ludicrous for him to assert that *x* is green and that he has no nonperceptual reason for believing this, but when asked whether he believes *x looks* green to him reply, "No, *x* looks red to me." Thus direct realism is not tenable if this sort of situation can arise. Direct realism is only plausible if one's beliefs about how things appear to him are incorrigible.[13]

7. The Principle of Implicit Reasons

I will now argue that the difficulty encountered by descriptivism, which led us to formulate direct realism, ceases to be a difficulty once we recognize a certain general principle about epistemic justification. Given this principle, it will be seen that descriptivism entails that if beliefs about the way things appear to us are incorrigible then direct realism is correct.

At first it is apt to seem that if *S*'s reason for believing-that-*P* is that *Q*, and on this basis *S* is justified in believing-that-*P*, then *S* must justifiably believe-that-*Q*. But this is not true. Quinton gives two helpful examples.[14] First, I may claim that my dog is ill. After staring at my dog in puzzlement for a while, I may suddenly notice that he has a glazed look in his eye and it will come to me that that is what led me to think he was ill. But on a conscious level I was previously unaware of the glazed look. In other words, my reason for thinking he is ill is that he has a glazed look in his eye, but as I did not consciously note the latter, I did not have the belief that he has a glazed look in his eye.

A second example: having known two people, *A* and *B*, for some time, I may believe that *A* dislikes *B*. I may be quite certain of this, and quite right, and yet be unable to cite any particular reason for believing it. I can be confident that I have observed behavior on the part of *A* which in fact supports my conclusion,

[13] This suggests that we should attempt to modify direct realism so that both the way we are appeared to and our beliefs about the way we are appeared to become relevant. This is in effect just what we get when we combine descriptivism with the principle of implicit reasons (see section 7).

[14] Quinton [1955]. Quinton uses these examples for a different purpose than they are used here, but they serve our purpose equally well.

and that this is what has caused me to believe that *A* dislikes *B*, but I cannot recall any particular instance of behavior, or not enough instances, to be able to give a good reason for my judgment. This sort of case is quite common. Except in extreme cases, how often can we actually give reasons for our judgments about people's feelings toward one another? The behavioral clues upon which we rely are generally so subtle that we are not consciously aware of them. And yet, we cannot withhold the term "knowledge" from these judgments. To do so would imply that we rarely know anything about other people's mental states, which is absurd. Granted, it is surely necessary here that I have observed instances of behavior which are such that if I *could* recall them all and sum them up in a single belief, that belief would be a logical reason for my judgment, but in fact I may be unable to do this. Yet my judgment may still be an instance of knowledge, so it is justified. Once again then, I have a reason which justifies my claim, but I do not have a corresponding belief.

Two elements are common to the above cases. First, where my reason for believing-that-*P* is that *Q*, the circumstances (at some time prior to the time I made the judgment-that-*P*) were such that I *could* have justifiably believed that *Q*. Second, in both cases, my having been in those circumstances is causally responsible for my believing-that-*P*. In the first case it was whatever perceptual state would justify me in thinking that my dog has a glazed look in his eye that caused me (psychologically) to acquire the belief that he was ill. In the second case it was whatever would justify me in thinking that *A* behaved in a certain way that caused me to believe that *A* dislikes *B*.

This suggests the following *principle of implicit reasons*:

(7.1) If the statement-that-*Q* is a logical reason for *S* to believe-that-*P*, and if at this time *S*'s justifiably believing-that-*Q* would justify him in believing-that-*P*, then if (possibly at some prior time) the epistemologically relevant circumstances are (or were) such that *S could* justifiably believe-that-*Q*, and *S*'s being (or having been) in those circumstances is the psychological cause of his believing-that-*P*, then he is justified in believing-that-*P*.[15]

[15] This principle abounds in unclear concepts. But perhaps it will be sufficiently clear for the purposes to which it is put here. This principle should

This principle seems to be completely general, holding in all cases. Consider an inductive example: I believe that a certain kind of cloud is generally accompanied by rain. My reason for this is surely that most such clouds that I have witnessed in the past have been accompanied by rain. But no matter how hard I rack my memory, I cannot now recall even a single specific instance of such a cloud. The specific observations that make up my inductive evidence must have registered on some level to make me believe what I do, but they did not register on the level of conscious recollection. Still, it would be preposterous to claim that I do not know that such clouds are generally accompanied by rain. I think that this is characteristic of most of our inductive reasoning. More often than not, when we believe a generalization on the basis of our general unorganized experience of the world (as opposed to the case where we set out explicitly to acquire evidence for a hypothesis), we move (psychologically) directly from our observations to the general belief without recalling most of those observations and without stopping to sum them up in a single belief. The justification for holding conclusions arrived at by such "implicit" inductive reasoning would be inexplicable without the principle of implicit reasons.

A different sort of inductive example is provided by a case in which we believe something on the basis of an inductive generalization but are unable to articulate the generalization. For example, I may believe that a certain painting is a van Gogh because it "looks like a van Gogh", but I may be totally unable to say what is involved in looking like a van Gogh. This is a common psychological phenomenon. There is a classical experiment in psychology in which subjects are told to classify Chinese characters into two groups—*A*'s and non-*A*'s—without being told what it is to be an *A*. (In fact, *A*'s are those characters containing a certain subcharacter.) At first the subjects are told to guess, and each time they are told whether they are right. The subjects quickly acquire the ability to classify the characters reliably, and this happens long before they themselves are aware of what principle they are using to

---

also be generalized to allow for the case in which *Q* is a conjunction, each conjunct of which could have been justifiably believed at a different time, but we will not pursue the details of that here.

classify the characters. Similarly, in the case of the painting, I am able to classify paintings as van Goghs and non-van Goghs without being able to articulate the way in which I do it. Are we to say that my judgment is unjustified? We can hardly say that—the phenomenon is too common. I would propose that precisely the same phenomenon occurs in recognizing robins, oak trees, my mother, and just about anything else. In each case we classify the object in question on the basis of its appearance, although its appearance is only contingently connected to its identity. Thus we are relying upon a contingent generalization, but it is not one that we can articulate. We can hardly say that all such judgments are unjustified. What justifies them is the principle of implicit reasons. The generalization in question is in each case an implicit reason. We have observed inductive evidence which would justify us in accepting the generalization were we to formulate it, and it is because we have observed such evidence that we classify the object as we do. Once more then the principle of implicit reasons is indispensable to our ordinary reasoning.

Problems arise regarding the nature of the causal connection involved in the principle of implicit reasons. The difficulties are the same as those that arise in section 3.5 of Chapter Two in attempting to analyze "believes on the basis of". We must restrict the connections allowed to those "ordinary psychological causes" that are normally involved in what philosophers have so frequently called "unconscious reasoning". It is not very clear just what the limits of these causes are, but fortunately this will not prove to be a difficulty for those applications to which the principle is put in this book.

It might be supposed that we can avoid the principle of implicit reasons by appealing to dispositional beliefs. That is, one might urge that whenever *S* is justified in believing-that-*P* on the basis of the implicit reason *Q*, *S* will have a dispositional belief that *Q*, and so we can regard the chain of justification as proceeding entirely in terms of beliefs. I do not find the concept of a dispositional belief terribly clear, but one thing at least seems clear—if one has a dispositional belief-that-*Q*, then he must have the disposition to occurrently believe-that-*Q* whenever he considers the matter. For example, when I am not consciously thinking about mathematics, I still have the dispositional belief that two plus two is four. At least part of what this means is that whenever I consider the matter, I will have the occurrent belief that two plus two is four. In other words, a dispositional belief is one that can be made occurrent simply by considering the matter. Now recall the case in which I judge that a painting is a van Gogh on the basis of its appearance, but am unable to articulate what it is about its appearance that is characteristic of van Gogh. My implicit reason is that paintings which look that way tend to be van Goghs. But do I have a dispositional belief to that effect? The answer can only be "No". In this example, it is supposed that I cannot even articulate the implicit reason. If I cannot articulate it, then simply reflecting on the matter will not automatically lead me to believe it. Consequently, the principle of implicit reasons cannot be supplanted by appeal to dispositional beliefs.

The principle of implicit reasons allows us to resolve the difficulty that arose for descriptivism in section 5 and led to the construction of direct realism. It was objected that descriptivism might be right as far as it goes—a person's belief that things appear a certain way to him constitutes a prima facie reason for him to believe that things are that way—but that this cannot be a complete account of perceptual knowledge because we do not generally have any beliefs about the way things appear to us when we judge perceptually how they are. Given the principle of implicit reasons, however, descriptivism does give a complete account. For example, because the statement that x looks red to me is a prima facie reason for me to believe that x is red, it follows that if the circumstances are such that I could justifiably believe that x looks red to me and these circumstances are the psychological cause of my thinking that x is red, then I have an (implicit) reason for thinking that x is red. There is no necessity for me to actually believe that x looks red to me.

8. Reconsideration of Direct Realism

Next it will be demonstrated that, given the principle of implicit reasons, descriptivism entails that if beliefs about the way things appear to us are incorrigible then direct realism is correct. (We have seen that if these beliefs are not incorrigible then direct realism is wrong, so in that case there is no reason why it should be obtainable from a correct theory of perceptual knowledge.) Suppose that beliefs about the way things appear to us are incorrigible. Given that assumption, let us ask what are the circumstances under which one could justifiably believe that he is appeared to redly. A necessary condition of my justifiably believing that I am appeared to redly is that I do believe I am appeared to redly, which in turn entails (by virtue of incorrigibility) that I am appeared to redly. Thus a necessary condition of my justifiably believing that I am appeared to redly is that I am appeared to redly. Conversely, if I am appeared to redly, then were I to form a belief concerning whether I am appeared to redly, I would have to believe that I am (because of incorrigibility). It seems clear that an incorrigible belief is also incorrigibly justified, so my belief that I am appeared to redly would also be justified. Thus the circumstances under which we could justifiably believe that we are appeared to redly consist simply of our being appeared to redly. Therefore, it follows from descriptivism, with the help of the principle of implicit reasons, that whenever we are appeared to redly and have no reason[16] for thinking that $\sim$ (we are appeared to redly $=>$ there is something red before us), and that is the cause of our believing that there is something red before us, then we are justified in believing that there is something red before us. This is just direct realism.

Given incorrigibility, descriptivism entails direct realism. It is a trivial matter to see that on the assumption of incorrigibility the converse entailment also holds. For suppose I believe that I am appeared to redly and have no reason for thinking that $\sim$ (I am appeared to redly $=>$ there is something red before me), and on that basis I believe that there is something red before me. Then, on the assumption of incorrigibility, I am appeared to redly, and it follows from direct realism that I have a prima facie reason for thinking that there is something red before me. But this means that "I am appeared to redly" is a prima facie reason for me to believe that there is something red before me, which is just descriptivism. Consequently, if beliefs about the way things appear to us are incorrigible, then descriptivism and direct realism are equivalent. However, there is still a sense in which descriptivism is more

16 "Have no reason" here must be understood as "believes no proposition which is a reason".

fundamental than direct realism. Descriptivism will remain true if beliefs about the way things appear to us are only prima facie justified rather than incorrigible, but direct realism will not.[17]

9. Reconsideration of Naive Realism

Finally, let us consider the only other theory of perceptual knowledge of which we were unable to dispose in the course of our earlier discussion. This is the version of naive realism elaborated in section 2 according to which beliefs of the form "I see that there is something φ before me" are prima facie justified, and from them one infers logically that there is something φ before him. It can now be seen that, rather than being a competitor of descriptivism, this theory is actually equivalent to descriptivism, and this time it makes no difference whether beliefs about the way things appear to us are incorrigible or prima facie justified, provided that they are one or the other.

First, we can dispose of the objection that one does not customarily judge, e.g., that he *sees* that there is something red before him, before he judges that there *is* something red before him, by appealing to the principle of implicit reasons. Even if he does not make such a judgment, that may be his implicit reason.

Now suppose descriptivism is correct, and it will be shown that it follows that naive realism is correct. It seems that the perceptual use of "*S* sees that there is something red before him" can be analyzed as "*S* knows, on the basis of being appeared to redly, that there is something red before him", which in turn means "*S* knows that there is something red before him, and his logical reason for believing that is that he is appeared to redly".[18] Consequently:

(9.1) One is justified in believing that he sees that there is something red before him, when and only when he is justified in believing on the basis of the prima facie reason (functioning as a prima facie reason) "I am appeared to redly" that there is something red before him.

[17] However, this point is academic because I will argue in Chapter Four that beliefs about the way things appear to us are incorrigible.

[18] The reader who denies the existence of a perceptual use of "sees that" can regard this as a stipulative definition rather than as an analysis. It makes no difference to the ensuing argument whether the English language actually contains such a use of "sees that."

This cannot be a merely implicit reason. Being appeared to redly is part of seeing that there is something red before one, and a person could not be said to understand what it means to say that he sees that there is something red before him unless he realized this. Thus if he (justifiably) believes that he sees that there is something red before him, he must believe that he is appeared to redly.

S is justified in believing on the basis of the (explicit) prima facie reason "I am appeared to redly" that there is something red before him, just when he is justified in believing that he is appeared to redly and has no reason for believing that $\sim$ (he is appeared to redly $\Rightarrow$ there is something red before him).[19] But any reason for believing the falsity of the latter conditional is a reason for believing that he does not see that there is something red before him. And conversely, any reason for thinking that he does not see that there is something red before him is a reason for denying that conditional.[20] Thus:

(9.2) A person is justified in believing that he sees that there is something red before him just in case he is justified in believing that he is appeared to redly and he has no reason for thinking that he does not see that there is something red before him.[21]

[19] This is just principle 3.5 of Chapter Two. Note that the person might have a reason for denying the conditional, but an overriding reason for affirming it (see n. 20, below). But if a person needs an independent reason for believing the conditional, then "I am appeared to redly" is not functioning as a prima facie reason, and he does not simply *see* that there is something red before him.

[20] This may be only a defeasible reason. For example, a person might know that his optic nerves have been temporarily severed and his visual cortex is being stimulated artificially by a computer. Then he knows that he is not seeing that there is something red before him. But he may also know that the neurologists who are running the experiment are so managing the way things appear to him that things really are the way they appear. Then if he justifiably believes that he is appeared to redly, he is justified in believing that there is something red before him. But in this case, "I am appeared to redly" is functioning not as a prima facie reason but only as a contingent reason. The full logical reason is the conjunction of "I am appeared to redly" and the conditional, because in this case the person needs an independent reason for believing the latter.

[21] This implies that "I am appeared to redly" is a prima facie reason for me to believe that I see that there is something red before me.

Now it can be shown that "*S* sees that there is something red before him" is prima facie justified for *S*. Suppose *S* believes he sees that there is something red before him. Assume in addition that *S* has no reason for thinking that he does not see that there is something red before him. It is to be shown that it follows from this that he is justified in thinking he sees that there is something red before him, thus establishing that that belief is prima facie justified. It was just argued that *S*'s believing that he sees that there is something red before him entails that he believes that he is appeared to redly. Now there are two cases to consider: (1) If *S*'s belief that he is appeared to redly is incorrigible, then *S* justifiably believes he is appeared to redly, and hence by principle 9.2, as he has no reason for thinking that he does not see that there is something red before him, he is justified in believing that he does see that there is something red before him. (2) *S*'s belief that he is appeared to redly might be prima facie justified rather than incorrigible. If *S* had a reason for thinking that he is not appeared to redly, this would also be a reason for thinking he does not see that there is something red before him, and we have assumed that he has no such reason. Thus *S* has no reason for thinking that he is not appeared to redly, and it follows that his belief that he is appeared to redly is justified. But then by 9.2 he is again justified in believing that he does see that there is something red before him.

Therefore, on either alternative, if *S* believes he sees that there is something red before him, and he has no reason for thinking that he does not, then he is justified in believing that he does. In other words, "I see that there is something red before me" is prima facie justified. Consequently, descriptivism entails this version of naive realism.

The converse entailment also holds. Assuming the correctness of naive realism, suppose a person justifiably believes he is appeared to redly and has no reason for thinking that $\sim$ (he is appeared to redly $=>$ there is something red before him), and on this basis believes that there is something red before him. As we have seen, something is a reason for thinking that $\sim$ (he is appeared to redly $=>$ there is something red before him) if and only if it is a reason for thinking that he does not see that there is something red before him. Consequently, he has no reason for thinking that he does not see that there is something red before him. Therefore, it follows from naive realism that were the person to believe he sees that there is something red before him he would be justified in that belief. Consequently, if the circumstances are such that the person could believe he sees that there is something red before him, the circumstances are also such that he could justifiably believe that. For him to see that there is something red before him is just for him to know on the basis of being appeared to redly that there is something red before him. Thus it seems clear that he *can* believe he sees that there is something red before him whenever he can believe he knows on the basis of being appeared to redly that there is something red before him. But all that is logically required for believing the latter is that he does believe he is appeared to redly, and by hypothesis he does. So it follows that the circumstances are such that he could justifiably believe he sees that there is something red before him. The latter belief entails, and hence is potentially an implicit reason for him to believe, that there is something red before him. Thus if his being in these circumstances is the cause of his believing that there is something red before him, then the latter belief is justified. But the circumstances consist simply of his believing he is appeared to redly, and by hypothesis that is the cause of his believing that there is something red before him. Therefore, the latter belief is justified, and hence "I am appeared to redly" is a prima facie reason for one to believe that there is something red before him, i.e., descriptivism is correct.

This conclusion seems strange. Which belief is epistemologically basic: "I am appeared to redly" or "I see that there is something red before me"? An epistemologically basic statement is one that a person can be justified in believing without having a reason for believing it. By principle 9.2 it follows that I cannot justifiably believe that I see that there is something red before me unless I have the prima facie reason "I am appeared to redly" (see above, note 20). Thus it follows that "I see that there is something red before me" is not epistemologically basic. Consequently, although when naive realism is formulated as a thesis about certain beliefs being prima facie justified it is true, when it is formulated more traditionally as a thesis about epistemologically basic beliefs it is false.

10. Conclusions

To summarize the results of this chapter, we have found that two of the basic theories of perceptual knowledge, phenomenalism and scientific realism, fail. There are important connections between the remaining theories. Descriptivism seems to give a correct account of perceptual knowledge, and is equivalent to naive realism when the latter theory is construed as a theory about certain beliefs being prima facie justified. When naive realism is construed more traditionally as a theory about epistemologically basic beliefs, however, it is incorrect. Furthermore, if beliefs about the way things appear to us are incorrigible, then descriptivism is also equivalent to direct realism, although the latter theory is false if those beliefs are not incorrigible. One of the most important results of this chapter is that it is misleading always to think of epistemic justification in terms of beliefs. Given the principle of implicit reasons, however, we lose no generality by formulating theories of knowledge in terms of the conditions of justified belief. These investigations have assumed that beliefs about the way things appear to us are epistemologically basic and hence either incorrigible or prima facie justified, but no attempt has been made to decide which status they actually have. That is the topic of the next chapter.

Chapter Four

Incorrigibility

1. Preliminaries

IT WAS argued in Chapter Two that our judgments about physical objects are based upon epistemologically basic beliefs, at least some of which have something to do with perception. In Chapter Three it was argued that beliefs ascribing perceptual attributes to physical objects are based upon beliefs about how we are appeared to. These two conclusions together suggest (but do not entail) that beliefs like "I am appeared to redly" are epistemologically basic, and hence either incorrigible or prima facie justified. This was assumed in several places in the last part of Chapter Three. But this is an unpopular position. Perhaps most contemporary epistemologists would disavow it. The objective of this chapter is to defend this view. Furthermore, it will be defended in its strongest possible form. It will be argued that beliefs about how we are appeared to are not just prima facie justified—they are incorrigible.

Those who deny that beliefs about how we are appeared to are epistemologically basic have sometimes urged that a belief like "I am appeared to redly" involves a comparison of the way I am presently appeared to with the way I am appeared to when I see something red. In other words, it is maintained that "I am appeared to redly" means "I am appeared to in the way I am normally appeared to when I see something red". A belief of this latter sort cannot be epistemologically basic because it involves knowing how red things normally look, which, it is argued, we can only know inductively.

Chisholm replies that we must distinguish between "comparative" and "noncomparative" uses of words that are used to describe ways in which we are appeared to.[1] Construed comparatively, "*x*

[1] Chisholm [1966], p. 35.

looks red to me" means "*x* looks to me the way red things normally look to me", and this belief cannot be incorrigible. But, according to Chisholm, there is another "noncomparative" use of these words, and when a belief is understood in that way it is incorrigible. To illustrate the noncomparative use of these words, Chisholm asserts that the sentence "Red things normally look red" can be understood in a way that makes it contingently true, but when "looks red" is construed comparatively, this latter statement would be trivially analytic. The implication is that "looks red" construed noncomparatively refers directly to a particular phenomenological state, and it is a contingent fact that red things tend to elicit this state in their observers.

I think that the distinction Chisholm is trying to get at is sound, but his example is inadequate. Furthermore, his discussion suggests (although he might disavow this) that there are two *meanings* of "looks red", which seems to me quite definitely wrong. The distinction can be illustrated better by picking another example. Hydrogen sulfide is noted for its characteristic "rotten egg" smell. This odor is quite distinctive. One can easily imagine a group of chemistry students who encounter this odor for the first time but do not know of what it is the odor. They might come to call it among themselves "that rotten odor". Here it is clear that they are identifying the odor purely phenomenologically, without reference to what things characteristically have the odor. Later, upon discovering that this is the smell of hydrogen sulfide, they might report either "I smell something that smells like hydrogen sulfide" or "I smell that rotten odor". In the first case their words would be functioning in the way Chisholm calls "comparatively", and in the second case noncomparatively. The distinction here is not between two ways a single word or phrase may function, but between two ways of referring to a way of being appeared to. We may refer to a way of being appeared to as the way we are normally appeared to under certain circumstances (where these circumstances are not simply defined in terms of that way of being appeared to), or we may refer to it using a word or phrase we have associated directly with the phenomenological state, as in the above example. It is only when φ is a word or phrase used in this latter way that a belief of the form "I am appeared to φly" can possibly be either incorrigible or prima facie justified.[2]

[2] It seems clear that "red" acquires its meaning by being associated di-

It would be a mistake, however, to suppose that all such statements involving noncomparative reference are incorrigible or prima facie justified. As we shall see, some are and some are not. Consider one of the chemistry students again. If he were to state, "I smell that rotten odor", however sincerely, there is still a way his statement could be false. This could result from his using the wrong words to refer to the phenomenological state he has in mind. Suppose, for example, that, because of some peculiar air currents in the room, he was in fact smelling a different odor than the other chemistry students. For example, it might have been the odor of ammonia. In this way he would come to use the words "that rotten odor" to refer to the wrong odor. Thus if he again smelled the odor he smelled on that earlier occasion, and reported, "I smell that rotten odor", his statement would be false. This does not show however that his *belief* is incorrect. Or better, there is one sense in which he holds an incorrect belief, and another sense in which his belief is correct.

To see more clearly how this works, let us consider a different example. Suppose we send a person in the next room to find out what color the wallpaper is. Suppose it is red, but mistakenly thinking that the color is called "green", he reports that it is green. In one clear sense he believes that the wallpaper in the next room is green. In this sense, he holds a mistaken belief. But there is another sense in which he knows perfectly well what color the wallpaper is—for example, he can pick out other things of the same color—but he does not know what to call it. In this sense, he does believe that the wallpaper is red, but does not report this belief correctly. The sense in which the person believes that the wallpaper is red, even though he reports that it is green, can be expressed as:

$$(\exists x)\ (x \text{ is the color red } \&\ S \text{ believes that the wallpaper is } x).$$

---

rectly with a perceived color. In other words, "red" functions noncomparatively. There is no comparative sense of "red". On the other hand, it is also true that I am appeared to redly if and only if I am appeared to the way I am normally appeared to when I see something red. But this does not imply that I must make an inductive generalization about how red objects look before I can know that I am appeared to redly. This is because a red object is *defined* to be one that normally looks red. ("Normally" is not to be identified with "usually"; it should be understood in terms of prima facie reasons.)

The sense in which the person believes that the wallpaper is green can be expressed as:

$(\exists x)$ S believes that (x is the color green & the wallpaper is x).

In the latter case, S holds a belief that is a conjunction, and the first conjunct is false. The quantifiers range over colors identified phenomenologically.[3]

To have a clear way of distinguishing between these two senses of belief sentences, let us write "S believes$_E$ that . . . red . . ." to mean

$(\exists x)$ (x is the color red & S believes that . . . x . . .)

and "S believes$_I$ that . . . red . . ." to mean

$(\exists x)$ S believes that (x is the color red & . . . x . . .).

Belief$_E$ is "external belief"—the identity of the color is not part of the belief. Belief$_I$ is "internal belief". The person identifying the color of the wallpaper believes$_E$ that the wallpaper is red, and is correct, but believes$_I$ that the wallpaper is green, and is incorrect.

We can apply this same distinction to the student who is mistaken about what odor is properly called "that rotten odor". There is a sense in which he holds a mistaken belief when he reports, "I smell that rotten odor". This is that be believes$_I$ that he smells that rotten odor. But there is another sense in which he knows quite well what odor it is that he smells but he is calling it by the wrong name, and in this sense his belief that he does smell that odor is correct. This is that he believes$_E$ that he smells the odor of ammonia (although he does not know that it is the odor of ammonia).

We have not yet determined whether the student's belief is either incorrigible or prima facie justified, but we are somewhat clearer on what kind of belief *might* be one or the other. The important thing is that the way the student thinks he is appeared to is somehow picked out "directly" by a kind of mental pointing, a focusing of attention, and then he thinks to himself, "I am appeared to

[3] It is fashionable to maintain that this kind of quantification into belief contexts is somehow illegitimate. That it is not is obvious when we consider statements like "There are colors on this chart which S believes he has seen before, but he doesn't know what they are called." The only reasonable rendering of this statement is: $(\exists x)$ (x is a color on this chart & S believes that he has seen x before & S does not know what x is called).

that way". The reference to the way of being appeared to must be demonstrative—the reference cannot be secured by a description or an expression whose denotation is fixed by its conventional meaning. In other words, his belief$_E$ that he smells the odor of ammonia may be incorrigible, but his belief$_I$ that he smells that rotton odor cannot be. Similarly, my belief$_I$ that I am appeared to redly can be neither incorrigible nor prima facie justified, although my belief$_E$ that I am appeared to redly might (as far as we know yet) be either. The traditional epistemologist has long been aware of the possibility of verbal error but has steadfastly maintained that, for the beliefs he is talking about, the possibility of verbal error does not arise. This has sometimes led to a rather confusing wrangle over private languages, but all that can be avoided. The belief in which the traditional epistemologist has really been interested, but which he has formulated badly, is just "I am appeared to that way", where the reference of "that" is secured demonstratively as described above.[4] If that way of being appeared to is redly, then it is the belief$_E$ (as opposed to the belief$_I$) that he is appeared to redly that has interested the traditional epistemologist.

2. A Demonstration of Incorrigibility

However, none of this answers the question whether these beliefs are either incorrigible or prima facie justified. Indeed, it may seem on cursory reflection that none of this has gotten us anywhere at all. When I think to myself, "I am appeared to *that* way", it appears that the phenomenological demonstrative reference involved is to the way I *think* I am appeared to, not necessarily to the way I am actually appeared to, and consequently the question of what the relationship is between thinking I am appeared to in a certain way and actually being appeared to in that way arises all over again.

The way out of this is to consider just what it means to say that I am appeared to in a certain way. Epistemologists have com-

[4] "I am appeared to that way" should not be confused with "I am appeared to the way I am appeared to" where the definite description functions attributively rather than referentially (for a discussion of the attributive/referential distinction, see Donnellan [1966]). The difference is that the reference of "that way" is secured demonstratively; "that way" refers to a specific way of being appeared to, not to *whatever* way we happen to be appeared to.

monly assumed that it is perfectly clear what this means, but that is doubtful. I propose to give an account of what *I* mean by "appeared to" and show that when "I am appeared to *that* way" is understood as I propose to understand it, it is in fact incorrigible.

Suppose I arrive at my childhood home and look at an old gnarled oak that I remember only dimly, and mutter to myself, "So *that* is the way that tree is shaped". To what does "that" refer? Clearly, it refers to the shape of the tree, but how does it acquire its reference? Before attempting to answer this question, let us change the example. Suppose the tree is in my own backyard and I am quite familiar with it, but I have been experimenting with drugs. I may look at the tree and exclaim to myself, "But *that* is not the way that tree is shaped". "That" refers to the same shape as in the previous example, but now it is no longer the shape of the tree. Furthermore, the mechanism by which "that" acquires its reference is the same in both cases. "That" refers demonstratively to a shape to which I am attending.

Now I will introduce "appeared to" as a piece of technical terminology. Whenever "that" acquires its reference as above to a particular shape or color or whatever, so that I might think to myself either "*That* is the way things are", or "*That* is not the way things are", I will say that *I am appeared to that way*; "that" refers to the way I am appeared to. So understood, "I am appeared to *that* way" is incorrigible. For suppose I think to myself, perhaps while gazing at my backyard, "I am appeared to *that* way". By the meaning of "appeared to", whenever "that" acquires its reference in this way it refers to one of the ways I am appeared to. Thus if I believe I am appeared to that way, it is true that I am appeared to that way. A precondition of "that" having the reference it does in "I am appeared to that way" is that I am actually appeared to that way. The truth of the sentence is a necessary condition of its having the meaning it does.

This argument may have the appearance of verbal hocus-pocus, so let us go over it again. The essential point of the argument is the following. Suppose I believe "I am appeared to that way", and on some grounds someone denies this, saying that I only *think* I am appeared to that way. This involves a misunderstanding concerning how "that" acquires its reference. "That" acquires its reference in the same way regardless of whether I am really appeared to that way or "only think I am appeared to that way". In both cases it refers to a shape (or color, etc.) that is somehow "before my mind". Thus by the meaning of "appeared to", in either case I am appeared to that way. There can be no such thing as "only thinking I am appeared to that way".

The above point can be put more picturesquely but less clearly by saying that we see the world "through our visual field". What we are initially aware of in perception is the physical world, but circumstances may cause us to retreat and focus our attention on the images in our visual field instead. We are aware of the *same* kind of things (shapes, colors, etc.) in either case, but in the one case we take them to be the shapes and colors of physical objects, while in the other case we do not. When I am aware of one of these shapes (colors, etc.), regardless of whether I take it to be the shape of an object, I am appeared to that way (i.e., I am appeared to as if there were something of that shape before me). If I believe I am appeared to that way, then I am aware of that shape, and so it follows that I am appeared to that way. In other words, my belief is incorrigible.

A possible objection to this is that because it is a *particular* shape we are aware of in this sort of case, this cannot be knowledge. Knowledge always involves universals.[5] But isn't a particular shape a universal? Or put another way, if we photographed the tree and then traced its shape exactly, and took our tracing to someone who had not seen the tree and informed him that that is the shape of the tree, would he not be acquiring knowledge?

3. The Electroencephalograph Argument

It is illuminating to reconsider the electroencephalograph argument against incorrigibility in the light of the above observations. This argument maintains that with the aid of the SEEG we might be able to tell that a person is mistaken when he thinks, for example, that he is appeared to redly, and thus that belief cannot be incorrigible. This is not a strong argument against incorrigibility because it begs the question. We interpret the data of the SEEG in terms of a theory about the neurophysiology of perception. In order for us to be able to hold that theory in the fact of the SEEG's telling us that a person is wrong about how he is appeared to, we

[5] Sellars employs a similar argument in connection with sense data in "Empiricism and the philosophy of mind" in Sellars [1963].

must already presuppose that people's judgments about how they are appeared to are not incorrigible. Nevertheless, the argument is persuasive. It seems somehow unsatisfactory to suppose that such a neurological theory could not be constructed and used just like any other scientific theory.

The above conclusions regarding incorrigibility lead to a way out of this quandary. Beliefs like my belief$_I$ that I am appeared to redly are not incorrigible; only those like my belief$_E$ that I am appeared to redly are incorrigible. These are beliefs of the form "I am appeared to *that* way" in which the way I am appeared to is picked out demonstratively. Thus the neurological theory could be constructed, and it would be quite possible for us to determine that a person is wrong in believing$_I$ that he is appeared to redly. On the other hand, the theory could never be of any help in deciding whether a person is right in a belief of the form "I am appeared to *that* way". Before the neurophysiologist could do anything with the latter belief, he would have to know what way "*that* way" is. Only the subject can identify it for him. If the subject identified it as redly, and the neurophysiologist subsequently ascertains that the subject is not appeared to redly, all that he can conclude is that *either* the subject is not appeared to the way he thinks he is *or* he is wrong about what to call the way he is appeared to. But empirical considerations could never lead to a choice between these two alternatives. Only logical considerations can do that, and they tell us that the first alternative is never possible and hence that the neurophysiologist should opt for the second alternative.

4. Conclusions

My conclusion is that beliefs$_E$ of the form "I am appeared to φly" (for suitable φ) are incorrigible, and that they are the only possible candidates for epistemologically basic beliefs among my beliefs about the way I am appeared to. In particular, beliefs$_I$ about the way I am appeared to are not epistemologically basic.[6] But are the incorrigible beliefs$_E$ strong enough to act as a foundation for perceptual knowledge? They are extremely weak beliefs, as indeed they must be to be incorrigible. However, my belief$_E$ that I am

[6] To be justified in believing$_I$ that, for example, there is something red before me, I must know that the color I now see is called "red", and that involves both memory and induction.

appeared to φly constitutes a prima facie reason for me to believe$_E$ that there is something φ before me. This is a belief about the physical world that is justified on the basis of my incorrigible beliefs about the way things appear to me. Consequently, those incorrigible beliefs about how things appear to us can get us started on the road to justifying our beliefs about physical objects. But by themselves they do not get us very far. Before we can make much progress we must be able to reidentify the ways we are appeared to, so that we can relate the way we are appeared to on one occasion (and hence the way we judge things to be on that occasion) with the way we are appeared to on other occasions. This latter knowledge is going to involve both memory and induction. These topics will be taken up in later chapters. But there is no difficulty in principle here. Once we have investigated and understood knowledge based on memory and induction, we will then be able to go on and give an account of more complicated beliefs about physical objects. In the meantime, we have at least seen how the simplest sort of knowledge about physical objects is possible.

It follows from the incorrigibility of my beliefs$_E$ about the way I am appeared to that descriptivism, naive realism, and direct realism all give equivalent accounts of perceptual knowledge (see section 10 of Chapter Three). The correctness of direct realism is probably the most important consequence of incorrigibility. Although the three theories are equivalent, direct realism gives a much more direct account of perceptual knowledge than descriptivism or naive realism does. Descriptivism and naive realism only give complete accounts when coupled with the principle of implicit reasons, whereas direct realism gives a complete account all by itself.

Chapter Five

Perceptual Attributes

1. Introduction

In Chapter One it was argued that there are many *ostensive* concepts that can be analyzed in terms of their justification conditions. An ostensive concept is one that can be explained to a person with the help of an ostensive definition. It seems quite clear that the concepts of perceptual attributes are ostensive concepts. Any attempt to give a verbal definition of a concept like "red" is doomed to failure. The concept of a red object can only be explained to a person by pointing out red objects and non-red objects. Accordingly, the only way to analyze the meaning of a concept like "red" is in terms of its truth conditions. We have already made a good start on this task. It was argued in Chapter Three that given any perceptual attribute φ, "*S* is appeared to φly" is a prima facie reason for *S* to believe that there is something φ before him. This constitutes the core of the justification conditions for the concept of something being φ. The purpose of this chapter is to complete the account of the justification conditions for perceptual attributes.

There are two reasons for undertaking this task. First, it is of some intrinsic interest. A number of important features of our perceptual concepts will come to light in the course of the investigation. But after a while this sort of discussion does tend to become rather dull and tedious. For this reason it will generally be avoided in later chapters when we discuss knowledge of other minds, knowledge of the past, etc. But there is an important reason for undertaking this task here, and that is simply to show that it can be done. I have proposed a program of epistemological analysis. Many such programs have been proposed in the history of philosophy, and they have generally looked good when first sketched. But their downfall has always been that the details of the proposed analyses have been impossible to carry out. Thus it is important to show that the details of my analyses can be carried out. Having carried out the details in one area—perception—it will not then be so necessary to carry them out in other areas. Following the model of perceptual knowledge, it will be pretty obvious how to carry out the details in the other areas of knowledge without actually doing so.

As yet, no attempt has been made to give a precise definition of "perceptual attribute". Roughly, these are attributes of physical objects which, like color, shape, size, weight, temperature, texture, etc., can be judged to be present or absent in an object directly by perception of the object. Perceptual attributes are to be contrasted with attributes like "flammable" or "bachelor" whose presence or absence generally cannot be judged simply by perceiving the object. At this stage it is difficult to be any more precise about what a perceptual attribute is. The above remarks cannot be taken as a definition, although they should suffice to indicate what sort of attributes we are talking about. It is notoriously unclear what it means to say that the presence or absence of an attribute can be "judged directly by perception". In section 7 it will become possible to give a precise definition of "perceptual attribute", but for the present we must be content to work with this rather rough characterization.

2. "There is something red before me"

Let us begin by considering the existential statement, "There is something red before me". It has already been argued that "I am appeared to redly" constitutes a prima facie reason for me to believe this statement. This observation constitutes a partial analysis of the existential statement, but to give a complete analysis we must give a complete description of the justification conditions of this statement and its denial.

2.1 *A Perceptual Criterion*

Initially it seems that there is also a simple prima facie reason for the negation of this statement, viz., "I am not appeared to redly". But this turns on an ambiguity in the statement "There is something red before me". When we say that something is red, do we mean that it is red all over, or only that it is at least partly red? Construed in the first manner, it seems correct that "I am not appeared to redly" is a prima facie reason for me to think that there is nothing red before me; but then it is incorrect to suppose that "I am appeared to redly" is a prima facie reason for me to think that there is something red before me. Just because something looks red to me from this angle, it does not follow that I am justified in judging it to be red all over. I have only a perceptual reason for a judgment of the color of a particular surface of an object insofar as I can see that surface. Consequently, if "I am appeared to redly" is to be a prima facie reason for me to think that there is something red before me, "red object" must be taken to mean "object that is at least partly red". However, so construed, "I am not appeared to redly" cannot be a prima facie reason for me to think that there is nothing (at least partly) red before me, because one of the objects that I see may be red on the back side.

We must modify our original observation in the following manner. "I am appeared to redly" is a prima facie reason for me to believe "There is an object before me having a red surface facing me", or more briefly, "There is a red surface before me". Furthermore, "I am not appeared to redly" is a prima facie reason for me to think that there is no object before me having a red surface facing me, i.e., there is no red surface before me.

This also suggests that we should be a bit more precise in describing the way in which we are appeared to. For the sake of precision, I propose to change my terminology so that "appeared to" takes a propositional object, i.e., I will write "*S* is appeared to as if *P*". Rather than writing "*S* is appeared to redly", I will write "*S* is appeared to as if there is a red surface before him".

When *P* is a prima facie reason for *S* to believe *Q* and $\sim P$ is a prima facie reason for *S* to believe $\sim Q$, let us say that *P* is a *criterion* for (*S* to believe) *Q*. Our conclusions about existential statements involving "red" can now be stated by saying that "*S* is appeared to as if there is a red surface before him" is a criterion for *S* to believe "There is a red surface before *S*".

2.2 *Other Reasons*

We have found a perceptual criterion for "There is an object before me having a red surface facing me". But this perceptual criterion does not constitute the only reason one may have for such a belief. For example, I may hold the belief because I have been told this by someone I consider to be reliable. Or I may believe this as a result of a measurement of the wave length of light reflected from some object before me. Or I may believe this on the basis of a chemical analysis of paint scrapings taken from an object before me. These are all contingent reasons for thinking that there is something red before me. They are only reasons for me to believe this if I also justifiably hold some other beliefs, viz., that my informer is reliable in this sort of case, that objects reflecting light of this wave length are red, and that objects coated with paint having this chemical composition are red. These later statements all have the characteristic that our grounds for them must be at least indirectly inductive. A person may be justified in believing these statements as a result of having carried out an inductive generalization concerning the past reliability of this speaker, or the connection between color and the wave length of light, or the connection between color and the chemical composition of paint. Or one might have other beliefs that constitute conclusive reasons for believing these statements. These conclusive reasons would be based upon some more general natural laws that would in turn entail, e.g., that paint of this composition will reflect light of a certain color. But then one's reasons for holding these more general beliefs will have to be inductive. Thus there is a large class of possible reasons one may have for thinking that something is (or is not) red that are inductive in the sense that they either are the result of a direct inductive generalization or else are based upon other more general beliefs that were in turn justified inductively. The possibility of carrying out these inductive generalizations presupposes that one can judge colors independently of these inductive reasons, but this is just what the existence of the perceptual criterion guarantees.

Are there any other sorts of reasons that one can have for thinking that there is or is not something red before him? In the next chapter it will be argued that there is one such reason. It will be shown that an object's having a certain perceptual attribute at one time is a prima facie reason for thinking that it has that attribute at any other time. For example, "*x* was red five minutes ago" is a prima facie reason for thinking that *x* is now red. This entails that "There is something before me that was red five minutes ago" is a prima facie reason for me to think that there is now something red before me. Similarly, "Nothing before me was red five minutes ago" is a prima facie reason for thinking that there is no red surface before me now. These prima facie reasons result from the way in which we reidentify physical objects over time. We will have more to say about these reasons shortly.

Thus far we have found three kinds of reasons that I may have for judging that there is or is not a red surface before me: (1) those arising out of the perceptual criterion; (2) those arising out of an inference from the past; (3) those arising out of inductive generalizations. There are innumerable other logical reasons. For example, "The sky is blue and there is a red object before me" is a logical reason for me to believe that there is a red object before me. But this is not an interesting kind of logical reason. Given any statement *P*, there will be many logical reasons *Q* for believing-that-*P* which have the characteristics that (1) *P* itself occurs somewhere within *Q*, and (2) replacing all occurrences of *P* in *Q* by any other statement *R* gives us a logical reason for believing *R*. Let us say that such a statement *Q* is a *universal* logical reason for believing *P*. For example, (*T* & *P*) is a universal logical reason for believing *P*, because given any statement *R*, (*T* & *R*) is a logical reason for believing *R*. Logical reasons that are not universal are *essential.* In describing the logical reasons for believing a statement, it is only necessary to list the essential ones, because the universal ones are the same for all statements. The above list of reasons for color judgments should be viewed as a list of essential logical reasons. It seems likely that there are no other essential logical reasons for those color judgments. It does not seem that any mode of intuition other than color vision and memory could provide such an essential logical reason.

2.3 *Defeaters*

To complete our account of the justification conditions for "There is a red surface before me", we must describe the defeaters for the prima facie reasons involved in the perceptual criterion. However, it is convenient to postpone that discussion until the next section where it can be handled simultaneously with a discussion of the defeaters for the prima facie reasons involved in attributive statements.

3. "*x* has a red surface facing me"

Now let us turn to attributive statements, i.e., statements that attribute to a particular object the property of having a red surface facing one. What are the justification conditions for such a statement?

3.1 *A Perceptual Criterion*

As a first approximation, it seems clear that "*x* looks red to *S*" is a prima facie reason for *S* to believe that *x* has a red surface facing him. Again, we have to ask ourselves just what we mean by "*x* looks red to *S*". It is not necessary that *all* of *x* looks red to *S*—it is only necessary that part of the surface of *x* looks red to *S*. So we can say more precisely that "Part of the surface of *x* looks red to *S*" is a prima facie reason for *S* to believe that *x* has a red surface facing him.

At first it might seem that this is actually a criterion, i.e., "No part of the surface of *x* looks red to *S*" is a prima facie reason for *S* to believe that *x* does not have a red surface facing him. But this is not quite right; *x* might fail to have any part of its surface look red to *S* simply because *S* does not see *x*. If *S* does not see *x*, then he certainly cannot conclude that because *x* does not look red to him it is not red. The prima facie reason for *S* to believe that *x* does not have a red surface facing him must be "*S* sees *x* and no part of the surface of *x* looks red to him".

"Part of the surface of *x* looks red to *S*" entails "*S* sees *x*", so the latter can be added as a redundant part of the prima facie reason for believing that *x* has a red surface facing *S*. Then we have:

(3.1) (1) "*S* sees *x* & part of the surface of *x* looks red to *S*" is a prima facie reason for *S* to believe that *x* has a red surface facing him; (2) "*S* sees *x* & no part of the surface of *x* looks red to *S*" is a prima facie reason for *S* to believe that *x* does not have a red surface facing him.

In order to state this more compactly, let us generalize the notion of a criterion:

(3.2) *Q* is a *criterion* for *S* to believe that *R*, and *P* is a *precondition* for the criterion, iff (1) (*P* & *Q*) is a prima facie reason for S to believe that R, and (2) $(P \,\&\, \sim Q)$ is a prima facie reason for S to believe that $\sim R$.

Then we can restate 3.1 succinctly by saying that "Part of the surface of x looks red to S" is a criterion for S to believe that x has a red surface facing S, and "S sees x" is a precondition for the criterion.

The criteria discussed in section 2 required no preconditions. Let us call such criteria *type I criteria*, and those requiring preconditions *type II criteria.*

3.2 *Other Reasons*

Just as in the case of existential judgments, there are other possible reasons for one to believe that x does or does not have a red surface facing oneself. The same kinds of inductive considerations are relevant here as were relevant for the judgment that there is a red surface before S. Similarly, inferences from the past provide reasons for such judgments. That is, "Five minutes ago, x had a red surface facing S" is a (type I) criterion for S to believe that x now has a red surface facing him.

3.3 *Defeaters*

Now let us consider the nature and source of defeaters for our perceptual criteria for existential and attributive color statements. Let us begin with type I defeaters for the positive judgments that x has a red surface facing S. These are reasons for thinking that x has no such surface despite the fact that it has a surface that looks red to S. As we have seen, nonperceptual reasons for thinking that x does not have a red surface must be either inductive or an inference from the fact that, e.g., x had no such surface five minutes ago. As we will see in the next chapter (and this seems obvious anyway), the latter reason is weaker than the perceptual reason. If x had no red surface five minutes ago but has a surface that looks red now, and we know nothing else about the situation, the only reasonable conclusion is that x now has a red surface. So a type I defeater cannot arise simply out of an inference from the past state of x. But it seems that such a defeater cannot arise inductively either. Suppose we discovered inductively that whenever x has a red surface, it is in state A. Then it seems that x's not being in state A should be a type I defeater. But faced with an object that appears to have a red surface but is not in state *A*, why don't we take this as refuting the generalization rather than concluding that the object does not really have a red surface? It seems that this would be the reasonable thing to do, or at least that this would be just as reasonable as concluding that the object does not have a red surface.

It seems that the only way to avoid this would be to have available a type II defeater which undermines the perceptual reason and allows us to accept the generalization or the inference from the past without worrying about *x*'s looking red to us. Given such a type II defeater, it becomes possible to discover inductively that when an object is in a certain state then it is not red even though it may look red to us. This seems to be the only way we could establish such an inductive generalization, and hence seems to be the only way that type I defeaters become possible. Type I defeaters are parasitic on the existence of type II defeaters.

Let us turn to type II defeaters. A type II defeater is not a reason for thinking that *x* has no red surface—it is merely a reason for thinking that under the circumstances *x*'s having a surface which looks red to *S* is not a reliable indication of whether *x* has a surface that is actually red. Examples of such defeaters are "*x* is illuminated by red lights", "*S* is wearing rose-colored glasses", "*S* is hypnotized", or "*S* is under the influence of drugs". These defeaters can be classified as those that are facts (at least partly) about *S*, and those that are not facts about *S* but, rather, facts about *x* and the general circumstances. Let us call these *personal* and *impersonal* defeaters, respectively. "*x* is illuminated by red lights" is an impersonal defeater, while "*S* is hypnotized" is a personal defeater.

How might I find a type II defeater? It seems that the only way I could possibly discover that under certain circumstances a surface's appearing red to me is not indicative of its being red is by knowing inductively that under such circumstances surfaces often appear red to me without being red. This is only possible if I have some way of telling that an object does not have a red surface despite the fact that it appears to, which in turn is only possible through the use of type I defeaters. It seems that type II defeaters are possible only if we already have access to some type I defeaters. But we saw that type I defeaters in turn presuppose the existence of type II defeaters. This seems to indicate that there is no way to establish either type I defeaters or type II defeaters. But this is absurd. We know of many type I and type II defeaters. Something must be wrong with the above argument.

Perhaps the solution is that we do not *discover* defeaters at all—they are conventional. Or more accurately, perhaps they arise from logical reasons peculiar to the concept of a perceptual attribute (essential logical reasons rather than universal logical reasons). This cannot be true of all defeaters. Type I defeaters are such things as "The light reflected from x has a wave length of 5,972 angstroms", or "Jones says that x is not red", and it is not plausible to regard these as anything but inductive. However, it is not so implausible to suppose that type II defeaters are conventional.

Type II defeaters cannot be completely conventional. There is some element of discovery involved. Consider how we might discover a new type II defeater. Scientists might find that an exaggerated Zeeman effect can be produced by imposing a very strong magnetic field on an object—so exaggerated that the color of the object appears to change.[1] As long as the apparent color of the object returned to normal when the field was removed, we would conclude that the color had not really changed, and hence that the presence of such a field constitutes a type II defeater. This cannot be regarded as the introduction of a new convention—it is an outright scientific discovery. However, the discovery may amount merely to establishing that the imposition of a very strong magnetic field instantiates some more general defeater which is conventional. Let us examine this possibility.

It is essential to the above example that the apparent color of the object returns to normal when the magnetic field is removed. If it did not, we would conclude that the magnetic field has changed the color of the object. Similarly, we know that illuminating an object with colored lights does not change the actual color of the object—only its apparent color. It is essential for this that when the colored lights are removed the apparent color of the object returns to normal. Once again, if when the lights were removed the apparent color did not change back, we would judge that the color has been altered by shining the lights on the object. Roughly, if doing something to an object makes its apparent color change, but

[1] The normal Zeeman effect is a slight splitting of the spectral emission lines of a substance in a magnetic field.

the apparent color changes back when we quit doing it, we judge that the actual color was not affected by what we did; but if the apparent color does not change back when we quit whatever we are doing, we judge that what we did altered the color of the object. Only when what we do results in a relatively permanent change in the apparent color do we judge that the actual color of the object has been altered. There appears to be a logical presumption of stability in the concept of the color of an object, and only those apparent changes that are stable or relatively permanent are judged to be real. In the background here there seems to be a general type II defeater which is something like the following:

> The circumstances are of a type which are often accompanied by a change in the apparent color of an object and whose cessation is then generally accompanied by a return of the apparent color of the object to what it was before the circumstances obtained.

This appears to be a logical type II defeater for perceptual judgments of the color of an object.

The above proposal is drawn a bit too broadly. For example, one kind of circumstance which satisfies it is that of being coated with paint, but we want to count that as creating an actual color change and not as being a defeater. There must be limits put upon the circumstances that fit this formula. The circumstances have to be "transitory"; they have to be circumstances that do not generally last long. When an object is coated with paint it usually remains so coated for a number of years. But when an object is illuminated with colored lights, it does not generally remain so illuminated for very long. This is why we say that painting an object changes its color, but illuminating it with colored lights does not. If paint characteristically flaked off an object in a matter of minutes, we would say that painting an object red only made it look red, it did not actually change its color. Similarly, some surfaces appear darker when they are wet. We say that rain makes them *look* darker, not that it changes their color. This is only because objects tend to dry rapidly. If once an object became wet it remained wet for years, we would say that the rain changed the color of the object and did not merely make it look darker. To take another example, the exaggerated Zeeman effect discussed above would only change the apparent color of an object, not its actual color, because being in a very strong magnetic field is only a transitory circumstance. But if an object placed in a magnetic field of sufficient strength to produce this effect tended to become magnetized so as to permanently retain the field and hence the color, we would judge that the color of the object actually changed when exposed to the field. These observations suggest that our defeater has the form:

(3.3) "The present circumstances are of a type which are generally transitory and are often accompanied by a change in the apparent color of an object to red and whose cessation is then generally accompanied by a return of the apparent color of the object to what it was before the circumstances obtained" is a logical type II defeater for the perceptual judgment that an object is red.

Certain features of this principle seem most peculiar. Why should the transitoriness of the circumstances have anything to do with whether they constitute a defeater? And must this principle be regarded as a basic feature of the concept of a red object, or can it be derived from some more basic feature of that concept? Both of these questions can be answered simultaneously. The principle can be derived from something more basic, and the derivation will explain why transitoriness enters the picture.

Principle 3.3 amounts to a presumption of stability for the color of an object. If the color of an object seems to fluctuate rapidly, we tend not to count the change as real. This presumption of stability results from the already mentioned fact that an object's having a certain perceptual attribute at one time t is a prima facie reason for thinking it has the same attribute at any other time t', where the strength of this reason is a function of the interval between t and t'. That there is actually such a prima facie reason will be seen in the next chapter. This reason itself amounts to a presumption of stability. Let us suppose that over a long interval prior to time t an object x looks red to S. Then at time t the color of x appears to S to change to purple. At that time S has a perceptual reason for thinking that x is purple, and a temporal reason for thinking that it is still red. The perceptual reason is stronger, so the reasonable conclusion at that point would be that x is purple. But now suppose that at time $t + 30$ sec. the apparent color of x changes back to red. Now S has a stronger reason for thinking that between t and $t + 30$ sec. x was red rather than purple. He has two distinct reasons for believing this, viz., "x was red before t", and "x was red after $t + 30$ sec." Both of these are prima facie reasons for thinking that x was red between t and $t + 30$ sec. By itself, neither is strong enough to defeat the perceptual reason for thinking that x was not red, but together they may be strong enough. The shorter the interval between the two changes in apparent color, the stronger will be the reason for thinking that the changes were not real.[2] This conclusion can be further strengthened by inductive considerations. For example, let us suppose that x is a red wall, and between t and $t + 30$ sec. it is illuminated with strong blue lights so that it looks purple. We suppose that S knows nothing about how colored lights can make an object look a different color than it is. Simply on the basis of the rapid fluctuation, S has a good reason for thinking that the color of the wall did not really change. But he may know other things that are also relevant. For example, he may know inductively that the color of a wall is determined by the color of its paint or wallpaper. He observes that between t and $t + 30$ sec. the wall was neither repainted nor repapered, so these inductive generalizations constitute a reason for judging that the color of the wall did not really change. By themselves, these generalizations would not be strong enough to defeat the perceptual reason for thinking that the color did change, but they can add strength to the reason based on stability. On the combined grounds of the presumption of stability and the inductive reasons for thinking that the wall was red, S is justified in concluding that the wall was red despite the fact that it looked purple. And given that it is possible for S to discover this, there is no problem about his discovering inductively that this happens whenever blue lights are shined on a red object.

In general, given some circumstances C, if these circumstances tend to be of short duration, and if when an object is placed in these circumstances its apparent color tends to change and when it is removed from the circumstances its apparent color tends to return to what it was prior to being placed in those circumstances, then a person can discover inductively on the basis of the presumption of

[2] At first this looks like a logical type I defeater for the perceptual judgment that x is purple. However, it is not a reason for thinking that x *is* not purple; it is a reason for thinking that x *was* not purple. In other words, it is a defeater for a certain kind of judgment about the past.

stability plus possibly inductive considerations that objects placed in these circumstances only appear to change color. In this way a person can inductively justify a defeater of the form of principle 3.3. This is the basis of 3.3. That principle does correctly formulate a logical type II defeater, however that defeater can be derived from other simpler facts about our concept of a red object. This explains how type II defeaters are possible, and as we have seen, given the possibility of type II defeaters, type I defeaters can be established inductively.

Notice that the logical reasons formulated in principle 3.3 are defeasible. That is because of the defeasibility of the logical reasons involved in the inference from the past on which 3.3 is based. The defeaters for the reasons involved in 3.3 are just the defeaters for that inference from the past. These defeaters will be examined more closely in the next chapter.

Is principle 3.3 the sole source of type II defeaters for the perceptual judgment that an object is red? That principle seems completely adequate for the derivation of all impersonal type II defeaters. What about the personal ones? Consider "*S* is wearing rose-colored spectacles". That this is a defeater can be established on the basis of principle 3.3. Glasses can be taken on and off easily and quickly with a resultant change in apparent color. Considerations of stability indicate that these changes are not real. Furthermore, in the case of most personal defeaters we have a rather strong inductive reason backing up the presumption of stability. We know inductively that when the color of an object changes it is extremely unlikely that the colors of all other objects in our field of vision will simultaneously change in the same direction. However, donning rose-colored glasses or taking drugs which affect color vision has precisely this effect. Combining this with considerations of stability gives us a strong reason for thinking that the apparent changes are not real. It does not seem that we need anything other than principle 3.3 and inductive considerations to account for our personal type II defeaters. Principle 3.3 opens the door to a vast number of borderline cases. To take an example made famous by J. L. Austin,[3] one may observe of a woman who dyes her hair, "That isn't the real color of her hair." But suppose hair dye characteristically lasted only five minutes, after which

[3] Austin [1962], p. 65.

time it faded. We would then say of a blond woman whose hair is dyed black, "Her hair is blond; it only looks black." Now suppose that someone invents an absolutely permanent hair dye. Once a person's hair is dyed with it, it never has to be redyed. New hair, as it comes in, has the dyed color. We would then say of the woman, "Her hair is black, but its *original* color (as opposed to its *real* color) was blond." The actual state of the art of hair dyeing lies midway between these two extremes. Dyed hair remains dyed for a fairly long period, but not indefinitely. This generates a borderline case. We are not happy saying that the woman's hair is black, because its color is not *all that* stable; but we are not happy saying that it is blond either, because its black appearance is fairly stable. We have reasons both for saying that her hair is black and for saying that it is blond, and they are of approximately equal weight, so we are unable to decide which to say. Of course, our language is rich enough to accommodate us here. We don't say either. Instead we distinguish between "the real color of her hair" and "the color her hair is now". Although we will happily say, "Her hair is now black", we are not so happy with "Her hair is black".

There are other difficult cases. A chameleon does not change its appearance quite so readily as people often believe. A chameleon usually looks green but on occasion changes its apparent color to brown or orange. However, suppose we discovered a "super chameleon" that had no usual color. At all times the apparent color of this strange beast would closely approximate that of whatever surface it rests upon. Now consider a super chameleon sitting upon a blue object. What color is it? Because it looks blue, we would ordinarily say, "It is now blue". But this is not to be taken literally. If someone asked "Is it really blue, or does it only look blue now?" we would not know how to decide. Here we have a perceptual reason for thinking that it is blue. But we also have a defeater for that reason—instability. However, that defeater ordinarily functions by giving us a reason for thinking the object is some color other than it looks—whatever color it stably had prior to the fluctuation in its appearance. But in the case of the super chameleon, there is no such color. So the defeater is also partially undermined. The result is a borderline case. We do not know what to say.

The existence of borderline cases is inevitable for any concept whose justification conditions are constructed out of prima facie reasons. For such concepts, there will always be conceivable circumstances in which, if we know everything relevant there is to know about an object, we may still be unable to decide whether the concept applies to that object. This is because the prima facie reasons are defeated, and no other reasons for making a judgment are provided by the circumstances. That our analysis of "red" leads to such borderline cases is a virtue, not a vice. The borderline cases are real. It is a logical feature of the concept of a red object that under certain circumstances, even if we know everything that is relevant, we will be unable to judge whether an object is red. Any analysis which eliminated these borderline cases would automatically be wrong.

To summarize our results, we have found that type II defeaters for the perceptual judgment that an object has a red surface facing us are all either instances of principle 3.3 or inductive generalizations made possible by establishing other defeaters with the help of 3.3. Type I defeaters are all inductive, and are made possible by the prior establishment of type II defeaters.

Now let us consider the defeaters for the existential perceptual judgment "There is an object before me having a red surface facing me." Such a perceptual judgment can only be made if one can also judge that some particular thing he sees has a red surface facing him. Consequently, any type II defeater for the latter is also a type II defeater for the former. In addition, any reason for thinking he really does not see the object he seems to see will be a type II defeater. These seem to be the only type II defeaters for the existential judgment. So the above account is equally an account of type II defeaters for the existential judgment.

Now consider type I defeaters for the existential judgment. One sort is inductive, and includes such things as "Jones told me that there is no object before me having a red surface facing me." Another sort is generated by the type I defeaters for the attributive judgment. Suppose that *S*'s perceptual judgment that there is an object before him having a red surface facing him is based on his being in a position to judge perceptually that some particular object *x* which he sees has a red surface facing him. Suppose *R* is a type I defeater for that attributive statement. *R* is not by itself a defeater of any kind for the existential judgment. However, R conjoined with "x is the only thing that appears to S as if it has a red surface facing him" is a (defeasible) reason for S to think that there is nothing before him having a red surface facing him, and hence is a type I defeater for the existential judgment. These seem to exhaust the type I defeaters.

Parallel considerations apply to the negations of the existential and attributive judgments. The following analogue of principle 3.3 clearly holds:

(3.4) "The present circumstances are of a type which are generally transitory and are often accompanied by an object's ceasing to appear red and whose cessation is then generally accompanied by the object's coming to appear red again" is a logical type II defeater either for the perceptual judgment that there is no object before one that has a red surface facing one, or for the perceptual judgment that some particular object which one sees has no red surface facing one.

Similarly, type I defeaters are inductive and parasitic on the existence of type II defeaters.

3.4 *Objective Appearance*

We have discussed the relation between an object's looking red to a person and its being red. Intermediate between these two concepts is another—that of an object *looking* red, not to any particular person, but objectively, to any "normal" observer. For example, we may have a wall which (1) is white, (2) looks red because it is illuminated by red lights, and (3) looks purple to Jones who is wearing blue spectacles.

There are roughly two sorts of things that can make an object look red to a person when it is not red: (1) there may be something wrong with the person (e.g., he may be color blind, hallucinating, wearing colored glasses, etc.); (2) there may be something wrong with the object (e.g., it may be illuminated by colored lights, or heated to the point where it glows red), or with the medium by which we see it (e.g., it may be enclosed in a case of colored glass). Both sorts of circumstances can make an object look red to a person without being red, but only the first kind can make it look red to a person without looking red objectively. The circumstances of the second sort are precisely those that make a non-red object look red (objectively).

How can we analyze the concept of an object looking red? The first temptation is to try to define it in terms of a "normal" observer: *x* looks red iff *x* would look red to any normal observer. But what is a normal observer? We cannot define "normal observer" by simply listing those conditions that in fact make a person an aberrant observer and then stipulating that a normal observer is anyone else, because however long our list there is always at least the logical possibility that other conditions may be discovered which also make things look red to particular individuals when they do not look red to anyone else. Furthermore, it is only a contingent fact that any of these conditions have this effect, so they cannot be involved in the *definition* of "normal observer". A normal observer can only be defined to be one to whom objects look red iff they look red objectively. But then any definition of "looks red" in terms of normal observers is circular.

It is hopeless to try to give a *definition* of "looks red". We must seek an analysis of "*x* looks red" in terms of its justification conditions. Such an account is easily given. Just as for "red", "*x* appears to *S* as if it has a surface that is red" is a criterion for *S* to believe that *x* looks red, and "*S* sees *x*" is a precondition for the criterion. What differentiates "looks red" from "red" are the defeaters for this criterion. The circumstances in which an object can look red without being red are precisely those enumerated by the impersonal type II defeaters for the perceptual judgment that *x* is red, and the circumstances in which the object can look red to *S* without looking red are those enumerated by the personal type II defeaters for the perceptual judgment that *x* is red. Thus the perceptual judgment that *x* looks red inherits its type II defeaters from the perceptual judgment that *x* is red—they are simply any *personal* type II defeaters for the latter. *Im*personal type II defeaters no longer count. As in the case of "red", all other type II defeaters for the perceptual judgment that *x* looks red are inductive, and all type I defeaters are inductive. Thus it is easy to give an account of the objective sense of "looks red" in terms of its justification conditions.

4. Nonspatial Perceptual Attributes

A number of attributes can be considered in a broad sense "spatial". These include at least shape, size, and location. Spatial attributes involve unique problems, so let us postpone their consideration for the moment. The above account of the justification conditions for "red" generalizes immediately to the other nonspatial perceptual attributes of objects. These attributes include color, temperature, texture, taste, and weight. For each of these there is a perceptual criterion, and defeaters arise out of a presumption of stability which is based upon an inference from the past state of an object to its present state. This all seems obvious, and little discussion is necessary.

Thus far we have only considered perceptual attributes of *physical objects*. However there are perceptual attributes that are not attributes of objects at all. For example, it is often said that sounds and smells are perceptual attributes. But this is not quite accurate. A sound is not an attribute, it is a thing. An auditory attribute would be something like "piercing", or "C-sharp". Similarly, an olfactory attribute would be something like "pungent". These are attributes of sounds and smells, respectively, not of objects. No doubt what is in the mind of those who regard these as attributes of things is that the sound is caused by an object, and so the attribute of the sound can be considered derivatively an attribute of an object; and a smell is the smell of something, so the attribute of the smell is derivatively an attribute of an object. But it is not to be supposed that every sound is caused by an object or that every smell is the smell of an object. The sound of the wind is not caused by an object, and the smell of sewer gas is not the smell of an object. Still, for those sounds that are caused by objects and those smells that are smells of objects, we can define corresponding attributes of objects. However, so defined, these are not perceptual attributes. We cannot, just by perceiving an object, tell whether it is causing a C-sharp tone. This is a causal attribute, and can only be judged to inhere in an object in whatever way objects are found to be causes of things. Whatever way this is, it is not simply by a perceptual criterion. Similarly, "having a pungent odor" is not a perceptual attribute, it is a causal attribute.

Although attributes like "pungent" and "C-sharp" are not perceptual attributes of objects, they are perceptual attributes of odors and sounds, respectively. That is, where x is a sound, "x sounds like C-sharp to S" is a criterion for S to believe that x is C-sharp, and a precondition is "S hears x". Analogously, if x is an odor, "x smells pungent to S" is a criterion for S to believe that x is pungent, and "S smells x" is a precondition. Thus, there are perceptual attributes of things other than physical objects.

5. Spatial Attributes

Now let us turn to spatial attributes. These attributes are more complicated than might at first be supposed, and they are not all perceptual attributes.

5.1 *Length*

Length is always the length of some line. For example, the length of an object is the length of a line drawn across the extremities of the object. There are different kinds of judgments we can make regarding the length of a line. We can make relative judgments, judging that one line is the same or longer than another line, or we can make numerical judgments, judging, e.g., that a line is 3.8 inches long. Numerical judgments result from measurements, which are relative judgments, relative to a standard length.

On what basis do we judge that two lines are of equal length? We can often do this by eye. But it is apt to seem that this can only be a learned ability, justified inductively. Some people are good at this, and others are not. Those who are good at it have learned inductively that they are, and this is what justifies their judgments. They determine whether they are good at it by comparing their judgments with the result of more careful judgments based on actually measuring the lengths in question. It seems that it is measurement that gives us the basic way of judging lengths.

But in what does measurement consist? In order to determine that a line AB is the same length as a line CD, we lay a rigid rod alongside AB, mark the length of AB on the rod, and then lay the rod alongside CD to see if the marking coincides with the end point of CD. Of course, the rigid rod might be AB or CD itself if either is satisfactorily rigid and mobile. In order to perform such a measurement, we must be able to tell when a rod is rigid, and we must be able to tell when the point marked on the rod coincides with the end point of *CD*. The latter is a judgment of location and will be discussed in section 5.4. But the judgment that the rod is rigid itself seems to involve judgments concerning length. To say that the rod is rigid is to say that we cannot easily alter its length. But how can we know this without repeatedly measuring the length of the rod, which would involve us in an infinite regress?

One possibility would be that, like perceptual attributes, there is a logical presumption that the length of a rod is stable. In other words, in the absence of any reason for thinking that a rod is not rigid, we are justified in supposing that it is. However, if length must be established by measurement then it is not a perceptual attribute. The argument in the next chapter whereby we establish the existence of such a presumption for perceptual attributes cannot be made to apply to nonperceptual attributes. Consequently, it is hard to see why there should be any such presumption of stability for measured length.

This suggests that making judgments of relative length ("Rod *AB* is longer than rod *CD*") must, after all, be a purely perceptual matter. It must be a matter, simply, of examining the lengths perceptually and seeing which appears longer. This accords with the obvious fact that a child can judge sizes long before he learns about measurement or rulers. The child's judgment is purely perceptual.

But there are difficulties regarding such a perceptual judgment. We learn inductively that the apparent size of an object varies as our distance from it increases or decreases. Thus in making a perceptual judgment of the relative size of two objects, it makes a difference whether they are the same distance from the observer. In fact, we know that they appear their correct relative sizes when they are the same distance from us and do not appear their correct relative sizes when they are different distances from us. But we could never discover this inductively without having some independent way of telling when they appear their correct relative sizes. All we could discover inductively is that their relative distances from us influence their apparent relative sizes. If we cannot discover inductively that the objects must be the same distance from us, then this must be built into the concept itself. That is, apparent relative size is only a logical reason for a judgment of relative size when the two objects are the same distance from us. But now another difficulty arises. To know that the two objects are the same distance from us ordinarily involves another judgment of length (a judgment of their distances). The only time it does not is when the two objects are actually adjacent to one another. Thus it seems that at most we have:

> "Lines *AB* and *CD* are adjacent to one another and appear to be the same length" is a logical reason for judging that they are the same length.

Clearly, the logical reason is only a prima facie reason. It can be turned into a criterion as follows:

(5.1) "Lines *AB* and *CD* appear the same length to *S*" is a criterion for *S* to believe that they are the same length, and "*S* perceives lines *AB* and *CD* and they are adjacent" is a precondition for the criterion.

Analogously, we must have:

(5.2) "Line *AB* appears to *S* to be longer than line *CD*" is a criterion for *S* to believe that it is longer, and "*S* perceives lines *AB* and *CD* and they are adjacent" is a precondition for the criterion.

Principles 5.1 and 5.2 indicate that relative length is a perceptual attribute. They explain how we can judge relative length for objects that are adjacent. But now we must explain how we can make such judgments for objects that are not adjacent. Obviously, we do this either by bringing them together so that they are adjacent, or by comparing each to a third object (e.g., a ruler) which we transport between the two. But how do we know that moving an object around for purposes of comparison does not change its size? This is just the problem of how we know we have a rigid measuring rod all over again. But now the answer is easy. By virtue of 5.1 and 5.2, relative length is a perceptual attribute. There is a presumption of stability for perceptual attributes. Having once compared the relative lengths of two objects, and having no reason for thinking that they have changed relative size, we are automatically justified in supposing they have not. This constitutes a logical presumption of rigidity and explains why we are justified in supposing that moving an object about to compare its length with that of another object does not ordinarily change its size.

But of course, sometimes moving an object about will change its size. How can we discover that moving *AB*, which was originally the same length as *CD*, has resulted in its now being longer than *CD*? We can only do this by comparing *AB* with other lengths whose sizes relative to *CD* are already known. Generally, we use measuring rods for that purpose. The situation is the following. Suppose that two adjacent lines *AB* and *CD* are the same length. We move *AB* away from *CD*. We then place a third line *EF*, which we use as a measuring rod, alongside *CD* and judge that they are the same length. Next we transport *EF* to a position adjacent to *AB* and judge that it is shorter than *AB*. We want to conclude that *AB* has become longer than *CD*. But how can we? On the one hand, because *AB* and *CD* were previously the same length, we have a reason based on stability for thinking they are still the same length. On the other hand, because *EF* was the same length as *CD* we have a reason for thinking that it still is, and because *EF* is shorter than *AB*, this gives us a reason for thinking that *CD* is shorter than *AB*. In other words, we have conflicting reasons. We have one reason for judging that *AB* and *CD* are the same length, and another for judging that *AB* is longer than *CD*. How do we decide which to accept?

If we know nothing more about the situation, there is no way we can decide which to accept. But in fact, we will generally know something about the rigidity of the measuring rod *EF*. We discover inductively that given a rod constructed of the same material and in the same manner as *EF*, if we repeatedly compare its length with other objects, moving it around freely, we tend to get the same result each time we compare it with the same object. (Of course, this would not be possible if it were not for the contingent fact that in our world most objects are relatively rigid.) In this way we establish a rather strong inductive reason for thinking that if the rod is the same length as some particular object at one time, it will remain so at any subsequent time. This gives support for saying that *EF* is still the same length as *CD*, and hence justifies us in concluding that *AB* is now longer than *CD*. This is the basis for our saying that the relative length of *AB* has changed.

In the above reasoning we argued that if *EF* and *CD* are the same length, and *EF* is shorter than *AB*, then *CD* is shorter than *AB*. In our judgments about length, we assume the following principles:

(5.3) (1) *AB* is longer than *CD* iff *CD* is shorter than *AB*.
(2) *AB* is the same length as *CD* iff *AB* is neither longer nor shorter than *CD*.
(3) If *AB* is longer than *CD*, and *CD* is longer than *EF*, then *AB* is longer than *EF*.
(4) If *AB* is longer than *CD*, then it is not shorter than *CD*.

From these principles we can derive others:

(5.4) (1) If *AB* is the same length as *CD*, and *CD* is the same length as *EF*, then *AB* is the same length as *EF*.
(2) If *AB* is the same length as *CD*, and *CD* is shorter than *EF*, then *AB* is shorter than *EF*.

What is the justification for the principles under 5.3? Quite simply, they are part of the concept of the length of an object. They are involved in the justification conditions of that concept. One might instead suppose that they are discovered inductively on the basis of repeated applications of the perceptual criteria, but that quickly leads to insoluble problems. Suppose we had to establish these principles inductively. Then consider once more the case in which we want to establish that moving *AB* away from *CD* has resulted in its becoming longer. We acquired one reason for thinking that *AB* was still the same length as *CD*, but stronger reasons for thinking that *EF* was the same length as *CD* but shorter than *AB*. The use of 5.4(2) then enabled us to conclude that *AB* was actually longer than *CD*. But if 5.4(2), or the principles from which it is derived, had to be justified inductively, then the apparently conflicting reasons for judgments regarding the length of *AB* would no longer conflict. They would simply be good reasons for judging that *AB, CD,* and *EF* are all the same length, and *EF* is shorter than *AB*. This would constitute a counterexample to the inductive generalizations involved in 5.3 and 5.4, and hence would refute them. Therefore, if the principles contained in 5.3 and 5.4 are merely inductive generalizations, then (1) cases like the above would constitute good reasons for thinking they are false, and (2) it would be impossible ever to justifiably judge that the length of an object relative to a second object has been altered in the process of moving it away from that second object. But of course, both of these results are preposterous.

We must conclude that the principles in 5.3 and 5.4 are not justified inductively on the basis of repeated application of our perceptual criteria. Rather, we appeal to them to correct conflicting judgments based upon those criteria.

In the example in which we judged that the length of *AB* relative to *CD* increased when it was moved away from *CD*, we made use of a measuring rod of which we had established inductively that it tended to retain the same length relative to other objects. We want to say of that rod that it is *rigid*—its length cannot easily be altered. This introduces a new concept—the (absolute) length of an object as opposed to its length relative to some other particular object. It has traditionally been supposed that the absolute length of an object is still relative—it is the length of the object relative to some standard length. This standard length will be the length of some standard object. But the choice of such a standard object is not merely conventional. We discover that an object is suitable for this purpose by discovering that, at least under specifiable circumstances (such as fixed temperature and pressure), its length is absolutely stable. But now this seems circular. We are defining absolute length in terms of an object whose absolute length is discovered not to change.

How do we choose a standard of length? We do so by repeatedly comparing its length with other objects and seeing whether we keep getting the same result. We cannot expect to always get the same result, because the other objects may change in length. But we must pick our standard in such a way that we maximize the extent to which we obtain the same result upon repeatedly measuring the same object. We can then judge whether the absolute length of another object has changed by comparing it with the standard.

However, the existence of an object having a standard length is only a convenience. If there were no such object, we could still talk about the absolute length of an object. To see this, let us examine the character of those judgments we make with the help of the standard. If at one time the length of an object *AB* bears a certain relationship to the length of the standard *CD*, we have a prima facie reason for thinking it will continue to do so at any later time. Suppose now that we compare *AB* with two other objects *EF* and *GH*, and find that their relative lengths have remained the same but the length of *AB* relative to each of them has changed. Again, we have a prima facie reason for thinking that the length of each of *EF* and *GH* relative to the standard has remained the same. These each provide us with a reason for thinking that the length of *AB* relative to the standard has changed. These two reasons together outweigh the single reason based on stability for thinking that the length of *AB* has not changed. Now notice that we can completely circumvent all talk about the standard here. We arrive at the same judgment, in the same way, by simply applying the following principle regarding absolute length:

(5.5) "The length of *AB* bears the same relationship to the lengths of most other objects as it did previously" is a criterion for believing that the length of *AB* has not changed.

In order to apply this principle we must know that the length of *AB* has remained the same relative to most of the objects in the universe. This seems like a big task, but it is made possible by the presumption of stability for relative length. We compare *AB* with other objects with which we previously compared it, and see whether the comparison gives the same result as before more often than it gives a different result. We have a prima facie reason, based on stability, for thinking that each object with which we compare *AB* is the same length relative to each object in the universe as it was previously. Thus if *AB* remains the same length relative to most of the objects with which we compare it, this gives us a reason for thinking that it remains the same length relative to more of the objects in the universe. This in turn is a good reason for thinking that the length of *AB* has not changed.

In the light of principle 5.5, what role does an object of standard length play? An object of standard length is one that we have discovered inductively to be maximally stable regarding the comparison of its length to the length of other objects. Thus if the length of *AB* has not changed relative to the length of the standard, we can conclude that there are more objects relative to which it has not changed than there are objects relative to which it has changed, and hence by 5.5 we are justified in concluding that the absolute length of *AB* has not changed. Thus 5.5 explains the role of a standard length. But it is also clear that we could make judgments of absolute length even if the length of every object underwent abrupt change at regular intervals differing for each object. This would hamper us in judging absolute length but it would not make such judgments impossible. Under such circumstances, we could even have objects that we accepted provisionally and temporarily as standards of length, although we would have to be prepared for them to change eventually.

Principles 5.1, 5.2, and 5.5 give us perceptual criteria for judgments of relative and absolute length. We have seen that other judgments of relative length are based upon a presumption of stability and on inductive considerations. Because judgments of absolute length are based upon judgments of relative length, the same thing is true of judgments of absolute length.

We can now clear up an old puzzle apparently due to Poincaré: how can we know that overnight everything did not abruptly shrink to half its original size? It is apt to seem that we could not know this, because any standards of length would also shrink. But in fact, it is quite simple how we know this. Such a change would not alter relationships of relative size between objects. If the size of an object this morning relative to most other objects is the same as it was last night, then I automatically have a prima facie reason for thinking that its absolute size has not changed. As it is true of most objects that there has been no change in their relative sizes, I have a prima facie reason for thinking it is false that everything abruptly shrank to half its original size.

But notice that I have only concluded that we would have a prima facie reason for thinking that everything did not shrink overnight. Many philosophers have wanted to go further and maintain that there is something logically absurd about everything shrinking uniformly. Their reasoning is based upon the assumption that length must always be defined in terms of a standard, which we have seen to be false. On the contrary, we can imagine circumstances in which our prima facie reason would be defeated and we would have a good reason for thinking that everything did shrink to half its original size overnight. Suppose the universe were divided up into several thousand cone-shaped regions all extending outward infinitely far from the center of the star Alpha Centauri. We could discover inductively that at regular intervals each region pulses, all linear dimensions within the region collapsing to one half their original size and all objects moving halfway to the apex of the cone. After a short interval, the dimensions then return to their original size. Having observed that all the other regions behave in this way, if we also observed that at regular intervals all the regions other than our own simultaneously appeared to double in size, we could reasonably conclude that this was due to our own region shrinking to half its original size. In this way we would discover inductively that all of the regions behave in this way. Furthermore, suppose that the period of these pulsations is completely regular, so that we can predict to the microsecond when one of these pulsations will occur. On this basis we might discover that there will come a time when the pulsations of all of the regions will occur simultaneously, so that everything in the universe will simultaneously shrink to one half its original size. Although we would observe no change, we could know inductively that this is occurring. Thus there is nothing logically absurd about this hypothesis.[4]

I have argued that our judgments of relative length are based upon a perceptual criterion. They seem to arise in precisely the same way as do defeaters for nonspatial perceptual attributes. Type I defeaters are inductive, and presuppose the existence of type II defeaters. Type II defeaters arise out of considerations of stability. For example, a type II defeater for a judgment of relative length would be "*AB* is behind a magnifying glass". That is, if *AB* looks bigger than *CD* but is behind a magnifying glass, we cannot tell on the basis of how it looks whether it really is bigger. We discover this defeater just as we discover that colored lights can make an object look a different color than it is. That is, we discover that placing the magnifying glass before an object results in an immediate change in its apparent size, and removing the glass causes the apparent size to return to normal. Considerations of stability indicate that such a rapid change is unreal, and so we conclude that only the apparent size changed. In this way we discover inductively that placing a magnifying glass before an object can alter its apparent size and hence constitutes a type II defeater.

In general, type II defeaters for judgments of length arise out of considerations of stability just as do type II defeaters for other perceptual attributes. And type I defeaters arise inductively and presuppose the existence of type II defeaters.

[4] This argument is adapted from a similar argument on a different topic in Shoemaker [1969].

There is one final point that must be discussed regarding our perceptual criterion. Principles 5.1 and 5.2 are phrased in terms of "perceives" and "appears". What do these terms mean? It seems that there are two distinct ways of making perceptual judgments of length—visually and tactually. Are both visual and tactual judgments involved in the perceptual criterion, or is only one involved? For large objects, visual judgments are much more useful, but for fine discriminations concerning the lengths of objects lying alongside one another tactual judgments may often be better. Can they both be involved in our perceptual criterion?

It is plausible to suppose that 5.1 and 5.2 each comprise two distinct principles, one in which "perceives" and "appears" are interpreted as "sees" and "looks", and the other in which both are interpreted as "feels". At first it seems that there is an argument which establishes that this cannot be correct. If P is a prima facie reason for Q, then $\sim Q$ is a prima facie reason for $\sim P$. By 5.1, "x and y feel the same length to S" is a prima facie reason for S to think that x and y are the same length, and "x and y do not look the same length to S" is a prima facie reason for S to think that x and y are not the same length. By contraposition and transitivity, we obtain the result that "x and y feel the same length to S" is a prima facie reason for S to believe that x and y would also look the same length to himself. But surely this is impossible. Any correlation between distinct modes of intuition can only be inductive. There can be no logical presumption that such a correlation exists.

Fortunately, the above argument involves a mistake. It overlooks the preconditions for the criteria, and these preconditions are part of the prima facie reasons. All we obtain by contraposition and transitivity is that "x and y are adjacent and feel the same length to S" is a prima facie reason for S to believe that *if* he sees x and y *then* they look the same length to him. But the latter involves him in knowing that the objects he feels are the same as the objects he sees. How do we establish such an intrasensory identification? Apparently we do so by observing that the objects we see are in the same places as the objects we feel, and in general that they stand in the same spatial relations to one another as the objects we feel. How can we know this? Only by using the perceptual criteria for spatial relations. We have discovered those criteria for relative length, and criteria for other spatial relations will be discussed below. These criteria give us ways of judging that seen objects stand in certain spatial relations to one another, and also that felt objects stand in certain spatial relations to one another. We discover inductively that there is an isomorphism between objects we see and objects we feel. That is, there tends to be a correspondence between seen objects and felt objects such that, whenever two seen objects stand in a certain spatial relation to one another, the corresponding felt objects also stand in that relation to one another. We then identify each seen object with its corresponding felt object. This is our concept of visual-tactual identity. A seen object x is identical with a felt object y iff y is the object that corresponds to x in the visual-tactual isomorphism.[5]

In order to judge that we both see and feel the same object, we must have discovered inductively that the visual-tactual isomorphism exists, which in turn gives us a reason for thinking that any objects that we both see and feel will both look and feel like they stand in the same spatial relations to one another. Consequently, the existence of two distinct perceptual criteria for judgments of relative length, one a visual criterion and the other a tactual criterion, cannot create any conflict between the two modes of intuition. The two criteria can only be applied to the same objects if we already have an inductive reason for thinking they will both give the same result.

5.2 *Volume and Area*

We have discussed one kind of size—length. Two other kinds of size are volume and area. No doubt one's first inclination is to attempt to handle them in a manner analogous to the treatment of length by introducing perceptual criteria. But a difficulty quickly arises. There is a logical connection between the concept of length and the concepts of volume and area. For example, the area of a square or the volume of a cube is a function simply of the length of its sides. Thus if we were to attempt to found judgments of area and volume on perceptual criteria, it would be possible to arrive at conflicting judgments of area or volume using our different

[5] This must be qualified a bit. It will become apparent in Chapter Six that the fact of correspondence only provides a prima facie reason, but I will not pursue the details of this.

modes of intuition (perception of length, and perception of area or volume). This suggests that judgments of area or volume must be based upon judgments of length, and hence there is no perceptual criterion for judgments of area or volume.

This suggestion conflicts with some rather simple facts. The ability to compare volumes or areas in terms of lengths requires the numerical comparison of lengths ("*AB* is three times as long as *CD*"), and subsequent numerical computation of volumes. This is a rather sophisticated ability. Young children do not have it, and yet they are able to compare volumes or areas. This shows that judgments of relative volume or area need not be based upon such computations.

Our concept of volume is in terms of "how much it takes to fill the volume". Crudely put, we judge that one volume is smaller than another if it would take fewer small units of volume to fill the one than to fill the other. More precisely, an object *x* occupies a smaller volume than an object *y* iff the volume occupied by *x* can be partitioned into smaller volumes which can then be rearranged and recombined in such a way that the resulting volume lies entirely within the volume occupied by *y*. This, basically, is our concept of volume. When we compare the volumes of two objects, we go through a kind of mental rearrangement of the volumes to see which will fit inside the other. Clearly, the child can have and exercise this ability without being able to compute volumes numerically. This suggests that our concept of volume is characterized by the following principle:

(5.6) One volume *X* is smaller than another volume *Y* iff each can be partitioned into (possibly) smaller volumes with the result that to each volume in the partition of *X* there corresponds a congruent volume in the partition of *Y*, but the partition of *Y* contains one volume over and above those corresponding to the volumes in the partition of *X*.

To be able to apply this principle, we must be able to judge when two volumes are congruent. They are congruent when they are of precisely the same size and shape. But this is simply a matter of their having precisely the same linear dimensions, i.e., length, and that is an attribute that has already been investigated.

What is the connection between principle 5.6 and the various mathematical formulas that we use for computing the numerical values of volumes? In essence, principle 5.6 is what justifies those formulas. For this purpose, we must introduce numerical comparisons of volume. This can be done as follows:

(5.7) One volume X is the same size as another volume Y iff neither is smaller than the other.

(5.8) One volume X is n times the size of another volume Y iff there is a volume Z the same size as X which can be partitioned into n volumes each congruent to Y.

Principles 5.6–5.8 logically imply the various mathematical formulas for the computation of volume.

The answer to our initial puzzle then is that a mathematically untutored individual can make judgments of relative volume by applying principle 5.6. With mathematical sophistication will come the ability to make numerical judgments of volume, but this only builds upon principle 5.6. It does not supplant it, nor can it lead to conflicting judgments of relative size. The same considerations apply to judgments of relative area.

The above considerations indicate that, unlike length, volume and area are not perceptual attributes. Careful judgments of volume and area must be made by actually partitioning the volumes or areas in question. In fact, we quickly acquire the ability to do this mentally, "moving the elements of the partitions about in our mind", so to speak. But this latter ability is only an acquired ability, not logically connected with the concepts of volume or area, and our reliability at this sort of judgment can only be established inductively. Some people are much better at it than others.

It may seem artificial to suppose that a child actually begins judging volumes and areas by partitioning them into smaller parts. But consider how a child does learn to make such judgments. He does not begin by immediately making mental judgments of relative volume or area. His first judgments of volume are made by seeing whether one thing will fit inside another. This case is that of the simplest possible partition—a two element partition. Later the child learns to judge volume by comparing how many smaller objects he can fit inside different volumes. Here the volumes of the smaller objects constitute the partition. When we point out to the child that this is not reliable unless the things are tightly packed so that there are no air spaces, he learns to judge volumes using still smaller objects, e.g., grains of sand. Here each grain constitutes an element of the partition. Only with considerable practice does the child acquire the ability to judge relative volumes without actually carrying out some such physical partitioning.

Still, this cannot be the whole story. It is unreasonable to suppose that whenever we compare volumes or areas we indulge in such a mental partitioning. It is undeniable that we can sometimes see at a glance that one volume or area is larger than another. In such a case, we are not applying principle 5.6. We seem to be making a direct perceptual judgment. And yet, we have seen that there can be no perceptual criterion for judgments of relative volume or area. The correct explanation must be that there is a way of being appeared to, which we can call simply "looking larger", which we discover inductively to be a fairly reliable guide to relative size. This cannot be a logical reason for judgments of size, but once we discover inductively that it is reliably correlated with actual size, it becomes a contingent reason for such judgments. Judgments based upon this contingent reason are perhaps more frequent than judgments based upon the essential logical reasons formulated in 5.6. However, whenever the apparent sizes are approximately the same, so that it is hard to tell perceptually which is larger, we fall back on the more careful kind of judgment involved in 5.6, either carrying out the partitioning mentally, or actually measuring the sizes in question.

5.3 *Shape*

Another spatial attribute of objects is shape. On what basis do we judge the shape of an object? Talk about the shape of an object can always be translated into talk about the relative lengths of various linear dimensions of the object. Of course, these linear dimensions will not ordinarily be aligned in such a way that we can apply our perceptual criteria for judging their relative lengths, but we quickly develop the contingent ability to make perceptual judgments of the relative lengths of lines not adjacent to one another, and in this way we can judge shapes purely perceptually. However, the perceptual clues upon which we base such a judgment do not constitute a logical reason for the judgment, only a contingent reason. This is because they only constitute a contingent reason for the requisite judgments of relative length.

Just as in the case of size, we acquire the ability to make even briefer judgments of shape. It seems to be a contingent fact that each shape has a characteristic look and feel. This look or feel constitutes a reliable basis upon which to judge shape, and it is perhaps the most common basis upon which we make such judgments. For example, in judging that something is a cube, we do not generally either measure the lengths of the sides or mentally estimate those lengths. Something simply *looks* like a cube to us, and so we judge that it is. But such a look or feel can only be a contingent reason for judging that something is a cube. It would seem natural to suppose instead that an object looking like a cube is a prima facie reason for thinking that it is a cube, but that leads to an absurd result. We would then have the following:

1. "*X* looks to *S* like a cube" is a prima facie reason for *S* to think that *X* is a cube.
2. "*X* is a cube" entails that the sides of *X* are the same length.
3. "A measuring rod has been placed adjacent to each of two sides of *X* and looks the same length as one but not the other" is a prima facie reason for thinking that the two sides are not the same length.
4. By contraposition: "Two sides of *X* are the same length" is a prima facie reason for thinking that if a measuring rod is placed adjacent to each of two sides of *X*, then if it looks the same length as one side, it will also look the same length as the other side.
5. Hence, from 1 and 4: "*X* looks to *S* like a cube" is a prima facie reason for *S* to believe that if a measuring rod is placed adjacent to each of two sides of *X*, then if it looks the same length as one side, it will also look the same length as the other side.

Number 5 requires there to be a logical connection between the two distinct phenomenological states of something looking like a cube to me and two lines looking the same length to me. This is impossible. Any connection between distinct phenomenological states must be only inductive. There can be no *logical* presumption that one phenomenological state will generally be accompanied by another independent phenomenological state. We must reject either 1 or 3. But 3 is unassailable—it cannot be denied that the relation between the lengths of the sides of a cube is logically involved in the concept of something being a cube. So 1 must be rejected. An object's looking like a cube (or analogously, an object's feeling like a cube) can only be a contingent reason for thinking that it is a cube. "Looks like a cube" means literally "looks the way a cube generally looks", and it can only be discovered inductively what way that is. But once this has been discovered, it provides a way of judging whether something is a cube that is much simpler than going through the measuring operations involved in applying the direct logical reason for thinking that something is a cube.

5.4 *Location*

Finally, let us consider location. The location of an object is always its location *relative* to other objects. This would seem to be a matter simply of its distance from those other objects. Thus a judgment of location becomes a judgment of length.

For the most part this is correct—location is judged by judging the lengths of lines drawn between objects. But this cannot be the whole story, because judgments of length in turn presuppose certain judgments of location. Part of the precondition for a perceptual judgment of length is "*AB* and *CD* are adjacent". This is a judgment of the location of *AB* relative to *CD*. On pain of an infinite regress, it cannot in turn be based on judgments of length.

In general, there are two kinds of judgments we can make regarding location. Either we can judge that an object is at a certain previously specified location, or we can judge that it is a certain distance from certain other locations. The latter judgments are based on judgments of length, but the former cannot always be. We must, at least sometimes, be able to judge purely perceptually that a point on an object is at a certain location. When that location is defined as being adjacent to some point on the surface of another object, it must be a matter merely of perceiving the two objects and seeing whether the two points in question really are adjacent.

One's first inclination may be to suppose that we can literally see coincidence in three dimensions—that there is a way of being appeared to which constitutes a prima facie reason for judgments of coincidence. It is undeniable that there is a way of being appeared to upon which we do frequently base judgments of coincidence. Two objects often "look to be adjacent in three dimensions". But there is an old, and I think basically correct, tradition in epistemology according to which the connection between objects looking this way and their actually being adjacent is strictly contingent. The problem lies with depth perception. Many philosophers would agree that we have a direct logical ability to judge visually whether two points are adjacent in two dimensions (let us say they are "radially coincident"), but would deny that we have such an ability to tell whether they are the same distance from us. According to this view, depth perception is only a learned ability. It is felt that depth perception relies upon perceptual clues that are only contingently connected with distance from the observer. I think that this view can be defended as follows.

First, notice that it is possible to judge whether two points are adjacent without relying upon depth perception. To do this we simply judge whether they are radially coincident, and then move to another location in any direction at an angle to the line drawn to the points in question and judge whether they are radially coincident from that location too. If they remain radially coincident, we have a prima facie reason for thinking they are coincident in three dimensions. We have only a prima facie reason because we must presuppose that the objects have not moved with respect to one another while we changed location, but we are prima facie justified in believing this because of the logical presumption for stability of lengths, which in turn entails a logical presumption for stability of location (if the distances between objects remain the same, their relative positions remain the same).

Given that it is possible to judge whether two points are adjacent without relying upon depth perception, it becomes a substantive question how reliable a guide depth perception really is. As such, this must be settled inductively and cannot be a matter of logic. Hence depth perception cannot be built into the concept of two points being adjacent.

Of course, the above discussion presupposes that it is possible to judge perceptually whether two points are radially coincident, but there seems to be no problem about that:

(5.9) "*X* and *Y* look radially coincident to *S*" is a criterion for *S* to judge whether *X* and *Y* are radially coincident, and "*S* sees *X* and *Y*" is a precondition for the criterion.

In order to identify a seen object with a felt object, it must be possible to tell whether they are in the same position, which means that we must be able to make judgments of spatial location both visually and tactually. We have already seen that there are tactual criteria for judgments of relative length, but that is not enough to secure tactual judgments of spatial location. We must also be able to judge tactually when two objects are adjacent. Unlike the case of vision, we can make simple tactual judgments of coincidence in three dimensions:

(5.10) "*X* and *Y* feel adjacent to *S*" is a criterion for *S* to believe that *X* and *Y* are adjacent, and "*S* feels *X* and *Y*" is a precondition for the criterion.

It is of some interest to note that we can construct logical reasons for judgments of absolute location (as opposed to location relative to other objects) on analogy to our treatment of absolute length:

(5.11) "*X* is in the same position relative to most other objects as it was previously" is a prima facie reason for believing that the absolute position of *X* has not changed.

However, as a matter of contingent fact, this reason never holds. When it was thought that the stars constituted a fixed system, this prima facie reason could be employed to yield judgments of absolute location, and such location became simply location relative to the fixed stars. However, with the discovery of the red shift, its interpretation in terms of an expanding universe, and the supposition of an infinite universe, it follows logically that no object can ever remain in the same position relative to most other objects in the universe. Thus, although there is nothing absurd about the Newtonian notion of absolute space, as a matter of contingent fact that is a concept which cannot be employed.[6]

[6] Similarly, the concept of absolute length can only be used because of the contingent fact that most objects tend to remain the same lengths relative to one another.

5.5 *Phenomenal Attributes*

I have argued that spatial attributes are not generally perceptual attributes. One only has a logical reason for a perceptual judgment of the relative lengths of two objects when they are adjacent to one another. The ability to make perceptual judgments of the lengths of nonadjacent objects is only contingently connected with the concept of length. Similarly, the concepts of volume and area involve partitioning, and once again the ability to make direct perceptual judgments of relative volume or area is only contingently connected with the concepts of volume and area. Shape concepts are ultimately defined in terms of lengths. As such, the "look" of a shape cannot be logically connected with the concept of that shape, and once again the ability to make direct perceptual judgments of shape is only contingently connected with the concept of shape.

In each of these cases we do have the ability to make direct perceptual judgments, and in fact most of our judgments are made in that way. It is only when we are being unusually careful or the circumstances are such as to make direct perceptual judgment difficult or unreliable that we fall back upon the basic logical reasons that are involved in these concepts. Notice that the ways of being appeared to that are involved in these different perceptual judgments may not all be logically independent of one another. For example, the look of a cube would seem to include the edges looking the same length. Perhaps all "apparent shapes" consist of combinations of "apparent relative lengths", where these relative lengths are just the lengths that would be involved in defining the shape in question. Still, the look of a shape cannot be logically connected with the concept of that shape, because the way of being appeared to that is involved in the judgments of relative length cannot be logically connected with the concept of length.

In general, we have a number of ways an object may look or feel. Some of these are logically involved, as criteria, in judgments about attributes of the object. Others are only contingently connected with attributes of the object. But now, suppose that we had not found such a contingent connection for some aspect of the appearance of an object. Suppose that there were some way an object could appear to us which we had not discovered inductively to be a reliable indicator of whether the object has any already defined attribute. Let us describe this by saying that the object "looks φ". There is no reason at all why we could not define a new attribute of objects in a manner completely analogous to ordinary perceptual attributes. We could specify the new attribute φ by saying that an object's looking φ to us is a criterion for "x is φ". Defeaters for this criterion could be established precisely as they are for our ordinary perceptual attributes. "Being φ" would then be a perceptual attribute completely analogous to color, texture, etc.

But now, simply because "looking spherical" is inductively connected with being spherical is no reason why we cannot anyway define a new perceptual attribute by taking this look as a criterion for the attribute. In this way we define a new perceptual attribute of "quasi-sphericality". Then the discovery that an object's looking spherical is indicative of its being spherical amounts to discovering that objects tend to be spherical iff they are quasi-spherical.

But is this all the discovery amounts to? In fact, it amounts to much more. It establishes not just that sphericality and quasi-sphericality *tend* to go together; it establishes that they *always* go together. Because objects tend to appear spherical iff they are spherical, we would at first conclude inductively that objects are spherical iff they are quasi-spherical. When we later encounter a case in which a spherical object does not look spherical, we are faced with either rejecting the generalization or accepting it and using it as a defeater for the perceptual judgment that the object in question is quasi-spherical. As is always the case for perceptual attributes, which decision we make will be dictated by considerations of stability. As a matter of contingent fact, those circumstances in which a spherical object does not look spherical are transitory, and hence considerations of stability always go in the direction of identifying sphericality and quasi-sphericality. So we are led to conclude inductively that an object is spherical iff it is quasi-spherical.

For each aspect of an object's appearance we can construct corresponding perceptual attributes. Some of these will be the ordinary perceptual attributes of color, texture, etc., but others will correspond inductively to the spatial attributes of shape, size, and location. The latter can be called *phenomenal spatial attributes.* Thus quasi-sphericality is the phenomenal attribute corresponding to sphericality.

It seems that we do not ordinarily operate with the concepts of the phenomenal spatial attributes. This is because they would come to the same thing as our ordinary *metrical* spatial attributes. We would end up correcting our perceptual judgments of phenomenal attributes in terms of our nonperceptual judgments of metrical spatial attributes, so in the last analysis it would be only the latter we would really use anyway. In addition, our metrical spatial attributes lend themselves much more readily to quantification, which is an important consideration given the uses to which these concepts are actually put. Nevertheless, it is arguable that not all of these concepts are as foreign to us as we might suppose. For regular geometric shapes it seems quite clear that our shape concepts are the metrical ones defined in terms of relative length. But is this so obvious for irregular shapes? For example, my concept of that shape which is the shape of my typewriter would seem to be a perceptual one. My judgment of whether another object has that same shape would be a purely perceptual judgment. Of course, if I wanted to be very precise about it, I could always measure the various linear dimensions of the two objects and see whether they are the same, but my measurement of the linear dimensions of my typewriter would amount to a *discovery* about that shape. The relative lengths of those linear dimensions is not part of my concept of that shape. This seems to indicate that my concept of the shape of my typewriter is the concept of a phenomenal attribute, not the concept of a metrical spatial attribute. In relying upon measurement to make a very accurate judgment of whether a certain object has that shape, I am only appealing to the inductive discovery that phenomenal attributes and metrical spatial attributes precisely correspond to one another. In general it seems that our collection of shape concepts is a mixture of phenomenal and metrical. Such a mixture is possible because we know that there is a precise correspondence between phenomenal and metrical shape concepts. For those shapes whose metrical characterization is simple, e.g., spheres or cubes, it is much more useful to employ the metrical concepts. But for complex shapes like that of my typewriter, the metrical concepts are unwieldy, and pragmatic considerations lead us to employ the phenomenal concepts.

Just as for shape, it is possible to have both metrical and phenomenal concepts for other spatial attributes. A phenomenal concept of "same length" would allow us to make perceptual judgments of the relative length of nonadjacent objects. And a phenomenal concept of relative location would allow us to make direct perceptual judgments of that. But unlike the case of shapes, there would be no advantage to employing such concepts. The metrical concepts in these cases are very simple. Still, we could have such concepts, and we would discover in each case that the metrical and phenomenal concepts coincide in their application.

6. Perception

The preconditions for the perceptual criteria for perceptual attributes all involve statements of the form "*S* perceives *X*". Consequently, in order to give a complete account of perceptual attributes, we must give an account of such perception statements.

Let us begin with vision. There have been many attempts in the history of philosophy to analyze the concept of visual perception. Those attempts have commonly yielded something like the following:

(6.1) If φ is a visual perceptual attribute, then *S* sees something φ iff (1) there is something φ before *S*, (2) *S* is appeared to as if there is something φ before him, and (3) *S*'s being appeared to in that way is caused by there being something φ before him.

Before criticizing this analysis, let us reformulate it using some traditional jargon. When we are appeared to as if there is something φ before us, let us say that we are "presented with an apparent object that looks φ to us". For example, if I am appeared to as if there is a mighty oak before me, I will say that I am "presented with an apparent oak tree". Talk about the appearance of the presented object is thus a convenient way of specifying the way of being appeared to. This way of talking should not be taken as implying that there are two things of which I am aware in perception—the real object, and the presented object. Rather, the entire expression ("I am presented with an apparent object that looks φ to me") is to be understood merely as specifying the way I am appeared to.

In this terminology, analysis 6.1 can be rephrased as follows:

(6.2) S sees something φ iff (1) there is something φ before S, (2) S is presented with an apparent object which looks φ to him, and (3) S's being presented with that apparent object is caused by there being something φ before him.

There is something wrong with each clause of this proposal. First, it is not a necessary condition of vision that the object seen be before the perceiver. Chisholm gives the example of a person who sees a distant star which may no longer exist by the time the light reaches earth.[7] The person does see the star, even if it no longer exists. A different sort of counterexample to the first clause is provided by a person who sees an object in a mirror. He does see the object, but it need not be before him.

Second, clause 2 is not a necessary condition. In seeing a red object, I might be presented with an apparent object which looks purple because there are blue lights shining on the object. Thus the presented object need not, at least, look *exactly* like the perceived object. This might suggest that the appearance of the presented object must be only approximately the same as that of the real object. But even that is not correct. If the circumstances are sufficiently unusual, there may be no feature of the appearance of the presented object which is at all like that of the real object. For example, if we are viewing a tree through a tinted and malformed lens, this may change its apparent color, size, shape, and location, all at once. Hence the appearance of the presented tree will be totally unlike that of the real tree, but still, we do see the real tree.

When we view the tree through the strange lens, the reason we are willing to agree that we see the tree is that we can explain all of the differences in appearance between the real tree and the presented tree in terms of our knowledge regarding the causes of perceptual error. If there were a number of differences that we could not explain in this way, e.g., if the real tree were an oak but the presented tree looked like a Douglas fir, we would not agree that we see the tree. To say that we can explain the differences in appearance in terms of our knowledge of perceptual error is just to say that the presented tree looks the way we would expect the real tree to look under these circumstances if we were to see it. This suggests replacing clause 2 by:

[7] Chisholm [1957], p. 153.

(2′) S is presented with an apparent object that looks to him the way a φ object would look to him were he to see it.

Unfortunately, putting this into the analysis makes it circular.

Finally, there are problems regarding the causal connection. Not just any causal connection will do. For example, our neurophysiologists might have wired *S*'s brain in such a way that whenever a small object is placed before him, he is presented with an apparent orange. Purely by chance, an orange of appearance identical to that of his presented orange is placed before him, thus causing him to be presented with an apparent orange. We certainly would not agree that he sees the orange. The problem is that the cause of *S*'s being presented with that apparent object must be the ordinary one of perception. But we cannot put this into the analysis without being circular. Thus a number of philosophers have attempted to specify precisely what kinds of causal connections are involved in perception, and then put that description into the analysis. I do not think that any of these attempted descriptions have been entirely successful, but that is not the most important objection to this maneuver. The difficulty is that the details of the causal connections involved in perception are contingent facts, and cannot be included as part of the concept of perception. For example, the most sophisticated proposal of this form that I know about is due to Chisholm.[8] But his characterization of the causal connection builds in the fact that vision proceeds in terms of light. This cannot be part of the concept of seeing. It is an important discovery that vision proceeds in terms of light rather than somehow involving a direct unmediated awareness of the object.

It seems that we cannot build a characterization of the normal causal connections in perception into the analysis of the concept of perception. The details of such a characterization must be left as contingent facts about perception. But, on the other hand, we cannot leave the causal clause out of the analysis either. If S is presented with an apparent object that looks exactly like a real object before him, but the cause of his being presented with that apparent object is not the ordinary one in perception, then he does not see the object before him. Thus any correct truth-condition analysis of the concept of perception must both contain the details of the causal connections involved in perception and not contain those

[8] Chisholm [1957], chap. 10.

details. It follows that it is impossible to give a reductive analysis of the concept of perception. As is the case with so many other concepts, the concept of perception must be an ostensive concept, and any correct analysis must be in terms of justification conditions rather than truth conditions. Once we accept this, the task of giving such an analysis becomes much simpler.

The first step in analyzing the concept of vision in terms of its justification conditions is to notice that we can reformulate the above proposed analysis in such a way that we avoid all of the objections to it except circularity.

(6.3) *S* sees *X* iff (1) *X* is situated relative to *S* in whatever way is necessary for vision, (2) *S* is presented with an apparent object that looks to him the way *X* would look to him were he to see *X*, and (3) *S*'s being presented with that apparent object is caused, in the way normal to visual perception, by *X*'s being so situated.

"Situated" here does not just mean spatially. It refers to whatever physical relationship must hold between an object and a person in order for the person to see the object.

As an analysis, the above equivalence is flagrantly circular. But it is nevertheless a correct equivalence, and provides us with a useful pair of conclusive reasons to be employed in judging whether people see things. If we can discover in some independent way what the normal causal connection in perception is, and how *X* should look, we can use 6.3 to judge whether *S* actually sees *X*. Principle 6.3 cannot be the whole of the concept of vision, because its use presupposes that we already have some prior knowledge about vision, but it is still an integral part of the concept of vision.

Obviously, we must augment 6.3 with some further principles regarding vision. What should they be? We shall see that it is simple to give principles for first-person judgments. Once we are able to judge in our own case whether we see things, we can then discover inductively all we need to know to employ 6.3 in making third-person judgments. Furthermore, 6.3 becomes automatically incorporated into the principles for first-person judgments, so in that context we need not consider it an independent principle. Thus the net result will be that we have a set of principles which provide the justification conditions for first-person perception statements, and then by using 6.3 we are able to extend our judgments to the third-person case.

The key to giving the desired account for first-person judgments of perception lies in a difficulty that arises for our previous account of existential statements regarding perceptual attributes. It was argued, where φ is a visual perceptual attribute, that "*S* is appeared to φly" is a criterion for *S* to judge whether there is something φ before him. But it was just pointed out that an object need not be before *S*, in the sense of being physically in front of him, in order for *S* to see it. After all, it is a contingent fact that we see with our eyes, and hence that a particular orientation with respect to our body is generally (but not always) necessary for an object to be seen. Accordingly, it seems unreasonable to suppose that "*S* is appeared to φly" is a logical reason for *S* to think there is something φ *before him*. Fortunately, there is a way out of this difficulty. There is another reasonable interpretation of "before *S*" which is not subject to this difficulty. "*X* is before *S*" can be taken to mean "*X* is so situated that it is possible for *S* to see *X*". It is best, at this point, to simply stipulate that that is what we mean by "before *S*" as it appears in our criteria. So interpreted, both the distant and no longer extant star, and the object seen in a mirror, are before *S*.

Why should *S*'s being appeared to φly be a logical reason for him to think there is something so situated that it is possible for him to see it? The answer is obvious—because it is a prima facie reason for him to think that he actually does see it. If a person is presented with an apparent object, he automatically has a prima facie reason for thinking he sees such an object:

> (6.4) "*S* is presented with an apparent object that looks φ to him" is a prima facie reason for *S* to think that he sees something φ.

It seems equally clear that *S*'s not being presented with such an object is a prima facie reason for thinking he does not see such an object. (It is not a conclusive reason because an object need not look the way it really is.) So we have:

> (6.5) "*S* is presented with an apparent object that looks φ to him" is a criterion for *S* to judge whether he sees something φ.

No mention of the cause of *S*'s being presented with the apparent object is contained in this criterion, but mention of the cause seemed very important when we were attempting to give a reductive analysis of the concept of perception. Should this be built into our criterion? It cannot be, on pain of an infinite regress. We must discover inductively what the normal causal sequence in perception is, and we could not do that unless we could sometimes judge independently of that knowledge that we do or do not see things. Knowledge of the causal connection must enter as a defeater rather than as part of the criterion. That is, if we are presented with an apparent object of a certain sort, then we judge provisionally that we do see such an object. If we subsequently discover that the cause of our being presented with that object is not the normal one in perception, we take that as a defeater, establishing that we do not, after all, see what we seemed to see. This defeater is really just a special case of a general inductive defeater. That is, we discover inductively that a particular thing (in this case, a particular cause) is necessary for perception, and hence its absence becomes a defeater. For example, how do we discover that it is necessary for our eyes to be open in order for us to see anything? We discover that when we close our eyes the presented object goes away. When we open them we are again presented with an apparent object of the same appearance. In this way we become inductively justified in thinking we do not see objects when our eyes are closed.

In addition to the causal defeater, all the defeaters we have already seen for the criteria for perceptual attributes will be defeaters for principle 6.5. These seem to exhaust the defeaters for the positive half of 6.5, but they do not exhaust the defeaters for the negative half of 6.5. We often know that we see something φ even though we are not presented with any apparent object that looks φ. Recall once more the tree seen through the tinted and malformed lens. What makes it possible for us to know that we do see the tree is our knowledge of visual illusions. We know inductively how the tree would look to us under those circumstances if we were to see it, and we have a strong inductive reason for thinking that whenever there is an object immediately in front of us, our eyes are open, etc., and we are presented with an apparent object that looks to us the way the real object would look to us were we to see it, then we do see the real object. How do we acquire the latter inductive reason, and how do we acquire our knowledge about visual illusions? The way in which we acquire knowledge of visual illusions is simple. Using 6.5, we ascertain that we see something θ (for some perceptual attribute θ). We observe that this thing we see does not look φ to us, but we also discover on the basis of our inductive reasons for ascribing perceptual attributes that the thing really is φ despite its appearance. We inductively generalize on the basis of a number of such cases, and discover general facts about perceptual error. Then, appealing first to those cases in which the appearance of the presented object differs from that of the real object in perhaps only one respect (e.g., color), we discover inductively that we do see the real object when differences between its appearance and that of the presented object can be accounted for in terms of our knowledge of perceptual error.

Unfortunately, the above reasoning cannot be justified by appealing merely to 6.5. This reasoning requires us to make a number of different judgments about one and the same object. To acquire our knowledge of perceptual error, we must be able to judge of one and the same object that we see it, that it does not look φ to us, and that it really is φ; 6.5 does not enable us to know this. Using 6.5, we can know that we see some object which is θ, but how do we know that it is the same object as the one that does not look φ to us? Of course, there is really no problem here. That it is the same object is determined by our phenomenological state itself. We are presented with a particular apparent object, and on that basis we judge that we see an object. If that same *presented* object looks θ, then we judge (barring any defeaters) that the object we see is θ. In this way we can judge that that object we see has a number of distinct perceptual attributes. Combining this knowledge with our inductive knowledge about perceptual attributes, it becomes possible to discover that the same object is not φ, although the presented object, and hence the object seen, looks φ to us. In general, it is the identity of the *presented* object that allows us to tie a number of perceptual judgments together as all being about the same *real* object.

Let us examine more closely the role of the presented object in perception. If I am presented with a certain object, I may attend to it and think to myself "I see that". Here "that" refers demonstratively to the object I take myself to be seeing. For example, I may be appeared to as if there is a large tree before me, and then think to myself, "I see that tree". Assuming that my perception is veridical, "that" refers to a tree that I see. But now, suppose I am hallucinating and there is no tree before me. Upon discovering that I am hallucinating, if my hallucination lingers on, I may exclaim to myself, "I guess I don't see that tree after all". The point here is that I can meaningfully talk about "that tree" even though there is no tree. In the case in which there is no tree, "that" refers to the presented object. The reference of "that" is secured the same way in both the veridical and nonveridical cases. In each case "that" refers demonstratively to something to which I am attending. But in the one case it is a real object, and in the other case it is only a presented object. As far as the way of being appeared to is concerned, there is no difference. Thus, it seems that in the veridical case the presented object simply *is* the real object. This should not seem remarkable. What makes an apparent perception veridical is that the object with which we are presented is real. In both the veridical and the nonveridical cases we are aware of the same thing, but in the one case it is real and in the other case it is not.

The above facts have suggested to some philosophers that in perception we do not really see a physical object—all we see are "sense data", or "percepts". But there are not two things in veridical perception—the presented object and the real object. On the contrary, the presented object *is* the real object. However, this is not to say that in the nonveridical case the presented object is something else. There is a perfectly good sense in which, in the nonveridical case, the presented object is nothing at all. This is underscored by noting that in the nonveridical case it makes no sense to talk about what color or shape the presented object "really has". It only makes sense to talk about its apparent color or shape. In the nonveridical case, talk about the presented object is still merely a convenient way of describing how we are appeared to.

Now let us put the above observations together into precise epistemic principles. It seems clear that 6.5 can be generalized to yield:

(6.6) "I am presented with that apparent object" is a prima facie reason for me to judge that I see that object.

The determination of what perceptual attributes are possessed by the object that is seen can be left to our criteria for judgments about perceptual attributes. We have already defended the following:

(6.7) If φ is a visual attribute, then "That looks φ to me" is a criterion for me to judge whether that is φ, and "I see that" is a precondition for the criterion.

The positive half of 6.5 follows from 6.6 and 6.7. That is, if I am presented with an apparent object that looks φ to me, then by 6.6 I have a prima facie reason for thinking I see it, and by 6.7 I have a prima facie reason for thinking it really is φ. The negative half of 6.5 follows from 6.7 together with the observation that in order for me to see an object I must be presented with it. Making the latter explicit:

(6.8) "X is not one of the objects with which I am presented" is a conclusive reason for me to think that I do not see X.

Then if I am presented with no object which looks φ to me, it follows from 6.8 that no object I see looks φ to me, and then by 6.7 I have a prima facie reason for thinking that each object I see fails to be φ, i.e., that I do not see something φ.

It is now clear how we can know that we see a particular object which is identified as one with which we are presented, and how we can know what perceptual attributes it has. This makes it possible to explain more ordinary perception judgments. Most commonly, our judgment that we see some particular object A is based upon our identifying A with some particular presented object we think we see. That is, our reasoning has the form, "I see that, and that is A; so I see A." Thus, in order to explain these judgments, all that remains is to give an account of the identity statement "That is A". Clearly, no one account will suffice for all different terms A. For example, identity statements involving proper names will be different from identity statements involving definite descriptions, and in turn different kinds of definite descriptions will generate different kinds of identity statements. No attempt will be made in this book to give an exhaustive account of all possible identity statements of the form "That is A". Some statements of this form will be discussed, particularly in the next chapter, but many will be left without mention.

The above remarks only concern seeing an object, but precisely analogous considerations apply to feeling an object, hearing a sound, or smelling an odor. We need not discuss these other modes of perception directly.

One final point must be mentioned in connection with the perceptual criteria for perceptual attributes. These criteria are statements of the form "X appears φ to S". How do we determine whether such a statement is true? At first, one might be tempted to suppose that all such statements are incorrigible. But it is rather obvious that at least most such statements are not incorrigible. For example, I can certainly be wrong in believing "Farmer Jones's barn looks red to me". The way in which I can be wrong is that I can be mistaken in thinking that what I am perceiving is Farmer Jones's barn.

Generally, in employing the perceptual criterion for judging that Farmer Jones's barn is red, I will proceed by identifying Farmer Jones's barn with a particular presented object, judge that I see that object, and judge that that object looks red to me. In such cases, the criterion I employ is not "Farmer Jones's barn looks red to me", but rather "That looks red to me", where "that" refers to a presented object. *This* statement *is* incorrigible. To say "That looks red to me" is merely to say "I am appeared to as if that is an object before me, and it looks red to me". This is a comment about the way I am appeared to, and as such is incorrigible. Thus, although statements of the form "X appears φ to S" are not generally incorrigible, they are incorrigible in the special case in which X refers demonstratively to a presented object. And that is all we need for perceptual judgments of the color of an object.

We have now seen both how we can know the truth of the precondition for the criterion for a perceptual attribute and how we can know the truth of the criterion itself. As such, we have explained how it is possible for us to know what perceptual attributes an object possesses. We have solved the Problem of Perception.

7. Perceptual Attributes

Throughout this chapter we have been content to talk about perceptual attributes without giving any precise definition of the concept of a perceptual attribute. We began by characterizing perceptual attributes rather roughly as those attributes which can be judged to be present or absent in an object simply by perceiving the object. At the time this characterization was given, it was not terribly clear what it meant to say that we can tell whether an object has a certain attribute "simply by perceiving the object". However, it is now obvious how to explicate this and give a precise definition of the concept of a perceptual attribute. The way in which we can tell directly by perception whether an object possesses a certain perceptual attribute is that perceptual attributes have perceptual criteria. If φ is any perceptual attribute, then "X appears φ to S" is a criterion for "X is φ". I propose to take this as a definition of "perceptual attribute":

(7.1) φ is a perceptual attribute iff "X appears φ to S" is a criterion for S to judge whether X is φ.

This has the consequence that we must change slightly our talk about some purported perceptual attributes. For example, "red" is not a perceptual attribute; the perceptual attribute is "has a red surface facing S". But with such minor modifications, this definition fits our preanalytic notion of a perceptual attribute pretty well.

8. The Concept of a Physical Thing

In this chapter we have been concerned with examining perceptual judgments about the physical world. Now, what can we say about the objects of perception, the things perceived? At first it may appear that these are simply physical objects.[9] But the concept of a physical object is both broader and narrower than the concept of an object of perception. First, there are physical objects like viruses and electrons that are not objects of perception. Second, rainbows, shadows, and flashlight beams would not ordinarily be counted as physical objects, but they can be seen and so are objects of perception. Thus perceptual judgments cannot be said simply to be about physical objects. Nevertheless, perceptual judgments are always about residents of the physical world, so the latter concept is broader than that of a physical object. Let us call it the concept of a *physical thing*. Then it is true that objects of perception are

[9] This is certainly false for most modes of perception. For example, we hear sounds and smell odors, but those are not physical objects. Physical objects are perceived by only two modes of perception—sight and touch. But I will restrict my attention in this section to these two modes of perception.

always physical things, although there are still physical things that are not objects of perception. It is rather curious that our concept of a physical object is narrower than that of a physical thing. It would seem that the more basic concept is that of a physical thing. Starting with that concept, some physical things, e.g., rainbows and shadows, are excluded from the category of physical objects because of the contingent fact that they are not enough like other physical objects. For example, rainbows do not even have locations. The apparent position of a rainbow varies depending upon where it is viewed from. Shadows are two-dimensional, and flashlight beams are too dependent for their existence on the transitory states of other physical things (in particular, flashlights).

Leaving aside the concept of a physical object, what can we say about the concept of a physical thing? Although because of size and other considerations not all physical things are objects of perception, I believe that the same justification conditions apply to judgments about all physical things. Objects of perception are just physical things that we happen to be able to perceive, but the way we acquire knowledge about all physical things is ultimately the same. Let me explain more fully what I mean. There are many average-sized physical things that we never perceive because we never happen to be in a position to perceive them. We can still acquire knowledge about their attributes, both perceptual and nonperceptual. We do this first by relying upon inductive generalizations that we have established by appealing to physical things we have actually perceived. For example, we can learn about unperceived objects with the help of photographs, and what justifies us in interpreting photographs as we do is our having confirmed inductively that photographs of objects constitute reliable representations of those objects. This latter generalization is established by appealing to photographs of objects that we have actually perceived. Once we have established some of these "indirect" inductive reasons for judgments about physical things, we can go on to discover new inductive generalizations about physical things by employing data gathered both from knowledge of objects perceived and from indirect knowledge of unperceived objects. To establish new inductive generalizations we do not have to keep returning to actually perceived objects. For example, having learned about the reliability of photographs, one can make inductive generalizations about a class of objects by appealing exclusively to photographs of those objects and never actually perceiving one of them. Thus an ornithologist might make a discovery about a certain kind of bird found only in China without ever having seen one. Similarly, if we did not know about the relation between wave length and the color of light, we could discover that relation by comparing color photographs of objects with measurements of the wave lengths of light reflected by the objects. It would not be necessary for us to actually perceive the objects. In this way we would have acquired a new inductive reason for color judgments without ever perceiving any of the objects that constitute our data.

The possibility of using inductive reasons to establish new inductive reasons for ascribing perceptual or other attributes to objects is all quite obvious and apparently uninteresting when we are thinking only about normal-sized objects. But when we turn to judgments about the microcosmos it becomes more interesting. Just as it is a contingent fact that we never perceive certain objects because we are not in a position to do so, it is also a contingent fact that we never perceive certain objects because they are too small. In neither case does this mean that we must have some special new logical reasons for making judgments about the objects. In both cases we simply use what we have learned inductively starting ultimately from objects we have perceived. For example, beginning with objects we perceive, we discover that optical lenses (in magnifying glasses) make such objects appear larger and that what we see through those lenses is really there. We can then apply this inductive generalization to stronger lenses which allow us to see things we could not see with the naked eye and conclude that those things are really there too. We use our inductive generalization about magnifying glasses to justify our use of optical microscopes to acquire knowledge about objects that we could not previously see. We can then use data acquired through the use of optical microscopes to confirm that electron microscopes also give us correct information about objects. That is, we verify that insofar as we can check (i.e., for sufficiently large objects) the information supplied by the electron microscope is correct (because it agrees with the information obtained through the use of optical microscopes). We can then conclude inductively that electron microscopes give us correct information about small objects, and go on to use electron microscopes to acquire knowledge about objects too small to be seen with optical microscopes. We can then repeat the process using electron microscopes to justify the use of some other instruments for acquiring knowledge about even smaller objects, and so on. What is happening here is that as we progress down the scale of sizes our perceptual criteria cease to be used, not because they are logically inapplicable but just because we happen no longer to be able to perceive the objects in question (and this is a contingent fact arising out of the contingent limits of human vision). But we do not then turn to some radically new and different way of acquiring knowledge about the small objects. We must rely upon all that is left for us when we can no longer employ our perceptual criteria—inductive generalizations confirmed *ultimately* by appeal to objects that we can perceive.[10] I would urge that in this way we can proceed all the way down the scale of sizes to even the smallest subatomic particles. It is just a matter of descending the scale and at each step using generalizations established at the previous levels.[11]

I have given an account of our knowledge of physical things. But what are physical things? Philosophers will not be content with knowing how we can have knowledge about them. They will want an analysis of the concept of a physical thing itself. It is vain to hope for a reductive analysis. It seems just obvious that we cannot *define* the concept of a physical thing in terms of anything

[10] One feature of the instruments that we actually use in acquiring knowledge about small objects may mislead us into thinking that when we get to electron miscroscopes and similar instruments we are suddenly doing something quite different from before. This is that, although the use of optical microscopes is justified inductively, nevertheless we do literally *perceive* objects through them. We discover this through the use of principle 6.3. But this is an inessential feature of our knowledge of small objects. It would change nothing if instead of optical microscopes we had some other nonvisual instruments for acquiring knowledge of microbes and similar-sized objects.

[11] This contradicts received views in the philosophy of science concerning the hypothetico-deductive method and theoretical entities. I will argue in Chapter Eight that those received views are wrong, the hypothetico-deductive method being nothing but a philosophers' fiction. But in the meantime we need not beg any questions. We can certainly go quite a way proceeding as I have described, and however far we go, these things are physical things. If we cannot go all the way to electrons and protons, then electrons and protons should not be counted as physical things in the same sense as tables and chairs are.

more basic. But the concept of a physical thing is not an ostensive concept either. This is because it is not an ascriptive concept. We do not first seize upon an object and then *decide* whether to ascribe the concept "physical thing" to it. Anything which *might* be a physical thing *must* be a physical thing. Our way of picking out objects which are physical things automatically guarantees that they are physical things. There is never any question about this to be settled by appeal to justification conditions.[12]

If the concept of a physical thing is not an ostensive concept, then it must be possible to give a verbal definition of it. Nothing could be simpler: Physical things are those things about which we can acquire knowledge in the way described above. This is all we have to say to characterize the concept of a physical thing. Of course, this is not the kind of answer the traditional philosopher was seeking, but there is no reason to think that any "deeper" answer is possible. This is a perfectly satisfactory verbal definition, and that is all that is necessary to legitimize the concept of a physical thing. To analyze the concept of a physical thing is not to somehow "take physical things apart into their metaphysical constituents" but is, rather, to explain how we operate with the concept. And that is simply to explain how we acquire knowledge about physical things. Thus to analyze the concept of a physical thing is really to analyze all possible statements about physical things. Every time we analyze a particular statement about the physical world, we are partially analyzing the concept of a physical thing.

[12] I will argue in the next chapter that the analogous thing is true in general of many "sortal concepts".

Chapter Six

The Reidentification of Physical Things

1. Introduction

I AM typing this page on my typewriter. It is the same typewriter I used yesterday. But how do I know this? Philosophers have often been puzzled about how one can possibly know that an object observed at one time is the same object as one observed at another time. In the case of my typewriter, how do I know that between yesterday and today it has not been replaced by another typewriter of identical appearance? My judgment seems to be based simply on the appearance of the typewriter I used yesterday and the one I am using now. But if I have not had my typewriter under continual observation, if it has been out of sight for even a moment, then it seems that there is no way I could know that the typewriter I have now is the same one as I had yesterday. And for that matter, even if I have had my typewriter under continual observation, how does that help? Couldn't my typewriter have been replaced by another one, the exchange occurring too rapidly for the eye to see?

When we identify an object *X* observed at one time with an object *Y* observed at another, we say that we are *reidentifying* the object in question. The problem then is how reidentification is possible: how can we ever know of such objects *X* and *Y* that they are the same object? In order to solve this problem, we will seek an analysis of the concept of identity over time. We have two related questions: (1) How can we ever know that two temporally separated objects are one and the same object? (2) What does it mean to say that they are one and the same object? Perhaps the second question can be answered by giving a truth condition analysis, and then an answer to the first question obtained from that analysis. Or it may be that, like most epistemological problems, truth conditions cannot be given and we must approach the first question directly. In that event, an answer to the first question is also an answer to the second question.

There are two divergent traditions concerning the problem of reidentification. One tradition identifies the problem with that of analyzing the concept of a physical thing. We do not know how to analyze "same physical thing", but surely, it is felt, we know what "same" means, so the problem must lie with "physical thing". The second tradition simply reverses the claims of the first. We know perfectly well what physical things are—they are those things we perceive and things like them. What we are unsure about in "same physical thing" is how to analyze "same". This second tradition maintains that there are two concepts of identity. On the one hand there is "strict" or "logical" identity which holds between objects identified at a single instant of time, and on the other hand there is "temporal" identity which is what is involved in reidentification. For example, in "My desk is the only wooden object in this room", the "is" is supposed to be that of logical identity, whereas in "The book in his hand is the one I bought yesterday", the "is" is that of temporal identity.[1] It is agreed that we know what "same" means insofar as it refers to logical identity, but that is not the sense of "same" that is involved in reidentification. Temporal identity is a weaker relation than logical identity: it holds between discrete individuals identified at different times. All we are aware of in perception are *temporal slices* of physical things. It is a mere convention that we tie all these slices together in a certain way and call them stages of a single object. The proponent of this view is apt to go on to maintain that there really are no physical continuants—physical things do not persist through time. Our language gives the illusion that they do because it uses "same" for both logical and temporal identity, but temporal identity is a relation between distinct objects. In order for physical things to persist through time, an object X observed at one time would have to be *logically* identical with an object Y observed at another time, and that is logically impossible—it conflicts with the very definition of logical identity.

Both of these traditions contain an element of truth, but they both go badly wrong too. First, it is ridiculous to say that physical things do not persist through time—that an object observed at one time can never in any literal sense be the same object as one ob-

[1] The latter example is from Strawson [1959], p. 31.

served at another time. This sort of case is a paradigm of what we mean by "same". Part of the concept of a physical thing is that it is the sort of thing that persists through time. The philosopher who claims that physical objects do not persist may have in mind a different sense of "same" than the ordinary one, but then he should make his claim in a less misleading way so that it does not seem to fly in the face of common sense.

Second, it is simply a mistake to suppose that in perception we are presented with discrete temporal slices of objects. Perception is not instantaneous—it takes place over the specious present. It does not consist of a sequence of discrete presented objects. The apparent objects presented to us are ongoing, evolving things. As such it is not merely a convention that we tie temporal slices together into a single object. We have no choice, because our perception is perception of objects as enduring things; it is not perception of temporal slices. Although we are not aware of temporal slices in perception, we can certainly define this concept, and for some purposes it is useful to do so. But the concept of a physical object is logically prior. We must define the concept of a temporal slice in terms of the concept of a physical object, and not vice versa.

Third, the view that there are two kinds of identity, logical and temporal, common though it is, is incoherent. In certain cases we can make a distinction of this sort, but in most cases these two concepts are welded inseparably into a single concept, which is simply that of identity. A distinction between logical and temporal identity can only be drawn for identity sentences of the form "*A* is *B*" when the terms *A* and *B* in some way involve reference to a time. For example, "the book in his hand" can be taken to involve reference to a time, namely now, and "the book I bought yesterday" involves reference to the time yesterday when I bought a book. But where is the temporal reference in "Nixon was the thirty-seventh president of the United States", or "van Gogh's self-portrait is the only painting of his ever to hang in the Allbright-Knox art gallery"? The supposed distinction between logical and temporal identity trades on the fact that a term *may* pick out its referent by describing it as the only thing satisfying a certain description at a certain time. But not all terms pick out their referents in this way. A proper name does not, and a definite description *may* pick out its referent by giving some timeless description of it (e.g., "the only thing that was ever φ").

The difference between purported cases of logical identity and temporal identity is not in the concept of identity but in the mode of reference. Within the limited context of identity sentences whose terms involve temporal reference, we can draw a distinction between logical and temporal identity. When the terms A and B involve reference to the same time, let us write "Con('A', 'B')" ("'A' and 'B' are contemporary"). We can then define logical identity as

$$\text{“}A \equiv B\text{” for “}A = B \ \& \ \mathrm{Con}(\text{‘}A\text{’}, \text{‘}B\text{’})\text{”}$$

and temporal identity as

$$\text{“}A \approx B\text{” for “}A = B \ \& \sim \mathrm{Con}(\text{‘}A\text{’}, \text{‘}B\text{’})\text{”}.$$

Notice however that so defined, "$A \equiv B$" and "$A \approx B$" are referentially opaque. These sentences may not even remain meaningful, much less retain their truth value, when we substitute other terms having the same reference for A and B. They are only meaningful insofar as A and B involve temporal reference. Nevertheless, these two concepts of identity will prove useful. If A and B are terms involving temporal reference, then clearly we have:

(1.1) $A = B$ iff $(A \equiv B \vee A \approx B)$.

Furthermore, "$=$" and "Con" are each both transitive and symmetric, which implies that the following principles hold:

(1.2) $A \approx B \ \& \ B \approx C \ \& \sim \mathrm{Con}(\text{“}A\text{”}, \text{“}C\text{”}) . \supset A \approx C.$

(1.3) $A \approx B \ \& \ A \not\approx C \ \& \sim \mathrm{Con}(\text{“}A\text{”}, \text{“}C\text{”}) . \supset B \not\approx C.$

(1.4) $A \approx B \ \& \ B \approx C \ \& \ \mathrm{Con}(\text{“}A\text{”}, \text{“}C\text{”}) . \supset A \equiv C.$

(1.5) $A \approx B \ \& \ A \not\equiv C \ \& \ \mathrm{Con}(\text{“}A\text{”}, \text{“}C\text{”}) . \supset B \not\approx C.$

These principles will be of particular importance later in this chapter.

If one or both of A and B are terms that do not involve temporal reference, then no distinction can be made between logical and temporal identity. Identity is simply identity—it does not bifurcate. Nevertheless, if we ask how one can know that $A = B$, logical and temporal identity reenter the picture. For example, consider how we might know that the tallest man in the room is John Smith. This identity statement cannot be classified as logical or temporal, because there is no temporal reference in "John Smith". In order to ascertain the truth of this identity statement, I will characteristically look around and find who the tallest man is. In other words, I locate the tallest man perceptually. Then, perhaps having met John Smith yesterday, I identify the man I met yesterday with the man I have picked out as tallest. This is reidentification. In thus affirming the truth of "$A = B$", the way I proceed is to identify A and B with certain perceived objects, and then determine whether the perceived objects are the same. The latter judgment is one of either logical or temporal identity depending upon the temporal relation of the perceived objects. The way in which we identify A and B with perceived objects will depend upon what sorts of terms A and B are. This is straightforward in the case of definite descriptions but more difficult in the case of proper names. However, we need not enter into those difficulties here.

The above identification proceeded by identifying A and B with perceived objects and then identifying the perceived objects with one another. However, that is not the only possible way to know that $A = B$. For example, I might be presented with a list of the heights of all the men in the room, and read off from it that John Smith is the tallest. But here I am proceeding inductively. I must have an inductive reason for believing that every man in the room is represented on the list. Characteristically I will accept this on the authority of the person presenting me with the list. But in order to originally acquire any such inductive reason, I must first be able to make identity judgments independently of it, and it seems that these judgments will always proceed as above by identifying A and B with perceived objects. Consequently, although it may not be possible to classify some particular identity statement in terms of the logical/temporal distinction, that distinction plays an important role in our ways of discovering whether the identity statement is true. It is noteworthy that those temporal identities to which we ultimately appeal in affirming other identities are temporal identities between perceived objects. These identities form the basis for all other judgments of identity. Thus the problem of reidentification can be regarded ultimately as the problem of reidentifying perceived objects.

We must conclude from the above discussion that in analyzing "same physical thing" we are not merely analyzing a special weak sense of "same" which relates distinct physical things. The sense of "same" that occurs here is that perfectly ordinary sense that we always employ. Should we conclude then, in the manner of the first tradition, that it is "physical thing" that is to be analyzed? To a certain extent, this is correct. The ensuing analysis will not lead to anything like a *definition* of "physical thing", but to analyze the concept of a physical thing is to get clear on how we can know all the different kinds of things we do know about physical things. Insofar as identity statements are statements about physical things, an analysis of identity statements is a partial analysis of the concept of a physical thing. But of course, a complete analysis of that concept will not be achieved until we have an adequate account of *all* categories of physical-thing statements. That will certainly not be forthcoming from this analysis.

The first tradition contains a grain of truth. In analyzing "same physical thing", we are in part analyzing the concept of a physical object. But the negative implications of the first tradition go badly astray. It is implied that it is *only* "physical thing" that we must analyze—not "same". On the contrary, it will be found that what must be analyzed is the entire concept "same physical thing". That cannot be split into two concepts, "same" and "physical thing", which can be treated separately. Furthermore, the problem with which we are specifically concerned in this chapter is reidentification, so we will only be concerned with those identity statements whose terms do involve temporal reference to different times. In other words, we are interested in identity statements that attribute temporal identity. Thus in a very real sense we are analyzing the concept of temporal identity, but this in itself is part of the process of analyzing the concept of a physical thing.

Our basic question is how it is possible for us to know that one object is temporally identical to another object. It is sometimes fruitful to reformulate this question in terms of the concept of a *time worm*. A *temporal stage* of a physical object is an ordered pair $<x, t>$ where x is the object and t a time when the object exists. A *time worm* is a sequence of temporal stages of physical objects, arranged in temporal order.[2] A *substantial* time worm is a time worm that consists of temporal stages of a single physical object. We then want to know: (1) how we can know that two perceived temporal stages belong to the same substantial time worm; (2) what it means to say that two temporal stages belong to

[2] The term "sequence" is not quite correct here, because the temporal ordering is not a well-ordering—it is a dense simple ordering.

the same substantial time worm. Of course, a trivial answer can be given to the second question, viz., "Two temporal stages belong to the same substantial time worm iff they are stages of the same object", but what we want is a nontrivial answer that throws some light on the concept of temporal identity. Stated in this way, these questions bear a distinct resemblance to the question, "By virtue of what do two experiences belong to the same Cartesian ego?", which arises for those Humean philosophers who identify a Cartesian ego with the class of experiences of a single person. The problem is, what is the principle of individuation which collects temporal stages together into a single substantial time worm?

2. Spatio-Temporal Continuity

It is perhaps generally thought that it is simple to give an analysis of temporal identity: a time worm is substantial iff it is spatio-temporally continuous. This means that an object x observed at one time is temporally identical to an object y observed at another time iff there is a temporal sequence of objects (i.e., a time worm) which contains x and y and is such that the spatial locations of the objects in the sequence, when plotted against time, constitute a continuous function. Common though this answer is, it is easily seen to be wrong. Spatio-temporal continuity is neither a necessary nor a sufficient condition for temporal identity.

To see that spatio-temporal continuity is not a sufficient condition for identity, imagine a world in which there are two kinds of matter. On the one hand there are objects just like the normal objects in our world, but on the other hand there are strange transparent basketball-sized spheres, faintly reminiscent of airborne jellyfish, which float about on the air currents and, although impenetrable by ordinary matter, when they meet one another pass right through each other as if they were insubstantial ghosts. Let us suppose that all of these spheres are of the same size but differ in color. Suppose further that the coefficient of elasticity of one of these spheres is a function of its color. For example, we can suppose that a red sphere has a coefficient of elasticity twice as great as that of a blue sphere. This means that if a red sphere and a blue sphere collide with a wall of ordinary matter while traveling at precisely the same speed, the speed at which the red sphere will rebound is twice the speed at which the blue sphere will rebound.

Because these spheres are impenetrable by ordinary matter, a person could easily capture both a red sphere and a blue sphere, and push them together with his hands so that they come to occupy precisely the same region of space. The result (we can suppose) would be a sphere that looks purple. Under these circumstances, the individual spheres would still retain their identity rather than coalescing into a single object, because due to their differing coefficients of elasticity they could be separated again at will. For example, we could simply swat the combined sphere with a baseball bat and the red sphere would bound away twice as rapidly as the blue sphere. While they were held together, the red sphere and the blue sphere would have precisely the same spatial location, so it follows that, at any later period, either sphere is spatio-temporally continuous with both spheres before they were brought together. But clearly the final red sphere is identical with the original red sphere, and not with the original blue sphere; and the final blue sphere is identical with the original blue sphere, and not with the original red sphere. Consequently, spatio-temporal continuity is not a sufficient condition for temporal identity.

That spatio-temporal continuity is not a necessary condition for temporal identity follows from the fact that teleportation is not a logical absurdity. There is no logical reason why physical objects cannot perform discontinuous spatial jumps. If we were watching a brightly colored butterfly flit about the garden on a warm summer afternoon, and it suddenly appeared to jump three feet to the left without appearing to occupy space intermediate between the two positions, our immediate question would be, "How did it do that?" —not "What happened to the butterfly I was watching, and where did that new one come from?" If we thought about the situation for a while, we might conjecture that what in fact happened was that the butterfly simply moved too rapidly to be seen by the naked eye. But we could become dissuaded of this (for example, by appealing to high-speed photography), and in that case we would still be at least as likely (and probably much more likely) to believe that it was the same butterfly and that it made a discontinuous spatial leap as we would be to believe that somehow one butterfly instantaneously ceased to exist, without leaving a trace, and another identical butterfly came into existence.

To take another example, we can imagine a person who claims to have a version of the ability called psychokinesis. He claims that, more or less at will, he can make small objects change position instantaneously and discontinuously. To test his ability, we place a small, ornately carved, brightly painted oriental box to the left of an otherwise empty tabletop. On command, the box on the left side of the table disappears, and an identical box appears on the right side of the table. No doubt, because we believe ourselves to be residents of a world in which objects do not make discontinuous spatial jumps, we would suspect that some trick had been pulled and that the box on the right is not really the same box as the one with which we began. But we could become dissuaded of this by examining the box very carefully. We might see that minute chips and scratches that we carefully recorded beforehand are the same, that the lid sticks just as it did on the original box, that personal letters whose contents are known only to us are still contained in a cleverly concealed secret compartment, etc. All of this goes to show that teleportation involves no logical absurdity, and consequently that spatio-temporal continuity is not a necessary condition for identity.

A different sort of consideration which leads to this same conclusion is that there is no logical absurdity in the idea of an object going out of existence and then coming back into existence again. For example, we can imagine discovering that every object, at regular intervals of four microseconds, disappears for one microsecond and then reappears. Then the maximum length of uninterrupted existence would be three microseconds. But we would not be at all tempted to conclude that no object exists for more than three microseconds. This discovery would be irrelevant to the question whether the typewriter on my desk today is the same one as was there yesterday. But given such a gap of nonexistence, the object on one side of the gap is not spatio-temporally continuous with the object on the other side. Consequently, as temporal identity can span such gaps of nonexistence, it follows once more that spatio-temporal continuity is not a necessary condition for identity.

3. Reidentification

Having disposed of what may be regarded as the more or less traditional theory of reidentification, what are we to put in its place? The best way to approach this problem is to ask what we do in fact accept as a good reason for reidentification. This question can be split into two parts: (1) When we have had an object under continual observation over a certain period of time, on what basis do we judge that the object at the end of the period of observation is the same as the object with which we began? (2) On what basis do we make such a reidentification when we have not had the object under continual observation? Let us call the latter case that of *discrete observation.*

3.1 *Continual Observation*

There is some temptation (I think mistaken) to suppose that the answer to question 1 will be simpler than that to 2, so let us begin with 1. Philosophers of a Humean turn of mind are apt to suppose that in the case of continual observation we can simply *see* that we are dealing with the same object throughout the period of observation, whereas in the case of discrete observation we can only conclude this (if at all) inductively on the basis of things we learn from the case of continual observation. This is a persuasive view. It does appear that often we can simply *see* that it is one and the same object we have had under observation over a certain interval. Upon reflection, however, this seems hard to justify. We can certainly be fooled; two objects could be interchanged so quickly that we would be completely unaware of the change even if we were closely scrutinizing them at the time. What is it that ordinarily justifies us in thinking this has not happened?

Consider a case in which you are watching an automobile approach, go by you, and disappear in the distance. Suppose you never take your eyes from the automobile during this process. You have the automobile under continual observation. What is your reason for thinking that the automobile at the end is the same as the one you began watching? It seems that this is something you know perceptually. The apparent objects with which you were presented during the period of observation just flowed into one another with no discontinuous breaks. There were changes in appearance but no discontinuous changes. In other words, if we examine the time worm constituted by the objects observed, when we plot the perceptual attributes of these objects against time we obtain continuous functions. This is the perceptual basis upon which we judge that it was one and the same object we were observing throughout the period of observation. It was pointed out earlier that our perception is not of temporal slices of objects but of enduring objects. For our perceptual state to be one of "being appeared to as if we are presented with a single enduring object" is for the apparent objects with which we are presented to constitute a time worm exhibiting continuity of perceptual attributes, and we ordinarily regard this as being a reason for judging that our perception is of a single enduring object. This would seem to be a logical reason for temporal identity. In this sense, temporal identity is as much "given" in perception as are colors or shapes, and perception provides us with a logical reason for reidentification just as it does for judgments of perceptual attributes.

It is worth pointing out that what is relevant here is the actual perceptual attributes of the object and not just how it looks to us. If we knew the object's perceptual attributes indirectly, e.g., by seeing it on television, this would be just as good a basis for reidentifying. Furthermore, if we could be persuaded that the perceptual attributes of an object did change continuously even though, through some perceptual aberration, they appeared to us to change discontinuously, we would reidentify on the basis of the continuous change.

I am persuaded by the above considerations that continuity of appearance[3] is a logical reason for reidentification. That, after all, is the basis upon which we do reidentify. But one might protest that this is too meager a basis upon which to reidentify, and maintain that besides the perceptual attributes of an object we must also check (some of?) its nonperceptual attributes in order to reidentify it. There is a very simple reason why this cannot be the case. Many attributes are such that we cannot ascertain whether they are possessed by an object without first being able to reidentify the object. For example, the attribute of being red all over is of this sort. There are only two ways of determining whether an object is red all over: (1) by systematically examining all sides of the object and seeing whether they are all red; (2) by relying upon inductive reasons (e.g., being told by someone reliable that it is red all over, or examining it with mirrors placed so that you can see all sides of it at once). In order to employ the first alternative, we must be able to know that the object we are viewing at the end of the examination is the same as the one with which we began, which requires that we reidentify it. And in order to have an

[3] By "appearance" I mean the perceptual attributes the object possesses, not how it appears *to* someone.

inductive reason we must have related something else (e.g., mirrors) to the results of examining objects directly in a number of cases. Thus the possession of such an inductive reason presupposes the ability to reidentify because direct examination does. It is clear that in order to reidentify an object we cannot be required first to check whether it has an attribute like this—otherwise we would be involved in an infinite regress. The only attributes we can be required to check in reidentifying are those which can be known to be possessed or not possessed by an object without reidentifying the object. In order for an attribute to satisfy this condition, the process of ascertaining whether it is possessed by an object cannot take place over an extended interval of time—otherwise we would have to be able to reidentify the object throughout the interval of the examination to know that we were examining the same object throughout. This means that, in order for an attribute to be one we must check in reidentification, it must be possible for us to "take in in an instant" whether it is possessed by an object. The only such attributes are perceptual attributes. Hence we can only be required to check the perceptual attributes of an object in reidentifying it.

Although we cannot be required to check the nonperceptual attributes of an object in order to reidentify it, this is not to say that they are irrelevant to reidentification. Although they cannot be something we have to check first, they are nevertheless relevant as defeaters. In other words, continuity of appearance is a prima facie reason—not a conclusive reason. This is really quite obvious. Recall once more the oriental box in the teleportation example. One test that it was the same box after it was teleported was that it still contained certain letters in a secret compartment. Its containing such letters is not a perceptual attribute. To ascertain whether it contains such letters we must do more than just perceive the box—we must carry out an operation on it. Nevertheless, if the box after the purported jump had been found not to contain the letters, we would have taken this as indicating that it was not the same box, even though it was identical in appearance to the original box. This is not yet an example in which all of the perceptual attributes of a time worm change continuously and yet we deny substantiality on the basis of some nonperceptual attributes, because the location of the box relative to other perceived objects changes discontinuously. But we can turn it into such an example by supposing that, instead of there being just one box, there are two boxes of identical outward appearance and their positions are interchanged. Then if we consider the time worm consisting of all temporal stages of boxes on the left side of the table (and similarly for the right side), the perceptual attributes of that time worm change continuously. But supposing that we already know teleportation to be possible so that we do not have a general inductive defeater undermining the judgment that the boxes have interchanged position, we would conclude on the combined basis of the report of our psychokineticist and the secret contents of the boxes that the boxes have changed position in spite of the fact that outwardly nothing seems to have happened. The upshot of this is that continuity of appearance is not a conclusive reason for reidentification. It is a prima facie reason:

(3.1) "$<X, t>$ and $<Y, t'>$ are members of a time worm whose perceptual attributes undergo no discontinuous changes" is a prima facie reason for judging that $X \approx Y$.

The defeaters for this prima facie reason are inductive. Reidentifying on the basis of this and other reasons yet to be elicited, we discover that under specifiable circumstances certain other attributes (such as the presence of personal documents in a secret compartment) are relatively stable, and hence the failure of these attributes to be preserved in a time worm becomes an inductive reason for denying substantiality.

We have seen that continuity of appearance is a prima facie reason for reidentifying. Is it also a criterion? In other words, does the existence of a discontinuity of appearance constitute a prima facie reason for denying temporal identity? Somewhat surprisingly, it does not. For example, if the color of my typewriter suddenly changed to a fluorescent orange, but it remained otherwise the same, I would have no difficulty in reidentifying it. I would reidentify it on the basis of its other perceptual attributes remaining the same or changing only continuously. It may even be possible to reindentify an object if all of its perceptual attributes change discontinuously at the same instant, provided the changes are not too great. For example, suppose we are viewing an oriental figurine on a table. There is a flash of light, and suddenly the figurine has moved several inches to the right, has shrunk slightly and become somewhat misshapen, its color has darkened a bit, etc. Even given all of these simultaneous discontinuous changes, there would be little tendency to deny that it is the same figurine. Clearly, the reidentification is made on the basis of the similarity of the appearance of the figurine before and after the flash.

It might be supposed that when we reidentify in the face of discontinuous changes in appearance, we are doing so on the basis of an inductive reason rather than a logical reason. This would require us to discover inductively on the basis of the case of continuous change that similarity of appearance is indicative of temporal identity, and then apply this inductive conclusion to the case of discontinuous change. But a simple argument suffices to show that this cannot be the case. It is at least logically possible that *all* change might be discontinuous. It is quite possible that we might discover that all change takes place in terms of quantum jumps. Or if it is objected that quantum jumps are so small that at the macroscopic level such changes in appearance should still be regarded as continuous, we might suppose instead that all change in appearance takes place by means of very rapid discontinuous overcorrections. High-speed photography might reveal to us that, for example, when the color of a cooling piece of iron appears to be varying slowly and continuously from red to gray over a period of three minutes, the color change actually occurs in large discontinuous steps. When the object appears to have darkened just slightly, what has actually occurred is that it has abruptly become *much* darker, held that state for 10^{-6} seconds, and then discontinuously changed back to almost the original color and held that for 10^{-3} seconds; then the process repeats with the iron coming out a slightly darker color than before, and so on for approximately 180,000 times until finally the color is that of cold iron. We might discover that all changes in perceptual attributes proceed by this kind of discontinuous overchange and correction, so that there is no such thing as true continuous change of perceptual attributes. In this case it would not be possible to inductively conclude on the basis of the case of continuous change that certain things are indicative of temporal identity because there would be no continuous change.

But, in point of fact, this would not hamper us in our ability to reidentify physical things. Consequently, the reason to which we appeal in the case of discontinuous change must be a logical reason. What does that reason amount to? We reidentify across a discontinuous change in appearance on the basis of the appearance of the object before the discontinuous change being sufficiently like the appearance of the object after the change. There is a "critical degree of similarity" such that if the objects bear at least that degree of similarity we have a reason for reidentifying them, and if they are not that similar we do not have a reason. So we have:

(3.2) "X and Y are substantial time worms, Y beginning when X ends, and the final stages of X bear at least a critical similarity to the initial stages of Y" is a prima facie reason for thinking that the concatenation of X and Y is substantial, the strength of the reason being a function of the degree of similarity.

Notice that principle 3.1 is just a special case of principle 3.2. In fact, it is just the limiting case in which the degree of similarity is total throughout the time worm. Consequently, we do not need principle 3.1 as a special principle—it is a corollary of principle 3.2.

What happens if more than one object contemporary with Y bears a critical similarity to X? Clearly, we reidentify X with the object to which it is most similar. This comes immediately out of principles 3.2 and 1.5. According to 1.5 it is a necessary truth that

$$X \approx Y \,\&\, Y \not\equiv Z \,\&\, \mathrm{Con}(`Y\text{'}, `Z\text{'}) \,.\supset X \not\approx Z.$$

Now suppose that Y and Z are two contemporary objects each temporally contiguous with and bearing a critical similarity to X, but suppose Y is more similar to X than Z is. By virtue of 3.2 we have a prima facie reason for thinking that $X \approx Y$, and we have a prima facie reason for thinking that $X \approx Z$, the former being the stronger of the two. Combining this with the above necessary truth, our reason for believing that $X \approx Y$ is also a reason for believing that $X \not\approx Z$, and our reason for believing that $X \approx Z$ is also a reason, although a weaker one, for believing that $X \not\approx Y$. Summing these up, we have a strong reason for believing that $X \approx Y$ and a weak defeater for this, and we have a weak reason for believing $X \approx Z$ and a strong defeater for this. Consequently, we are justified in believing that $X \approx Y$ and $X \not\approx Z$.

3.2 *Discrete Observation*

Thus far we have only considered the case of continual observation, on the assumption that reidentification would prove simpler in that case than in the case of discrete observation. Now let us turn to discrete observation. On what basis do we judge that an object perceived at one time is temporally identical to an object perceived at a later time when we have not had the objects in question under continual observation throughout the interval? Hume seems to have given the right answer—we judge identity on the basis of similarity. If Y perceived at t is sufficiently like X perceived at t', where t is later than t', we have a reason for judging that X and Y are temporally identical. If X and Y are not sufficiently alike, then we have a reason for judging that they are not temporally identical.

Before attempting to make this reason for reidentification precise, let us ask whether it is a logical reason or only a contingent reason. It has frequently been supposed that only in the case of continual observation can we judge identity on the basis of a non-inductive logical reason—in the case of discrete observation we must rely upon clues discovered inductively in the case of continual observation. This view gains its plausibility from the fact that in the case of continual observation we can sometimes literally "see" temporal identity. But this phenomenon only occurs when the changes in appearance are continuous, and there is no logical guarantee that they will be. We have seen that we need a logical reason (principle 3.2) broad enough to cover the case of discontinuous change. Once we have admitted that we must have a principle as broad as that, it is not so obvious that we may not have an even broader logical reason which is applicable to discrete observation as well as continuous observation. So let us consider objectively whether we could get by without such a logical reason.

The alternative to having a logical reason applicable to cases of discrete observation would be for us to proceed entirely inductively in cases of discrete observation. According to this view, by considering objects that we have had under continual observation for long periods we discover inductively that certain attributes of physical objects (e.g., a certain specific gravity) tend to be stable—if an object has the attribute it tends to keep it, and if it lacks it it tends not to acquire it—and other attributes (e.g., wetness) tend to be unstable. Then when we encounter an object Y and want to know whether it is temporally identical with an object *X* perceived earlier, we consider some set of stable attributes of *Y* that are sufficient to individuate *Y* from any other simultaneously existing object. As these attributes are stable, we have an inductive reason for thinking that whatever object was temporally identical to *Y* at the time we perceived *X* also had those attributes. It is assumed that these attributes are sufficient to individuate an object, so at most one such object could have had them all. Therefore if *X* had those attributes, we have an inductive reason for thinking that *X* and *Y* are temporally identical.

There are at least two difficulties with this view. First, as a matter of contingent fact we do not generally keep a single object under continual observation for a period long enough to learn that any attributes are stable for more than a few minutes. But then we would be unjustified in applying anything we learn in that way about the stability of attributes to reidentification over an interval of days or even years. Even more serious, as we noted before it is conceivable that we might discover that every object, at regular intervals of four microseconds, disappears for one microsecond and then reappears. The maximum length of continual observation would be three microseconds, which would not be long enough to establish anything inductively, but this would not create any difficulties for our ability to reidentify objects.

Second, in order for us to be able to reidentify in the above manner, it must be possible for us to find a set of attributes which are (1) stable, and (2) sufficient to individuate an object from any of its contemporaries. If we are allowed to include spatial location among these attributes, this will not be a problem (although as we have seen, it is only a contingent fact that two objects never occupy the same space). But spatial location is always relative to a reference point. The simplest reference point is the observer himself. But observers move about rather freely, much more so than inanimate objects, and hence location relative to the observer is not a particularly stable attribute. Location relative to most inanimate objects is much more stable, but to know an object's location relative to a set of such objects we must first reidentify those objects. Generally, if an object has been out of sight for a while, so have any nearby objects that can serve as a reference system. While we sleep, all objects are out of our sight. Consequently, reestablishing the reference system is itself a matter of reidentification under conditions of discrete observation. Therefore, such reidentification cannot rely upon our prior ability to locate an object in such a reference system. This indicates that spatial location cannot be one of the attributes contained in our set of stable individuating attributes. But if spatial location cannot be included, it is extremely doubtful whether it will be possible to find a set of stable attributes that will individuate and are such that we can know whether an object possesses them without having to first reidentify the object under conditions of discrete observation. In that case, the most our knowledge of stable attributes can do is tell us when *dis*similarity is a reason for thinking that two objects are *not* temporally identical. It cannot help us judge when similarity is a reason for thinking that they are temporally identical. The upshot of this is that similarity must be regarded as a logical reason for reidentification in the discrete case just as it is in the case of continual observation. It cannot be justified by appealing to the case of continual observation.

We must agree that there is a logical reason for reidentification which is applicable to cases of discrete observation, and that reason seems to be similarity. In the case of continual observation, the similarity that constituted a logical reason was just similarity with respect to perceptual attributes. That was because the perceptual attributes of an object are the only ones we can check without reidentifying the object. But this same argument does not apply to the case of discrete observation. For example, it might seem that in reidentifying under conditions of discrete observation we should at least examine objects from different angles. Our ability to do this presupposes our being able to reidentify the objects while we turn them around to examine them, but that can be reidentification under conditions of continual observation, which we have already secured. Furthermore, it is apt to seem that the perceptual attributes of an object constitute a very meager basis upon which to reidentify it. It is not implausible to suppose that something more stringent is required under conditions of discrete observation.

However, there is a very simple reason why nothing more stringent can be required. We can again appeal to the logical possibility that all objects might disappear and reappear at regular short intervals of several microseconds. If this were the case, any observation of an object over an interval of more than a few microseconds would be discrete observation. Hence there would simply not be time to turn objects around to examine them from other angles, or do anything else that requires reidentification. Once more, until we could reidentify objects we could know nothing about them other than their perceptual attributes. Under these circumstances we would still reidentify objects just as we do now. For example, I would feel no temptation to maintain that the chair in which I am sitting changes its identity every few microseconds. Consequently, our reidentification must once more be based simply on the perceptual attributes of the objects in question:

(3.3) "The appearance of X bears at least a critical similarity to the appearance of Y" is a prima facie reason for thinking that $X \approx Y$.

This is not nearly so meager a basis for reidentification as we might first suppose. When we think of perceptual attributes we generally think of nonrelational ones like color or shape. But among the perceptual attributes of an object are numbered its (phenomenal) spatial relations to other nearby objects, themselves having complex arrays of perceptual attributes. Because of this we rarely reidentify objects "in a vacuum". As a general rule we reidentify whole groups of objects simultaneously. For example, if called upon to reidentify my footstool in unfamiliar surroundings, I might have difficulties. But if I see it in its normal surroundings I will have no difficulty. Under those circumstances I will see and reidentify not only the footstool but the chair and the table it stands by, the nearby fireplace, and all the other normal furnishings of the room. This provides me with a very rich body of perceptual information all of which is relevant to the reidentification of the footstool in accordance with principle 3.3.

As a matter of contingent fact, reidentification under conditions of discrete observation is a somewhat riskier business than reidentification under conditions of continual observation. We are more often wrong. For this reason we do often strengthen our basis for reidentifying by examining more than just the perceptual attributes of the objects in question. We examine them from different angles, examine their interiors, etc. But it is only a contingent fact that this helps. For example, we may learn that there are a number of oriental boxes just like ours. But we know inductively that it is highly unlikely for any of them to contain the same personal documents in the secret compartment. Consequently, upon checking a box for the presence of those documents and finding that they are there, we have considerably strengthened our reason for reidentifying. But we only need do this when we have some concrete reason for thinking that similarity of appearance may not be a sufficient indication of temporal identity.

3.3 *A Single Criterion*

In discussing reidentification we have progressed from what seems to be the most secure case—that of continual observation and continuous change of appearance—to the most problematic case—that of discrete observation. But in each case our reasons have turned out to be generalizations of our previous reasons. Principle 3.1 was a special case of 3.2, and 3.2 is a special case of 3.3. Thus it seems we need only one logical reason for reidentification—principle 3.3—and this suffices to account for all of our judgments of reidentification.

It is worth seeing in some detail just how principle 3.1 arises out of principle 3.3. At first it might seem that 3.3 is even incompatible with 3.1, because 3.1 can give us a reason for judging that $X \approx Y$ even when X and Y are completely unlike one another in appearance, provided that the one has grown out of the other through continuous changes. This ability of continuity to override final dissimilarities arises out of principle 1.2, according to which temporal identity is transitive, i.e., $[(X \approx Y \,\&\, Y \approx Z) \supset X \approx Z]$ is a necessary truth. This means that "$X \approx Y \,\&\, Y \approx Z$" is a conclusive reason for believing that $X \approx Z$. Consequently, although Z's being similar to X may be a reason for thinking that $X \approx Z$, if we know of a Y existing between the times the objects X and Z are being considered, and the appearance of Y is midway between the appearances of X and Z, then we have a stronger reason for judging that $X \approx Y$ and that $Y \approx Z$, and that in turn is a logical reason for believing that $X \approx Z$. By thus interposing additional objects between X and Z we can rely upon closer similarities and thus make our reason for reidentification stronger. Going one step further, X and Z may be quite unlike one another in appearance, but by breaking up the temporal interval between them we may find objects $Y_1, \ldots, Y_n$ such that $X \approx Y_1 \approx Y_2 \approx \ldots \approx Y_n \approx Z$, where each of these temporal identities is judged on the basis of almost perfect similarity. Then we have a very strong reason for thinking that $X \approx Z$, even though X and Z are not similar in appearance. This indicates that the significance of continuity is that it allows us to appeal to arbitrarily great similarities by appealing to arbitrarily short intervals of change, and hence makes our judgment of identity maximally strong. Thus continuity is not a reason independent of similarity; it arises out of similarity. It is in effect the limiting case of similarity. Consequently, we need list only one prima facie reason for reidentification—similarity of appearance.

We have seen that similarity is a prima facie reason for reidentification. It also seems clear that dissimilarity (i.e., less than a critical degree of similarity) is a prima facie reason for denying temporal identity. In the case of discrete observation, if the appearance of an object Y is quite unlike that of an object X perceived at some earlier time, and we have no particular reason for thinking that they are the same object, we do not simply withhold judgment about whether they are the same—we judge that they are not the same. This means that at least in the case of discrete observation, similarity of appearance is actually a criterion for temporal identity. This remains true when we turn to cases of continual observation. Clearly, in the case of a time worm that is continuous except for one point, if the discontinuity is sufficiently great (i.e., the dissimilarity is sufficiently great), then we have a reason for denying temporal identity. On the other hand, if we have a continuous time worm whose end points are not similar, this by itself would be a reason for denying temporal identity, but if we know about the continuity this is a stronger reason for affirming identity and hence defeats the original reason. Thus in general, similarity of appearance is a criterion for temporal identity:

(3.4) "The appearance of X bears at least a critical similarity to the appearance of Y" is a criterion for judging whether $X \approx Y$.

This single criterion gives us an elegant and unified account of reidentification.

In the last chapter we made extensive use of a purported logical presumption of stability for perceptual attributes. That there is such a presumption follows from our criterion for reidentification. According to that criterion, similarity of appearance is a prima facie reason for identifying an object X perceived at one time with an object Y perceived at another time, and dissimilarity of appearance is a prima facie reason for denying that identity. An equivalent way of putting this is to say that for each perceptual attribute, sameness or similarity of X and Y with respect to that attribute is a weak reason for reidentification, and difference or dissimilarity with respect to that attribute is a reason for denying identity. In deciding whether to identify X with Y, we sum up all of these individual reasons. Notice that dissimilarity with respect to a single attribute is a stronger reason for denying identity than similarity is a reason for affirming it. If we know nothing about X and Y except that X was red and Y is not, then we would be (rather weakly) justified in judging that $X \not\approx Y$. But if all we know is that X and Y are both red, this would not be sufficient to justify us in thinking that $X \approx Y$. It takes much more than similarity with respect to a single attribute to justify reidentification. This is also obvious if we consider the overall degree of similarity of appearance that is required to justify reidentification on the basis of the criterion. It is clearly insufficient that X merely have as many perceptual attributes like Y as it has unlike Y. There must be a clear preponderance of perceptual attributes in which X and Y are alike before reidentification is warranted.

If φ is a perceptual attribute, and X and Y are objects identified at distinct times, then "X is φ but Y is not" is a weak prima facie reason for judging that $X \not\approx Y$. By contraposition, it follows that "$X \approx Y$" is a weak prima facie reason for judging "If X is φ then so is Y". In other words, given any object X, its being φ at one time is a prima facie reason for judging that it is φ at any other time. This is our presumption of stability for perceptual attributes. It arises out of our criterion for reidentification.

3.4 *Defeaters*

To complete our account of the essential justification conditions of the concept of temporal identity, we must describe the defeaters for our criterion. A type I defeater for the positive judgment is a reason for thinking that $X \not\approx Y$. Such a defeater is provided by principle 1.5, i.e., "$X \approx Z \;\&\; Y \not\asymp Z \;\&\; \mathrm{Con}(Y, Z)$" is a conclusive reason for believing that $X \not\approx Y$. We have already seen one example of how this defeater is employed. It is by virtue of this defeater that we identify an object with at most one earlier object—the single object that it is most like. There is one other essential type I defeater for the positive judgment, this one arising out of principle 1.3. By that principle, "$X \approx Z$ & $Z \not\approx Y$ & $\sim$ Con(Y, Z)" is a conclusive reason for believing that $X \not\approx Y$. An application of this defeater comes in the case in which X is observed at time t, Y at time $t + 10$ min., and Z at time $t + 1$ min. X and Y are very similar, X and Z are equally similar, Z is more like X than anything else we observed at that time, and we know on some basis (perhaps we carried Z away with us) that $Z \not\approx Y$. Then, because of the greater temporal proximity between X and Z than between X and Y, we have a stronger reason for thinking that $X \approx Z$ than we do for thinking that $X \approx Y$. On this basis we would judge that $X \not\approx Y$. These appear to be the only essential type I defeaters for the positive judgment. Any other type I defeater will be inductive. We have already noted examples of several inductive type I defeaters. For example, if we discover inductively that φ is a stable property of objects, then the presence of φ in X and its absence in Y is an inductive reason for thinking that $X \not\approx Y$.

An essential type I defeater for the negative judgment is provided by principle 1.2. That is, "$X \approx Z$ & $Z \approx Y$ & $\sim$ Con(X, Y)" is a conclusive reason for believing that $X \approx Y$. We have seen that this defeater provides the key to understanding why our judgments are more secure in the case of continuous change during continual observation. This appears to be the only essential type I defeater for the negative judgment. Any other type I defeater will be inductive.

A type II defeater for the positive judgment will be a statement P such that we are justified in believing that, when P is true, X and Y may be quite similar without being identical. This may be discovered inductively, or it may be a logical consequence of our type I defeaters. In order for it to be possible to make such an inductive discovery, it must be possible for us to judge that $X \not\approx Y$ exen though X and Y are very similar. Thus the discovery of such a type II defeater presupposes the existence of type I defeaters. An example of an inductive type II defeater might be "I am witnessing a play and the actors are heavily made up", where X is one of the actors. Or X might be a painting by Cézanne and P the statement, "A number of forged Cézanne paintings have turned up lately and were obtained from the same source as X". An example of a noninductive P would be "There are a number of things just like X around here". By virtue of our type I defeaters, we know that at most one of these things can be identical with Y, and we we have just as good a reason for identifying any of them with Y as we do for identifying X with Y. Hence, X may be just like Y and still not be identical with it.

Type II defeaters for the negative judgment will be completely analogous to those for the positive judgment. For example, if X is a robust young criminal and Y is a withered old man, we would have a prima facie reason for thinking that they are different people, but an inductive type II defeater would be "X is a master of disguise".

4. Sortals and Composition

4.1 *Fission and Fusion*

There is a class of examples which appear to create difficulties for the preceding account of reidentification. These examples involve fission, fusion, and the parts of objects.

My typewriter is held off the desk by four little rubber feet. Suppose someone steals those feet. Do I still have the same typewriter? Of course I do. I would protest that someone has stolen the feet off my typewriter, but it would never occur to me to protest that someone has destroyed my typewriter and left another (the top part of the first one) in its place. And yet there is an argument which seems to establish that that is precisely what has happened. The object T which remains on my desk after the feet have been stolen off my original typewriter T_0 is the top part T^* of my original typewriter. That is, T is temporally identical with T^*. But T^* was a proper part of, and hence not logically identical with, my original typewriter T_0. By principle 1.5, as we have $T \approx T^*$ & $T^* \not\equiv T_0$ & Con('T_0', 'T^*'), we must conclude that $T \not\approx T_0$, i.e., what remains on my desk is not the same object as my original typewriter. Insofar as it is still a typewriter, it is a different typewriter than the one I had before. The one I had before no longer exists. If this is correct, something must be wrong with the account of reidentification set forth in section 3. That account leads us inexorably to reidentify the typewriter on my desk with the one I had before. That this is the judgment we really would make suggests that it is the above argument rather than the account of reidentification that is in error.

That there is some mistake in the above argument seems inescapable. By a precisely analogous argument, we can conclude that whenever a part is removed from an object, or a piece broken off of it, the object that remains is not the same object as the one with which we began. Let us call these cases of "fission". Similarly, in cases of fusion where something is added to an object, we must conclude that the product of the fusion is a different object from either of its constituents, no matter how small and insignificant one of these constituents might be. If a screw falls off of my car, I no longer have the same car; or if a window breaks in a giant skyscraper, it is no longer the same building. Surely this is absurd. The problem is to explain what has gone wrong in this argument.

4.2 *Composition*

Our problem can be solved by making a distinction. When a screw falls off my car, what remains is the same car but a different quantity of matter. That it is the same car seems inescapable. But that something is different is equally inescapable, and what is different is the quantity of matter which constitutes the car. Where the argument goes wrong is in assuming that the car is to be identified with this quantity of matter and hence when the quantity of matter changes so does the identity of the car.

4.2.1. *Composition and identity.* What is the relation between the car and the quantity of matter of which it is composed? I think it is fair to say that this has generally been supposed to be the identity relation. Most philosophers have assumed that the quantity of matter is the same thing as the car. But this cannot be correct for at least two reasons. First, it seems undeniable that the matter can change without our thereby having a different car. Second, the car and the matter may have different attributes. To simplify the example, suppose the car is made out of a single lump of plastic. The plastic may have come into existence long before the car. The car was made by Ford Motor Company, but the plastic was not. The car may be a work of art, but the plastic is not. The plastic was made in a factory in Ohio, but the car was not. If the car were the same thing as the plastic, they would have to share these attributes. It must be concluded that an object cannot be identified with the matter of which it is composed.[4]

This relation of composition is important in a number of philosophical respects. I shall argue that it is the same as the relation between a statue and the lump of clay from which it is molded, the relation between a club and the set of its members, the relation between a body of water and a collection of H_2O molecules, the relation between lightning and an electrical discharge, and the relation between a person and his body. Thus the clarification of this relation is of considerable importance quite apart from a defense of the above account of reidentification.

At this point let me dispel one misconception. It may be felt that the argument which leads us to distinguish between the car and the lump of plastic will work for any predicate just as readily as for "car". Given any two predicates A and B, the A at a certain location cannot be the same thing as the B at that location, because the B could continue to exist after the A has ceased to exist. For example, it might be argued that the car before me cannot be the same thing as the *red* car now before me, because if the color were changed the red car would no longer exist but the car would continue to exist. This would constitute a reductio ad absurdum of the argument, because it would establish that no object can simultaneously satisfy two different predicates. But it is pretty obvious that this generalization of the argument is incorrect. If we were to repaint the red car, the red car would still exist (that is, the thing which is now a red car would still exist) but no longer be red. To say that the red car would still exist is just to say that the car which is now red would still exist. To reidentify the red car is just to reidentify the car. Not so for the car and the plastic. If we melt it down, the car will genuinely cease to exist, although the lump of plastic may continue to exist. Furthermore, unlike the lump of plastic and the car, the car and the red car share all the same attributes. Thus the argument cannot be generalized to absurdity.

[4] If there were only the first of these two reasons for denying identity, one might instead be inclined, with Geach [1962] and [1967], to relativize identity and say that there is just one thing there, but although it may be the same lump of plastic as one perceived earlier it is not the same car. However, the fact that the lump of plastic and the car have genuinely different attributes precludes our saying that they are the same thing.

However, the argument can be employed more generally than might be suspected. It usually works for those concepts philosophers have called *sortals*. Sortals are difficult to characterize precisely. They are those concepts which refer to "kinds of substances". Terms for sortals are generally such that they take the definite or indefinite article—"a tree", "the bucket", "a car", as opposed to "a red". The difference is approximately that between a noun and an adjective.

Working for the moment with just this rough intuitive notion of a sortal, we can observe that the above argument usually (not invariably) works for pairs of sortals. A horse is to be distinguished from the structure of flesh and bones at that place because the horse can die and thereby cease to exist although the organic structure remains. For the same reason, the horse is also to be distinguished from the collection of molecules occupying that region of space. However, some sortals are related as genus to species, and for them the argument fails. For example, the horse cannot be distinguished from the animal occupying that same region of space.

The way in which the argument works in connection with sortals points the way to constructing a rough but workable notion of a sortal. The argument forces us to distinguish between the *A* and the *B* only when *A*'s and *B*'s are reidentified in different ways. The reason it works for sortals is that sortal concepts have built into them criteria for reidentification.[5] For example, the way we reidentify cars is different from the way we reidentify lumps of plastic, and the way we reidentify horses is to be distinguished from the way we reidentify organic structures, which in turn is to be distinguished from the way we reidentify collections of molecules; but the way we reidentify horses is not to be distinguished from the way we reidentify animals. Thus "car" is a sortal, because to understand what a car is we must understand how to reidentify cars. But "red" is not a sortal, because there is no single way to reidentify red things—red cars are reidentified differently from red lumps of plastic.

Because sortals have criteria for reidentification built into them, one object cannot fall under two sortals having different criteria

[5] I use the term "criteria" loosely here—not in our technical sense.

for reidentification. Still, we want to locate objects falling under different sortals at the same place. For example, the car and the lump of plastic occupy the same volume of space but cannot be identified with one another because of the different criteria for reidentifying cars and lumps of plastic. The objects falling under different sortals are intimately connected but not identical. This is the origin of our notion of one object being composed of another.

4.2.2 *The analysis of composition.* What is this relation of composition wherein one object is composed of another? As a first approximation, for the first object to exist is for the second object to have certain attributes. For example, for the car to exist is for the plastic to have a certain structure. The existence of the composed object is dependent upon the structure or attributes of the composing object. Furthermore, the location of the composed object is determined by the location of the composing object. The car is located wherever the matter composing it is located. This suggests, where A and B are sortals:

(4.1) The A at location l is composed of the B at location l iff there is an attribute φ possessed by the B at l such that there being a unique B at l and that B's being φ entails that there is a unique A at l.

Thus the car is composed of the lump of plastic because the lump of plastic has a certain structure φ and a lump of plastic's having that structure entails that there is a car located where that plastic is located.

As a piece of additional terminology, when X is composed of Y, let us say that Y *constitutes* X. Thus the plastic constitutes the car.

Proposal 4.1 is only a first approximation to a correct analysis. The first difficulty is that, if 4.1 were correct, the expression "X is composed of Y" would be referentially opaque. This is because the A at l might also be the C at l, and although the B at l being φ might entail that there is a unique A at l, it might not entail that there is a unique C at l. Letting "$A_l x$" symbolize that x is an A at l, and taking "$\rightarrow$" for entailment, and "$(\exists !x)$" for "there is a unique x", we can rectify this difficulty of 4.1 as follows:

(4.2) X is composed of Y iff $(\exists A)\ (\exists B)\ (\exists l)\ (\exists \varphi): X = \imath x A_l x\ \&\ Y = \imath x B_l x\ \&\ \varphi(Y)\ \&\ [(\exists !x) B_l x\ \&\ \varphi(\imath x B_l x). \rightarrow (\exists !x) A_l x]$.

Here and throughout this section, "A" and "B" range only over sortals.

Proposal 4.2 avoids the referential opacity of 4.1 but is subject to another difficulty. This is that if 4.2 were correct the composition relation would be symmetric. That is, it would be true that if X were composed of Y, Y would also be composed of X. This cannot be right. The lump of plastic is not composed of the car. To see that this does follow from 4.2, suppose the A at l is composed of the B at l. Then letting φ be "is composed of the B at l", the A at l has the attribute φ, and this entails the existence of a unique B at l. Thus by 4.2 it would follow that the B at l is composed of the A at l.

The reason the composition relation should not be symmetric is that when one object is composed of another it is in some sense *something more than* the other. Its existence *consists* of the other's having some structure or attributes. This suggests adding to the analysis the requirement that if the B at l didn't exist or weren't φ, the A at l wouldn't exist. For example, if the lump of plastic either didn't exist or didn't have the structure required to make a car, the car wouldn't exist. This blocks the symmetry argument: it is not true that if the A at l either didn't exist or didn't consist of a B, then the B at l wouldn't exist. For example, it is not true that, if the car either didn't exist or weren't composed of the lump of plastic, the lump of plastic wouldn't exist. The lump of plastic might easily have existed but simply not been formed into a car. Let us symbolize a counterfactual "if it weren't true that Q it wouldn't be true that P" as "$P \Rightarrow Q$". Then my next proposal becomes:

(4.3) X is composed of Y iff $(\exists A)\ (\exists B)\ (\exists l)\ (\exists \varphi): X = \imath x A_l x\ \&\ Y = \imath x B_l x\ \&\ \varphi(Y)\ \&\ [(\exists !x) B_l x\ \&\ \varphi(\imath x B_l x). \rightarrow (\exists !x) A_l x]\ \&\ [(\exists !x) A_l x \Rightarrow .(\exists !x) B_l x\ \&\ \varphi(\imath x B_l x)]$.

Proposal 4.3 is still not entirely satisfactory. To see that it is not, consider a piece of ice sculpture. The ice sculpture is, of course, composed of a piece of ice, but it is also composed of a collection of H_2O molecules. The difficulty is that there is no attribute φ

possessed by this collection of molecules which satisfies 4.3. If we let φ be "consists of H_2O molecules having spatial arrangement S and temperature less than 0° C." (where S describes the volume occupied by the ice sculpture), then the collection's having attribute φ does not *entail* the existence of the ice sculpture. There is no entailment because it is a contingent fact that ice consists of H_2O molecules. We can create an entailment by adding to the generalization, "and at whatever location there is a collection of H_2O molecules at less than 0° C., there is also ice." But then the last clause of 4.3 fails. If the collection of molecules did not have the attribute φ, this might come about by virtue of the generalization's being false. And there is no reason to think that if the generalization were false, the ice sculpture would not exist. Consequently, we can find no φ satisfying both the entailment and the counterfactual required by 4.3, but we still want to say that the ice sculpture is composed of a collection of molecules. The solution to our difficulty lies in noticing that, with our first choice of φ, although the collection's having attribute φ does not entail the existence of the ice sculpture, it does nevertheless "necessitate" it in the sense that the following counterfactual is true: if the ice sculpture did not exist, either the collection of molecules would not exist or it would not have the attribute φ. This indicates that the requirement of an entailment is too strong. We should replace the entailment by the counterfactual: if there were no unique A at location l, then either there would not be a unique B at location l or that B would not be φ, i.e.,

$$[(\exists !x)B_l x \; \& \; \varphi(\text{℩}x B_l x) . => (\exists !x)A_l x].$$

This is the converse of the counterfactual we have already required. Thus if we write "$<=>$" for the counterfactual biconditional which is the conjunction of the two counterfactual conditionals, we have:

(4.4) X is composed of Y iff $(\exists A)\ (\exists B)\ (\exists l)\ (\exists \varphi)$: $X = \text{℩}x A_l x \;\&\; Y = \text{℩}x B_l x \;\&\; \varphi(Y) \;\&\; [(\exists !x)B_l x \;\&\; \varphi(\text{℩}x B_l x). <=> (\exists !x)A_l x]$.

To avoid any misunderstanding, let me emphasize that the biconditional in this analysis is simply a symbolization of the following English sentence: "If there were no unique A at location l, then either there would be no unique B at location l or that B would not be φ; and if there were no unique B at location l or that B were not φ, there would be no unique A at location l." It is perhaps unfortunate that this analysis makes such thoroughgoing use of counterfactual conditionals. Those who abhor counterfactuals will abhor this analysis. But there is nothing to be done about this—the counterfactuals appear to be essential to the analysis.

Although I see no way to prove this, the composition relation, as analyzed by 4.4, does not seem to be symmetric. For example, the argument that demonstrated the inadequacy of 4.2 fails for 4.4: If the A at l is composed of the B at l (under the attribute φ), then letting φ^* be "is composed of the unique B at l", we certainly have $\varphi^*(\imath x A_l x)$, and we have $[(\exists !x)A_l x \;\&\; \varphi^*(\imath x A_l x). \Rightarrow (\exists !x)B_l x]$. But the converse fails. Without the additional assumption that the B at l is φ, there being a unique B at l is no guarantee of the existence of a unique A at l which is composed of that B.

As one would expect, the composition relation is transitive:

(4.5) If the A at l is composed of the B at l, and the B at l is composed of the C at l, then the A at l is composed of the C at l.

For example, if the car is composed of a certain piece of plastic, and the piece of plastic is composed of a certain collection of molecules, then the car is composed of the collection of molecules. That this is true in general can be seen by letting the attribute φ which connects A and C be "constitutes a B which constitutes an A".

4.2.3 *Examples of composition.* Given analysis 4.4, we can now verify that the examples proposed in section 4.2.1 are indeed examples of composition. It is immediate that this is the relation between a statue and the lump of clay from which it is molded. The second case is more problematic. It seems to me intuitively that the relation between a club and the set of its members is the same as the relation in the other examples of composition. But it is not clear how to apply 4.4 to this case, because it is not immediately clear what is to count as the location of a club and the set of its members. I propose that we take the location both of the club and of the set of its members to be the total volume of space occupied by its members. Given this convention, we can apply 4.4. For the club to exist is for the set of its members to be non-empty, so letting φ be "is non-empty", it follows from 4.4 that a club is composed of the set of its members. Turning to the next case, it has frequently been maintained that the relation between a body of water and the corresponding set of H_2O molecules is one of identity. There are several reasons why this cannot be. First, the criteria for re-identification for bodies of water and for sets of molecules are quite different. The identity of a set is determined by the identity of its members. Changing one molecule is sufficient to change the identity of the set of molecules, but it is certainly not sufficient to change the identity of the body of water. Second, it verges on a category mistake to say that a body of water is a set of anything. The body of water is a physical thing, but a set is an abstract entity. Connected with this is the fact that the body of water and the set of molecules have different attributes. For example, the set of molecules may have cardinality 10^6, but the body of water has no cardinality. Thus the body of water cannot be identified with the set of molecules. Instead, the relation is one of composition. That the body of water is composed of the set of H_2O molecules follows immediately from 4.4, in this case letting φ be "has as members all of the molecules at location *l*".[6] Of course, this does not preclude that the body of water and the set of H_2O molecules also stand in some stronger relation to one another, but I think it does remove the temptation to suppose they do. The one being composed of the other suffices to explain the intimate connection we feel between the two things.

Perhaps what tempts us most to suppose that the body of water is to be identified with the set of H_2O molecules is that we ordinarily *say* "Water is H_2O". But we also say "That piece of clay is a statue", where the relation is even more obviously not one of identity.[7] It must be recognized that "is" can mean more than one thing. There is an "is" of composition just as there is an "is" of identity.

[6] Perhaps we should add something about temperature and density here too.

[7] It is noteworthy in this connection that although we say "The piece of clay is a statue", we do not say "The statue is a piece of clay". The relation expressed by "is" is not symmetric.

Turning to lightning, it is certainly composed of an electrical discharge, but this does not automatically preclude the lightning's being identical to the electrical discharge,[8] and most philosophers have supposed that this is an identity. But there are several reasons why it cannot be. First, the criteria of reidentification for lightning and electrical discharges differ. As a matter of fact, the electrical discharge generally begins (comes into existence) several minutes before the lightning and builds up slowly. Furthermore, a single discharge could give rise to two consecutive bolts of lightning if it had an interval of very low discharge in the middle. Second, the lightning has attributes not possessed by the discharge. The lightning is yellow and pointed, but an electrical discharge cannot have a color or be pointed. Thus, once again, this cannot be an instance of identity. The lightning must simply be composed of the electrical discharge.

Finally we come to persons and their bodies. Philosophers have often thought that this was an identity, but we can demonstrate that it is not in the same way we demonstrated that the above are not identities. First, persons have attributes not shared by their bodies. A person may be in pain or know the president, but his body cannot be in pain or know the president. Second, the sortals "person" and "human body" have different criteria for reidentification. This is demonstrated by the fact that the body characteristically outlasts the person. Philosophers have traditionally wondered what the relation between a person and his body can be if it is not one of identity. What is it for a person to *have* a certain body? The answer is that it is for him to be composed of that body. That a person is composed of his body follows immediately from 4.4. A suitable φ might be "is a human body and encompasses all of the points of proprioceptive sensation of some person". This would seem to be an entirely adequate explanation of the intimate connection we feel between a person and his body.

4.3 *Reidentification*

Objects falling under different sortals are in general reidentified in different ways. It follows that the account of reidentification given in section 3 cannot be applied in general to all physical things. We were led to talk about sortals to resolve one difficulty for that account, but this had led us to another difficulty, this time

[8] Composition is reflexive—everything is composed of itself.

insurmountable. If the account in section 3 is correct for one sortal, it must be incorrect for most others. No single account of reidentification is adequate for cars, lumps of plastic, trees, and statues. In light of this we must reexamine our earlier account. We must ask what sort of thing is reidentified in the way described. What sortal is our account about?

More or less following Strawson,[9] let us say that *basic particulars* are those objects which can, in principle, be reidentified without first reidentifying anything other than the object under consideration. To avoid an infinite regress, there must be basic particulars. If we ask how basic particulars are to be reidentified, all of the arguments of section 3 immediately become relevant. There must be some logical reason for reidentification which proceeds exclusively in terms of attributes we can know the object to possess or not to possess without first reidentifying the object. The only such attributes are perceptual attributes, so there must be a perceptual prima facie reason for reidentifying basic particulars. This prima facie reason will clearly be just the reason described in section 3. Section 3 is an account of the reidentification of basic particulars.

But what are basic particulars? It is easier to say what they are not. They are not trees, cars, statues, typewriters, etc. The criteria of reidentification for all of these sortals are more stringent than those for basic particulars. For example, consider cars. We cannot reidentify cars perceptually. Or more precisely, there is no perceptual logical reason for reidentifying cars. This is because the attribute of being a car is not a perceptual attribute. It is quite true that we can often tell perceptually that a car we see at one time is the same car as one we saw at another time. But this is only because of certain contingent facts we have learned about cars. For example, suppose we witness a car coming toward us, passing us, and then disappearing into the distance. We can tell perceptually that we were seeing the same car all along. But this is only true because, as a matter of contingent fact, cars have characteristic appearances. We can generally tell whether something is a car by looking at it. This is relevant because a necessary condition for the car we see at the end of the period of observation to be the same as the one we began looking at is that what we were watching was a car all along. If at some point it ceased being a car, and then later became a car again, it could not be the same car. To get a

[9] Strawson [1959], p. 38.

concrete example of this, suppose we are projected 100 years in the future and presented with fantastically shaped plastic cars quite unlike anything we have ever seen before. Because of our lack of familiarity with them, we may be unable to tell whether something is a car just by looking at it. Let us suppose further that in this future time there are factories that remanufacture cars. Old worn-out cars are placed on a conveyer belt which carries them first through a microwave oven where they are melted down into pliable lumps of plastic, and then the lumps of plastic are formed into new cars by passing through invisible force fields. The cars coming out of the factory are not the same ones as those that went in. The ones going in are destroyed, and the ones coming out are entirely new. Now suppose we are able to witness this entire process from some point above the conveyer belt. We may be quite unable to tell that what goes in ceases to be a car when it passes through the oven. To us, all the cars look like formless lumps of plastic. Hence we cannot tell perceptually whether what comes out is the same car as what went in. Therefore cars are not basic particulars.

Next notice that although a different car comes out of the factory than went in, something has persisted throughout the remanufacturing process. There was an object which we could see and identify perceptually throughout the process. For example, if we just happened upon this factory without knowing that those plastic things were cars, we would observe a single object enter the factory, slowly have its shape changed, and emerge. It would never occur to us to deny that it was one and the same object throughout its sojourn in the factory. This object was (i.e., constituted) at first a car, then ceased to be a car, and then became (i.e., came to constitute) a new car. We watched one and the same object undergo all of these changes. What is this object which persists when the car does not? It is the lump of plastic. It is one and the same lump of plastic which first constituted the old car and then constituted the new car, and it is this lump of plastic that we reidentify perceptually. In general, what we might call lumps, hunks, pieces, or agglomerations of material are basic particulars.[10] For want of a better

[10] These are the only basic physical particulars, but they are not the only basic particulars. It will follow from the account of the concept of a person given in Chapter Nine that persons are also basic particulars.

term, I will call these *perceptual objects*, because they are objects that can be reidentified perceptually.[11]

The lump of material which is a basic particular is not to be identified with a *quantity* of material. If in the remanufacturing process the lump of plastic is converted into a lump of a different kind of plastic, it is still the same lump but not the same quantity of material. If even a single molecule is altered, we presumably have a different quantity of material, but not a different lump. In talking about basic particulars, the emphasis is on "lump", not "material". It is the lump itself that is reidentified perceptually, not the material. The relation between the lump and the material is simply one of composition—the lump is composed of the quantity of material.

Although we are generally more interested in cars and statues than the basic particulars of which they are composed, the basic particulars are of preeminent conceptual importance. For example, on what basis do we ordinarily reidentify a car over an interval of continual observation? We judge perceptually that there is one and the same thing there all along, and we judge that it is (i.e., constitutes) a car throughout the interval of observation. This one and the same thing we judge to be there all along is a perceptual object. It is not the car, because it would still be there if at some point the car slowly melted down into a lump of metal. In general, the reidentification of nonbasic particulars is, in ways like this, parasitic on the reidentification of perceptual objects. Perceptual objects play an essential role in our thinking about other objects.

This discussion of the reidentification of cars suggests a general logical reason for reidentifying nonperceptual objects. Where A is a sortal, it might seem that a conclusive reason for judging the A perceived at t_1 to be the same A as the one perceived at t_2 is that the perceptual object of which the first A was composed is the same as the one of which the second A is composed, and that perceptual object constituted an A throughout the interval from t_1 to t_2. This does seem to be correct for "car" and many other sortals,[12] but it is not correct in general. There are sortals

[11] This is not meant to imply that only perceptual objects can be perceived. We can perceive the car just as readily as the lump of plastic.

[12] I do not mean to imply that this is the only reason we can have for reidentifying a car. If it were, it would be impossible to disassemble a car and then regain the same car by reassembling it.

for which it fails. For example, consider "piece of sculpture". Suppose I am artistically naive and have never seen any abstract sculpture. I witness a man working a lump of clay into a weird shape. He then leaves it sitting on a pedestal. Along comes another man who reworks the shape in subtle ways. I do not realize that these are pieces of sculpture. As far as I know the two men are just idly manipulating the clay. If asked whether both men were working with the same object, I would certainly agree that they were. There is a perceptual object which persists throughout this process. In addition, there are the abstract sculptures. The first man created an abstract sculpture out of the clay. Thus the lump of clay, which is a perceptual object, came to constitute a piece of sculpture. When the second man came along and changed the shape, he thereby destroyed the first piece of sculpture and created a new one. Furthermore, his changes could have been such that at no point did the piece of clay cease to constitute a piece of sculpture. Every minute change left a piece of sculpture. But clearly the final piece was distinct from the first one. Thus, although the perceptual object continually constituted a piece of sculpture, the final piece cannot be identified with the original piece. Hence the sortal "piece of sculpture" does not have the same kind of criteria for reidentification as do sortals like "car". Different sortals function in different ways, and there is no reason why we should expect them all to be the same as regards reidentification.

Although reidentification functions differently for different sortals, all sortals whose objects are "physical" are alike in one respect—their reidentification presupposes the reidentification of perceptual objects. This is because, by definition, to reidentify any nonperceptual object we cannot proceed simply on the basis of perceptual attributes. To reidentify that object we must know that *something* has some nonperceptual attribute. That something cannot be the object in question, because to know that it has the nonperceptual attribute would presuppose a prior ability to reidentify it, and we would have an infinite regress. But obviously the something cannot be an arbitrary object; it must be an object intimately connected with the object we are reidentifying. The only way to achieve this is to appeal to something which constitutes the object in question. For example, to reidentify a car we must at least know that the object we are considering is still a car. If we could only know this by reidentifying the car, we would have an infinite regress. Instead we know it by knowing that the lump of plastic composing the car has a certain structure. We can know this without reidentifying the car. The plastic's having this structure is also a nonperceptual attribute, so to know it we must reidentify the lump of plastic. But this we can do without reidentifying anything else, because the lump of plastic is a basic particular. In general, in reidentifying one object we may appeal to the attributes of another object of which it is composed; and to do that we may have to reidentify the second object by appealing to a third object of which it is composed. And so on. But this cannot go on indefinitely. At some point we must come to something we can reidentify without having to reidentify anything else—a basic particular. Otherwise we could never get started on the process of reidentifying the first object. This is why perceptual objects are conceptually necessary. Other physical sortals cannot stand on their own feet. Their reidentification must always lead us back ultimately to the reidentification of perceptual objects. Thus although the other sortals may be more interesting, perceptual objects are indispensable to their functioning.

4.4 *Emergence and Inheritance*

We have seen a number of examples of composition, but there is an important difference between two kinds of composition. Sometimes it is a necessary truth that anything of one sort (anything falling under one sortal) must be composed of something of another sort. For example, it is a necessary truth that statues are composed of pieces of material—perceptual objects. Let us call such cases ones of *analytic composition.* Analytic composition can be defined precisely as composition in which the counterfactual biconditional of analysis 4.4 can be replaced by logical equivalence:

(4.6) X is analytically composed of Y iff $(\exists A)\ (\exists B)\ (\exists l)\ (\exists \varphi)$: $X = \imath x A_l x\ \&\ Y = \imath x B_l x\ \&\ \varphi(Y)\ \&\ [(\exists !x) B_l x\ \&\ \varphi(\imath x B_l x) . \longleftrightarrow (\exists !x) A_l x]$.

It should be noticed that to say X is analytically composed of Y is not to say that it is a necessary truth that if X exists then it is composed of Y. For example, our plastic car is analytically composed of a piece of plastic, but it might have been composed of something else. The composition is analytic because it is a necessary truth that cars are composed of perceptual objects, and in this case the perceptual object at the location in question is a piece of plastic.[13] To say that *X* is analytically composed of *Y* is to say that *X* and *Y* fall under *some* sortals (not necessarily the ones involved in the terms "*X*" and "*Y*" if these are definite descriptions) such that it is a necessary truth that anything falling under the first sortal must be composed of something falling under the second.

Composition which is not analytic I will call *contingent composition*. Water is only contingently composed of H_2O and lightning is only contingently composed of an electrical discharge. Furthermore, I will argue in Chapter Nine that persons are contingently composed of their bodies. Many philosophers would maintain that this is an instance of analytic composition. Which kind of composition it is is the question whether it is a necessary truth that persons have bodies. I shall argue that ghosts and other immaterial beings are logically possible, and hence that the composition in question is contingent.

In analytic composition we encounter an interesting phenomenon which might be called *emergence*. The existence of the analytically composed object cannot be known noninductively except by knowing something about the object which constitutes it. What it means for the composed object to exist is for the constituting object to have a certain attribute. The existence, the location, and the identity of the composed object are logically parasitic on the existence, location, and identity of the constituting object. In this sense the composed object is a "logical construction" out of the constituting object. It "emerges out of" the constituting object through the constituting object's coming to acquire certain attributes. Furthermore, the emergent object is conceptually superfluous. We could say everything we want to say about the world by talking merely about the constituting object. It is convenient to be able to talk about the emergent object, but not essential.

A second interesting phenomenon connected with analytic composition might be called *inheritance*. The emergent object acquires certain attributes simply from the definition of what it is for it to exist. Among these will be the time of its creation and the time of its destruction, and attributes connected with these (e.g., "con-

[13] Although "perceptual object" and "piece of plastic" are distinct sortals, they are related as genus to species and hence can both apply to a single object.

ceived by Michelangelo", "destroyed by a maniac"). But if these were the only attributes possessed by the emergent object, it would be a rather naked object. Instead we fill out its list of attributes by simply transferring most of them from the constituting object. For example, the car weighs what the lump of plastic weighs, has the color the lump of plastic has, has the shape of the plastic, the location of the plastic, etc. The emergent object "inherits" any attributes it can consistently be taken to have. The restriction of consistency rules out the emergent object's inheriting the date of creation or destruction of the constituting object, its sortal, the history of the constituting object prior to the creation of the emergent object, and a few other things. But in general the emergent object is taken to have all the attributes of the constituting object which it can have.

Somewhat surprisingly, inheritance also occurs in contingent composition. In contingent composition the objects are independently identifiable, and so already have full ranges of attributes. But if they are of quite different sorts, some attributes possessed by the constituting object may be undefined for the composed object. The composed object then inherits them (providing it can do so consistently). For example, consider lightning and the corresponding electrical discharge. The lightning inherits the voltage of the discharge. If the voltage of the discharge is 10,000 megavolts, we also say that the voltage of the lightning is 10,000 megavolts. Independently of the composition, the lightning has the attribute of having a certain voltage measurable across its extremities. This is something we could ascertain without knowing that the lightning is composed of the electrical discharge. But this is to attribute the voltage to a discharge across the space occupied by the lightning and is not to attribute the voltage to the lightning itself. It is only after discovering that the lightning is composed of the electrical discharge that we can actually attribute the voltage to the lightning.

Perhaps in most cases of contingent composition, little if any inheritance takes place because the composed object and the constituted object are sufficiently alike that the same attributes are already defined for both and hence no new attributes can be consistently inherited. The requirement of consistency may also rule out the inheritance of some attributes not previously defined for the composed object. For example, a gas is composed of a collection of molecules. It inherits the energy of that collection of molecules, which is something not previously defined for the gas. But it does not inherit the cardinality of the collection of molecules. This is because the gas is also composed of other sets. For example, every object consists of the set whose only member is itself—for the object to exist is for the collection of all things identical to it to exist and be non-empty. Thus if the gas could inherit the cardinality of a set composing it, it would inherit different cardinalities from different sets and we would have an inconsistency.

Perhaps the most interesting case of inheritance concerns persons. Philosophers have traditionally been puzzled about how persons can have physical attributes like weight or height if they are not identical with their bodies. The answer is now obvious. Although a person is not identical with his body, he is composed of his body. Consequently he can inherit the physical attributes of his body. Thus a person weighs 200 pounds and is six feet tall because his body has these attributes. To say that he has these attributes is not just a shorthand way of saying that his body has them—he really has them. But he only has them *because* his body has them.

4.5 *Conclusions*

In discussing the reidentification of physical things we must distinguish between different physical sortals. No one account of reidentification is adequate for all sortal concepts. A general account of reidentification would have to proceed piecemeal by examining different sortals one at a time and giving a separate account of each. Such a task is far beyond the scope of this book. Instead I have been content to examine that physical sortal which is logically simplest and epistemologically most basic—the concept of a perceptual object. This is the most important of all physical sortals because the knowledge of any physical thing reduces ultimately to knowledge of perceptual objects. The account of reidentification in section 3 is an account of the reidentification of perceptual objects.

Chapter Seven

Memory and Historical Knowledge

1. Introduction

I HAD eggs for breakfast this morning. How do I know this? I remember that I did. But why is that a reason for believing that I did? Memory is not infallible. People are often mistaken in what they think they remember. What reason is there for thinking that memory is *ever* reliable? Of course, there are other ways to acquire knowledge about the past. We can examine old newspapers or documents, or talk to other people. But how do we know that what they report actually happened? As Bertrand Russell asked,[1] how do we even know that there was a past? How do we know that the world did not come into existence five minutes ago, complete with all our purported memories and records of a nonexistent past? We cannot resurrect the past bodily,[2] so how can we get at it to find out what actually occurred? This is the philosophical problem of historical knowledge.

As I shall use the term, "historical knowledge" refers to any knowledge of the past, either recent or distant. Knowledge that I had eggs for breakfast this morning is as much historical knowledge as is knowledge that Caesar crossed the Rubicon. Of course, we do have historical knowledge. That much cannot reasonably be doubted. But the puzzling question is, how is that knowledge possible? The past is past, and as such it seems to be beyond our reach.

A great deal of our historical knowledge is based upon memory. Most of the mundane and rather uninteresting historical facts that we know are things that we remember. I remember that I had eggs for breakfast this morning, that it began raining about five minutes

[1] Russell [1921], p. 159.

[2] The phrase is from Russell [1921].

ago, and that I read a certain journal article last night. More interesting and more distant facts I know on the basis of the reports of other people, history books, old newspapers and documents, archaeological evidence, etc.

Among the ways in which one can have knowledge of the past, philosophers have generally attached particular importance to memory. Most philosophers have felt that the basic source of historical knowledge is memory, and that other sources can only be justified inductively on the basis of memory. It is by no means true that this opinion has been universal,[3] but it has been pretty general. Let us examine it carefully.

There are many ways other than memory in which I can acquire historical knowledge. These include being told something about the past by another person, reading about a past event in a history book, finding events reported in old newspapers, interpreting archaeological remains, etc. But none of these can be more than contingent reasons for judgments about the past. In order to be justified in accepting another person's report, I must have a prior reason for thinking that what he says is probably true. We have a general inductive reason for thinking that anything we are told by another person will probably be true, and so do not need special evidence regarding each person; but we do, nevertheless, rely upon an inductive generalization in accepting another person's report. Analogously, my reason for accepting what I find in a history book is that I have been told by people I consider reliable that the book is generally correct, and this again involves my knowing inductively that these people are reliable. Similarly, my reason for believing a report in an old newspaper is that I know inductively that newspaper reports are generally correct. Were I competent to interpret archaeological remains, I could only do so in terms of some general laws about both people and the natural sciences. My acceptance of those laws must either be justified inductively or be on the authority of someone else whom I am justified in taking to be reliable. In every case, in acquiring knowledge of the past on some basis other than memory, I must appeal to inductive generalizations.

A very simple argument suffices to show that such inductive reasoning is not possible unless we have an independent reason to trust our memory of the past. In order to be justified in accepting

[3] Ayer [1956] denies this. He seems to hold a version of the nebula theory regarding historical knowledge.

some general proposition, I must have observed several particular instances that confirm the generalization. Consider what those instances are like. For example, suppose we have not yet justified any contingent sources of historical knowledge, and then consider how we would justify accepting the reports of other people about the past. In order to do this, we must observe that, insofar as we can check their reports, they are generally correct. This checking must provide us with knowledge that *particular* reports about the past were true. Such checking cannot without circularity involve other contingent sources of historical knowledge. Thus the checking must be done solely in terms of our own experience. But how is that possible? What must be checked is that what another person reports about the past was true. But to know that is to have historical knowledge. This indicates that the particular instances we call upon to justify the generalizations regarding the reliability of the various contingent sources of knowledge about the past are themselves statements partly about the past. So it follows that inductive knowledge of the past is possible only if noninductive knowledge of the past is possible. The only plausible source of noninductive knowledge of the past is memory, so memory must provide logical reasons for judgments about the past.

2. Theories of Historical Knowledge

Given that historical knowledge is based upon memory, we must ask just how it is so based. We can propound theories of historical knowledge that are completely analogous to the theories of perceptual knowledge. There are four possible kinds of theories of historical knowledge: naive realism, reductionism, scientific realism, and descriptivism. We can deal with them rather briefly by appealing to our discussion of the corresponding theories of perceptual knowledge.

2.1 *Naive Realism*

Naive realism maintains that some statements about the past are epistemologically basic, and hence either incorrigible or prima facie justified. Clearly, there are no incorrigible statements about the past. We can always be wrong. If we turn to prima facie justified statements, the only plausible candidates are certain memory statements. It is conceivable that some statements of the form "I remember that *P*" are prima facie justified. The statement "I remember that *P*" entails that *P*, so it is at least indirectly a statement about the past.

At this point it should be recognized that philosophers have often used the expression "I remember that *P*" in such a way that it does not entail that what is remembered is true. Their intention has been to use "remember" to refer merely to the phenomenological aspect of remembering. However, their detractors have pointed out that this is not the way "remember" is ordinarily used by the nonphilosopher. To remember-that-*P* is one way of knowing-that-*P*, and as such it entails the truth of *P*. This seems to be true, but not particularly important. What is important is that there are two different things philosophers have wanted to use "remember" to mean. On the one hand they have wanted to use "remember" to refer to a certain kind of knowledge, and on the other hand they have wanted to use it to refer to the phenomenological state which is involved in that kind of knowledge. A number of recent philosophers have questioned whether there is any such phenomenological state, and that is a matter that we will have to investigate. But in the meantime, it is important to have suitable ways of talking about both of these things. However, whether the language we adopt for this purpose is in complete accordance with ordinary usage is of no importance at all. Consequently, I propose to use "recollection" to refer to the phenomenological state (if there is such a state), and "remember" to refer to the kind of knowledge. Thus "*S* remembers that *P*" entails both that-*P* and that *S* recalls that *P*. But "*S* recalls that *P*" is merely a remark about *S* and does not entail that *P*.

Naive realism regarding historical knowledge can be formulated precisely as the claim that some statements of the form "I remember that *P*" are prima facie justified. It will be argued below that the statement "*S* remembers that *P*" can be analyzed as "*S* knows-that-*P* on the basis of recalling that *P*". Just as for perceptual knowledge, the thesis that such a statement is prima facie justified is equivalent to the thesis that "*S* recalls that *P*" is a prima facie reason for *S* to believe that *P*.[4] Thus once again, naive realism

[4] This assumes that "*S* recalls that *P*" is either incorrigible or prima facie justified. This can be established by a slight variation on the argument of Chapter Four. More will be said about this in Chapter Nine.

is equivalent to descriptivism. Consequently, we can leave the further discussion of naive realism until we come to descriptivism.

2.2 *Reductionism*

Reductionism is analogous to phenomenalism, and claims that statements about the past are entailed by statements about the present. These statements about the present will presumably be statements about our present evidence for our beliefs about the past. These will include our recollections, and perhaps some other beliefs.

It is manifest that statements about present records and artifacts cannot entail statements about the past. It is only a contingent fact that they bear the relationship they do to the past. The only present evidence which can conceivably bear a *logical* relation to the past is recollection. Let us ask then whether any statements about our present recollections can entail statements about the past. That they cannot is indicated by the same sort of considerations that demonstrated the falsity of phenomenalism. Recall once more the poor soul whom we have wired into a computer. Given sufficient knowledge of brain physiology, we can manipulate his recollections in any way we wish, but changing them will have no effect on what is actually true of the past. Consequently, statements about his present recollections cannot entail statements about the past. I quite agree with the reductionist that there must be a logical connection of some sort between recollection and the past, but this connection cannot be an entailment.

2.3 *Scientific Realism*

The scientific realist claims that our beliefs about the past can be justified inductively. Clearly this cannot be a matter of enumerative induction. That would require us to have observed in many cases that what we recall is true, which is only possible if we can already have knowledge of the past on some other basis. Although enumerative induction will be of little help here, it might be supposed that something like the hypothetico-deductive method will suffice. The use of the hypothetico-deductive method would amount to concluding that the best way to explain what we know about the present is to suppose that there was a past of a certain sort. But a little reflection shows that this is preposterous. What we can know about the present without presupposing some knowledge of the past is minuscule. We can know the way we are presently appeared to, and on this basis make judgments about the perceptual attributes of objects in our immediate vicinity. We can also know what we are presently recalling, if anything. In fact, at any given time we are *able* to recall very many things, but we are not actually doing so, and to know that we are able to recall these things we must reason inductively, which in turn requires historical knowledge. Thus what we are able to recall cannot be taken as data to be explained—only what we are actually recalling. This is not nearly enough to allow us to frame any comprehensive theories about the existence of a past. We simply do not have at our disposal enough present data to get scientific realism off the ground.

2.4 *Descriptivism*

Just as in the case of perception, we must conclude that there is a connection between recollection and the past, but that it is a matter neither of induction nor of entailment. This is descriptivism. According to descriptivism, our reasons for historical judgments are constitutive of our concept of the past, that concept being ostensive.[5] In spelling out those reasons, we are analyzing our concept of the past. It seems rather likely that those reasons can be characterized by saying that recollection provides prima facie reasons for judgments about the past. But before we can establish this we will have to examine recollection itself more closely.

We seem to have a strong argument for descriptivism, and it does seem almost obvious that the concept of the past is an ostensive concept. There seems to be no way to define this concept in terms of other more basic concepts, and hence it must be ostensive. However, this has been challenged in an interesting way by Ayer. Ayer maintains that "the relation of temporal precedence is 'given' to us in experience. As a matter of empirical fact, one can see or hear *A*-following-*B*, in the same immediate fashion as one can see *A*-is to the left of-*B*."[6] It does seem beyond dispute that we

[5] This cannot be taken quite literally. The concept of the past is not the concept of a *kind*, so it cannot, strictly speaking, be an ostensive concept. Rather, the judgments whose justification conditions we seek are those of the form "It was true that *P*", so the ostensive concept is that of being something true of the past.

[6] Ayer [1956], p. 152.

can perceive temporal precedence over a sufficiently short interval. Let us call this short-interval precedence "temporal succession". The argument is then that as we can perceive temporal succession, it can be explained ostensively without appeal to the past. Then temporal precedence can be defined as the ancestral of the relation of temporal succession, i.e., *A* precedes *B* iff *A* succeeds *B*, or there is an event *x* such that *A* succeeds *x* which succeeds *B*, or there are *x* and *y* such that *A* succeeds *x* which succeeds *y* which succeeds *B*, or . . . . Then the event *A* is past iff *A* precedes the present.

At first, this argument is persuasive. But we must balk at the very first step. Ayer maintains that the concept of temporal succession can be explained ostensively—we can simply perceive temporal succession. But this only gives content to the concept if it is intended to mean that the concept of temporal succession is a perceptual concept—that there is a way of being appeared to which is a criterion for judging that *A* succeeds *B*. There is such a way of being appeared to *provided A* and *B* are within (this) specious present. But there is clearly no such way of being appeared to when *A* and *B* are both some distance in the past. The perceptual concept is simply "*A now* succeeding *B*", whereas what we need to define the concept of the past is the *timeless* relation of *A* succeeding *B*. This must be defined in terms of the tensed relation together with the concept of the past, i.e., as " '*A* is now succeeding *B*' *was* true". However, if we thus explain the concept of temporal succession in terms of the concept of the past, we cannot then use the concept of temporal succession to give a noncircular definition of the concept of the past. Thus Ayer is wrong in thinking we can define the concept of the past in this way. We must be content with the concept of the past being an ostensive concept whose meaning must be given by its justification conditions. To state those justification conditions is the task undertaken by descriptivism.

3. Two Kinds of Memory

We have a "theoretical" argument to the effect that memory must provide us with prima facie reasons for historical judgments. It was argued that, otherwise, historical knowledge would be impossible. But before we can be confident of this conclusion, we must actually produce those reasons, and make it clear that they are reasons.

In order to do this, we must become clearer about both memory and recollection. We remember many different kinds of things—our mother's face, how to ride a bicycle, what we had for breakfast, the decimal expansion of *pi*, that Caesar crossed the Rubicon, etc. It is difficult to say what all of these instances of remembering have in common, but fortunately that will not prove necessary for the task at hand, which is that of explaining historical knowledge. We need only concern ourselves with two kinds of memory.

3.1 *Propositional Memory*

When philosophers talk about memory as a source of historical knowledge, they often have in mind what may be called *propositional memory*. To have propositional memory is to remember-that-*P*, for some proposition *P*. The descriptivist who fixes upon propositional memory as our fundamental source of historical knowledge is then committed to saying that recalling-that-*P* is a prima facie reason for one to think it true that *P*. There are two problems regarding this position.

First, in what does recalling-that-*P* consist? By definition, this is the phenomenological state contained in remembering that *P*. But it is not clear that there is any phenomenological state so contained other than simply believing-that-*P*. If this is correct, then recalling-that-*P* amounts simply to believing-that-*P*, in which case this version of descriptivism comes down to saying that believing-that-*P* is a prima facie reason for one to believe that *P*. This is at least peculiar.

The second and more serious difficulty for this version of descriptivism concerns the propositions remembered. Propositional memory is not predominantly about the past. To be sure, I can remember that I had eggs for breakfast this morning, but I can also remember facts about the present (e.g., that my wife is now shopping), facts about the future (e.g., that some friends will be coming over this evening), and timeless facts (e.g., that two is the square root of four). Philosophers have sometimes mistakenly supposed that talk about remembering other than historical facts must be elliptical for talk about remembering acquiring whatever grounds one has for believing those facts. But that is clearly wrong. I can remember that *pi* is approximately equal to 3.14159 without having the slightest idea how I came to know that. I have simply forgotten what my original grounds for that belief were. Nevertheless, I do remember that that is the value of *pi*.

The reason this constitutes a difficulty for descriptivism is that descriptivism must justify the existence of its prima facie reasons by saying they are constitutive of our concept of the past. But this will only work insofar as what we remember is about the past. Descriptivism can give no such rationale for saying that, where *P* is a statement not about the past, my recalling-that-*P* is a prima facie reason for me to believe that *P*.

Perhaps the way to save descriptivism is by narrowing its scope and saying that my recalling-that-*P* is a prima facie reason for me to believe-that-*P* only when *P* is a statement about the past. But it seems that even this cannot be true. My warrant for accepting my recollection of many historical facts is precisely the same as my warrant for accepting my recollection of general truths of mathematics and physics. I know that George III was king of England during the American Revolution in precisely the same way I know that "$s = \frac{1}{2} at^2$" is the correct formula for computing the distance covered by an accelerating body. In both cases, I originally acquired this knowledge from textbooks (I presume; I cannot now remember doing so), and now I simply recall it. Surely my warrant for the one belief is the same as my warrant for the other. Thus not all propositional memories, even about the past, constitute logical reasons for believing the propositions recalled.

It appears that propositional memory does not have the characteristics necessary for it to be our basic source of historical knowledge. I shall argue below that propositional memory can be successfully defended against the above objections. But to make this more plausible, it is first necessary to dispose of another important contender for the role of being our basic source of historical knowledge.

3.2 *Personal Memory*

There is a kind of memory which is more intimately connected with the past than propositional memory is. I can often recall *events* from my own past. For example, I can recall having eggs for breakfast, or more remotely, I can recall living in a certain apartment house as a child. It is quite plausible to suppose that this sort of recollection does provide me with logical reasons for judgments about the past. My connection with the events recalled in this way is much more intimate than my connection with the historical facts generally remembered in propositional memory.

Let us call this form of memory *personal memory*. Personal memory is memory of features of my own past. Personal memory is not always memory of what would be regarded as an event. I have personal memory of the apartment house in which I lived as a child. I can recall cracks in the stucco, the wooden stairs in back, the shape of the yard and placement of some of the trees, etc. None of this is memory of events. I can also recall running into one of those trees while riding my bicycle, and that is personal memory of an event. Personal memory is appropriately described as memory-*of* rather than memory-*that*. I have personal memory of the cracks, the stairs, and running into the tree. We can express personal memories using gerund clauses. I recall my having eggs for breakfast, my running into a tree, the stucco walls of the apartment in which I lived having cracks, that apartment having wooden stairs, etc. Any personal memory can be expressed in this form, and so expressed we will understand it as personal memory rather than propositional memory. These gerund clauses can be said to describe "states of affairs". We can then say that personal memory is always memory of a state of affairs. Personal memory always has the form "I remember its being the case that *P*".

Notice that not all memory of features of my own past is personal memory. Having been told by my parents that at age three I wandered off and got lost, I now remember that I did, but I do not remember doing so. My memory of this event is simply propositional memory, not personal memory.

The descriptivist can surmount his earlier difficulties by maintaining that it is personal recollection, rather than propositional recollection, which provides prima facie reasons for judgments about the past. On this view, my recalling its being the case that *P* would be a prima facie reason for me to think it was the case that *P*. Such judgments are inherently about the past, and so we could regard the existence of such a prima facie reason as being partially constitutive of our concept of the past.

But now the descriptivist is beset with new difficulties. The first difficulty is suggested by cases of what appear to be personal memories not containing any knowledge about what is remembered. Benjamin [1956] gives the example of a painter who, upon being asked to paint an imaginary scene, proceeds to paint an accurate picture of a scene his parents recognize as something he witnessed in childhood. He thinks he is imagining the scene, but given the accuracy of his portrayal it seems that he is really remembering it. Similarly, Malcolm gives the example of a child who has recurring nightmares of masked figures grappling with him and carrying him away.[7] It turns out that when he was very young he was kidnapped by masked men, but he no longer remembers that it happened. This case is less clear, but at least it is not obviously wrong to say that when he has the nightmares he is remembering the kidnapping. Most people feel some reluctance to describe the cases of Benjamin and Malcolm as cases of remembering, although in the end I think we should. This reluctance stems from the fact that there is no propositional memory involved. If we exclude these as genuine cases of personal memory, then we are simply building into the concept of personal memory the requirement that it contain propositional memory. But either way, it is clear that it is only insofar as a personal memory is accompanied by or contains as part of it some propositional memory that it can give one knowledge of the past. This suggests that, although propositional memory in general does not give us logical access to the past, insofar as a propositional recollection is part of a personal memory, it does give us logical reasons for judgments about the past. The presence of the rest of the personal memory would somehow validate the propositional memory.

What is there about a personal memory that might play this validating role? It must be something other than the propositional memory itself, so what must there be, over and above the propositional memory, for a person to have a personal memory? A natural suggestion is that personal memory involves images—in personal memory I resurrect an image of a past event and read off features of that image. Then the suggestion would be that it is the presence of the image which validates the accompanying propositional memory. But there are extensive difficulties here. First, not just any image will do—it must be a *memory* image. For example, when I recall that Caesar crossed the Rubicon, this is accompanied by an image of Roman cavalry fording a river; but this image is

[7] Malcolm [1963], pp. 213-214. Malcolm arrives at what seems to me to be the wrong conclusion regarding this example, viz., that the child remembers *that* the kidnapping occurred.

obviously imaginary. Such an imaginary image cannot turn propositional memory into personal memory, and hence cannot play the desired validating role. It might be supposed that this creates no real problem, because there is a clear phenomenological difference between imaginary images and memory images—we can always tell whether an image is a memory image, and hence can always tell whether it validates corresponding propositional memories. Unfortunately, this is false. It is not uncommon to have an image associated with a personal recollection but to be uncertain whether that image is the product of memory or imagination. For example, I remember that I met my great-grandmother once when I was very young. Associated with this memory is an image of a very old lady sitting on a screened-in porch. I do not know, and probably will never know, whether that is really a memory image or only an image supplied by my imagination. This creates a real problem, because if a memory image is to supply us with knowledge of the past, we must recognize it as a memory image. This involves, at least, remembering that that is an image of the way things were. This is really no different from being presented with a picture of a long-forgotten event and remembering that that is the way the event looked. This remembering is propositional memory. Thus, rather than the image validating the propositional memory, it is propositional memory which must validate our acceptance of the image. Consequently, images cannot play the necessary validating role.

A further difficulty for the role of images in personal memory is that there are people who claim they never have memory images.[8] We might question whether they are right about themselves, but it seems undeniable that there *could* be such people. There would be no logical absurdity in supposing there are people whose memories are devoid of images. We can suppose that their memories would be entirely propositional. For them, remembering

[8] This sounds very suspicious. If they do not have them, how do they know what it is that they do not have? I would be very skeptical about this claim were it not for the fact that a friend who always claimed that he did not have memory images came up to me one day and announced that he had suddenly begun having them. He had always thought that I was misdescribing my own phenomenological state until he suddenly found himself in the same sort of state. There are some mysterious facts to be investigated here, but I am content to agree that some people do not have memory images, while others do.

would consist simply of retaining past knowledge. Are we to say that such people have no personal memory? If so, they constitute a counterexample to the descriptivist's claim that knowledge of the past must arise ultimately out of personal memory, because we would feel no temptation to deny that they have historical knowledge as long as their propositional memory concerning past events functions as well as ours.

However, I do not think we would say that such people have no personal memory. For them, to have personal memory of a state of affairs would consist merely in having very detailed propositional memory of the state of affairs.[9] That this is right can be seen by noting that, even for those of us with rich visual imagery, a personal memory *may* consist merely of such propositional memories. For example, when I remember developing a film in my darkroom, my memory is accompanied by a visual image of what went on, but that image is imaginary because I was working in total darkness. My remembering developing the film consists simply of my remembering in considerable detail what happened, and that is propositional memory.

This leads to grave difficulties. If personal memory can consist merely of detailed propositional memory, and personal memory gives us logical access to the past, then propositional memory must give us logical access to the past. Thus the present version of descriptivism reduces to the previous version according to which propositional recollection constitutes a prima facie reason for making judgments about the past. We have not, after all, escaped the difficulties that arose for that position.

It seems that this version of descriptivism is not a viable alternative to the original version. Insofar as personal memory can consist of merely detailed propositional memories, such memory only gives logical access to the past if propositional memories do so; insofar as personal memory consists of or contains images, (1) we could do without it, and (2) we require the prior validity of propositional memory to justify us in accepting something as a personal memory.

We have seen that if historical knowledge is to be possible, then

[9] It must also be required that this propositional memory in some sense stems from the person's having originally witnessed the state of affairs. It is difficult to make this requirement precise, but it will turn out that we do not have to for the purposes of this investigation.

memory must provide us with logical access to the past, and we have seen that if any memory can do that, propositional memory must do it. We must go back and reexamine the arguments which led us to reject the view that propositional recollection in general provides logical reasons for believing the propositions recalled. If it does not, we are forced to skepticism regarding historical knowledge, which is certainly preposterous.

3.3 *Reconsideration of Propositional Memory*

The most serious difficulty for the position that recalling-that-*P* is always a prima facie reason for believing-that-*P* was that *P* need not be a proposition about the past, and hence we cannot justify the existence of such a prima facie reason by saying that it is partially constitutive of our concept of the past. I think that there is an easy way around this difficulty. I propose instead that the recollection is a prima facie reason for thinking that it *was* true that *P*. For example, not only is my recalling that I had eggs for breakfast a reason for thinking I had eggs for breakfast; my recalling that my wife is now shopping is a reason for thinking that it was true that my wife would now be shopping; my recalling that some friends will be coming over this evening is a reason for thinking it was true that some friends will be coming over this evening; and my recalling that two is the square root of four is a reason for thinking it was true that two is the square root of four. From these propositions about the past, I can then logically infer conclusions about the present and future. Its having been the case that some friends will be coming over this evening entails that that is still the case; its having been true that two is the square root of four entails that two is still the square root of four; etc. On this view, propositional recollection only constitutes logical reasons for judgments about the past (and hence this can be partially constitutive of our concept of the past), but some of those statements about the past entail statements about the present and future. Whether such an entailment holds has to do with the content of the statement itself and has nothing particular to do with memory. Thus the descriptivist can avoid the first of the two difficulties that originally seemed devastating.

The second difficulty concerned the identity of the phenomenological state of recollection. Is recalling-that-*P* any different from simply believing-that-*P*? That there is a difference between recalling-that-*P* and believing-that-*P* can be seen by considering some examples. The first example shows that it is possible to recall-that-*P* without believing-that-*P*. Consider a physicist who has spent years working on a certain project. He has proposed an intricate theory to explain some previously puzzling observations, and both he and the scientific community at large have performed a truly vast number of diverse experiments all of which confirm the theory. The result is that the theory has become a well-entrenched part of physics. However, when the physicist was a young research assistant, he performed a single, at the time inconsequential, experiment whose results contradict his later theory. Now, on the eve of receiving a Nobel Prize, the physicist thinks back over his long career, and suddenly he recalls that early experiment. Because that experiment, as he recalls it, conflicts with such a huge body of subsequent evidence, he might reasonably and with complete justification mistrust his memory and be absolutely convinced that his recollection is in error. This illustrates that one can recall-that-*P* without believing-that-*P*, and hence the two states are distinct.

For another example, consider what is involved in remembering the value of *pi*. I recall that *pi* is approximately 3.141592653589-793. Is my recalling this any different from my simply believing it? It is different. First, we could propound a case similar to the above in which I have the recollection, but mistrust my ability to remember such a long number and think it quite unlikely that I have got it right. Or even if I do accept my recollection, the recollection adds something to the belief. My having the recollection tags the source of the belief as being memory rather than present calculation or the result of reading the value off of a table presently before me or simply pulling the number out of the air at random. For example, suppose I have the bad habit, when asked for the value of various mathematical and physical constants, of confidently spieling off numbers at random without at all trying to remember their correct values, and furthermore, I believe each time that I have got them right. I am invariably wrong, but I remain unrepentant. Then some unsuspecting soul asks me the value of *pi* and I reply at random "3.141592653589793".[10] Phenomenologically, picking a number out of the air like this and believing

[10] The explanation for my getting it right is almost surely that I do remember the value, but this is not to say that I remember *that* that is the value.

that it is the right number "feels" very different from recalling that that is the desired number. Thus once again, recollection is to be distinguished from belief.

A further example to illustrate the phenomenological state of recollection is provided by considering a case in which a person remembers-that-*P* as a result of now being told-that-*P*. He had forgotten-that-*P*, but now as a result of being reminded he remembers again. There is a clear phenomenological difference here between remembering and simply accepting what you are told. For example, upon meeting someone, you may be told that you met him once before at a convention in Philadelphia. You may simply take your informant's word for this and on this basis know that you met the man in Philadelphia. But it may also happen that your memory is jogged by your being told you met the man in Philadelphia, and you now remember that you did. The difference between these two cases is a purely phenomenological one. In the latter case, you are led to recall that you met the man in Philadelphia, and you then believe this on the basis of your recollection. This difference would be inexplicable if there were no such phenomenological state as recollection.

It must be concluded that propositional recollection is a distinct phenomenological state.[11] But it remains to be shown that recollection provides us with prima facie reasons for historical judgments. What is it that justifies a memory claim? The natural response is that it must be some feature of my present state which justifies me in thinking I remember, and recollection is the only possible candidate for such a feature. This would seem uncontroversial were it not that a number of recent philosophers have maintained that what justifies a memory claim is whatever justified me originally in believing what I now remember. The argument is that in remembering-that-*P*, what I do is *retain* my original knowledge-that-*P*.[12] What now justifies me in believing-that-*P* must be whatever justified me in believing it earlier. Hence my

[11] This does not mean that there is some *feature* of recollection which sets it apart from other phenomenological states. It is just different. You cannot say in what the difference consists any more than you can say what the difference is between something's looking red to you and its looking blue to you. The difference is manifest but indescribable.

[12] See Squires [1969].

reason is not my recollection; it is whatever my original reason was.[13]

Although this position is initially plausible, it cannot be right. It would mean that the justification conditions for judgments about the past are the same as the justification conditions for judgments about the present, and this would rob our concept of the past of all content. To see why it fails, let us turn to concrete examples. I had eggs for breakfast this morning. At the time, I knew I was having eggs because I was appeared to in certain ways. I still remember how I was appeared to, and so can reasonably say that my reason for now believing I had eggs for breakfast is that I was appeared to in certain ways (but this is now a statement about the past and hence is not quite the same as my original reason).[14] But what is my present reason for thinking I was appeared to in those ways? At the time it happened, I did not need a reason for thinking I was appeared to in those ways, because that judgment was incorrigible. But the past-tense judgment that I *was* appeared to in those ways is certainly not incorrigible. I must have some reason for believing that, and the only reasonable candidate is my recollection that I was appeared to in those ways. So at least in this sort of case my recollection must constitute a logical reason.

Next suppose I no longer remember how I was appeared to when I had eggs for breakfast. This is certainly the more common case. Characteristically, I remember for a while how I was appeared to, but then that memory fades and I only remember *that* I had eggs for breakfast. If I am convinced that I do remember that I had eggs for breakfast, and I have no good reason for doubting my memory, then certainly I am justified in my claim. But my being so justified is not at all influenced by whether my original judgment that I was having eggs was justified. Whether I am presently justified in thinking I had eggs for breakfast is a function simply of my present state. If my wife blindfolded me this morning and made me guess what I was eating on the basis of taste, which is something that most people are surprisingly bad at, I might have erroneously and without sufficient justification concluded

[13] This is defended in Malcolm [1963], pp. 229-230.

[14] It seems to be true that whenever *P* is a logical reason for *S* to believe *Q*, "It was true that *P*" is a logical reason for *S* to believe "It was true that *Q*".

that I was eating eggs. I have now forgotten about being blindfolded (I am only half-conscious in the morning anyway), and I simply recall (erroneously) that I had eggs. As long as I do not remember the circumstances of my original judgment, they cannot make my present judgment that I had eggs for breakfast any the less justified than if I had been more careful in my original judgment. All that I have to go on in making my judgment is what I presently recall. If I recall that I had eggs, and I have no present reason for doubting my recollection, then I have done the best I can and cannot be epistemically reprehensible for believing that I had eggs, i.e., my belief is justified. Thus what justifies my present judgment is not what justified or failed to justify my previous judgment. It is my recollection that justifies my present judgment.

But, it may be objected, surely the warrant for my originally believing something which I now recall is relevant to whether I should accept my present recollection. In remembering-that-*P*, what I do is recall my previous belief-that-*P*. My present recollection is caused by my earlier belief. But it makes no difference to the causal connection, and hence to the existence of the recollection, whether my earlier belief was true or even justified. It is merely the existence of that earlier belief that was required for me to have my recollection. If I am in the habit of rashly jumping to conclusions and holding myriad unjustified beliefs, then I will recall as true many propositions which I never had any good reason for believing. How then can my present recollection be a good reason for believing those propositions when it stems simply from an earlier unjustified belief?

This objection must be wrong—if it were correct it would make it impossible for us to have the knowledge of the past that we do have. We have seen that our knowledge of the past must arise ultimately out of memory, and that the form of memory involved must be propositional memory. Thus propositional recollection has to provide us with logical reasons for historical judgments. Still, it cannot be denied that the warrant for our originally believing something which we now recall is somehow relevant to whether we should accept our present recollection. But there are different ways in which it can be relevant. Its relevance need not consist of its being something we must check before we accept a memory—indeed, it cannot consist of that, on pain of skepticism regarding historical knowledge, because to check it requires historical knowledge, and hence involves us in an infinite regress. We must distinguish here between what is required for me to be *justified* in thinking I remember something, and what is required for me to be *right*. My originally having been justified in believing-that-*P* cannot be a necessary condition for my now being justified in thinking I remember-that-*P*, but it is most certainly a necessary condition for the truth of my claim to remember. Consider the egg case again. Insofar as remembering requires previous knowledge, I am certainly *mistaken* in claiming to remember that I had eggs for breakfast, but nevertheless I am justified in that claim.

This is not to say that my original warrant is totally irrelevant to the justification of my present claim to remember. Although I need not first ascertain that I originally had a good reason for believing-that-*P* before I can justifiably claim to remember-that-*P*, nevertheless, if I discover somehow that I did not have a good reason, this entails that I do not remember, and hence defeats the justification of my claim to remember. Thus my original warrant is relevant, but only negatively, as a defeater.[15] If I recall-that-*P*, I have a prima facie reason for believing-that-*P*, but if I also know that my original belief-that-*P*, from which my present recollection stems, was unjustified, this defeats my prima facie reason. This is the only way in which my original warrant can be relevant to whether I am presently justified in thinking I remember.

It must be concluded that the following principle is correct:

(3.1) "*S* recalls that *P*" is a prima facie reason for *S* to believe that it was true that *P*.

This prima facie reason is partially constitutive of our concept of the past, and its existence suffices to make historical knowledge possible.

Thus far I have argued that historical knowledge must arise ultimately from propositional memory, and that recollection pro-

[15] This is analogous to the role of the causal connection in perception. We saw in Chapter Five that we cannot be required to know that our way of being appeared to is caused in the normal way before we can make a perceptual judgment, because that would make perceptual knowledge impossible. Instead, the causal connection is relevant as a defeater—our knowing that the causal connection is abnormal defeats the prima facie reasons provided by our way of being appeared to.

vides a prima facie reason for historical judgments. If recollection were an essential part of propositional memory, it would follow that recollection is all that is needed to justify that historical knowledge which constitutes propositional memory. On this basis I could urge that remembering-that-*P* can be analyzed as "knowing-that-*P* on the basis of recalling-that-*P*". This would make for a very tidy account of historical knowledge. Unfortunately, the structure of historical knowledge is not quite this tidy. The problem is that recollection is not an essential part of propositional memory. For example, it might be clear that a man remembered that he had put his hat in the hall, because he went directly there to get it after the meeting; but it might not be true that he recalled that he put it there—he might not have thought about the matter at all.[16] Consequently, there are cases of propositional memory in which the resultant belief does not derive its justification from the presence of a recollection, because there is no such recollection.

On the strength of examples like the above, we must distinguish between "occurrent" and "nonoccurrent" remembering. Those cases in which one is explicitly thinking about what is remembered constitute occurrent remembering. I would urge that recollection is an essential part of occurrent remembering. In those cases in which a person "searches his memory" to try to remember whether it was true that *P*, and as a result acquires the occurrent memory-that-*P*, it seems clear that he recalls-that-*P*. It might be supposed that this is not equally true of those cases in which one nonoccurrently remembered-that-*P* all along, and then simply "called the memory to consciousness" in an appropriate case. But I think that even in these cases the person must recall. For example, if the man went into the hall to get his hat and it was missing, this would result in his becoming aware of what he was doing and would lead him to occurrently remember that he put it there. He might say, "That's odd—I remember that I put my hat right there." It seems clear that he recalls that he put it there. I think it must be concluded that recollection is an essential part of occurrent remembering.

But what about nonoccurrent remembering? A person has historical knowledge in that case too, and in that case there is no question of his having a recollection. Thus it seems that some

[16] I am indebted to Norman Malcolm for this counterexample to my earlier view that recollection was an essential part of propositional memory.

historical knowledge constituting memory is not based upon recollection. However, this is a peculiar kind of knowledge in that it itself is nonoccurrent. The knowledge constituted by nonoccurrent remembering is nonoccurrent in the sense that one is not explicitly thinking about what it is that is known. When one consciously thinks about what it is that he knows, the memory, by definition, becomes occurrent. When philosophers have talked about knowledge, they have as a general rule only been thinking about occurrent knowledge. It is arguable that most of what we know at any given time we know nonoccurrently, but somehow this does not seem epistemologically important. It seems that what we want to know, as epistemologists, is how it is possible for us to have occurrent knowledge. The reason for this seems to be that nonoccurrent knowledge is parasitic on occurrent knowledge. Nonoccurrent knowledge introduces no new sources of knowledge. We cannot have nonoccurrent knowledge-that-*P* unless we *can* also have occurrent knowledge-that-*P*. Roughly speaking, to nonoccurrently know-that-*P* is, in some sense, to have the ability to call up the occurrent knowledge-that-*P*. Perhaps "ability" is the wrong word here, because we cannot *try* to occurrently know-that-*P*. Rather, we have a disposition to just naturally have the occurrent knowledge whenever it is appropriate. To make this precise would be difficult, but that does not seem necessary for present purposes. The point is that epistemologists are interested in knowledge at a conscious rational level. Nonoccurrent knowledge consists merely of a certain kind of disposition to have occurrent knowledge, and does not add anything to what it is possible for us to know or how it is possible for us to come to know it. Thus, in analyzing historical knowledge, it is only occurrent memory with which we must concern ourselves. The analysis of nonoccurrent memory is an interesting problem for the philosophy of mind, but it does nothing to further elucidate the structure of historical knowledge.

I think it can be concluded that principle 3.1 constitutes the explanation of how historical knowledge is possible. Recollection provides prima facie reasons for historical judgments, and without recollection historical knowledge would not be possible. To complete our account of both historical knowledge and our concept of the past, we must supplement principle 3.1 with an account of what defeaters there are for this prima facie reason. We have already seen that one such defeater consists of knowing that our original belief-that-*P* was unjustified. The simplest way to complete the task of enumerating the possible defeaters is to turn to the concept of (occurrent) propositional memory itself and attempt to analyze it.

4. An Analysis of Propositional Memory

It seems clear that "*S* occurrently remembers that *P*" means "*S* knows-that-*P*, on the basis of recalling-that-*P*". This at least requires (1) that *S* believes that *P*, and *S*'s reason for believing-that-*P* is that he recalls that *P*; or more compactly, *S* believes-that-*P* on the basis of recalling-that-*P*. Furthermore, *S*'s recollection cannot be accidental—it must be brought about by what he knew before. The natural way to fill this out is to require (2) that *S* knew that *P*, and (3) that *S*'s recalling-that-*P* is caused by his having known that *P*. The conjunction of these three clauses gives us a more or less traditional analysis of occurrent propositional memory. However, as we will find, it is not entirely adequate as it stands.

A few philosophers have objected to clause 2, the "previous awareness condition".[17] I do not find the objections raised in the literature persuasive, but nevertheless I think that this condition must be modified. Every student in introductory psychology is familiar with the fact that a person can often see something without realizing it and then later remember seeing it. For example, a person whose brakes fail while driving at high speed in heavy traffic will be concentrating on controlling his careening automobile to the exclusion of all else, his attention rigidly fixed on the road and surrounding cars. But later, after his miraculous escape, he may literally relive his terrifying experience and recall with great clarity things like what was written on a billboard beside the road, although at the time of his near accident he did not notice the billboard. Here we have a case in which a person remembers that he saw the billboard, but did not know he was seeing it at the time he saw it.

It is easy to see what is required in order for this to be a legitimate case of remembering. The driver was appeared to in the ways necessary for him to be able to know that there was a bill-

[17] See Martin and Deutscher [1966].

board of a certain description beside the road, but did not make any judgments on that basis. Later, his having been appeared to in that way caused him to recall the billboard, and this is the reason we are willing to say he remembers it. Let us say that *S implicitly knows*-that-*P* iff the epistemologically relevant circumstances are such that he could justifiably believe-that-*P*, and that belief would be an instance of knowledge.[18] Then we can deal with our counterexample by altering our proposed equivalence to read as follows:

> *S* occurrently remembers-that-*P* iff (1) *S* believes-that-*P* on the basis of recalling-that-*P*, (2) *S* implicitly knew that *P*, and (3) *S*'s recalling-that-*P* is caused by his having implicitly known that *P*.

A different sort of putative counterexample is provided by remembering that I have seen a certain object before. The fact remembered in this case is essentially about both the present (the object I am now perceiving) and the past. As such it could not generally have been known before now (unless I had some way of predicting what object would be before me at this time), and hence my remembering that I have seen it before cannot require that I previously knew this in some other way. However, I think we can avoid this counterexample without modifying the proposed equivalence. It is plausible to take the claim to remember having seen the thing before as elliptical for something else, viz., "I remember that I have seen an object of such-and-such appearance, and that object was the same as the one now before me." Here the strictly memory part of the claim is something that I knew before. It seems that we do not have a genuine counterexample here.

We can find many other examples which at first look like counterexamples to the previous-awareness condition, but I think they can all be reconstructed along lines like the above. The only genuine counterexamples I have been able to find are those of the first sort, and as we have seen, they can easily be met by modifying the previous-awareness condition to require implicit knowledge rather than explicit knowledge. The modified previous-awareness condition must be allowed to stand.

[18] This definition is intended to include the ordinary case of knowledge—if *S* knows-that-*P*, then *S* implicitly knows-that-*P*.

However, another difficulty arises for our analysis of propositional memory. To remember-that-*P* is to know-that-*P* on the basis of recalling-that-*P*. As such, one must at least be justified in believing-that-*P* on the basis of his recollection, which means that the prima facie reason provided by his recollection must not be defeated. Our analysis makes explicit what the defeaters are for the prima facie reason. For example, either my not previously having known-that-*P*, or my recollection-that-*P* not being caused by my previous knowledge, is a defeater. Consequently, in order for me to know-that-*P* on the basis of my recollection-that-*P*, neither of these defeaters can be true. This much is already provided by our proposed analysis. But we saw in Chapter Two (section 3.4) that it is not sufficient simply to require that no defeaters be true. If a person believes a defeater, even though it is false, this is still enough to defeat the prima facie reason. For example, if I recall-that-*P*, believe-that-*P* on the basis of that recollection, and my recollection is caused by my having previously known-that-*P*, but I am perverse enough to also believe that I could not have previously known-that-*P*, this latter belief will prevent my belief-that-*P* from being justified by my recollection, and hence precludes my recollection from being an instance of remembering. To take care of this, we must add a clause to our analysis:

> *S* occurrently remembers-that-*P* iff (1) *S* believes-that-*P* on the basis of recalling-that-*P*, (2) *S* implicitly knew-that-*P*, (3) *S*'s recalling-that-*P* is caused by his having implicitly known-that-*P*, and (4) *S* does not believe that his recollection is not caused in this way.

Clause 3 in this analysis, the "causal" requirement, has been the subject of much debate. Some philosophers have rejected it on the grounds that memory is not the acquisition of new knowledge but rather the retention of old knowledge.[19] As such the knowledge is not caused anew by anything. But this objection misses the target. First, we are not saying that *S*'s *knowledge* is caused by his previous knowledge, but rather that his *recollection* is so caused. His recollection is something that he most assuredly did not have originally, and so it must be caused by something. Furthermore, it is not very clear what is meant by saying that memory

[19] See Malcolm [1963] and Squires [1969].

is not the acquisition of new knowledge. This is true if we differentiate "pieces of knowledge" solely by their content—what is known in memory is the same thing as was known before. But if we also differentiate in terms of grounds, we must say that in memory we have new knowledge. In memory the ground is recollection, which is not what the ground was for the original knowledge.

A more serious difficulty for the causal condition is analogous to what we encountered in analyzing perception. Not just any causal connection is sufficient to make *S*'s recollection genuinely memory. Weird causal connections must be prohibited. For example, suppose that Jones, an astronomer, learns about unusual sunspot activity occurring on the sun. He resolves to drive to an observatory deep in the desert two days hence so that he can discuss this event with some colleagues. In the ensuing two days he forgets why he wanted to go to the observatory but remembers that there was some good reason, so he goes anyway figuring that he will remember the reason once he gets there. While driving through the desert he has car trouble, and while attempting to walk back to civilization he becomes sunstruck. This results in his having delusions which take the form of recollections concerning events that supposedly happened two days earlier. He has delusive memories of riding pink and purple elephants through space and doing battle with interstellar warriors armed with spears and mounted on green giraffes. An incidental part of his fantasy involves the offending warriors attempting to drive him toward the sun where, according to the fantasy, giant sunspots reach out to gobble him up. He thus recalls that there was unusual sunspot activity two days ago, but with his recollection being embedded as it is in a pure fantasy, it is clear that he does not remember that there was unusual sunspot activity. Nevertheless, his having the recollection is caused by his having previously known what he now recalls, because that previous knowledge caused him to get into the situation in which the fantasy occurs.

Apparently not just any causal connection between previous knowledge and current recollection can make the recollection an instance of remembering. Some restrictions are necessary on the nature of the causal connection. But now we become impaled on the horns of a dilemma. If we are not *quite* specific about the nature of the causal connection, we will not succeed in eliminating the counterexamples. But if we are quite specific, we will build into our analysis what are only contingent facts about remembering. For example, although we know it does not, there would be no *logical* absurdity in supposing that memory proceeds in terms of magnetic tapes in the stomach, or in terms of rays from the sun. For that matter, I see no reason why memory could not be an occult process in which there is no intervening mechanism between the original knowledge and the present recollection. We would still say that the original knowledge caused the present recollection, but there would be no answer to the question of how it caused it. It would be a kind of unanalyzable action at a temporal distance. Some philosophers profess to find this unintelligible, but I can see nothing wrong with it. If we were to discover that memory is such an occult process, this would still be useful in ruling out recollections caused in other ways. In such a case, if a recollection were caused by some traceable process, we would conclude that it is not a genuine remembering.

This is suggestive of the role the causal clause actually plays in deciding whether people remember. We discover inductively what the actual causal mechanism is in memory (or less ambitiously, we discover that certain causal mechanisms are not part of the normal causal mechanism), and then we rule out those recollections resulting from aberrant causal mechanisms. But how can we do this? We can only discover what the actual causal mechanism is if we can tell when people remember, and it seems we cannot do that until we already know what the causal mechanism is. The solution is that knowledge of the causal mechanism functions negatively, as a defeater. If a person satisfies conditions 1, 2, and 4, we take that as a prima facie reason for thinking he remembers. On the basis of judgments made in this way, we discover inductively what the normal causal mechanism is in memory, and then go back and use that as a defeater to possibly rule out some of our earlier judgments that people remembered.

We can explain the existence of this prima facie reason as follows. To begin with, as far as the causal clause in the analysis of memory goes, it seems that the most we can say is that the causal mechanism must be the *normal* one in memory.[20] This gives us:

[20] This should not be taken as implying that the causal mechanism in all possible creatures must be the same. The normal connection may be a disjunction of connections.

(4.1) *S* occurrently remembers-that-*P* iff (1) *S* believes-that-*P* on the basis of recalling-that-*P*, (2) *S* implicitly knew-that-*P*, (3) *S*'s recalling-that-*P* stands in whatever causal relation is normal in memory to his having implicitly known-that-*P*, and (4) *S* does not believe that this recollection is not caused in this way.

As an analysis this is a failure, because it is circular, but it still seems to be a correct equivalence, and it is of supreme importance to the concept of remembering. This equivalence can be regarded as giving us a pair of conclusive reasons for judging when people remember things or fail to remember things. If we can somehow ascertain whether a person's recollection is caused in the way normal to memory, we can use 4.1 to determine whether he remembers. At first, ascertaining this may seem problematic. Even now, neurologists know almost nothing about the causal mechanisms involved in memory, so how can we who are not even neurologists know that a person's recollection is caused in the way normal to memory? An example demonstrates that there is really no problem here. When most people dial a telephone they are quite certain both that their doing so will cause a telephone to ring at the other end and that the causal mechanism will be the normal one involved in telephones, although they have no idea what that causal mechanism is.[21] It seems to be a logical truth about the concept of a cause that if a phenomenon recurs many times in a particular context, we automatically have a prima facie reason for thinking that the causal mechanism is the same each time. Consequently, in applying 4.1 we do not have to worry about the causal clause except insofar as we have a specific reason for thinking it is violated. This generates the prima facie reason we noticed above.

The fact that we do not ordinarily have to look at the causal clause in our equivalence suggests that 4.1 does after all constitute a noncircular analysis of remembering. It seems that this equivalence gives us all we need to be able to judge whether people remember things. We simply look at the noncausal clauses and see whether they are satisfied. We need only take the causal clause into account when we have an inductive reason, arising from previous judgments made by ignoring it, for thinking that

[21] The example is taken from Martin and Deutscher [1966], p. 175, and the point to be drawn from it was suggested to me by their discussion.

the causes of the present recollection are abnormal. But notice that what this amounts to is that given the above principle regarding the justification conditions for certain causal judgments, our equivalence generates a noncircular account of the justification conditions for judgments regarding whether people remember things. Our equivalence still does not give a noncircular account of the truth conditions for such judgments.

We set out to give a truth condition analysis of the concept of propositional remembering, but our proposed analysis has degenerated into an account of the justification conditions for that concept. The problem is that the causal clause must be an essential part of any truth condition analysis of remembering, but that clause cannot be correctly stated without making reference to what happens normally in remembering. It is impossible to give a noncircular truth condition analysis of remembering. I think it must be concluded that the situation with regard to memory is completely analogous to that with regard to perception. As in the case of perception the concept of propositional memory is itself an ostensive concept, just like the concept of the past, and must be analyzed in terms of its justification conditions. Principle 4.1 makes a large contribution toward providing this kind of analysis.

Principle 4.1 by itself does not give a complete account of the justification conditions for the concept of propositional memory. The problem is that it does not give an adequate account of our first-person judgments. Consider some proposition *P* which I remember. If the only way I can know that I remember it is by applying 4.1, then I must somehow know that at an earlier time I implicitly knew-that-*P*. This is not itself something that I would ordinarily remember. Except in extraordinary cases, I merely remember-that-*P*—I do not remember that I knew-that-*P*. Thus 4.1 would provide me with no basis for judging that I remember-that-*P*. But clearly, in this sort of case, I can reasonably judge that I do remember-that-*P*. My recalling-that-*P* gives me a reason not only for thinking-that-*P* but also for thinking that I remember-that-*P*:

(4.2) "*S* recalls that *P*" is a prima facie reason for *S* to think that he remembers that *P*.

Thus in the first-person case we need not apply 4.1.

Nevertheless, principle 4.1 is of importance in the first-person case because it generates what defeaters there are for the prima facie reasons formulated in both principles 4.2 and 3.1. First, look at 3.1. It has been argued that "*S* recalls that *P*" is a prima facie reason for *S* to believe that *P*. A defeater for this prima facie reason is any reason for thinking that *S* does not know-that-*P* on the basis of recalling-that-*P*, i.e., any reason for thinking that *S* does not remember that *P*. Thus the defeaters for 3.1 are the same as those for 4.1. Reasons for thinking that *S* does not remember-that-*P* are provided by the negations of the clauses in principle 4.1. For example, suppose that I recall-that-*P* and on that basis believe-that-*P*. Then by virtue of 4.1, any reason for thinking that I did not previously implicitly know-that-*P* will be a defeater, and any reason for thinking my recollection is not caused in the normal way will be a defeater. No new defeater comes out of the negation of clause 4, because if I believe that I believe that my recollection is not properly caused, then I believe that my recollection is not properly caused, and hence I have a defeater of the sort that arises out of clause 3. These seem to exhaust the logical defeaters for this prima facie reason.

I believe that principles 4.1 and 4.2 together give us a complete account of the justification conditions for the concept of propositional remembering. Principle 3.1 and the defeaters provided by principle 4.1 give us a complete account of the justification conditions for statements about the past. This explains how historical knowledge is possible.

Chapter Eight

Induction

1. The Problem of Induction

THE traditional problem of induction was that of justifying induction. This is just one more instance of the traditional attempt to justify sources of knowledge. In the case of induction it is almost obvious that nothing could possibly count as a justification. We cannot justify induction inductively, and, as Strawson remarked, to attempt to give a deductive justification of induction is to attempt to turn induction into deduction, which it is not.[1] This, of course, is just what has always made the traditional problem of induction so puzzling. But the lesson to be learned from all this is that the attempt to justify induction is wrongheaded and must be forsaken. This is because the principles of induction are instrumental in our making justified judgments about the world, and as such are involved in the justification conditions of our concepts. Insofar as the principles of induction are involved in the justification conditions of our concepts, they are partially constitutive of the meanings of these concepts. It is simply part of the meaning of these concepts that one can inductively generalize in connection with them. To *justify* induction would be to somehow derive the justification conditions of these concepts from something deeper, but there is nothing deeper. It is in principle impossible to justify induction, and there is no reason why things should be otherwise. The traditional problem of induction is best regarded as a pseudo-problem.

However, there does remain an important and difficult problem concerning induction. Just as it is difficult to state precisely what are the justification conditions for perceptual judgments or his-

[1] Strawson [1952], chap. 9.

torical judgments, so it is extremely difficult to state in a precise way what are correct principles of induction. The problem of explicating the principles of inductive reasoning is just what Goodman [1955] has called "the new riddle of induction". This is the task to be undertaken in the present chapter.

2. The Confirmation Relation

Principles of induction take the form of saying that certain particular observations *confirm* certain generalizations. For example, it seems reasonable to say that observation of a number of *A*'s which are *B*'s confirms the generalization that all *A*'s are *B*'s. Before we can attempt to make the principles of induction precise, we must get clearer about this relation of confirmation.

It was argued earlier that inductive reasons are always prima facie reasons, and this makes it possible to state principles of induction without using the term "confirms". For example, rather than saying that observation of a number of *A*'s which are *B*'s confirms the generalization that all *A*'s are *B*'s, we might instead say that a (sufficiently long) conjunction of statements of the form $(Aa \,\&\, Ba)$ constitutes a prima facie reason for $(x)(Ax \supset Bx)$. In this way we could eliminate all talk about confirmation and talk merely about prima facie reasons. But despite this, it is convenient to introduce the weaker notion of confirmation. Not only do we want to say that observation of sufficiently many *A*'s which are *B*'s justifies us (in the absence of any defeaters) in believing that all *A*'s are *B*'s; we would also like to say that observation of a single *A* which is a *B* gives *some* justification for believing that all *A*'s are *B*'s, although it does not usually provide enough justification all by itself to make us justified in believing that all *A*'s are *B*'s. We want to say that each instance of an *A* which is a *B* adds a little justification, and then putting a lot of these together we get something strong enough to qualify as a prima facie reason. We customarily express this by saying that each instance *confirms* the generalization, and then a conjunction of enough confirming instances constitutes a prima facie reason. How are we to define this notion of confirmation?

We first define the notion of a *logical protoreason* as something which is weaker than a logical reason in the same way that confirmation is weaker than a prima facie reason:

(2.1) The statement-that-*P* is a *logical protoreason* for *S* to believe the statement-that-*Q* iff, necessarily, if *S* justifiably believed-that-*P* and held whatever beliefs are necessary to justify his belief-that-*P*, and held no other beliefs, then he would be more justified in believing-that-*Q* than if he did not believe-that-*P*.

(2.2) The statement-that-*P* *elementarily confirms* the statement-that-*Q* iff the statement-that-*P* is a defeasible logical protoreason for a person to believe-that-*Q*.

Logical reasons become the limiting case of logical protoreasons, and hence prima facie reasons become the limiting case of the elementary confirmation relation. So defined, elementary confirmation is not exclusively *inductive* confirmation. Elementary confirmation proceeds in terms of anything which is like, but possibly too weak to be, a prima facie reason.

Elementary confirmation is not, by itself, the relation that we want to call "confirmation". What we might call the "traditional notion of confirmation" is the notion of how one can become justified in believing a general hypothesis on the combined basis of inductive inference and deductive inference. This concept of confirmation is the concept that allows us to describe how scientists justify beliefs in general hypotheses. It is a combination of straightforward induction from instances (which proceeds in terms of elementary confirmation) and drawing deductive conclusions from the inductive conclusions. One might attempt to define this notion of confirmation as the deductive closure of elementary confirmation (that is, say that something is confirmed iff it is entailed by propositions that are elementarily confirmed). Unfortunately, the deductive closure will generally be inconsistent, because as a general rule our evidence will elementarily confirm different incompatible hypotheses, although not all to the same degree. A scientist, rather than accepting all of the deductive consequences of what is confirmed by his evidence, only accepts a hypothesis if the evidence supports it more strongly than it supports any incompatible hypothesis. We can make this precise as follows:

(2.3) *P supports Q* iff there is a statement *R* logically equivalent to *P* which elementarily confirms *Q*.

(2.4) *P confirms Q* iff there are statements $R_1, \ldots, R_n$ such that:

(1) P supports each R_i;

(2) $(R_1 \& \ldots \& R_n) \rightarrow Q$;[2]

(3) it is false that there are statements $S_1, \ldots, S_m$ such that:

(*a*) P supports each S_j;

(*b*) $(S_1 \& \ldots \& S_m) \rightarrow \sim Q$;

(*c*) there is an i such that each S_j is as strongly supported by P as is R_i.

In this definition of confirmation we can think of $R_1, \ldots, R_n$ as the premises of an argument leading to Q. An argument is only as strong as its weakest premise, so we require that there be no premises $S_1, \ldots, S_m$ entailing $\sim Q$ each of which is as strongly supported as the weakest premise of $R_1, \ldots, R_n$. This definition is intended to capture the way in which the scientist actually proceeds in combining inductive and deductive reasoning to decide whether the evidence confirms the hypothesis Q.

In defending this analysis of confirmation, we must not commit an error that has been committed all too frequently in the literature. This is the error of supposing that there is only one logical relation which might reasonably be called "confirmation". That supposition is demonstrably false. For example, it seems reasonable to call elementary confirmation a confirmation relation too. Another important confirmation concept is what Carnap [1950] called "positive relevance". Positive relevance is of particular importance in discussing statistical confirmation, but it is not the same as the concept defined in 2.4. All too frequently an author has adopted one concept of confirmation and then criticized a second author on the grounds that what the second author said about confirmation was not true of the confirmation concept adopted by the first author.[3] But that is no basis for criticism unless both authors claim to be talking about the same concept of confirmation.

From definition 2.4 we can obtain a number of important logical features of our concept of confirmation:[4]

[2] I use the arrow for logical entailment—*not* the material conditional.

[3] For example, Carnap [1950] seems to be guilty of this in his criticism of Hempel [1945].

[4] This list of theorems is equivalent to the list of conditions of adequacy proposed by Hempel [1945].

(2.5) If P confirms Q and Q entails R, then P confirms R.

(2.6) If P confirms both Q and R, then P confirms $(Q \& R)$.

(2.7) If P confirms R and Q is logically equivalent to P, then Q confirms R.

(2.8) If P is logically consistent and P confirms Q, then $(P \& Q)$ is logically consistent.

It might also seem natural to suppose that if a proposition P entails a proposition Q, which confirms a proposition R, then P confirms R. But this is not the case. Confirmation is defeasible. A proposition may entail something which confirms some conclusion, but also entail a defeater for that confirmation. For example, suppose the predicates A and B are chosen so that $(Aa \& Ba)$ confirms $(x)(Ax \supset Bx)$. The proposition $(Aa \& Ba \& Ab \& \sim Bb)$ entails $(Aa \& Ba)$, but it also entails $(Ab \& \sim Bb)$, which defeats the confirmation.

3. Classical Attempts to State the Principles of Induction

3.1 *The Nicod Principle*

Now let us turn to the formulation of principles of induction. What is surely the most natural first suggestion is some principle of *enumerative induction* according to which a hypothesis of the form "All A's are B's" is inductively confirmed by observation of its "positive instances". Positive instances are those instances which, upon being amassed, lead to greater and greater confirmation of the hypothesis. Precisely what constitutes a positive instance is a matter of controversy. The simplest proposal is that a positive instance of the hypothesis $(x)(Ax \supset Bx)$ is any statement of the form $(Aa \& Ba)$. Following Hempel [1945] we can call this the *Nicod principle.* As Goodman [1955] has pointed out, there are some choices of the predicates A and B for which this principle cannot be defended. But let us leave aside for the moment the question of what kinds of restrictions should be placed upon the predicates A and B and consider other objections to this principle.

The first difficulty is due to Hempel [1945]. Hempel does not object that the Nicod principle is false; he objects simply that it is too restrictive. Hempel argues that we must say not only that $(Aa$

& Ba) is a positive instance of $(x)(Ax \supset Bx)$ but also that statements of the forms $(\sim Ab \,\&\, Bb)$ and $(\sim Ac \,\&\, \sim Bc)$ are positive instances. The argument involves the infamous "paradox of the ravens". Hempel begins by agreeing that the positive instances picked out by the Nicod principle are positive instances. Next he proposes that any correct theory of induction must satisfy the following equivalence condition:

(3.1) If P confirms Q, and Q is logically equivalent to R, then P confirms R.

In fact, 3.1 follows immediately from theorem 2.5. But given this, we can prove that a statement of the form $(\sim Ac \,\&\, \sim Bc)$ confirms the generalization that all A's are B's. By the Nicod principle, $(\sim Ac \,\&\, \sim Bc)$ confirms the generalization $(x)(\sim Bx \supset \sim Ax)$. For example, if A is "raven" and B is "black", the observation of non-black non-ravens confirms the generalization that all non-black things are non-ravens. But the latter statement is simply the contrapositive of $(x)(Ax \supset Bx)$. Hence, by the equivalence condition, amassing statements of the form $(\sim Ac \,\&\, \sim Bc)$ confirms $(x)(Ax \supset Bx)$. Thus these must also be positive instances of $(x)(Ax \supset Bx)$. For example, if we went to a factory manufacturing plastic garbage cans and observed that all of the cans coming off the assembly line were green, this would confirm that all ravens are black. This is at least peculiar. It does not seem that you can confirm generalizations about ravens by examining garbage cans. But it is extremely difficult to see how we are to avoid this conclusion, as it follows logically from such eminently reasonable premises. Hempel concludes that our initial intuitions are wrong and that we must simply accept this conclusion. His explanation of the situation is that what $(x)(Ax \supset Bx)$ says is that everything in the universe is either a non-A or a B. Thus observation of anything which is either a non-A or a B should confirm the generalization. This leads to the conclusion that not only does $(\sim Ac \,\&\, \sim Bc)$ constitute a positive instance of $(x)(Ax \supset Bx)$; so, too, does $(\sim Ab \,\&\, Bb)$. If anything, the latter result is more paradoxical than what it was intended to explain. Although it seems strange that $(x)(Ax \supset Bx)$ can be confirmed by observing non-B's that are non-A's, it is preposterous to suppose it can be confirmed by observing non-A's that are B's. Non-A's that are B's are simply irrelevant to the generalization, and so should neither confirm it nor disconfirm it.

This intuitive rejection of $(\sim Ab \mathbin{\&} Bb)$ as a positive instance of $(x)(Ax \supset Bx)$ can be given substance as follows. It seems to me that the error lies in supposing that the generalization which is confirmed in enumerative induction is properly symbolized using a material conditional. The difficulty is that observation of positive instances supports not only the generalization but also further instances of the generalization. More precisely, insofar as $(Aa \mathbin{\&} Ba)$ confirms $(x)(Ax \supset Bx)$, it also confirms the counterfactual "If we were to encounter another A, it would also be a B". This has often been put by saying that we confirm *laws*, not accidental generalizations.[5] If we were convinced that $(x)(Ax \supset Bx)$, if true, would be true only coincidentally, then we would not take the addition of positive instances to our evidence as confirming the generalization. We only take the addition of positive instances to add to the confirmation of $(x)(Ax \supset Bx)$ insofar as it also supports other instances, and hence confirms the generalized counterfactual "Given anything, if it were an A then it would be a B". Let us symbolize this as $(x)(Ax \Rrightarrow Bx)$. The accumulation of positive instances confirms this counterfactual, and it only confirms the material conditional derivatively, because it is entailed by the counterfactual. Herein lies the error in Hempel's argument. The generalization that is confirmed in enumerative induction does not simply say that everything is either a non-A or a B, and hence there is no reason to think it should be confirmed by everything which satisfies this disjunction. The generalization that is most directly confirmed by its positive instances is counterfactual, and hence stronger than this disjunction. Consequently, there is no reason to think it should be confirmed by $(\sim Ab \mathbin{\&} Bb)$.

Having brought counterfactuals into the picture, we are treading on notoriously slippery ground. I will make no attempt here to explain or clarify the counterfactuals involved. I can only hope that our rather fuzzy intuitions regarding counterfactuals will prove equal to the task of understanding at least those features of counterfactuals which are necessary for the present discussion.

By maintaining that what is confirmed in enumerative induction is the generalized counterfactual $(x)(Ax \Rrightarrow Bx)$, I have ex-

[5] I think the term "laws" is misleading here. It makes the nonaccidental generalizations sound more prestigious than necessary.

plained why $(\sim Ab \,\&\, Bb)$ should not be regarded as a positive instance. Can we perhaps dissolve the paradox of the ravens altogether by maintaining that $(\sim Ac \,\&\, \sim Bc)$ is not a positive instance either? To do this, it would suffice if contraposition failed for the counterfactuals involved. I think that contraposition does fail for these counterfactuals: in general, $(x)(Ax \Rrightarrow Bx)$ is not logically equivalent to $(x)(\sim Bx \Rrightarrow \sim Ax)$. For example, the following counterfactual is true:

> Any piece of chalk is such that, if dropped in a vacuum at the surface of the earth, it would accelerate at 32 ft/sec^2.

However, its contrapositive is:

> Anything which, when dropped in a vacuum at the surface of the earth, did not accelerate at 32 ft/sec^2 would not be a piece of chalk.

And this is false. If chalk did not behave in this way, the law of gravity would be false, and there would be no reason to think that anything else would behave in that way either.

As contraposition fails, the Hempelian argument no longer works and there is no reason to think that $(\sim Ac \,\&\, \sim Bc)$ is a positive instance of $(x)(Ax \Rrightarrow Bx)$. Unfortunately, this does not yet resolve the paradox of the ravens. This is because, although $(\sim Ac \,\&\, \sim Bc)$ may not confirm $(x)(Ax \Rrightarrow Bx)$, it does confirm $(x)(\sim Bx \Rrightarrow \sim Ax)$, which entails $(x)(\sim Bx \supset \sim Ax)$, and hence entails $(x)(Ax \supset Bx)$. Thus, although $(\sim Ac \,\&\, \sim Bc)$ may not confirm the counterfactual, it most certainly does confirm the material conditional $(x)(Ax \supset Bx)$, and that is just as paradoxical. For example, although observation of green garbage cans might not confirm "Any raven would be black", it seems that it must confirm "All actual ravens are black". We still have a paradox, and the paradox is seen to be independent of the question whether $(\sim Ac \,\&\, \sim Bc)$ is a positive instance of $(x)(Ax \Rrightarrow Bx)$. The final resolution of this paradox must wait until section 4. In the meantime, however, we have successfully defended the original Nicod principle from Hempel's attempt to enlarge it by adding many more positive instances.

Apart from the paradox of the ravens, it has been claimed that the Nicod principle suffers from another shortcoming. This is that it is only applicable to generalizations which are conditional in form. It has been claimed that we frequently deal inductively with generalizations which are at least not overtly of this form. Examples might be "Everything is soluble in something", "There exists organic life on other stars", and "Polio is caused by some virus".[6] Another source of counterexamples lies in scientific theories. If one accepts the dogma that theories are confirmed by the hypothetico-deductive method (about which more will be said in section 7) and cannot be confirmed by enumerative induction, then the Nicod principle is inapplicable to them.

I seriously doubt whether any of the above three examples are really counterexamples. The first can be paraphrased as "Given any chemical substance, there exists another chemical substance such that all instances of the first are soluble in instances of the second". This has the desired conditional form, and so can be handled by the Nicod principle. "There exists organic life on other stars" cannot be confirmed directly, either by the Nicod principle or by any other reasonable principle of induction. Rather, it must be deduced logically from other generalizations concerning, e.g., the conditions under which long organic molecules are apt to form, and these generalizations can be dealt with straightforwardly by the Nicod principle. "Polio is caused by a virus" is problematic because it introduces the concept of a cause, but that is not itself a problem for induction. The basis for judging that polio is caused by a virus would presumably be some generalization like "Everyone who has polio has virus X in his blood", and this once more can be dealt with in terms of the Nicod principle. Leaving aside theories for the moment, I am convinced that all those generalizations that are confirmed inductively[7] can be recast naturally in conditional form, and then the Nicod principle handles them nicely. Further support for the conclusion that we can only confirm conditionals comes from the observation that it is not $(x)(Ax \supset Bx)$ that we most directly confirm, but rather the counterfactual $(x)(Ax \Rrightarrow Bx)$. It is hard to see how this could be generalized to anything other than conditionals. Thus considerations of this sort do not require us to supplement the Nicod principle with something more inclusive.

[6] The latter two examples are from Hempel [1945].

[7] More precisely, those generalizations that are confirmed "directly", in the sense of being confirmed without being logically deduced from something else already confirmed, are always generalizations of conditionals.

3.2 *Explanatory Induction*

Nevertheless, there is another principle which has often been proposed as the correct account of induction, and that principle must be considered. This will lead us to a further generalization of the Nicod principle.

Frequently, in science and everyday life, we construct hypotheses to explain some data, and then we confirm the hypotheses by checking their testable consequences to see that they all come out true. We might call this *explanatory induction*. This is the model upon which the hypothetico-deductive method is based, but in fact it seems just as applicable to experimental laws and more mundane things as it is to scientific theories replete with theoretical entities. For example, consider a parapsychologist investigating a supposedly haunted house. The symptom of the haunting consists of ghostly howls in the night. These howls are never heard during the day. To explain these ghostly howls our parapsychologist hypothesizes that they are caused by wind in the chimney. To confirm his hypothesis he first observes that the howls are only heard when it is windy, and that in the region where this house is located it is only windy at night. Both of these observations are entailed by the hypothesis that the howls are caused by wind in the chimney, and observing them is confirmation for the hypothesis. The parapsychologist then goes on to make two further observations. First, he measures the length of the chimney and finds that it is the appropriate length for the wave length of the sound constituting the howls. Again, this is entailed by the hypothesis and constitutes strong confirmation for it. Finally, he observes the previously unnoticed fact that the howls are higher pitched in the winter than in the summer. This is because sound travels faster in the cold winter air, and thus the same wave length constitutes a higher frequency sound and hence a higher pitch. This latter observation would be very strong confirmation for the hypothesis. It appears that what we have here is a hypothesis being confirmed by verifying the truth of various propositions entailed by it.

This example of explanatory induction suggests the following *entailment theory* of confirmation:

If P entails Q, then Q confirms P.

As Hempel [1945] pointed out, stated thus baldly the theory leads to the absurd result that anything confirms anything. Given any two statements *P* and *Q*, the conjunction (*P* & *Q*) entails *P*, and so by the entailment theory, *P* confirms (*P* & *Q*). By principle 2.5, if a statement confirms another statement, it also confirms anything entailed by that statement. (*P* & *Q*) entails *Q*, so if *P* confirms (*P* & *Q*), *P* must also confirm *Q*. Thus according to the entailment theory, any statement *P* confirms any other statement *Q*. This is absurd, so the entailment theory is unacceptable at least in the above form.

This result is most peculiar because the entailment theory seemed merely to codify what we do in explanatory induction when we confirm hypotheses by verifying that various consequences of them are true. But if we think about it for a minute, it is obvious that the entailment theory is wrong anyway. Not all entailments of a hypothesis are relevant to its confirmation—just a few. For example, the wind-in-the-chimney hypothesis entails that if we planted roses in the garden, that would not result in the cessation of the howls. But we would not regard that as at all relevant to the hypothesis, and certainly would not take it as confirming the hypothesis. So the entailment theory cannot be correct. We must look elsewhere for an explanation of what is involved in explanatory induction. I think that the proper explanation can be found by turning our attention first to a difficulty that arises for the Nicod principle.

Suppose, on the basis of chemical theory, that we know we could produce an artificial gem in a certain way. We do not know whether such gems actually occur in nature. Suppose further that, although we cannot predict their color on the basis of their chemical structure, we can predict that all gems made in this particular way will be green. Suppose further that we know of no other way to produce them. If we then go ahead and create a number of these artificial gems (let us call them "runes"), we will have a number of green runes, and this will confirm the generalization that all runes are green.[8] But before we ever produced them, we

[8] One might be tempted to balk at this on the grounds that we do not *know* that there are no other ways runes might be produced, and hence have no basis for concluding that they must all be green. But this must be wrong. It cannot be required, on pain of skepticism, that before we can use a sample of *A*'s to confirm that all *A*'s are *B*'s we must first ascertain that there are no other ways of producing *A*'s than the ways represented by the *A*'s in our sample. This is because the only way to find out that there are no other ways of producing *A*'s is inductively, and hence we would

already knew that our samples were going to be green. Surely, then, it makes no difference to the confirmation whether we actually do produce the runes or not. If we know that we can "produce positive instances upon demand", this confirms the generalization just as much as actually producing those instances does.

Now let us take this one step further. Suppose that, although we know of this process which would result in the creation of these gems, we cannot actually carry it out because of the extreme temperatures involved. This would seem to make no difference to the confirmation. If knowing that all runes created in this way would be green confirmed the generalization before when we were able to actually carry out the process, it should confirm it just as much if we cannot carry out the process. All that is necessary for the confirmation is that the only known physically possible process which would result in the creation of runes would result in the creation of green runes. What confirms the generalization is our knowing of *possible* green runes and not knowing of any possible non-green runes. All that is necessary for confirmation is *possible* positive instances. As actual positive instances are automatically possible ones, they are also subsumed under this rule. Of course, this talk of possible positive instances should not be regarded as talk of possible objects in a metaphysically suspicious way. Being a little more careful, we can formulate the above observation as follows. Taking "$\underset{\mathrm{P}}{\Diamond}$" to symbolize "it is physically possible that":

$$\text{(3.2)} \quad \underset{\mathrm{P}}{\Diamond}(\exists x)(Ax \;\&\; Bx) \text{ confirms } (x)(Ax \Longrightarrow Bx).$$

As $(Aa \;\&\; Ba)$ entails $\underset{\mathrm{P}}{\Diamond}(\exists x)(Ax \;\&\; Bx)$ (and does not entail any defeaters), it follows that this also confirms $(x)(Ax \Longrightarrow Bx)$.

have an infinite regress. Applying this to the runes, the only way one could ever find out that there is no other way to produce runes is inductively, by finding that all runes are produced in *this* way. If one had to find out that there is no other way to produce runes before he could use this sample to confirm general conclusions about runes, we would have an infinite regress. Notice, however, that this is not to say that we need not know this—just that we need not know it *first*. Insofar as our sample confirms that all *A*'s are *B*'s, it also confirms that all *A*'s are produced in ways represented by the sample. In the case of the runes, our sample confirms not only that all runes are green but also that all runes are produced by this chemical process. But we do not have to know the latter *before* we can confirm the former—they are confirmed simultaneously.

Principle 3.2 can be regarded as constituting an extended Nicod principle.

We can now employ this extended Nicod principle to understand what is happening in explanatory induction. Suppose a scientist has a set of data, and he knows of only one physically possible mechanism that would produce that pattern of data. He would ordinarily take this as confirming that that is the mechanism actually responsible for the data. This can be justified on the basis of 3.2. Insofar as he knows of a physically possible mechanism which would produce data of this sort, he knows of physically possible instances of data of this sort being produced by that mechanism. He does not (we are supposing) know of any other possible mechanism which would produce such data, so he has "possible positive instances" of the generalization "All sets of data of this sort are produced by mechanisms of this sort". This, in turn, entails that the actual data were produced by the postulated mechanism. This is the basis upon which the scientist confirms that the postulated mechanism is the real one.

To take a concrete example, consider Planck's hypothesis regarding black-body radiation. Classical electromagnetic theory gave the wrong prediction concerning the energy radiated from a black body at a given wave length. Planck showed that if we suppose the electromagnetic oscillators to be "quantized" in the sense that they can only have energies which are integral multiples of a certain value, this yields a prediction that is exactly in accord with the experimental data. This was taken as confirming that the energy of the oscillators is quantized. We can explain this by saying that Planck showed that if his proposed mechanism were correct we would get data of the sort actually observed. Hence we have possible positive instances of the generalization that data of that sort always result from such quantized sets of oscillators. We know of no other mechanism which would yield such data, so we confirm inductively that such data are always produced by quantized oscillators. Hence we become justified in believing that the oscillators in black-body radiation are quantized.

In general, on the basis of principle 3.2 we can conclude:

(3.3) "We have data of type *S*, and the only known physically possible mechanism for producing data of type *S* is *M*"

> confirms that mechanism M is operative in producing the data we have.

Thus we do not need recourse to anything like the entailment theory to justify explanatory induction. All we need is the extended Nicod principle.

Now let us return to the example of the haunted house. This example introduces a further complication. We explain the ghostly howls as being caused by the wind in the chimney. But there is at least one other hypothesis that would also explain the data—there might really be ghosts. Furthermore, they might just be perverse enough to howl at a higher pitch in the winter than the summer, etc., just to confuse us. Still, we opt for the wind in the chimney. This is because we judge it to be much less likely for there to be ghosts than for there to be wind in the chimney. But how does that justify our conclusion? This sort of case is not particularly unusual. Frequently, we will be able to construct more than one possible mechanism which would yield our observed data, but if one of the mechanisms is deemed much more likely than the others, we conclude that it is probably the operative one. The justification for this seems to be the following. If we know of more than one possible mechanism for producing the data, we cannot use the Nicod principle to conclude that all data of this sort are produced by just one of these mechanisms; but we can use it to conclude that all data of this sort are produced by one or the other of these mechanisms. Thus we become justified in believing that one of a certain disjunction of mechanisms is operative. Then, if we know on the basis of some sort of statistical inference that one of these mechanisms is much more likely than the others, we can conclude that it is the mechanism that is probably operative in this case. In the case of the haunted house, we regard ghosts as much less likely than wind in the chimney because we have never encountered any ghosts but we have encountered wind in the chimney. We are justified on the basis of principle 3.3 in believing that there is either a ghost or wind in the chimney, and then our statistical beliefs about ghosts justify us in believing that the howls are probably caused by wind in the chimney.

The upshot of this is that we do not need anything like the entailment theory to justify the kinds of moves we make in explanatory induction. Our moves can all be justified by appeal to ordinary enumerative induction, using the extended Nicod principle.

4. Enumerative Induction

I have argued that the only kind of induction we need to explain scientific reasoning is enumerative induction. In this section I want to clarify just how enumerative induction works. It was noted in section 2 that the relation we called "confirmation" was really broader than inductive confirmation. This was because elementary confirmation includes more than just the confirmation of generalizations by their positive instances. If we can replace elementary confirmation by a more restrictive relation characterizing the confirmation of generalizations by their positive instances, then we can define a notion of "instance confirmation" which is precisely the logical relation used in enumerative induction. At the same time, we will be explaining just how enumerative induction works. Let us say that the evidence *directly confirms* a generalization when the evidence confirms the generalization by containing positive instances of it. Then we can define instance confirmation in a way completely analogous to our earlier definition of confirmation:

(4.1) P *instantially confirms* Q iff there are statements $R_1, \ldots, R_n$ such that:
- (1) P directly confirms each R_i;
- (2) $(R_1 \& \ldots \& R_n) \rightarrow Q$;
- (3) it is false that there are statements $S_1, \ldots, S_m$ such that:
  - (*a*) P supports each S_j;
  - (*b*) $(S_1 \& \ldots \& S_m) \rightarrow \sim Q$;
  - (*c*) there is an i such that each S_j is as strongly supported by P as is R_i.[9]

Note that in clause 3 we hark back to our original notion of "supports" rather than "directly confirms". There is no reason why the arguments against an inductive conclusion must themselves be inductive.

[9] It must be admitted that this definition (and also definition 2.4) proceeds partly in terms of an undefined notion, viz., degree of support. No attempt will be made here to explicate that concept.

Now what remains is to define direct confirmation. We will say that $(Aa \ \& \ Ba)$ directly confirms the generalization $(x)(Ax \Rrightarrow Bx)$. Or, more generally, we will say that $\underset{P}{\Diamond}(\exists x)(Ax \ \& \ Bx)$ directly confirms the generalization. However, this is not yet enough to define direct confirmation. We want to know when the generalization is directly confirmed in light of everything we know. For the generalization to be directly confirmed, we must not only have (at least possible) positive instances; we must *not* have any defeaters. So, where P represents our total knowledge and Q some generalization, P directly confirms Q iff P entails positive instances of Q, but does not entail any defeaters. Thus, in order to complete our characterization of direct confirmation, we must characterize the defeaters that operate in enumerative induction.

The simplest kind of defeater is a type I defeater, i.e., a reason for thinking that Q is false. But notice that there is a logical difference between type I defeaters for confirmation and type I defeaters for prima facie reasons. In order to defeat a prima facie reason, it suffices to have a reason for thinking that the conclusion is "quite possibly false". Our reason need not be strong enough to justify us in thinking that the conclusion is definitely false. All that is required is that our reason be strong enough that we can no longer be justified in believing the conclusion to be definitely true. But this is not the way defeaters for confirmation work. If we have a reason for thinking that Q is quite possibly false, this will certainly lessen the degree of confirmation, but it may not remove the confirmation altogether (particularly if we have *strong* inductive evidence supporting Q). It seems that in order to have a type I defeater for the confirmation of Q, our evidence must support the premises of an argument for $\sim Q$ at least as strongly as Q is supported by those of its positive instances that are contained in the evidence. The simplest and most common example of this occurs when the evidence actually entails $\sim Q$ by containing a counterexample for the generalization.

However, this picture must be complicated somewhat. As we will see shortly, there are also type II defeaters for instance confirmation. More generally, there are type II "diminishers" which diminish the degree of confirmation without defeating it altogether. If the evidence contains such diminishers, the degree to which Q is supported is lessened, and hence in order to have a type I defeater our evidence need not support the premises $S_1, \ldots, S_n$ of an argument for $\sim Q$ as strongly as if there were no diminishers. In other words, the support of $S_1, \ldots, S_n$ need only be as strong as the diminished support that Q receives from its positive instances conjoined with the diminishers that occur in the evidence.

We can schematize type I defeaters as follows. Our inductive evidence consists of observing a class Γ of (at least possible) A's and seeing that they are all B's, i.e., $(x)(x \varepsilon \Gamma \supset .Ax \ \& \ Bx)$. Let us abbreviate this as "$\Gamma(A, B)$". Let S be the conjunction of all type II diminishers entailed by the total evidence. Then the confirmation of $(x)(Ax \Longrightarrow Bx)$ is defeated if our total set of evidence also supports some statements $S_1, \ldots, S_n$ as strongly as $[\Gamma(A, B) \ \& \ S]$ supports $(x)(Ax \Longrightarrow Bx)$, and $(S_1 \ \& \ldots \& \ S_n) \rightarrow \sim Q$. Let us define:

(4.2) $\mathrm{Dft}_1(P, \Gamma, (x)(Ax \Longrightarrow Bx))$ iff, if S is the conjunction of type II diminishers entailed by P, then there are statements $S_1, \ldots, S_n$ such that P supports each S_i at least as strongly as $[\Gamma(A, B) \ \& \ S]$ supports $(x)(Ax \Longrightarrow Bx)$, and $(S_1 \ \& \ldots \& \ S_n) \rightarrow \sim (x)(Ax \Longrightarrow Bx)$.

Then P contains a type I defeater for the confirmation of $(x)(Ax \Longrightarrow Bx)$ by $\Gamma(A, B)$ iff $\mathrm{Dft}_1(P, \Gamma, (x)(Ax \Longrightarrow Bx))$.

Type I defeaters defeat the confirmation truth-functionally, by showing that the generalization must be false. But these are not the only defeaters operative in enumerative induction. There are also type II defeaters. These defeat the confirmation by attacking the fairness of the inductive sample. For example, suppose we are examining bananas to see whether they contain vitamin C. We examine several, find no vitamin C, and on that basis we conclude that bananas are devoid of that vitamin. But then it is pointed out that we only examined green bananas, and that even those fruits which are rich in vitamin C contain very little until they ripen. This indicates that our sample was not a fair sample—it was prejudiced in favor of finding no vitamin C. If the sample is just a little biased, this will not completely defeat the confirmation, but it at least diminishes the degree of confirmation. What we have here is a diminisher rather than a defeater. These diminishers take the following form. Our sample consists of a set Γ of objects all of which are A's, and we observe that they are all B's. This is supposed to confirm the generalization that all A's are B's. But then we observe (1) that all members of Γ were also C's, (2) that it is not true that all A's are C's (more accurately, $\sim (x)(Ax \Rrightarrow Bx)$), and (3) that A's which are C's are more likely to be B's than are A's which are not C's. For convenience, I will use the notation of the probability calculus and abbreviate clause 3 as: $\text{prob}(B/A \,\&\, C) > \text{prob}(B/A \,\&\, \sim C)$. However, I do not wish to assume that the likelihoods involved here are really subject to numerical computation. I would rather stay neutral on that subject.

As a second example of these diminishers, suppose we are examining cars with the objective of establishing that no car can go faster than 100 miles an hour. Suppose this is true of every car in our sample. This would confirm the generalization. But if we notice (1) that all cars in the sample have small engines, (2) that not all cars have small engines, and (3) that the probability of a car's having a top speed less than 100 miles an hour is greater if the car has a small engine than if it has a large engine, this significantly weakens the degree of confirmation.

Our characterization of these diminishers is not yet entirely adequate. It is necessary to put a restriction on the predicate C. The difficulty is that if there is some attribute F which everything in Γ possesses but not all A's possess, then we could define Cx to be $(Fx \,\&\, Bx)$. And we can always find such an F. For example, we might let Fx be '$x\varepsilon\Gamma$'. Clearly, this should not diminish the confirmation (if it did, all confirmation would be diminished). It seems that the restriction we need on C is: the way in which we know that $(x)(x\varepsilon\Gamma \supset Cx)$ does not presuppose our first knowing that $(x)(x\varepsilon\Gamma \supset Bx)$. A more precise formulation of this restriction must await a satisfactory analysis of knowing, which I am not now prepared to give.

Also, to avoid similar difficulties, it must be understood that the probability involved in condition 3 is the probability prior to knowing that everything in Γ is B. Otherwise, we could let Cx be '$x\varepsilon\Gamma$', and we would have $\text{prob}(B/A \,\&\, C) = 1$.

These diminishers are themselves defeasible. If C satisfies conditions 1–3, but there is a stronger predicate C^* entailing C such that (1) $(x)(x\varepsilon\Gamma \supset C^*x)$, (2) $\sim (x)(Ax \Rrightarrow C^*x)$, and (3) $\text{prob}(B/A \,\&\, C^*) \leq \text{prob}(B/A \,\&\, \sim C^*)$, then the degree of confirmation is not diminished after all. For example, if the cars we examined had a normal power-to-weight ratio despite their small engines, and the probability of a car's having a top speed less than 100 miles an hour given that it has a small engine but a normal power-to-weight ratio is no greater than if it did not have a small engine but a normal power-to-weight ratio, then the sample is not biased after all. (Here C^* is "has a small engine but a normal power-to-weight ratio".)

Next notice that the fairness of a sample can be attacked by showing that it is biased in favor of just part of the generalization. Suppose we are attempting to confirm $(x)(Ax \Longrightarrow .Bx \ \& \ Cx)$. If the sample is biased in favor of just one of the predicates B or C, this diminishes the confirmation just as strongly as if it were biased in favor of the conjunction. For example, suppose once more that we are examining bananas, but now our conclusion is that bananas are low in both vitamin C and vitamin D. Suppose that green fruits are generally apt to be very low in vitamin C but extraordinarily high in vitamin D. Then the sample is biased in favor of the bananas being low in vitamin C but is also biased against their being low in vitamin D. These may be balanced out so that the sample is not biased against the conjunction that the bananas are low in both vitamin C and vitamin D. Nevertheless, we would take this as diminishing the confirmation. You cannot shore up a biased sample by adding to your hypothesis antecedently unlikely things that you have already found to be true. If the sample is biased in favor of any part of the hypothesis, this diminishes the confirmation just as much as if it were biased in favor of the whole hypothesis. Of course, if we delete that part of the hypothesis which the sample unfairly favors, we can still use the sample to confirm the remainder of the hypothesis, but that is a different matter. In general, we have the following:

(4.3) If S is a diminisher for the confirmation of $(x)(Ax \Longrightarrow Bx)$ by $\Gamma(A, B)$, then $[\Gamma(A, B \ \& \ C) \ \& \ S]$ supports $(x)\ (Ax \Longrightarrow .Bx \ \& \ Cx)$ no more strongly than $[\Gamma(A, B) \ \& \ S]$ supports $(x)\ (Ax \Longrightarrow Bx)$.

There is a special case in which diminishers become defeaters. This is the case in which $\text{prob}(B/A \ \& \ C) = 1 > \text{prob}(B/A \ \& \sim C)$. For example, suppose we are attempting to confirm that all wooden chairs are made of oak. To collect our sample we visit a furniture factory manufacturing wooden chairs. The sample bears out the hypothesis. But then we discover that this factory manufactures only oak furniture, and we know that this is not true of all factories manufacturing wooden chairs. This would make the sample completely useless, and hence defeat the confirmation. The reason the confirmation would be defeated seems to be the following. If we let C be "was manufactured in a factory producing only oak furniture", then a chair's having this attribute *entails* that it is oak, and hence $\text{prob}(B/A \mathbin{\&} C) = 1$. This means that the chairs we examined could not have been anything but oak because of the way the sample was chosen, and hence the generalization could not have been false of the sample. For this reason, there was no chance of the sample not bearing out the generalization. The generalization ran no risk in this case, and hence that the sample did bear it out in no way confirms the generalization. So in this case we have a genuine defeater rather than just a diminisher.

To shorten our writing tasks, let us define:

(4.4) $\Psi(C, \Gamma, A, B)$ is the proposition "$(x)(x\varepsilon\Gamma \supset Cx) \mathbin{\&} \sim (x)(Ax \Longrightarrow Cx) \mathbin{\&} \text{prob}(B/A \mathbin{\&} C) = 1 > \text{prob}(B/A \mathbin{\&} \sim C) \mathbin{\&} \sim (\exists C^*)[C^*x \rightarrow Cx \mathbin{\&} (x)(x\varepsilon\Gamma \supset C^*x) \mathbin{\&} \text{prob}(B/A \mathbin{\&} C^*) \leq \text{prob}(B/A \mathbin{\&} \sim C^*)]$ & the way in which we know that $(x)(x\varepsilon\Gamma \supset Cx)$ does not presuppose our first knowing that $(x)(x\varepsilon\Gamma \supset Bx)$".

Our fair sample defeaters are then propositions of the form $\Psi(C, \Gamma, A, B)$.[10]

Our inductive evidence consists of observing that Γ consists of A's which are B's, i.e., $\Gamma(A, B)$. Then the confirmation of $(x)(Ax \Longrightarrow Bx)$ by this evidence is defeated by a proposition of the form $\Psi(C, \Gamma, A, B)$. However, this is not the only way it can be defeated by attacking the fairness of the sample. Just as in the case of diminishers, if B is itself the conjunction of two predicates, B_1 and B_2, then if the sample is prejudiced in favor of just one of these predicates, this still defeats the confirmation. For example, suppose once more that we are examining wooden chairs, but now

[10] I would propose that this characterization of defeaters is also adequate for the case in which our sample consists of *possible* A's that are B's. It may sound metaphysically outrageous to talk about a set Γ of possible objects, but all of this can be regarded as a shorthand way of saying that the physically possible way of producing A's that are B's would result in their also being C's, etc. This is the way $\Psi(C, \Gamma, A, B)$ is to be understood in such a case.

our conclusion is that they are both made of oak and have wicker seats. Once more, our sample comes from a factory producing only oak furniture. Then, although $\text{prob}(B_1/A \,\&\, C) = 1$, we would not expect to have $\text{prob}(B_1 \,\&\, B_2/A \,\&\, C) = 1$. Nevertheless, we would take the confirmation to be defeated. You cannot shore up a biased sample by adding unlikely things to your hypothesis. If the sample is prejudiced in favor of any part of the hypothesis, this defeats the confirmation. In general, defeaters which attack the fairness of the sample are propositions entailing $\Psi(C, \Gamma, A, B^*)$, where B^* is some predicate which is part of (i.e., entailed by) B. Let us define:

(4.5) $\text{Dft}_2(P, \Gamma, C, B^*, (x)(Ax \Longrightarrow Bx))$ iff $\{(B \rightarrow B^*) \,\&\, [P \rightarrow \Psi(C, \Gamma, A, B^*)]\}$.

These type II defeaters, together with the type I defeaters already noted, exhaust the defeaters for inductive confirmation. Consequently, we can define direct confirmation by saying that P directly confirms $(x)(Ax \Longrightarrow Bx)$ just in case P entails (possible) positive instances of $(x)(Ax \Longrightarrow Bx)$ and entails no defeaters. We must also require that $(Ax \Longrightarrow Bx)$ be "projectible". The meaning, and the reason, for this final requirement will be explained in the next section.

(4.6) *P directly confirms* $(x)(Ax \Longrightarrow Bx)$ iff $(Ax \Longrightarrow Bx)$ is projectible and $(\exists \Gamma)\{[P \rightarrow \Gamma(A, B)] \,\&\, \sim \text{Dft}_1(P, \Gamma, (x)(Ax \Longrightarrow Bx)) \,\&\, \sim (\exists C)(\exists B^*)\, \text{Dft}_2(P, \Gamma, C, B^*, (x)(Ax \Longrightarrow Bx))\}$.

Because of the particular nature of the defeaters involved in direct confirmation, it is possible to give a much simpler definition of instance confirmation than that provided by 4.1. In effect, clause 3 of 4.1 is rendered redundant by the character of type I defeaters:

(4.7) P instantially confirms Q iff there are statements $R_1, \ldots, R_n$ directly confirmed by P such that $(R_1 \,\&\, \ldots \,\&\, R_n) \rightarrow Q$.

Proof: If P instantially confirms Q, then the right side of 4.7 holds by 4.1. Conversely, if P directly confirms R, then P instantially confirms R. This is because if there were $S_1, \ldots, S_m$ supported by P as strongly as P supports R, and $(S_1 \,\&\, \ldots \,\&\, S_m) \rightarrow \sim R$, then we would have a type I defeater and P would not directly confirm R. And

> by theorems 2.5 and 2.6, anything entailed by a conjunction of instantially confirmed statements will also be instantially confirmed.

Thus, although we could not define the general concept of confirmation to be the deductive closure of elementary confirmation, we can define the more restrictive concept of instance confirmation as the deductive closure of direct confirmation. This completes our analysis of direct confirmation, and hence of instance confirmation.

Finally, let us return to the paradox of the ravens. This paradox can be resolved by appealing to our results concerning fair sample defeaters. The paradox arises because observation of non-A's that are non-B's directly confirms $(x)(\sim Bx \Longrightarrow \sim Ax)$, and hence instantially confirms $(x)(Ax \supset Bx)$. This becomes paradoxical when our sample consists, for example, of green plastic garbage cans, and we take that to confirm that all ravens are black. But, as Hempel observed, if we change examples this no longer seems so paradoxical. Consider "All good conductors of electricity are good conductors of heat". It is not in the least paradoxical to suppose we can confirm this by finding substances that are not good conductors of heat and ascertaining that they are not good conductors of electricity either. Furthermore, if we shift the setting a bit it is not paradoxical to suppose we can confirm that all ravens are black by observing non-black non-ravens. Suppose we are somehow provided with a catalog of everything in the universe listing certain of their important properties. If we go through the catalog picking out non-black things and then checking that they are not ravens, it certainly seems that we could confirm that all ravens are black.

Then why is it paradoxical to suppose we can confirm that all ravens are black by going to a garbage-can factory and checking that the cans are all green as they come out? I think the answer is that observation of green garbage cans really does not confirm that all ravens are black. More precisely, although "*c* is a non-black non-raven" directly confirms "All non-black things are non-ravens", "*c* is a green garbage can" does not, despite the fact that it entails "*c* is a non-black non-raven". The explanation is in terms of fair sample defeaters. Suppose our sample consists of green plastic garbage cans. The probability of being a non-raven given that something is a green plastic garbage can is 1. Thus our sample of non-black non-ravens is totally prejudiced against finding any ravens in it. There was never any chance of finding any ravens in it, so we have a fair sample defeater. This is why, intuitively, we would not regard this sample as confirming either that all ravens are black or that all non-black things are non-ravens. Thus we resolve the paradox of the ravens.

On the other hand, if we pick our sample of non-black things randomly from a catalog of everything in the universe, we will not automatically prejudice our sample against ravens, and for this reason we feel no reluctance about taking it to confirm that all ravens are black.

Also, we are now in a position to explain the often-voiced intuition that the reason it is harder to confirm that all ravens are black by looking at non-black things than it is by looking at ravens is that the proportion of non-black things in the universe is so much greater than the proportion of ravens. Because there are so many more non-black things, unless we pick our sample very selectively (e.g., choose only birds), it is very likely that we will find everything in our sample to have some attribute *C* which entails that it is not a raven. For example, picking things at random we are quite apt to end up with only inanimate objects, because most objects are inanimate, and a sample of non-black inanimate objects cannot confirm that all ravens are black.

It seems that there are really two paradoxes of the ravens. The original paradox concerned how observation of non-black non-ravens can confirm that all ravens are black. This paradox is resolved by appealing to fair sample defeaters. However, Hempel compounded the paradox by giving an incorrect explanation of it which then led him to maintain that observation of black non-ravens also confirms that all ravens are black. The latter is simply wrong, and arises out of supposing that the generalizations that are confirmed inductively are properly symbolized with material conditionals.

5. A Theory of Projectibility

5.1 *Nonprojectible Conditionals*

I have argued that some form of the Nicod principle is the only serious contender for a correct principle of induction. But now we come to what is the most serious difficulty for the Nicod principle. There are choices of the predicates A and B for which it clearly does not hold. Following Goodman [1955], let us say that the conditional $(Ax \Longrightarrow Bx)$ is *projectible* if it is directly confirmed by its positive instances. Contemporary philosophy owes a debt of gratitude to Goodman for bringing it irrevocably to our attention that there are conditionals which are not projectible. Goodman has pointed out at least three classes of nonprojectible conditionals:

1. In general, conditionals having disjunctive antecedents are not projectible. For example, consider the conditional "If x is either a mammal or a reptile then x is warm blooded". If this conditional were projectible, then having observed a number of warm blooded mammals we would have observed a number of positive instances of it, and so would have confirmation for the generalization of the conditional. But the generalization entails that all reptiles are warm blooded, so that would also have been confirmed. But surely observation of warm blooded mammals gives us no reason at all to think that all reptiles are warm blooded. Thus the conditional "If x is either a mammal or a reptile then x is warm blooded" is not projectible.

2. Goodman showed how to construct a class of peculiar predicates, which we can call "Goodmanesque" predicates, which in general cannot enter into projectible conditionals. Letting t be some particular time, e.g., 1:00 a.m., January 1, A.D. 2000, and given two predicates A and B, we can define a new predicate to mean

> x is now A, and it is now earlier than t, or x is now B, and it is not now earlier than t.

Using this format, we can define the Goodmanesque predicates "grue" (green now and it is now earlier than t, or blue now and it is not now earlier than t), "bleen" (blue/green), "gred" (green/red), "emeruby" (emerald/ruby), "condulates" (conducts electricity/does not conduct electricity). These predicates generate counterexamples to the Nicod principle. For example, consider the conditional "If x is an emerald then x is grue". Having observed many green emeralds, we have also observed many grue emeralds (given that it is now earlier than t, an emerald is grue iff it is green). If this confirmed the generalization that all emeralds are grue, then it would confirm the conclusion that all emeralds after t will be blue. But the observation of green emeralds certainly does not confirm that conclusion. Thus these Goodmanesque predicates cannot enter into projectible conditionals, except perhaps in some extraordinary ways.

3. There are also some quite ordinary predicates that are excluded from projectible conditionals. Examples would be "has been observed" or "existed prior to t". It is certainly true that all the emeralds we have observed have been observed, but this in no way confirms the generalization that all the emeralds there are have been observed. Similarly, all the robins we have observed have existed prior to the year 2000, but this gives us no reason to think there will be no new robins born after that time.

These examples indicate that the Nicod principle cannot be maintained in its full generality. On the other hand, it seems clear that for some choices of A and B it can be maintained. Some conditionals are projectible, and others are not. To get a correct account of inductive reasoning, we must give a characterization of those conditionals which are projectible, and then restate the Nicod principle so that it is restricted to those conditionals. This is why we defined direct confirmation as we did.

The discovery of nonprojectible conditionals was a surprising one, but once they have been pointed out we can see that we should have expected there to be nonprojectible conditionals. In the introduction to this chapter, I argued that induction receives its validity from the fact that principles of induction are built into the justification conditions of our concepts. But there is no reason why induction should have to be built into the justification conditions of all our concepts. It should be quite possible to have concepts which cannot be handled inductively, and these are precisely the ones that generate nonprojectible conditionals. If this is correct, it explains very simply why there are nonprojectible conditionals.

Goodman has shown that there are some nonprojectible conditionals. At this point it still seems likely that most conditionals are projectible, with only a few pathological ones failing to be projectible. However, in what follows it will be shown that *most* conditionals fail to be projectible. Most, and perhaps all, conditionals can be confirmed inductively, but only in ways more complex than countenanced by the Nicod principle. The projectible conditionals are those that receive their projectibility directly from the justification conditions of certain fundamental concepts into which the Nicod principle is built. Other conditionals can be dealt with inductively only insofar as this is a logical consequence of the projectibility of projectible conditionals.

In order to defend the above account, I will divide the theory of projectibility into two parts. On any theory of projectibility there will be the *basic projectible conditionals* which receive their projectibility directly from whatever the ultimate source of projectibility may be. Then by performing various logical operations on these basic projectible conditionals we can construct new projectible conditionals, and possibly other conditionals that are not projectible but can be dealt with inductively in more complex ways. Thus we can ask two questions: (1) Where do the basic projectible conditionals come from? (2) What logical operations allow us to construct new projectible conditionals from old ones, and by what means can we confirm nonprojectible conditionals that are built out of projectible ones? The answer to the second question constitutes the *logic of projectibility*. It is convenient to discuss the logic of projectibility before discussing the source of basic projectible conditionals, because this will give us some insight into the way projectibility functions. However, before we can do either we must construct a precise definition of projectibility.

5.2 *The Definition of Projectibility*

Roughly, projectible conditionals are those whose universal generalizations are directly confirmed by their positive instances. However, we cannot use "directly confirmed" in defining "projectible", because direct confirmation was defined in terms of projectibility. But we can use the more general notions of confirmation and elementary confirmation. A natural first attempt at defining "A/B" ("B is projectible with respect to A") would be:

$$A/B \text{ iff } (Aa \,\&\, Ba) \text{ elementarily confirms } (x)(Ax \Longrightarrow Bx).$$

However, this is not quite good enough. We want projectible conditionals to be elementarily confirmed by evidence containing their positive instances just in case that evidence directly confirms them.

This is what the notion of direct confirmation was intended to capture. The difficulty with the definition of projectibility proposed above is that $(Aa \,\&\, Ba)$ might elementarily confirm $(x)(Ax \Rightarrow Bx)$ only "indirectly" in the sense that $(Aa \,\&\, Ba)$ entails a positive instance of some more general conditional that entails $(x)(Ax \Rightarrow Bx)$. For example, let us define the Goodmanesque predicate "copronium" (copper/zirconium). Then the conditional (metal(x) & copronium(x). $\Rightarrow$ x conducts electricity) should not be considered projectible. If we already know that some metal does not conduct electricity, then observing copper which now conducts electricity in no way confirms the conclusion that zirconium after the year 2000 will conduct electricity. On the other hand, if c is a piece of copper, then "metal(c) & copronium(c) & c conducts electricity" does confirm the generalization that all pieces of metal which are copronium conduct electricity. In other words, the latter conditional is confirmed by its positive instances. This is because "metal(c) & copronium(c) & c conducts electricity" entails "metal(c) & c conducts electricity", which confirms "All metal conducts electricity", and the latter entails "All pieces of metal which are copronium conduct electricity". Thus, although the latter conditional is confirmed by its positive instances, this confirmation is "inherited" from the confirmation of "All metal conducts electricity" and hence is defeated by finding a single piece of metal, say a piece of nickel, which does not conduct electricity. If "All pieces of metal which are copronium conduct electricity" were *directly* confirmed by its positive instances, its confirmation should not be defeated by finding a piece of metal that is not copronium which does not conduct electricity, because this is not an instance of any of the kinds of defeaters built into the concept of direct confirmation. Thus, if our definition of projectibility is to capture this intuitive notion, it must preclude the existence of such defeaters as this. This can be accomplished by simply listing the conditions under which evidence containing positive instances of $(x)(Ax \Rightarrow Bx)$ may fail to confirm $(x)(Ax \Rightarrow Bx)$. This can happen only if the evidence contains either a type I or a type II defeater. Thus we can define projectibility as follows:

(5.1) A/B iff for any statement P and set Γ, if $P \rightarrow \Gamma(A, B)$ but P does not confirm $(x)(Ax \Rightarrow Bx)$, then either $\mathrm{Dft}_1(P, \Gamma, (x)(Ax \Rightarrow Bx))$ or $(\exists C)(\exists B^*)\ \mathrm{Dft}_2(P, \Gamma, B^*, (x)(Ax \Rightarrow Bx))$.

5.3 *The Logic of Projectibility*

Given our definition of projectibility, it becomes possible to establish a number of formal results. The major result will be that very few conditionals are projectible. However, it will also be shown that nonprojectible conditionals can be instantially confirmed, but not by using the Nicod principle. The way in which such a conditional can be confirmed will depend upon the conditional.

5.3.1 *Closure conditions for projectibility.* Now we can establish some simple results concerning how new projectible conditionals can be built out of conditionals we already know to be projectible. First, from theorem 2.5 and the definition of projectibility we have two equivalence principles. Letting "$\longleftrightarrow$" symbolize logical equivalence:

(5.2) *Theorem*: A/B & $B \longleftrightarrow C. \supset A/C.$

(5.3) *Theorem*: B/C & $A \longleftrightarrow B. \supset A/C.$

Next we prove that projectibility is closed under the conjunction of consequents:

(5.4) *Theorem*: If A/B and A/C then $A/(B \& C)$.

Proof:[11] Suppose A/B and A/C. Suppose $P \rightarrow \Gamma(A, B \& C)$, and $\sim$ $\mathrm{Dft}_1(P, \Gamma, (x)(Ax \equiv> .Bx \& Cx))$, and $\sim (\exists D)(\exists B^*)\ \mathrm{Dft}_2(P, \Gamma, B^*, (x)(Ax \equiv> .Bx \& Cx))$.

$\Gamma(A, B \& C) \rightarrow \Gamma(A, B)$, so $P \rightarrow \Gamma(A, B)$. Suppose $\mathrm{Dft}_1(P, \Gamma, (x)(Ax \equiv> Bx))$. Let S be the conjunction of type II diminishers entailed by P for the confirmation of $(x)(Ax \equiv> Bx)$ by $\Gamma(A, B)$. Then there are $S_1, \ldots,$ S_n supported by P at least as strongly as $[\Gamma(A, B) \& S]$ supports $(x)(Ax \equiv> Bx)$, and $(S_1 \& \ldots \& S_n) \rightarrow$ $\sim (x)(Ax \equiv> Bx)$. Then $(S_1 \& \ldots \& S_n) \rightarrow \sim (x)(Ax$

[11] As we are dealing with counterfactual conditionals, some of the logical moves made here and on the following pages may seem suspicious. For the rather strong counterfactuals symbolized by "$\equiv>$", the following principles seem to be true, and I assume them: (1) If $(P \equiv> R)$ and $(Q \equiv> R)$, then $(P \vee Q. \equiv> R)$; (2) if $(P \equiv> Q)$ and $(P \equiv> R)$, then $(P \equiv> .Q \& R)$; (3) if $(P \equiv> Q)$ and $(Q \rightarrow R)$, then $(P \equiv> R)$; (4) if $(P \& \sim Q. \equiv> R)$, then $(P \equiv> .Q \vee R)$.

$\Rightarrow .Bx \& Cx)$. $[\Gamma(A, B) \& S]$ supports $(x)(Ax \Rightarrow Bx)$ as strongly as $[\Gamma(A, B \& C) \& S]$ supports $(x)(Ax \Rightarrow .Bx \& Cx)$, by principle 4.3. Thus $\mathrm{Dft}_1(P, \Gamma, (x)(Ax \Rightarrow .Bx \& Cx))$, which is contrary to supposition.

Suppose that for some D, B^*, $\mathrm{Dft}_2(P, \Gamma, D, B^*, (x)(Ax \Rightarrow Bx))$. Then $B \rightarrow B^*$ and $\Psi(D, \Gamma, A, B^*)$. But then $(B \& C) \rightarrow B^*$, so $\mathrm{Dft}_2(P, \Gamma, D, B^*, (x)(Ax \Rightarrow .Bx \& Cx))$, which is contrary to supposition.

Therefore, P confirms $(x)(Ax \Rightarrow Bx)$. Similarly, P confirms $(x)(Ax \Rightarrow Cx)$. Thus P confirms $[(x)(Ax \Rightarrow Bx) \& (x)(Ax \Rightarrow Cx)]$, and this conjunction is equivalent to $(x)(Ax \Rightarrow .Bx \& Cx)$. Consequently, $A/(B \& C)$.

Goodman's observation that disjunctive antecedents create difficulties gives us:

(5.5) There are A, B, C such that A/C, B/C, but not $(A \vee B)/C$.

This gives us the rather surprising conclusion that projectibility is not closed under contraposition:

(5.6) *Theorem*: There are D, E such that D/E but not $\sim E/\sim D$.

Proof: Suppose otherwise. Choose A, B, C as in 5.5. Then $\sim C/\sim A$ and $\sim C/\sim B$. By 5.4, $\sim C/(\sim A \& \sim B)$, and hence $\sim(\sim A \& \sim B)/\sim\sim C$. Finally, by theorems 5.2 and 5.3, $(A \vee B)/C$, which contradicts the choice of A, B, C.

Theorem 5.6 indicates that we must be a bit careful what logical operations we perform on projectible conditionals in attempting to construct new projectible conditionals. Some operations work, e.g., we can conjoin consequents, but there are also some natural operations, such as contraposition, which do not work. Let us look at other natural operations.

When we refute a generalization of the form $(x)(Ax \Rightarrow Bx)$ by finding a counterexample, we often try to salvage things by either weakening the consequent or strengthening the antecedent. This suggests two possible principles: (1) $A/B \supset (A \& C)/B$; (2) $A/B \supset A/(B \vee C)$. Unfortunately, both of these principles fail. Using Goodmanesque predicates, we can easily construct counterexamples. For example, we have already seen that although (metal$(x) \Longrightarrow x$ conducts electricity) is projectible, (metal(x) & copronium$(x). \Longrightarrow x$ conducts electricity) is not projectible. Thus proposal 1 fails. It is equally simple to construct counterexamples to proposal 2.

It is natural to suggest that what went wrong with proposals 1 and 2 is that they were stated so generally as to allow the use of Goodmanesque predicates. Perhaps if they are stated in such a way that only projectible predicates are allowed, they will be true: (3) $A/C \,\&\, B/C. \supset (A \,\&\, B)/C$; (4) $A/B \,\&\, A/C. \supset A/(B \vee C)$. Proposal 3 may be correct. In fact, I conjecture that it is. However, proposal 4 fails. Astonishingly enough, projectibility is not closed under either the disjunction or the negation of consequents, nor is it under the formation of conditionals.

First, consider disjunctions. Suppose A/B and A/C. Suppose we have examined lots of A's, found many of them to be either B's or C's, and not ascertained of any A's that they are neither B's nor C's. Would we then be justified in thinking that all A's are either B's or C's? It might seem so, but consider more carefully. Suppose the way we proceeded was first to examine lots of A's to determine whether they were B's, and found that many were. But we did not go on to determine whether any of the A's that were not B's were C's. Analogously we examined lots of other A's and found that many were C's, but once again we did not go on to determine whether any of the A's that were not C's were B's. Under these circumstances, we have determined that many A's are either B's or C's, and have not determined that any A's are neither B's nor C's. But all we really know is that many A's are B's (and many are not), and many A's are C's (and many are not). There is no reason at all to think that the B's and C's exhaust the A's. To determine the latter, we must either examine many A's that are not B's and find that they are all C's, or examine many A's that are not C's and find that they are all B's. If we did this, we would get the desired result. But this is because we apparently have $(A \,\&\, {\sim} B)/C$ and $(A \,\&\, {\sim} C)/B$ and hence can determine inductively either that $(x)(Ax \,\&\, {\sim} Bx. \Longrightarrow Cx)$ or that $(x)(Ax \,\&\, {\sim} Cx. \Longrightarrow Bx)$. Either of these conditionals entails the conditional $(x)(Ax \Longrightarrow .Bx \vee Cx)$, so the latter can then be inferred logically. But the latter conditional cannot be confirmed directly by its positive instances. We must always deal indirectly with conditionals involving disjunctions, deriving them logically from other conditionals that are projectible. It follows that projectibility is not closed under the disjunction of consequents:

(5.7) There are A, B, C such that A/B and A/C but not $A/(B \vee C)$.

Nor is projectibility closed under the negation of consequents:

(5.8) *Theorem*: There are C/D such that C/D but not $C/\sim D$.
Proof: Suppose otherwise. Choose A, B, C as in 5.7. Then by hypothesis, $A/\sim B$ and $A/\sim C$, so by theorem 5.4, $A/(\sim B \ \& \sim C)$. By hypothesis again, $A/\sim(\sim B \ \& \sim C)$, and hence by theorem 5.2, $A/(B \vee C)$, which contradicts the choice of A, B, C.

Theorem 5.8 is surprising. I would have supposed initially that whenever it is possible to establish inductively that all *C*'s are *D*'s, it is also possible to establish inductively that no *C*'s are *D*'s, but this is precisely what is denied by theorem 5.8. The explanation for this will be seen in the next section.

Finally, we establish that projectibility is not closed under the formation of conditionals in the consequent:

(5.9) *Theorem*: There are C, D, E such that C/D, C/E, but not $C/(D \supset E)$.
Proof: Suppose otherwise. Choose A, B, C as in 5.7. Then by two applications of the hypothesis, $A/(B \supset C. \supset C)$. But $(B \supset C. \supset C)$ is equivalent to $(B \vee C)$, so $A/(B \vee C)$, which contradicts the choice of A, B, C.

5.3.2 *Some conjectures on projectibility.* We can pretty much sum up our discoveries regarding closure conditions for the consequents of projectible conditionals in two words: *Nothing works.* The only truth function we have found the consequents to be closed under is conjunction. Furthermore, closure under conjunction is of little practical importance. Whenever closure under conjunction allows us to establish a conditional $(x)(Ax \Rrightarrow .Bx \ \& \ Cx)$ inductively, we could just as well establish directly the two conditionals $(x)(Ax \Rrightarrow Bx)$ and $(x)(Ax \Rrightarrow Cx)$, and then infer

$(x)\ (Ax \Rrightarrow .Bx \,\&\, Cx)$ logically. Thus closure of the consequents under conjunction in no way increases the class of propositions that can be established inductively beyond what we have using those basic projectible conditionals with which we begin.

It seems likely that our basic projectible conditionals will be simple ones like (x is a raven $\Rrightarrow$ x has eight toes). Unfortunately, the universal generalizations of these simple conditionals are at least mostly false. In order to obtain useful projectible conditionals we must have ways of weakening these basic ones. This will involve either strengthening the antecedent or weakening the consequent. The most natural ways of weakening the consequent are by forming disjunctions or conditionals, but both of these moves are disallowed, by theorems 5.7 and 5.9. Let us turn instead to the possibility of strengthening the antecedent. The natural way to do this is by forming conjunctions. This takes us back to proposal 3, according to which if A/C and B/C then $(A \,\&\, B)/C$. I will state this as a formal conjecture:

(5.10) *Conjecture*: If A/C and B/C then $(A \,\&\, B)/C$.

This will give us more complicated conditionals like (x is a two-footed raven $\Rrightarrow$ x has eight toes), which will at least have more chance of having true universal generalizations. It seems that we must also be allowed to introduce the negations of predicates into the antecedents of projectible conditionals. This suggests another principle: (5) If A/B then $\sim A/B$. However, if we assume conjecture 5.10, we can easily prove that proposal 5 is false:

(5.11) *Theorem*: If conjecture 5.10 is true, then there are D, E such that D/E but not $\sim D/E$.

Proof: Suppose otherwise. Choose A, B, C as in theorem 5.5. Then by hypothesis, $\sim A/C$ and $\sim B/C$, so $(\sim A \,\&\, \sim B)/C$, and hence $\sim(\sim A \,\&\, \sim B)/C$. Hence by theorem 5.3, $(A \vee B)/C$, which contradicts the choice of A, B, C.

Proposal 5 is incorrect, but certainly we must be allowed to get negations in somehow. The trouble with proposal 5 is that it allowed us to negate conjunctions, thus forming disjunctions. It still seems reasonable to suppose that we can insert the negations of "simple" predicates into the antecedents. In an attempt to sort this out, I will now make a more far-reaching conjecture which, if correct, will explain just how negations can enter into projectible conditionals.

From this point on, I am going to restrict my attention to conditionals formulated exclusively from monadic predicates. A comprehensive treatment of projectibility would require discussion of more complicated conditionals, but that will not be attempted here. Among this restricted class of conditionals, examination of those which can plausibly be regarded as basic projectible conditionals yields the result that whenever $(Ax \Longrightarrow Bx)$ is such a conditional, so is $(Bx \Longrightarrow Ax)$. Furthermore, whenever $(Ax \Longrightarrow Bx)$ and $(Cx \Longrightarrow Dx)$ are such conditionals, so is $(Ax \Longrightarrow Dx)$; whatever is projectible with respect to one predicate is projectible with respect to any other predicate which enters into basic projectible conditionals. This implies that in constructing basic projectible conditionals, we simply begin with a class Π of "projectible predicates", and then any conditional $(Ax \Longrightarrow Bx)$ such that $A, B \varepsilon \Pi$ is a basic projectible conditional. In other words, it is not the conditionals themselves that are basic, but rather the class Π of raw material from which the conditionals are constructed. Against this it may be urged that projectibility is always relative, and that a predicate may be projectible with respect to one predicate and not with respect to another. To support this contention, one would presumably appeal to conditionals like (emerose(x) $\Longrightarrow$ gred(x)) which have been mentioned a number of times in the recent literature.[12] The argument is that this conditional (or more precisely, its universal generalization) is *lawlike*, in the sense of being a counterfactual, so it must be projectible. But why assume that lawlike conditionals are always projectible? This assumption apparently comes from Goodman, and has been accepted uncritically even by his dissenters. But it is obviously incorrect. The conditional (emerose(x) $\Longrightarrow$ gred(x)) is clearly not projectible. Having examined a number of emeralds prior to the year 2000 and found them all to be green, it does not follow that we have any reason at all for thinking that all roses examined after the year 2000 will be red. There is a clear distinction between projectibility and lawlikeness. It seems that all projectible conditionals are lawlike, but the converse is not true.

[12] See Davidson [1966].

I assume then that we begin with the class Π of predicates, and construct the antecedents and consequents of projectible conditionals out of members of Π. It seems clear that in constructing the antecedents of projectible conditionals, we should be allowed to conjoin members of Π to get long conjunctions. This is in accordance with conjecture 5.10. In addition, by virtue of theorem 5.4, consequents can be constructed by conjoining members of Π. What about negations? It seems clear that we can put negations of members of Π into both the antecedents and consequents. For example, (raven(x) & non-black(x). ⇛> white(x)) and (raven(x) ⇛> x cannot see colors) are certainly projectible. On the other hand, disjunctions, conditionals, etc., must be excluded. This leads to the following all-encompassing conjecture:

(5.12) *Conjecture*: There is a class Π of predicates such that for all A, B, A/B iff A and B are each equivalent to conjunctions of members of Π and negations of members of Π.

It is worth mentioning that Π will contain a general predicate "thing" true of everything, so that a hypothesis like "Everything is orange" (were it true) could be discovered to be true by observing lots of things that are orange and nothing that is non-orange. Such hypotheses can be considered degenerate conditionals.

5.3.3 *Indirect confirmation.* Not all generalizations (constructed from monadic predicates) that are established inductively have the form of conditionals that are projectible by conjecture 5.12, but those which do not can plausibly be regarded as being deduced logically from conditionals that are projectible according to that conjecture. For example, consider the nonprojectible "All pulsars are either neutron stars or white dwarfs". This cannot be confirmed simply by observing pulsars which are either neutron stars or white dwarfs, but it is entailed by "All pulsars which are not neutron stars are white dwarfs", and so can be confirmed indirectly by confirming the latter.

This way of dealing inductively with nonprojectible conditionals can be generalized as follows. To simplify the discussion let us recast things in an artificial language which is a monadic predicate calculus containing the additional connective "⇛>" and having as primitive predicates just the members of Π. This puts extreme limitations on what we can express, but it makes it possible to prove some theorems rather easily. The task of extending these theorems to richer languages is left for another time.

Let us define:

(5.13) $A//B$ ("B is pseudoprojectible with respect to A") iff $(Ax \Rrightarrow Bx)$ is entailed by a conjunction of projectible conditionals.

Pseudoprojectible conditionals are those that can be confirmed inductively, although not necessarily by observing A's which are B's. Assuming conjecture 5.12, it is trivial to show that every quantifier-free conditional (containing no individual constants) in our language is pseudoprojectible:

(5.14) *Theorem*: If A, B are any quantifier-free formulas of our language which contain no individual constants, then $A//B$.

A *simple universal sentence* is any sentence of the form $(x)Px$ where Px is a formula containing no quantifiers and no individual constants. A *simple existential sentence* is a sentence of the form $(\exists x)Px$ where Px is a formula containing no quantifiers and no individual constants. A *singular sentence* is one containing no quantifiers (hence all argument places of predicates are occupied by individual constants). Singular and simple existential sentences can be verified noninductively (except insofar as one may have to proceed inductively to determine that one of the predicates applies to a certain object). Every simple universal sentence is equivalent to the universal generalization of a quantifier-free material conditional containing no individual constants, and hence is entailed by a pseudoprojectible conditional, so it follows from theorem 5.14 that every simple universal sentence is amenable to at least indirect inductive confirmation. Furthermore, it is a well-known fact that in the monadic predicate calculus every sentence is equivalent to a truth-functional combination of simple universal, simple existential, and singular sentences. Therefore, it follows that *every* sentence of our language which cannot be verified directly is subject to at least indirect inductive confirmation. This is just what we would have expected initially. The negative theorems of section 5.3.1 do not constitute any real limitations on what we can confirm inductively. What they mean instead is that the way we must proceed in inductive confirmation is more complex than philosophers have traditionally realized. It is only the exceptional hypothesis that can be confirmed simply by observing positive instances of it. Although this is a rather radical departure from traditional confirmation theory, it is entirely in accordance with actual inductive practice. Once pointed out, the examples of non-projectible conditionals are all quite obvious. No scientist would ever dream of doing any of the things our theorems say he mustn't.

It must be pointed out that the positive results of this section have been established only for the simple case of a monadic predicate calculus in which the atomic predicates are members of Π. It seems likely that they can be extended to more complicated languages, but this has yet to be done. In particular, I would conjecture that in languages of arbitrary complexity it will remain true that every sentence is subject to at least indirect inductive confirmation. For example, "All emeralds are grue" cannot be formulated in our language, but there are circumstances under which even it would be regarded as inductively confirmed. It certainly cannot be confirmed by observing grue emeralds, but it could be confirmed by observing green emeralds and finding that due to some strange chemical condition they are all going to turn blue precisely at the turn of the century.

5.4 *Basic Projectibility*

We have divided the theory of projectibility into two parts—the logic of projectibility, and the theory of basic projectible conditionals. Although the last section was about the logic of projectibility, we also learned something important about basic projectible conditionals. This is that they are constructed out of a set of *projectible predicates*[13] each of which can occupy any place in a projectible conditional that can be occupied by any other. Thus the theory of basic projectibility is really the theory of projectible predicates. The question is, by virtue of what does a predicate come to be projectible?

There is a simple answer to how predicates come to be projectible. It is built into the justification conditions of a predicate

[13] Or more generally, projectible relations.

whether or not it is projectible, and hence is part of its meaning. For example, predicates ascribing perceptual attributes are projectible.[14] This arises out of their justification conditions in a very natural way. As we have seen, part of the justification conditions of perceptual attributes is that we can ascribe them to things on inductive grounds. If we could not do this, we would never be able to judge that an object is some color other than it looks, or differs in any way from the way it appears. This would make it impossible to establish any defeaters for the perceptual criteria involved in perceptual judgments, and the effect of this would be that such criteria would become conclusive reasons rather than merely prima facie reasons. But it is essential to the concepts of perceptual attributes that perception gives us only prima facie reasons for ascribing them to objects. Consequently, there are very fundamental reasons why we must be able to proceed inductively with respect to perceptual attributes, and hence why, simply by virtue of their meanings, predicates ascribing perceptual attributes must be numbered among the projectible predicates.

But then, why aren't nonprojectible predicates like "grue" projectible? Quite simply, because that is not part of their justification conditions. For example, "grue" is defined in terms of "blue" and "green", which are projectible, but the definition is not such as to preserve projectibility. Therefore, there is nothing to make "grue" projectible. Some modes of definition lead from projectible predicates to projectible predicates, and others do not. By way of illustration, it would seem that dispositions are projectible when defined in terms of manifest predicates which are projectible. But the mode of definition involved in constructing Goodmanesque predicates does not yield projectible predicates. Thus Goodmanesque predicates fail to be projectible for the simple reason that their definitions do not normally force projectibility into the justification conditions of the predicates so defined.

Apparently there is nothing mysterious, or even particularly surprising, about nonprojectible predicates. Whether a predicate is projectible is part of its meaning in much the same way as its entailments are part of its meaning. Some predicates will naturally be projectible and others not, because projectibility is built into the meaning of some and not into the meaning of others.

[14] For the sake of brevity, I will say that the attributes themselves are projectible.

6. Projectibility and Induction

The preceding account of projectibility sheds a new light on the nature of inductive reasoning. The traditional view of induction was that it was comprised of some general principles of reasoning universally applicable to all concepts. As such, induction was viewed as somehow "standing above" our conceptual framework, on a par with deductive logic. It was this very generality that made it difficult to see why inductive reasons were good reasons and led to the traditional Problem of Induction. But it now appears that this picture is mistaken. There are no principles of induction applicable to all concepts. What it takes to inductively confirm a proposition depends entirely upon what proposition is being confirmed. Those general propositions which can be confirmed simply by applying the Nicod principle are the exception rather than the rule. The Nicod principle can only be used in connection with projectible predicates. And in that connection it is not some pre-eminent principle standing above them, but is built into them as part of their meaning. For example, that we can reason inductively with respect to a perceptual attribute like "red" is just part of the meaning of the concept "red", and is completely on a par with such other features of the concept as that being appeared to redly is a criterion. The Nicod principle and the perceptual criteria are just two different reasons which go into making up the justification conditions, and hence the meaning, of the concept "red". The only respect in which the Nicod principle is more general than the perceptual criterion is that the Nicod principle recurs in more concepts, but it certainly does not have the status of a general principle applicable to all concepts.

7. Theories and the Hypothetico-Deductive Method

Thus far, in discussing induction, we have found nothing which deserves to be considered a serious competitor to enumerative induction. However, there is one area in which, according to received dogma in the philosophy of science, enumerative induction is in principle inapplicable. According to this dogma we must distinguish between scientific *theories* and scientific *laws*. The latter can be established by enumerative induction, but not the former. According to the "received view", scientific theories take the form of complex hypotheses about entities which are in principle unobservable, and they relate the states of these unobservable ("theoretical") entities to observable states in the world. In effect, a theory is just an abstract calculus having observable consequences.[15] On this view, whatever meaning the theoretical terms (the terms referring to unobservables) may have must somehow come out of the axioms of the theory itself. One is led to talk about the axioms "implicitly defining" the theoretical terms. This is reminiscent of a formalist philosophy of mathematics. Alternatively, one can maintain that the theoretical terms have no meaning, but are just uninterpreted symbols of use in systematizing observational regularities. On this alternative, theories are just "black boxes" of use in predicting relations between observables. This alternative has often been called *instrumentalism.*

I am inclined to regard instrumentalism as the more defensible of these two alternatives. I do not think it makes sense to talk about the axioms "implicitly defining" the theoretical terms. In Chapter One, I defended the view that the meaning of a term or concept must be provided by either (1) the justification conditions for ascribing it to things, or (2) an explicit definition of it in terms of other concepts or terms. Neither alternative is possible for theoretical terms. As they refer to things that are supposed to be in principle unobservable, we are unable to ascribe them to anything, so the first alternative is ruled out. And no one seems to believe that we can give explicit definitions of theoretical terms in terms of observables. Thus I feel that if one holds the received view of theories, one ought to be an instrumentalist. However, I will rest nothing on this contention.

On the received view of theories, it obviously follows that we cannot use enumerative induction to confirm what the theory says about the theoretical entities. The theoretical entities are in principle unobservable, so the only thing we can check about the theory is its observational consequences. Thus we are led inexorably to the conclusion that the way to confirm scientific theories is to find out that their observational consequences are true. (One might add other desiderata for what makes a "good" theory—simplicity, breadth, etc.—but that will not make any difference to the present discussion.) This view of the confirmation of scientific theories is

[15] See, for example, Campbell [1920] and [1957], Carnap [1956], Hempel [1958], and Nagel [1961].

called the *hypothetico-deductive method.* Letting "$O(p)$" mean that p is an observation statement, the hypothetico-deductive method tells us that to confirm a theory T we must inductively confirm the generalization:

$$(7.1)\quad (p)[O(p)\ \&\ (T \rightarrow p).\supset p \text{ is true}].$$

In a sense, this is to reduce theories to enumerative induction. If you are an instrumentalist, you stop here, having confirmed that your black box works. But if you are a realist, you go on and infer the literal truth of the theory from 7.1, which is to go beyond enumerative induction.

My position on theories, so construed, is that there are none. What's more, *there could be none.*[16] There is a very simple reason why there could be no theories: the generalization 7.1 is not projectible. This can be seen as follows. Choose two theories, T and T^*, which agree on something but disagree on something else. Thus we have observation statements p and q such that $T \rightarrow p$ and $T^* \rightarrow p$, but $T \rightarrow q$ and $T^* \rightarrow \sim q$. If we suppose 7.1 to be projectible, then "$O(p)\ \&\ (T \rightarrow p)\ \&\ p$ is true" confirms $(p)[O(p)\ \&\ (T \rightarrow p).\supset p$ is true]. But "$O(p)$" and "$T \rightarrow p$" are truths of logic. Consequently, "$O(p)\ \&\ (T \rightarrow p)\ \&\ p$ is true" is logically equivalent to p. Hence (by principle 2.7) p confirms $(p)[O(p)\ \&\ (T \rightarrow p).\supset p$ is true]. The latter entails $[O(q)\ \&\ (T \rightarrow q).\supset q$ is true], so this is also confirmed by p. But the antecedent of this conditional is a truth of logic, so the conditional is equivalent to q. Therefore, p confirms q.[17] By applying the same argument to T^*, we obtain the result that p also confirms $\sim q$. But p is a contingent statement, and as such cannot possibly confirm both q and $\sim q$. If it did, it would confirm their conjunction $(q\ \&\ \sim q)$, and we have proven (theorem 2.8) that this is impossible.

[16] Of course, I do not want to deny that, on a more reasonable construal of the term "theory", there are theories. I think that as the term is ordinarily used, there is no sharp distinction between theories and laws. Theories are just more general and less well confirmed. If a theory becomes sufficiently well confirmed, it becomes a law. What I am primarily concerned to deny in saying that there are no theories is that we need any principles of confirmation besides enumerative induction.

[17] This itself seems manifestly absurd. If T is at all comprehensive, p and q may be statements about very different subject matters, ostensibly unrelated. Then p could not possibly confirm q.

Consequently, generalization 7.1 cannot be projectible. But this means that if there were any theories they could not be confirmed because there would be no way to find out that their observational consequences are all true. Such theories would be worthless. Obviously, the actual theories of science are not like this. Real scientific theories are not "theories" in the sense of the received view.

Is there any way to modify the received view of theories so that theories become confirmable? I take it to be essential to this view that theories are about theoretical entities which are in principle unobservable. So clearly enumerative induction will not work. We cannot confirm the hypotheses of a theory by enumerative induction, because we have no way (except by assuming the theory, which begs the question) of finding out that what the theory claims about theoretical entities is true in particular cases. The hypothetico-deductive method looks superficially like explanatory induction, so it might be supposed that we can confirm theories by explanatory induction. But that will not work either. In order to use explanatory induction we must know that the relations between theoretical entities hypothesized by the theory constitute a physically possible mechanism for producing the observable data. But if the entities discussed by the theory are truly unobservable, so that our only access to them is through the theory, then we have no way of knowing whether what the theory proposes about them is physically possible. On the other hand, if we drop the requirement in principle 3.4 (the principle of explanatory induction) that we know the physical possibility of the mechanism for producing the data, the resulting principle is equivalent to supposing that generalization 7.1 is projectible, so that is not defensible either. It must be concluded that there simply is no way to confirm theories insofar as they are about entities which are in principle unobservable.

It seems inescapable that the real theories of science must not be about entities that are unobservable in the strong sense supposed by the received view. This conclusion can be defended on grounds completely independent of those adduced above. First we must make clear just what it is that the received view is affirming and we are denying. I think that the strong sense of "unobservable" embodied in the received view can be made precise as claiming that the only way to know of the existence or the states of a theoretical entity is by first confirming the theory. There is no way to know the states of such an entity prior to confirming the entire theory. Any weaker notion of "unobservable" would make it possible to confirm a theory by enumerative induction by ascertaining that what it asserts about the theoretical entities is true in particular cases. This construal of the observable/unobservable distinction requires it to be a sharp logical distinction. It has to do with the concepts of the entities, and not merely with contingent facts about them.

It must be emphasized that "observable" (i.e., "not unobservable") is not the same thing as "perceivable". There may well be entities that we cannot perceive with our senses that are nevertheless observable because we can know of their states without having to confirm any theories by the hypothetico-deductive method. An example would be the molten core of the earth. We cannot see it, but we know a lot about it just by using enumerative induction and (derivatively) explanatory induction.

There are at least two arguments to the effect that the actual entities of science are not unobservable in this strong sense. The first is a "slippery slope" argument, and the second is an appeal to actual scientific practice. Among the actual entities of science, there is no place to draw the line between observable and unobservable entities. It is undeniable that there is something different about the observability of tables and neutrinos, and one is tempted to record this difference by saying that the former are observable and the latter are not. But there is a continuum between tables and neutrinos. If a one-celled organism can only be seen through a microscope, is it a theoretical entity or an observable entity? What if some people can see it with the naked eye but others only with a microscope? For example, very nearsighted people can see hydras with the naked eye by holding a sample of swamp water very close to their eyes. Surely this is enough to make the hydra observable. But if all the nearsighted people in the world were suddenly to die, would the hydra become a theoretical entity? Certainly not if the observable/unobservable distinction is to be a logical distinction. Thus we must admit that entities seen only through microscopes can be observable. Then what about those entities which cannot be seen through optical microscopes but can be detected using an electron microscope? Surely the limits of resolution of optical microscopes are only contingent, and as such cannot contribute to a logical distinction between observable and unobservable entities. But even a single uranium atom can be observed through an electron microscope. By progressing further we can observe even smaller entities—electrons, mesons, etc.—using less "visual" instruments. As we progress down the scale of size, the entities do in some sense become less readily observable, but there is no point at which it makes any sense to draw a sharp line and say that those above the line are observable and those below the line theoretical. There is simply no basis for any sharp distinction between observable and unobservable entities. Such a slippery-slope argument is not fatal to most distinctions, because most distinctions are not intended to be sharp. But it is essential to the observable/unobservable distinction that it be a sharp distinction of logical kind if it is to do the work required of it by the received view, and as such the slippery-slope argument is fatal. Of course, none of this is to deny that there are differences between different kinds of entities which might be marked by saying that some are observable and others unobservable; but these differences are only differences of degree and do not yield a sharp distinction, and more important, the differences are not such as to force upon us some entirely new principles of confirmation like the hypothetico-deductive method.

I think it must be concluded that the observable/unobservable distinction, as traditionally construed, is an untenable dichotomy, and accordingly the hypothetico-deductive method is a philosophers' fiction. But if we are not allowed to use the hypothetico-deductive method to confirm scientific theories, how are they to be confirmed? This only seems to be a problem when we accept the theoretical/observable dichotomy. We confirm scientific theories just as we confirm anything else—by using enumerative induction and (derivatively) explanatory induction. Once it is granted that there are no entities which are in principle unobservable, there is no reason why we cannot determine directly whether the principles of a theory hold in particular cases, and then by enumerative induction we can confirm the theory. For example, how was it discovered that negative electric charge comes in discrete bundles, subsequently dubbed "electrons"? Physicists began by confirming (by enumerative induction) various physical laws such as Coulomb's law, laws governing the motion of a particle through a fluid, etc. These laws were confirmed by observation of macroscopic objects. Then Millikan performed his famous oil-drop experiment in which small negatively charged oil drops were subjected to an electrostatic field opposing the force of gravity. By measuring their rate of fall in a gas of known viscosity, Millikan was able to calculate the charges on the oil drops, and he confirmed (by enumerative induction) that all of the oil drops bore charges which were integral multiples of a certain small value. He thus confirmed inductively that negative electric charge came in discrete units. This is characteristic of the way in which physicists first acquired knowledge about atoms, molecules, and subatomic particles. They simply applied laws they had already confirmed inductively by appealing to larger objects, and in this way acquired knowledge about particular microscopic events. They then used this knowledge to confirm general laws about the microscopic world. These laws were subsequently used to acquire more particular bits of knowledge about the microscopic world, which in turn were used to confirm more general laws, and so on. For example, how would a contemporary physicist set about trying to establish a generalization regarding the production of muons under bombardment of a target by energetic protons? He would perform experiments which, in light of principles that have already been confirmed, would give him knowledge about particular instances of muon production. He would then use enumerative induction to confirm his general principle.[18]

I would urge that examination of the history of physics indicates that physicists have never used anything but enumerative induction (and explanatory induction) in establishing general principles about the microscopic world. There is no need for recourse to the hypothetico-deductive method or anything else more abstruse than enumerative induction to account for the reasoning that actually occurred in the history of physics. To support this contention in detail is an enormous task, far beyond the scope of this book, but I hope that the above brief discussion has at least made it plausible.

[18] Notice that this common sort of scientific practice would be completely mysterious to an instrumentalist. According to him, "statements" about theoretical entities are just tokens devoid of meaning (and hence not really statements). As such it would be in principle impossible to discover some new "law" about theoretical entities by enumerative induction, although scientists do this all the time.

Accordingly, one cannot defend the hypothetico-deductive method by saying that it is necessary to account for actual scientific reasoning. There is no good reason to think that scientific reasoning, or any other reasoning, requires any principles of induction other than those embodied in enumerative induction.

Chapter Nine

The Concept of a Person

I WITNESS a man hit by a truck. He is writhing about on the pavement and screaming. The splintered ends of broken bones are projecting through his torn flesh, and he is lying in a pool of blood. Being a philosopher, I ask myself, "How do I know that he is in pain?"

This is representative of one type of problem regarding the concept of a person. The task of this chapter will be to analyze that concept. Pretty obviously, the concept of a person cannot be defined in terms of other purely physical concepts. It might be possible to analyze the concept of a person in terms of some mental concepts, but those mental concepts cannot themselves be defined in terms of physical concepts.[1] This means that among our mental concepts there must be some ostensive concepts. Those concepts can be explained in terms of their justification conditions, and perhaps in no other way. Then it will be argued that, like the concept of a physical thing, the analysis of the concept of a person consists of giving an account of the justification conditions of propositions about persons.

1. Theories Regarding Our Knowledge of Other Minds

We will begin the discussion of the concept of a person with one of the most venerable problems of philosophy: the problem of "other minds". In this section and the next I will consider how we can know that a person is in any particular mental state. For example, how do we know that the man hit by the truck is in pain?

[1] This, of course, presupposes the falsity of behaviorism, but that will be discussed in more detail in section 1.3.

More or less following Strawson,[2] I shall say that an *M-state* ("M" for "material") is any state definable in the language of physics, and a *P-state* ("P" for "person") is any non-M-state of a person. This means that even such states as "going for a walk" or "trying to scale the North American face of El Capitan" are P-states. A *P-attribute* is the attribute of being in a P-state, and a *P-concept* is the concept of a P-state. Not all P-states can reasonably be called "mental states", but the problem of how we can have knowledge of other minds is readily extended to the question of how we can know what P-states another person is in. Let us begin by surveying the traditional theories regarding this problem.

1.1 *The Argument from Analogy*

Consider a statement ascribing a P-state to a person, e.g., "Jones is in pain". How do we determine whether such a statement is true? A traditional answer to this question is provided by the *argument from analogy*. According to this argument I discover inductively, on the basis of my own case, that in certain circumstances certain M-states tend to be accompanied by pain. When I subsequently witness a person in those circumstances manifesting those M-states, I have an inductive reason for thinking that he is in pain.

There is a traditional response to this argument. It is claimed that it is a very weak induction because it is based upon a single instance—myself. I observe that something is true in one case, i.e., I observe that these M-states are accompanied by pain in myself, and I conclude that this is true of everyone. The standard reply to this objection is that it is not an induction based upon a single instance; rather, it is based upon all those cases where I have observed a person in those M-states and have been able to judge whether he was in pain. That those were all cases involving myself is irrelevant to the inductive argument.

I think we must side with the defenders of the argument from analogy in this dispute. Their detractors seem to be assuming that the fact that all my inductive evidence concerns myself defeats the inductive argument. It could only do so if this were a reason for thinking my inductive evidence was not based on a fair sample. But the mere fact that the sample in question (my P-states) *might* not

[2] Strawson [1959] talks about M-predicates and P-predicates. These are predicates ascribing M- and P-states respectively.

be characteristic of others is not sufficient to constitute a defeater. If that were a defeater, all inductive arguments (regardless of subject matter) would be defeated analogously—it is always true that a sample *might* be uncharacteristic. What is required, to have a defeater here, is some concrete reason for thinking my P-states and M-states are not characteristic of people in general.[3] In other words, the burden of proof is on the detractors to show that it makes a difference that all of the evidence concerns myself. They have not tried to do this, and certainly no general argument could be given to this effect. I think it must be concluded that this traditional attack on the argument from analogy involves a misconception about induction.

Let us turn now to a more sophisticated objection that has been made to the argument from analogy. This objection has been raised by Malcolm [1958], and he attributes it to Wittgenstein [1953]. We can recast the objection in our own terms as follows. Before we can have an inductive reason for believing a statement, that statement must, of course, be meaningful. As I argued in Chapter One, this means that either we must be able to characterize the meaning of the statement in terms of its justification conditions, or else we must be able to state the truth conditions of the statement in terms of other statements whose meanings can be characterized in terms of their justification conditions. If the argument from analogy provides the only way to acquire knowledge of other minds, then it follows that we cannot give such an account of the truth conditions of "Jones is in pain", so the meaning of that statement must be given by its justification conditions, i.e., by specifying what are logical reasons for believing it. In other words, in order for it to be possible to have an inductive reason for believing that a person is in pain, that statement must be meaningful, and so it must be possible to have a logical reason for believing that the person is in pain. Malcolm then reasons that if the argument from analogy were the only way of finding out that a person is in pain, then there would exist only inductive reasons for believing that; there would not exist logical reasons for the statement. But then the statement "Jones is in pain", having no logical reasons, would be meaningless, and hence the argument from analogy could not justify us in believing it either. Consequently, the argument from

[3] See section 4 of Chapter Eight for a more precise discussion of these "fair sample" defeaters.

analogy cannot explain how we can know that another person is in pain. It is only possible to have an inductive reason for believing that if it is also possible to have a more direct logical reason for believing it.

Malcolm's argument contains an unstated presupposition. This is that the inductive reason itself cannot both be a logical reason for thinking that a person is in pain and be sufficient to determine the justification conditions of that statement. The phrase "the inductive reason" can be taken to denote either (1) the statement that Jones is behaving in a certain way under certain circumstances, or (2) the statement under clause 1 together with all of the evidence we have for thinking that people who behave in that way under those circumstances are in pain. Waiving for the moment any qualms about whether this is a good induction, we find that clause 2 is a logical reason, while clause 1 is a contingent reason. Let us ask whether clause 2 can exhaust the justification conditions of the statement "He is in pain".

In general, it is clear that we could not have *only* an inductive reason for ascribing a particular concept to objects. In order to use enumerative induction, we must first ascertain in some *other* way that the concept tends to be correctly ascribable to things under certain circumstances. But of course, this condition is satisfied in the case of pain. We do not use an inductive argument to ascribe pain to ourselves, so we do not have *only* an inductive reason for ascribing pain to objects. It is just that we may have only an inductive reason for ascribing pain to certain objects, namely, to persons other than ourselves. Unless we can show that there is something wrong with this, Malcolm's argument cannot be made to work. I do not, at this point, see any way to demonstrate that there is anything wrong with this.

However, there is another difficulty with the argument from analogy. The defenders of this argument are proposing that we can explain our knowledge of other minds without introducing any new epistemic principles having to do specifically with the mental. They are maintaining that our reasons for attributing P-states to others are derivative from general principles of induction which are universally valid, applying to all subject matter. But, as we saw in the last chapter, the principles of induction are not universally valid. There are many concepts, like "grue" and "bleen", which are not projectible, i.e., for which the principles of induction do not work. It was argued that insofar as induction is applicable to a concept, this is because the principles of induction are built into the meaning of the concept as part of its justification conditions. When inductive reasoning works for different concepts, the inductive reasons are formally analogous in each case; but they are still different reasons which must be posited anew for each concept. There is no underlying rationale which simultaneously justifies all inductive reasoning. If induction is to be applicable to P-concepts, this must be because it is built directly into the justification conditions of certain P-concepts. Thus, even if the argument from analogy is correct, it does not succeed in *explaining* our knowledge of other minds—it merely *describes* that knowledge. To say that our knowledge of other minds is inductive is not to base it upon something we already have but to propose a partial analysis of P-concepts. Thus it becomes incumbent upon the defender of the argument from analogy to show that P-concepts really are projectible and to show that it is possible for us to acquire all the knowledge we have of other minds by appealing to induction. This is not something we can take for granted. In other words, we need another argument to defend the argument from analogy. Rather than attempting to provide such an argument now, I suggest that it is best to examine the alternatives to the argument from analogy.

1.2 *Scientific Realism*

The argument from analogy attempts to give an inductive justification for our beliefs regarding the P-states of others. There is another type of inductive approach to this same problem. Some philosophers have argued that our beliefs about the P-states of others constitute a theory which is justified by the hypothetico-deductive method.[4] I have already argued on general grounds that the hypothetico-deductive method is a philosophers' fiction and plays no true role in rationality. However, quite apart from that, there seems to be a devastating objection to the hypothetico-deductive method as a way of justifying our ascriptions of P-states to others. The problem is that if this were a correct account of our reasons for such ascriptions, it would make the P-states of others theoretical entities. On this account statements about the P-states of others would have no meaning independent of the theory—they

[4] For example, Castañeda [1966].

would be given their meaning by the theory. But when we say that someone else is in pain, we mean to ascribe to him the same thing we ascribe to ourselves when we say that we are in pain. "Pain" means the same thing in both cases. When we learn to talk about pains, we do not have to learn two different meanings—one for ourselves and one for others. This implies that statements about the P-states of others cannot be *given* their meaning by the theory. Thus scientific realism cannot be correct. The only possible inductive argument of use in ascribing P-states to others is the argument from analogy.

1.3 *Behaviorism*

It cannot be denied that behavior and other M-states and physical phenomena provide us with good reasons for ascribing P-states to other persons. That, after all, is the basis upon which we make such judgments. These reasons must be either contingent reasons or logical reasons. The position that they are contingent reasons is just the argument from analogy. Let us investigate the other possibility—that they are logical reasons. Because philosophers have not traditionally recognized the existence of nonconclusive logical reasons, those who have supposed these reasons to be logical have generally supposed them to be conclusive. In other words, they have supposed that statements about the P-states of persons are logically entailed by statements about their various M-states. This is *behaviorism.* Behaviorists have generally gone further and maintained that statements about P-states are not just entailed by statements about M-states but are in fact logically equivalent to the latter. This is because they knew of no way to generate entailments except from truth conditions, and truth conditions always yield equivalences rather than mere entailments. For this reason, behaviorists have traditionally maintained that it is possible to analyze the truth conditions of statements about P-states in terms of statements about M-states. However, I will consider the weaker view which simply asserts that there are entailments here, leaving open the question of whether they are generated by equivalences.

To my mind, and I think it is generally agreed, the biggest problem with behaviorism comes from considering first-person ascriptions of mental states. For example, according to the behaviorist, there is some complex M-attribute P such that, if I have that attribute, it follows logically that I am in pain. But there can be no M-attribute the possession of which *logically* guarantees that I will feel a pain. What I feel and the way I behave are simply two different things. I can *imagine* behaving entirely differently than I do, perhaps consistently feigning pain to perfection when in fact I really feel nothing. No statement about my M-states can logically guarantee that I have any sensation at all. Consequently, my being in pain cannot be entailed by any statement about my M-attributes, and behaviorism fails.

It is not my intention to claim that behavioristic analyses must *always* fail. There are some instances in which behavioristic analyses are much more plausible than in the case of pain. For example, it is not unreasonable to suppose that a behavioristic analysis of depression might be given. The most important part of being depressed seems to be how one acts, not how one feels. And even if it should turn out that all behavioristic analyses fail, I am quite certain that some statements about P-states at least entail statements about M-states. For example, "Jones is going for a walk" obviously entails something about Jones's M-states. But then it also follows that at least some statements about P-states are entailed by statements about M-states. This is because if P is a statement about P-states and it entails Q, which is a statement about M-states, then it follows that $\sim Q$, which is also a statement about M-states, entails $\sim P$, which is a statement about P-states. To this extent, then, the behaviorist would appear to be correct. Sometimes statements about M-states entail statements about P-states. However, in order to give a complete account of our knowledge of the P-states of others, he must maintain that statements about those P-states are *always* entailed by suitable statements about M-states, and in that he is mistaken.

1.4 *The Criteriological Theory*

If the argument from analogy fails, then statements attributing certain M-states to a person must constitute logical reasons for attributing corresponding P-states to them. The position that these logical reasons are conclusive reasons is behaviorism, but behaviorism fails. Let us consider instead the descriptivist position that we have nonconclusive logical reasons here. This position has recently been held by a number of philosophers.[5] It has come to be

[5] Malcolm [1958] held this, and he attributed the view to Wittgenstein

called the *criteriological* theory, because these philosophers sought what they called "logically adequate criteria". What they seem to have meant by this term is simply what I have called "prima facie reasons".

According to the criteriological view, there are certain "basic" P-states such that, if X is one of them, then there corresponds a (possibly very complex) M-state Y such that a person's being in state Y is a prima facie reason for thinking he is in state X. Non-basic P-states are regarded as being composites of these basic P-states together with M-states. If one has rejected both the argument from analogy and behaviorism, this is the only possibility left—there must be such prima facie reasons. And this is indeed the basis upon which most adherents of the criteriological theory have defended their position.

But the criteriological theory is subject to an immediate difficulty. Whether there are criteria for P-states or not, it is at least clear that we do not ordinarily employ them when making self-ascriptions of P-states. I do not have to look at my own behavior to know whether I am in pain. Thus first-person and third-person ascriptions are made on entirely different bases. One cannot help but wonder how they get hooked together to make up the justification conditions for a single concept. This hooking together cannot be simply a matter of convention. We cannot construct a new P-concept by taking the mode of self-ascription from one (say, being in pain) but the third-person criterion from another (say, being happy). Such a conglomerate would not be a P-concept. If I ascribe a concept to myself because I feel pain, and to another because he acts happy, there is no reason at all to think that there is a P-state that we share. Thus we cannot construct P-concepts in such a haphazard way. There must be some connection between the means of self-ascription and the means of other-ascription. If we ask what the connection must be, the answer seems fairly clear: a P-concept must be "coherent" in the sense that, were we to use the means of third-person ascription on ourselves, we would get approximately the same result as we do with our actual means of first-person ascription. The only apparent way of finding out that a concept is coherent in this sense is by induction. Thus it seems

---

[1953]. Strawson [1959] argues for such a view, and it was endorsed by Shoemaker [1963].

that before we can even know whether we have a P-concept we must be able to discover inductively what M-states are correlated with the P-state in our own case (thus testing a proposed criterion for coherence with the means of self-ascription). But now the criterion drops out of the picture as irrelevant. We have the right criterion just in case it is what we would arrive at inductively, and in that case we do not need it because we could get the same result proceeding purely inductively. Thus the criteriologist seems to be forced into endorsing the argument from analogy.

A criteriologist might be tempted to agree that we have to proceed inductively in tying together a means of self-ascription and a criterion, but maintain that I have described things backward because we begin with the criterion rather than the means of self-ascription, and then proceed inductively to tie the means of self-ascription to the criterion rather than the other way around. But this only sounds different; it is not really different. In order to proceed inductively in establishing a correlation between two classes of things, we must be able to observe both classes of things independently. Thus, whether we start with the criterion or first-person observations of the P-state, we must be able to reidentify the P-state when it recurs in our own experience before we can relate it inductively to the criterion, and as long as that is possible, the criterion is unnecessary.

At this point a defender of the criteriological theory is apt to respond that we are not free to just make up new P-concepts at will. We are somehow constrained to use (only?) those already entrenched in our language as it now exists.[6] These come with the means of third-person ascription already built into them, because we are taught them in terms of those means of third-person ascription. For example, consider how we teach a child the concept of pain. When we judge that he is in pain, we say "You are in pain", and when he volunteers that he is in pain when we judge that he is not, we tell him that he is not in pain. In order to do this we must be able to tell when he is in pain, which, of course, we do in terms of some means of third-person ascription. We teach the concept of pain in terms of that means of third-person ascription, and consequently it cannot help but be built into the concept.

The above response only helps if it is supposed that it is not

[6] This response has been made to me by John Turk Saunders in correspondence on this topic.

incumbent upon us to check the coherence of those P-concepts we are taught by others as part of learning our language. The only reason I can see why that might be so is if coherence is, after all, at least partly a matter of convention. We saw that it cannot be entirely a matter of convention, but it might be proposed that it is a matter of convention for certain basic P-concepts (those entrenched in our language), and then the coherence of proposed new P-concepts can be tested against these basic concepts. For example, the reason we cannot build a P-concept by combining the means of first-person ascription of pain and the means of third-person ascription of happiness is that we already have two different concepts in our language which employ those means of ascription. If we did not, presumably, it would be open to us to construct the new concept described. So the basic assumption that is required to make the criteriological theory work is that the coherence of P-concepts is, at least ultimately, a matter of convention. We are only precluded from introducing a new P-concept in a certain way when doing so would conflict with our conventions regarding other P-concepts that we already use. Without this assumption, the criteriologist is inexorably driven in the direction of the argument from analogy.

The above position is plausible, but a little reflection indicates that it is mistaken. It is implied that there is no objective test of the coherence of a new P-concept other than its not conflicting with P-concepts we already employ. But this is obviously wrong when we consider the case of a person who acquires a new P-concept from his own experience, without it being taught to him by other people. Anyone who has been troubled by some peculiar recurring sensation and, perhaps fearing an impending heart attack or some other physical ailment, has attempted to talk to his doctor about it is in precisely the situation of acquiring the concept of a P-state from his own experience and looking about for corresponding M-states with the help of which to explain to his doctor what P-state he is in. Obviously, no M-states which might ultimately be found to be associated with the P-state can bear any *logical* connection with the concept of that state. I expect that some philosophers will profess to find this example unintelligible, and will ask how one could ever know that it was the same sensation that was recurring on several occasions if he were unable to relate it to any M-states. I can only reply that having been in this sort of situation myself, I can assure the reader that there is not the slightest difficulty in reidentifying such a sensation when it recurs, even though one has not yet found any M-states which tend to be associated with it.

Two lessons are to be learned from this example. First, given that a person in the above situation can and does proceed inductively in looking for means of third-person ascription of his P-state, it follows that there is an objective standard against which the coherence of a means of third-person ascription for this concept is to be tested, i.e., the inductive standard. A criteriologist might reply that this is only possible against the background of a basic set of P-concepts already entrenched in our language,[7] but in the proceedings just described, no other P-concepts were used at any point. It does not seem to make any difference whether we have any other P-concepts. Thus I think it is unreasonable to maintain that there is no objective standard of coherence for means of first-person and third-person ascriptions. Given this, there seems to be no way to defend the criteriological theory against the objection that it presupposes the validity of the argument from analogy. The second lesson to be learned is that no particular M-states need be built in as criteria in P-concepts that are acquired from our own experience, and hence the criteriological theory will not work for such concepts. But it is surely a contingent fact that we are taught any particular P-concept rather than acquiring it from our own experience, so it follows that the criteriological theory is mistaken in general.

The upshot of this is that there need be no logical connection (prima facie or conclusive) between a P-concept and any M-concepts. This does not mean that there are *no* P-concepts that bear any logical relationships to M-concepts. We have already seen examples of some that do, e.g., "is going for a walk". The conclusion is rather that there *exist* P-concepts that are not logically related to M-concepts. For the above reasons, it seems to be true in general that those states which we could reasonably call "phenomenological states" are not logically connected with any M-states.[8] On the other hand, if we turn to those P-states that are not phenomenological states, we find all sorts of connections between

[7] This is maintained in Saunders and Henze [1967], pp. 188-191.

[8] An attempt will be made in section 3 to say more precisely what a phenomenological state is and how P-states are related to phenomenological states.

them and M-states, and I think it is this that made the criteriological view initially plausible.

It must be concluded that the criteriological theory, as it is normally understood, does not give an adequate account of our knowledge of the P-states of others. There may be some P-states for which we can find the postulated prima facie reasons, but they do not exist for the vast majority of P-states. Nevertheless, I do not believe that the criteriological theory is completely wrong. I think that it errs only in the level of specificity of the prima facie reasons it postulates. Bleeding, grimacing, and crying out cannot be part of a prima facie reason for judging that a person is in pain, because it is only a contingent fact that persons in such M-states are usually in pain. There is a simple reason why this must be the case. The M-states which the criteriologist wants to employ as prima facie reasons are states of one's body. But it is only a contingent fact that persons have bodies at all like they do in fact have. There would be no logical absurdity in supposing persons to have bodies that are incapable of bleeding, grimacing, or crying out, or in general incapable of being in any particular M-state we may care to specify. If, as the criteriologist supposes, these prima facie reasons constitute the ultimate content of our P-concepts, then there would be no way to ascribe these concepts to persons whose bodies are very different from our own or to persons who lack bodies altogether. Is it a necessary truth then that persons have bodies like our own, or for that matter that they have bodies at all? Are ghosts a logical absurdity? I think not. Suppose that whenever people die the room is filled with a ghostly chill. This chill can be roughly located in terms of the spatial region in which it is felt, and it tends to move about. Furthermore, in the presence of this chill, one is apt to hear a voice, apparently emanating from empty space. It is possible to carry on conversations with this voice, and the voice is capable of informing us of facts regarding things that have happened both in the presence of the chill and in the presence of the person who died. The voice seems to evidence anger, pleasure, etc., associated with the goals and desires of the person who died, and in all respects behaves just as if it were the voice of that person. Can there be any doubt that we would judge that person to have become a ghost, a disembodied person?

Furthermore, if we lived in a world like this, and recognized the presence of ghosts, it would also become possible for us to discover the existence of ghosts that had never been embodied. This indicates that it is not only logically possible for a person to become disembodied, it is also logically possible for a person to have never had a body.

To take another example, suppose a world in which, rather than having corporeal bodies, persons have associated with them multicolored magnetic fields. These magnetic fields have definite shapes, are affected in predictable ways by their surroundings, and in turn are able to affect their surroundings in predictable ways. These persons would not be unlike we are, except that they would be acted upon and would in turn act upon their environment in terms of magnetic phenomena rather than mechanically. Although nonmaterial, these magnetic men would still have bodies of a sort—their magnetic fields—but the M-states of these bodies would be quite different from our own M-states.

The important thing about these examples is that it is only a contingent fact that we aren't like these incorporeal beings. We could just as well have been ghosts or magnetic men as human beings. And this would not hinder us in our ability to judge one another's P-states. For example, we could judge that a ghost is enraged either because he tells us that he is or because he begins making vases fall off shelves, lamps tip over, windows break, etc. This indicates once more that the way in which we make these judgments cannot be by appealing to particular M-states which constitute prima facie reasons for judgments about P-states. It is contingent what M-attributes we are even capable of possessing. Our magnetic men could not bleed. Although they might do something which, once we knew how to interpret it, we could call a "grimace", their grimaces need bear no physical resemblance to our own. This indicates that the concept of a grimace is not really an M-concept. The concept of a grimace is defined not in terms of its physical characteristics but rather in terms of the P-states to which it is generally a response. We might well discover that the grimaces of our magnetic men look more like our own smiles. Analogously, our magnetic men may cry out, but what constitutes crying out for them may be physically completely unlike our own crying out. They may communicate in terms of radio waves rather than sound waves, so that crying out for them would consist of emitting certain kinds of bursts of radio waves. We could only discover this by seeing what P-states tended to elicit such a response. This indicates that crying out is not an M-state either, but like grimacing it is a P-state. It is the P-state which consists of being in *whatever* M-state is generally elicited by certain other P-states (e.g., being in pain) and proceeds in terms of whatever channel of communication plays the role for them that vocal communication does for us.

The above indicates that although grimacing and crying out might be part of a logical reason for ascribing pain to others, they are not M-states. In order to make use of such a logical reason, we would first have to find out what M-states constitute instances of grimacing and crying out, and that we could only do inductively. The simple criteriological view, according to which there are always specific M-states which constitute prima facie reasons for ascribing P-states to persons, will not work.

If there is a physical prima facie reason for ascribing these P-states to others, it cannot involve any specific M-states. We *discover* what M-states are associated with what P-states. But perhaps therein lies a prima facie reason. The prima facie reason is that the various M-states which have been discovered to be connected with the P-state are possessed by the person in question:

(1.1) "*S* possesses an M-state which tends to be accompanied by being in the P-state *X*" is a prima facie reason for me to think that *S* is in state *X*.

The above seems to be the only way to make the criteriological theory work. More specific prima facie reasons than these cannot exist. But now, how do we discover what M-states are associated with a P-state? We must make this discovery before we can ascribe P-states to others, so the only possible answer is that we begin with our own case. We discover that in our own case certain M-states tend to be accompanied by the P-state in question, and then we can use this together with our prima facie reason to judge when others are in that state. Of course, this is generally made easy for us by the fact that we are usually taught the concept of the P-state in terms of the M-states that are connected with it, and so we learn both the concept of the P-state and what M-states are associated with it simultaneously.

This seems to be the only way to make the criteriological theory work, but it is an unfashionable view. Perhaps most contemporary philosophers would deny that one can begin from one's own case, and they give very sophisticated arguments to support this. For example, Strawson [1959], pp. 99-100, has argued that you cannot have a P-concept until you know how to ascribe it to others. Consequently, you cannot begin from your own case. I find Strawson's argument extremely opaque. There is a perfectly good sense in which the criteriological theory just elaborated does not violate Strawson's principle. If you have a P-concept, then you do know how to ascribe it to others—by seeing what M-states are associated with it in your own case and judging that others are in the P-state when they are in the corresponding M-states. I am sure that Strawson would disallow this, but then I do not know how to interpret his principle so as to make it defensible. The best way to cut through all of these arguments and see that one can begin from his own case is to find a clear example of this, and we do not have to look far to find such examples. Most P-concepts are *taught* to us, and when that happens there is an important sense in which we do not begin from our own case—we are taught the corresponding M-states right along with the P-concept. But sometimes we do acquire new P-concepts that have not been taught to us. Recall the man who was troubled by the recurring sensation that he wanted to tell his doctor about. That example indicates that it is quite possible to begin from one's own case in determining what M-states are associated with a P-state. All of the arguments which purport to disprove this must simply be wrong.

If we agree that the argument from analogy must be rejected, I think it must be concluded that there are physical prima facie reasons for ascribing P-states to others. After all, it is on the basis of their M-states that we do make such ascriptions, and our judgments are certainly defeasible. But where the "traditional" criteriological theory errs is in supposing that these prima facie reasons make reference to any *specific* M-states. Rather, the prima facie reason consists of the person being in *any* M-states which we have found are generally accompanied by the P-states in question. For example, philosophers have bandied about the term "pain behavior", supposing that to be some physically specifiable behavior such that when a person behaves in that way his so behaving constitutes a prima facie reason for thinking he is in pain. On the contrary, a person's manifesting pain behavior *is* a prima facie reason for thinking he is in pain, but we cannot specify a priori what constitutes pain behavior. Pain behavior is *whatever* behavior tends to be accompanied by pain, and we have to discover what kind of behavior that is.

2. Our Knowledge of the P-States of Others

Now I will try to bring some order to the above observations and provide a systematic account of our knowledge of the P-states of others.

2.1 *The Equivalence of the Argument from Analogy and the Criteriological Theory*

I have argued that there are only two possible theories regarding our knowledge of the P-states of others—the argument from analogy, and a watered-down version of the criteriological theory. But this does not yet solve the problem. We would like to know which of these two theories is the correct one. I shall now argue that both are correct, because they are equivalent. The apparent differences between them are chimerical.

We have here two theories regarding the justification conditions of statements about the P-states of others. The defenders of the criteriological theory give a fairly concrete account of those justification conditions. I have argued that the most defensible version of the criteriological theory is that proposing principle 1.1 (although, as we will see shortly, that principle must be modified a bit). On the other hand, the argument from analogy proposes merely that those justification conditions are derivative from the principles of induction. But what does this amount to? It amounts to saying that a person's being in the M-states picked out by principle 1.1 constitutes an inductive reason for thinking he is in the corresponding P-state. In other words, we get as inductive reasons just the prima facie reasons proposed by principle 1.1. But, of course, inductive reasons are prima facie reasons, so the argument from analogy yields precisely the prima facie reasons that are forthcoming from the criteriological theory.

Now the only apparent difference between the argument from analogy and the criteriological theory is that the former labels these prima facie reasons as inductive reasons, while the latter maintains that they are directly constitutive of the P-concepts themselves, giving, as they do, the justification conditions of those concepts. But what does this difference really amount to? The traditional defender of the argument from analogy would have denied that these reasons are constitutive of the P-concepts, because he thought of induction as consisting of universally valid principles standing above all concepts. But as we have seen, that is an erroneous picture of induction. Not all concepts are projectible. When a concept is projectible, this constitutes part of its justification conditions, and hence is partially constitutive of that concept. Consequently, a defender of the argument from analogy ought to regard these reasons as directly constitutive of the P-concepts. Once again, we find no dispute between the criteriologist and the defender of the argument from analogy.

In conclusion, I do not see any way to distinguish between the argument from analogy and the criteriological theory. Let us briefly rehearse the argument. The argument from analogy is the position that our reasons for judgments about the P-states of others are contingent reasons. The only alternative is to maintain that those reasons are logical. They cannot be conclusive reasons, so they must be only prima facie. Furthermore, these prima facie reasons cannot make reference to any specific physical attributes. What physical attributes are involved must be discovered inductively. Thus, a sufficiently general criteriological theory resolves itself into the original argument from analogy, and that becomes the only possible theory of our knowledge of the P-states of others.

2.2 *Persons and Bodies*

We have been discussing how we can know what P-states a person is in. This question presupposes the ability to identify something as a person, or to know that there is a person present. Now let us turn to the more general question of how we can know that there is a person present who is in a certain P-state.

A person is not the same thing as his body. When a person dies, he ceases to exist, but his body may continue to exist unchanged. And it will be argued in section 4 that it is logically possible for a person to change bodies. So we cannot say of a particular body that it *is* a person. Let us talk instead of bodies being inhabited.[9] How do we tell whether a particular body is inhabited? Clearly, we do so by seeing whether it behaves like an inhabited body. If it

[9] It was argued in Chapter Six that the relation between a person and his body wherein he inhabits the body is one of composition—the person is composed of his body.

exhibits pain behavior, acts angry, happy, bewildered, etc., under the appropriate circumstances, then we judge that the body is inhabited. Judging whether it behaves in these ways is a matter of judging, on the basis of principle 1.1, that *if* the body were inhabited, then its inhabitant would be in pain, angry, happy, bewildered, etc.

We distinguish between a person and his body. We seem to make an analogous distinction between a dog and its body, and even a lobster and its body. For any living thing, it is possible for it to die, and hence cease to exist, without its body ceasing to exist. Thus the living thing must be distinguished from its body. What makes something a living thing is that it has P-states. For example, lobsters at least feel pain. How do we tell when a lobster feels pain? He behaves in a manner not unlike we behave in situations analogous to those that would cause us pain. In other words, we use the same prima facie reasons to ascribe P-states to nonhuman animals as we do to persons. This indicates that we should reformulate principle 1.1 as a principle about bodies and living things, and not just about persons:

(2.1) "Body *B* possesses an M-state which tends to be accompanied by a living thing being in the P-state *X*" is a prima facie reason for me to judge that body *B* is inhabited by a living thing in state *X*.

A person is simply a living thing that exhibits sufficiently many and sufficiently complex P-states. A person must be capable of believing, thinking, desiring, contemplating, admiring, etc. I doubt whether any precise list can be made of the P-states that are necessary to make something a person—the concept is not that precise—but this should be sufficient to characterize this rather fuzzy concept.

Now another problem arises. Principle 2.1 can only be employed in connection with persons who have bodies, but it has already been argued that it is logically possible for persons to be disembodied. Ghosts are not a logical absurdity. But as long as they exhibit other physical manifestations, we would not find it too difficult to judge the P-states of disembodied persons. We would make these judgments on the same basis as our judgments regarding embodied persons—by seeing that they exhibited physical manifestations which we had found to be accompanied by the P-states in question. This indicates that we must generalize principle 2.1 so that it can be employed in connection with disembodied persons:

(2.2) "The present state of affairs is of a kind that I have found to be accompanied by the presence of a living thing in the P-state *X*" is a prima facie reason for me to think that there is present a living thing in state *X*.

2.3 *The Problem of Copersonality*

Principle 2.2 is not yet enough to account for all of our judgments concerning the P-states of others. By using principle 2.2 we can judge that there is a person present who is in some particular P-state. But we often want to judge of one and the same person that he is in several P-states. For example, using principle 2.2, we can judge that there is a person present who is in pain, and we can judge that there is a person present who is angry. How can we tell whether this is one and the same person? A simple answer might be that we use principle 2.2 in connection with the complex P-state consisting of being both angry and in pain. But this use of principle 2.2 would require us to have previously observed people in that complex state, which is unnecessary. It is only necessary that we have observed some in pain, and others angry. We can then put together what we have learned to tell that a person is both angry and in pain. How do we do this? This is the problem of *copersonality*—how do we determine that two P-states are states of the same person?[10]

Some philosophers have taken the problem of copersonality seriously. But they have generally thought that there was a problem for both the first-person and third-person judgments of copersonality, and have sought the solution in some phenomenologically discoverable relation of copersonality. Other philosophers have

[10] There are actually two problems of copersonality: what makes two simultaneous P-states states of the same person, and what makes the P-states of a person at one time copersonal with his P-states of a later time? We might call these "horizontal" and "vertical" copersonality, respectively. In this section I am only concerned with horizontal copersonality. Vertical copersonality becomes a special case of the problem of reidentifying persons and will be dealt with in section 4.

denied that there is a problem of copersonality,[11] on the grounds that we can only identify a P-state in terms of the person whose state it is, and hence to know of the existence of a P-state is automatically to know whose state it is. As we shall see, both of these views are in error. The latter philosophers are right that there is no problem in the first-person case, but there remains a difficulty in the third-person case.

Let us begin by considering first-person judgments of copersonality. Bertrand Russell [1914] found our ability to make such judgments mysterious, and in need of explanation. He sought such an explanation in the content of those P-states themselves, maintaining that there was a relation of "being experienced together" that we are aware of in our P-states, and that it is this relation which makes one's P-states all states of oneself. As Shoemaker points out, this leads quickly to absurdity. On this theory, if I were to feel a pain, but not observe it to stand in the relation of copersonality to my other P-states, I would have to conclude that it is not my pain. But if I feel it, then of course it is my pain.[12] In the first-person case, there simply is no problem. If I judge of each of two P-states that I am in them, then it follows automatically that they are copersonal. There is nothing further that I have to establish to know this.

It is tempting to suppose that the same thing is true of third-person judgments of copersonality. It may seem that we can only identify a P-state in terms of the person whose state it is. There is no way to refer to a P-state without making reference to the person who possesses it. Consequently, it seems that if we know of the existence of a particular P-state, we automatically know whose it is, and so the problem of copersonality cannot arise. Unfortunately, this is a mistake. Using principle 2.2, we may know of the existence of a person in a certain P-state, e.g., in pain. We know this on the basis of the person's body. In one sense, we do know who it is that is in pain—the person whose pain it is. This is a uniquely referring description. But of course, this is not a very informative answer. And we do not automatically know of another way to refer to the person in question. Whether that person is Jones is a substantive question which we have not yet seen how to settle. Analogously, we may know that there is someone who is angry. Then the question of whether the pain and anger are

[11] For example, Ayer [1964].

[12] Shoemaker [1963], p. 104.

copersonal is simply the question of whether the person who is in pain is the same person as the one who is angry. How can we know whether this is so?

It may seem that there is a simple solution to this problem. If, using principle 2.2, we judge the presence of a person in pain on the basis of the M-attributes of a body, we automatically know of another term referring to the person in question, viz., "the person whose body this is". Then if we judge, on the basis of that same body, that there is a person who is angry, we know that the person who is angry is also the person whose body this is. Thus it follows that the pain and the anger are copersonal. This is certainly correct as an account of our actual judgments of copersonality. We attribute two P-states to the same person iff it is the same human body that is involved in our coming to know of both P-states. If this is a logical reason for judgments of copersonality, then it seems that our problem is solved.

However, there are difficulties with the suggestion that copersonality is simply a matter of sameness of body. First, persons need not have bodies, but we could still make judgments of copersonality. It would not be particularly difficult to tell that a ghost is both embarrassed and angry. Second, even if we restrict our attention to embodied persons, our formula for copersonality will not work for two reasons: (1) it is a contingent fact what constitutes a body, and the ability to determine this presupposes the prior ability to make judgments of copersonality; (2) it is not a necessary truth that two persons cannot share a single body, in which case sameness of body would not be a guarantee of copersonality. Taking these points in order, first consider what it is for a certain physical object to constitute a person's body. A person's body is, roughly, the locus of those M-states which are regarded as manifestations of his P-states. If it were a necessary truth that a person's body must consist of a single physical object, this locus might not be difficult to find, but there is no such necessary truth. For example, we can imagine persons whose arms have wings which allow them to fly off and perform tasks remote from the rest of the body and then come back to roost on the shoulders. In general, there is no reason why a person's body might not consist of an extensive array of disconnected "parts" working in unison. To discover the extent of this array, we must discover, e.g., the extent to which pains exhibited by the different parts are copersonal. Thus judgments of copersonality cannot in turn presuppose judgments of sameness of body.

Going on to the second point, the human brain consists of two hemispheres joined together. To a large extent, the right hemisphere controls the left side of the body, and the left hemisphere controls the right side of the body. As a cure for severe epilepsy the two hemispheres are sometimes split apart. The results have been carefully studied, and are fascinating. The two hemispheres seem to communicate with one another via external clues. For example, the right hemisphere hears with the left ear what the left hemisphere is saying.[13] Now, suppose we have a child who is *born* with a split brain. Each hemisphere is dormant, asleep, for half of the child's waking day, and during that time the other hemisphere controls the child's entire body. Because different things happen during their distinct periods of control, the two hemispheres would be conditioned differently. They would exhibit different knowledge, different memories, different desires and aspirations, etc. When the child reaches maturity, a change occurs and the two hemispheres no longer sleep while not in control. Each still controls the body for half of the body's waking day, but each is able to report what went on while the other hemisphere was in control. Furthermore, because the two personalities are so different, a marked antagonism develops between the two hemispheres. The one hemisphere, who happens to have become a neurophysiologist, begins experiments designed to "drive that meddlesome intruder from my body". The other, who is an opera singer, goes to the police and asks them to prevent this happening. Is it not extremely plausible that here we have two persons in a single body?

So far, this indicates that it is logically possible for two persons to inhabit a single body. However, if this is to be an obstacle to judgments of copersonality, it must be shown that the single body can *simultaneously* exhibit the P-states of both persons. An addition to the above story yields the desired result. The neurophysiologist continues his experiments with the object of ultimately gaining permanent control of his body, and one day announces that he believes he has succeeded. The test will come when his twelve hours of control are up and the opera singer appears. But

[13] See Gozzaniga [1967] for a fascinating nontechnical discussion of some of these experiments.

the scientist is only partly successful. Different parts of the body seem to struggle against one another. The opera singer wishes to go to a party, so the body starts to walk into the bedroom to dress. But although the legs cooperate, the arms grasp wildly at furniture to drag the body back. The carefully modulated tones of the opera singer protest that something terrible is happening and that he cannot control his arms. But the voice breaks off in midsentence and the raspy voice of the scientist announces with glee that he is gaining control of the body. Then one of the arms suddenly begins cooperating with the legs and seeks to pry the other hand loose from the davenport to which it stubbornly clings. Would we not conclude that this body is inhabited by two persons each striving for dominance? Accordingly, although the body might exhibit both pain and anger, there is no guarantee that it is one and the same person who is both angry and in pain. Thus copersonality cannot be defined in terms of sameness of body.

Of course, we do base our judgments of copersonality on sameness of body. But we must be proceeding inductively. We discover that our own P-states are related in certain ways to a certain physical object—our body. We observe other similar objects around us which have sufficiently similar attributes to allow us to employ principle 2.2 and judge the presence of other persons. Then we discover that there is only one person associated with each of these bodies, and hence we can base subsequent judgments of copersonality on sameness of body.

But how do we discover that there is only one person associated with each body? The simplest way is to observe that this is true of our own body and then conclude inductively that it is true of others as well. But there must be other evidence that is relevant too—if this were the only relevant evidence it would be impossible for us to ever discover cases like the split-brain example in which sameness of body is not a guarantee of copersonality. To see what else is relevant, consider the scientist and the opera singer once more. If we know both well, we might not have too much trouble sorting out the different mental states exhibited by their common body and assigning each to the appropriate person. If the opera singer is a very meek but emotional person, and the body suddenly bursts into tears of despair, we would attribute the despair to the opera singer. If the scientist is renowned for his fiery temper, and the body begins throwing things about and bellowing with rage, we would attribute the rage to the scientist. If a curious mouse happens upon the scene, and the body jumps screaming upon an end table, we would attribute the fear to the opera singer (who is known to be afraid of mice). These attributions are based upon the "naturalness" of certain temporal sequences of P- and M-states. If a person has in the past exhibited both meekness and emotionality, we would not be surprised to see him burst into tears of despair in a difficult and threatening situation. A person who in the past has exhibited a tendency to become angry easily does not surprise us when he again becomes angry. If a person has previously acquired knowledge of certain facts, we expect him to act accordingly. If he has previously exhibited certain likes and dislikes, we expect his future behavior to be consonant with those likes and dislikes. And so on. What constitutes "acting accordingly" is something we learn inductively, starting ultimately from our own case. We learn that certain sequences of P- and M-states are common, and others, e.g., laughing when stuck with a pin, are extremely unlikely.

It is on the basis of the "naturalness" of the sequence of P-states that we can determine, at least to some extent, which P-states to attribute to the scientist and which to the opera singer, even though both concurrently inhabit the same body. The explanation for this is that (1) we have a strong inductive reason for thinking that copersonal states can be placed in "natural" sequences, and (2) we have a strong inductive reason for thinking that those P-states exhibited by a single body which can be placed in a natural sequence are copersonal. The latter is the basis upon which we group the states we attribute to the scientist and the states we attribute to the opera singer as we do. The former is the basis upon which we deny that they can all be grouped together as states of one person.

My conclusion is that our third-person judgments of copersonality are always inductive. This is the only way to explain the variety of situations that can arise regarding copersonality.

2.4 *How P-Concepts Are Possible*

I have given a rudimentary account of how we acquire knowledge of the P-states of others. But it may be felt that a difficulty arises for this account. Consider my ascription of pain to myself and to another person. I know that I am in pain because

I feel the pain, but I cannot feel another person's pain. I ascribe pain to him on the basis of his behavior. And both of these bases for ascribing pain seem to arise directly from the concept of pain. There is some temptation to suppose that in the first-person case I am simply reporting my feeling, but in the third-person case I am actually reporting the other person's behavior. But this cannot be right, because there is always the logical possibility that the other person is pretending. Whatever his behavior, it is not logically sufficient to guarantee that he is in pain. We want to say that it is not his behavior we are reporting but what he feels; but how can this be possible on the basis of his behavior? How can we be ascribing the same thing to ourselves and to others when we do so on such different bases?

Described in this way, P-concepts seem mysterious. How can there be one concept that is ascribed to different subjects in such totally different ways? However, the air of mystery disappears once it is realized that the line between the two ways of ascribing P-concepts is improperly drawn as the distinction between ourselves and others. We can, and do, ascribe P-concepts to ourselves in precisely the same way we ascribe them to others. For example, upon witnessing a home movie taken of myself several years ago, I may well judge on the basis of my behavior that first I was angry and then amused. My grounds for this judgment would be just the same as my grounds for making this judgment about someone else. In other words, the line between the two ways of ascribing P-states does not coincide with the distinction between my P-states and the P-states of others, but rather with the distinction between P-states I am currently experiencing and other P-states. The former category contains only P-states of myself, but the latter category contains P-states of both myself and others.

Once we have seen the proper place to draw the line, the two ways of ascribing P-concepts should no longer seem perplexing. P-concepts become completely analogous to other familiar concepts. For example, consider the concept of a red object. There are two ways of ascribing this concept to an object: (1) by seeing the object and judging its color on the basis of the way it looks to us; or (2) by appealing to various inductive reasons which we have acquired ultimately by using the first reason. Analogously, there are two ways of ascribing a P-concept to persons: (1) by experiencing the P-state and making a judgment on that basis; or

(2) by appealing to various inductive reasons which we have acquired ultimately by using the first reason. For either concept, our second kind of reason arises simply out of the fact that the concept is projectible. In the case of P-concepts, it has nothing special to do with other persons. It is, in effect, just a logical coincidence that this is the only way of ascribing P-concepts to other persons, and should be viewed as no more significant for the nature of the concept than the fact that we can only employ inductive reasons in ascribing colors to objects we do not see. The distinction between the two ways of ascribing P-concepts is just the distinction we should expect from the fact that they are projectible coupled with the fact that, in the relevant sense, we can only experience our own P-states.[14]

3. The Analysis of P-Concepts

3.1 *Projectibility*

In the above sections we constructed elaborate principles like 2.1 and 2.2 that were intended to formulate the actual inductive reasons which the defender of the argument from analogy or the criteriologist would propose. However, these principles are both too weak and unnecessary. First, they are too weak because there are ascriptions of P-states to others which do not proceed in terms of these principles. Once we can make some judgments about the P-states of others on the basis of principle 2.2, it then becomes possible to make other judgments about their P-states on a different basis altogether. Recall once more the example of the man who experienced a strange sensation in his chest but was unable to find any M-state associated with it. This makes principle 2.2 inapplicable, but does not guarantee that others will be unable to discover what sensation he has. Although he may not be able to find any M-states such that whenever he is in those states he has the sensation, he may nevertheless be able to *describe* the sensation quite well. He might be able to tell us, "It is a fluttery sensation I get in my chest, accompanied by a burning sensation in my throat. When I get it I feel light-headed, and get a panicky feeling as if I cannot breathe properly. When I lie down it goes away."

[14] My thinking on this was made much clearer by reading Ayer [1953].

Given a fairly detailed description of this sort, another person might respond, "I know exactly what you mean; I get the same sensation whenever I eat my wife's cooking." What is happening here is that through the use of principle 2.2 we learn what he means by the various elements of his report. Thus we can understand what attributes his sensation has even though we do not know what sensation it is. It is then possible for us to discover inductively that only one kind of sensation has all of those attributes, and hence we can identify his sensation on the basis of its attributes.

This identification of a P-state in terms of its attributes is something not covered by principle 2.2, so it seems that that principle should be augmented by another. However, this is unnecessary. We can replace any such principle, and also principle 2.2 at the same time, by a simple postulate of projectibility. What these principles do is attempt to formulate various aspects of our inductive reasoning about P-states, but all such principles can be eliminated in favor of a single principle saying that P-concepts are projectible. Such a principle of projectibility automatically licenses the reasoning carried out in accordance with these other principles.

However, slight reflection indicates that a postulate of projectibility must be restricted—not all P-concepts can be projectible. We can construct Goodmanesque P-concepts, and the strictures elaborated in the last chapter against disjunctions, conditionals, etc., apply just as much to P-concepts as to any other concepts. I shall argue that, among P-concepts, it is basically the concepts of phenomenological states that are projectible.[15] (Of course, the notion of a phenomenological state must be made more precise than it has so far been made.) What gives any P-concept its characteristic "mental flavor" is that it makes reference somehow to phenomenological states, generally mixing them with M-states. In general, P-states are hybrids of phenomenological states and M-states. Accordingly, inductive reasoning with respect to P-concepts other than those of phenomenological states is derivative from the projectibility of phenomenological concepts and physical concepts.

To defend this, I will examine phenomenological states more carefully. What is desired is a complete account of the justification conditions of statements ascribing phenomenological states to per-

[15] Although not exclusively—for example, we have already seen that the concepts of perceiving and remembering are projectible.

sons. This should make it clear that phenomenological concepts are projectible.

3.2 *Phenomenological States*

Phenomenological states (at least as I shall use the term) are those P-states that one can pick out introspectively. To use a phrase of Quine's, they are those that are "tinged with awareness". Phenomenological states are those that are subject to introspective demonstrative reference. In other words, they are those states to which the argument in Chapter Four is applicable. Accordingly, the external judgment "I am in that phenomenological state" is incorrigible.

The simple incorrigible external judgment that one is in a particular phenomenological state does not get us very far. We must compare states, reidentify them, label them (e.g., "This is a state consisting of my being appeared to redly"), identify them with the states of others, and correlate them inductively with M-states and other P-states. Let us consider how such judgments are possible.

3.2.1 *Identifying phenomenological states with one another.* We often identify two phenomenological states as being the same. For example, I may judge that the pain I now feel is just like the pain I felt yesterday. This sameness is not the sameness of the individual states themselves (i.e., we are not saying that one and the same state has recurred), but is rather sameness of type. This becomes clear when we notice that we can judge two simultaneously existing phenomenological states to be the same. For example, I may judge that I am simultaneously presented with the same color in two different parts of my visual field. This is the same notion of sameness as is employed in reidentifying a present state with an earlier one. Let us call this "phenomenological sameness".

Phenomenological sameness does not require that two states have *all* their attributes in common—otherwise it would be numerical identity rather than sameness of type. What it requires is that they be "phenomenologically indistinguishable". If we could lay them side by side, we would find no phenomenological difference between them. In other words, they have all their *phenomenological* attributes in common where phenomenological attributes are those attributes that are, in some sense, "directly discriminable". We have no difficulty deciding which attributes are relevant to whether two states are the same. For example, time of occurrence is not relevant, but, e.g., if the states involve visual objects, then the colors of the presented objects are relevant. However, we need a more precise characterization of phenomenological attributes. This is not difficult to come by. Phenomenological attributes are those which are relevant in judgments of phenomenological sameness, so they must refer to features of phenomenological states to which we have the same kind of direct access as we do to phenomenological states themselves, i.e., to those features which are subject to introspective demonstrative reference. This immediately gives us the following:

(3.1) An attribute *A* of phenomenological states is a phenomenological attribute iff our being in a state having attribute *A* is itself a phenomenological state.

Thus we can think of the phenomenological attributes of a state as referring to other simpler phenomenological states which are "logical parts" of the state in question. Furthermore, if we wish to judge that two phenomenological states are the same in certain phenomenological respects, although not entirely the same, this amounts to judging that certain states which are logical parts of the larger states are phenomenologically the same. For example, we may judge that two perceptual states are the same with respect to the presented object being red, although not in other respects. This amounts to saying that both perceptual states contain as parts of them states of being appeared to redly, where these latter states are phenomenologically the same.

Given two simultaneously existing phenomenological states, how is it possible for us to know that they are the same? This is a very perplexing question. The sameness of two states seems so manifest that it is hard to imagine anything more basic to which we might appeal. Nevertheless, as we shall see, there is something more basic. We have a definition of phenomenological sameness in terms of phenomenological attributes:

(3.2) The phenomenological states *X* and *Y* are phenomenologically the same iff they have the same phenomenological attributes.

Consequently, to ascertain whether two states are the same, we need merely check their phenomenological attributes. Unfortunately, this does not take us as far as we might suppose. The difficulty is that definition 3.2 is essentially circular. We defined the notion of a phenomenological attribute in terms of phenomenological states, in such a way that to say two states *X* and *Y* have all of their phenomenological attributes in common is merely to say that every phenomenological state which is logically part of *X* is phenomenologically the same as some state which is logically part of *Y*, and vice versa. Accordingly, we have defined phenomenological sameness in terms of phenomenological sameness. This is not to say that 3.2 is useless, but only that it is incomplete. Definition 3.2 still achieves something, because it relates the phenomenological sameness of composite states to the phenomenological sameness of their parts. But we still need some way of judging the sameness of those "simple" states which do not have other phenomenological states as parts. Being appeared to redly is an example of such a simple state.

In the case of simple phenomenological states, it seems there can be nothing more manifest than their distinguishability or indistinguishability. In other words, our ability or failure to distinguish between two simple phenomenological states in which we find ourselves is itself a phenomenological state. For example, upon being presented with two colors, our being able to distinguish between them is something that stands out clearly as an object of introspective awareness. So, too, is our not being able to distinguish between the colors. So these two states of being able to distinguish or not being able to distinguish are phenomenological states. And it seems clear that it is these states which provide the basis for our judgments of phenomenological sameness. If we cannot distinguish between two phenomenological states, we judge them to be the same, and if we can distinguish between them, we judge them to be different. The latter is clearly a conclusive reason:

(3.3) "*X* and *Y* are simple phenomenological states and I can distinguish between them" is a conclusive reason for me to think that *X* and *Y* are not phenomenologically the same.

Somewhat surprisingly, our inability to distinguish between two simple states is not a conclusive reason for judging them to be the same. It is well known that although two colors, sounds, pains, etc., may be indistinguishable by direct comparison, they may be distinguishable by comparison with a third object. For example, although two colors may seem exactly the same upon direct comparison, we may be able to find a third color which is indistinguishable from one of the original colors but distinguishable from the other. This is just the psychological phenomenon of "just noticeable differences". Clearly such "indirect" distinguishability is sufficient to guarantee that two indistinguishable phenomenological states are not phenomenologically the same. Hence indistinguishability cannot guarantee sameness. On the other hand, indistinguishability is certainly the basis upon which we judge sameness, so it must be a prima facie reason:

(3.4) "*X* and *Y* are simple phenomenological states and I cannot distinguish between them" is a prima facie reason for me to think that *X* and *Y* are phenomenologically the same.

The only defeaters for this prima facie reason seem to arise out of the above sort of indirect distinguishability. If *X* and *Y* are phenomenologically the same, then they ought to be distinguishable from precisely the same states:

(3.5) "There is a state *Z* which is distinguishable from one of *X* and *Y* but not the other" is a conclusive reason for thinking that *X* and *Y* are not phenomenologically the same.

By using this reason, we can discover inductively that two states are not the same because, although we are not now in such a state *Z*, we could be. For example, I may know that the colors of two adjacent slabs that look the same to me are different because, although there is no third color present with the help of which to distinguish between them, nevertheless it is possible for such a third color to be present. I may know of this possibility either directly, by having compared the slabs with such a third color on other occasions, or I may have some general inductive reason for this judgment based perhaps on a measurement of the wave lengths of the light reflected by the slabs.

The above principles seem to be correct, but at first glance they do not appear to explain how it is possible for us to know that two states *X* and *Y* are the same. The problem is that, in order to have this reason for judging them to be the same, we must know that we cannot distinguish between them. Our being unable to distinguish between them is itself a phenomenological state, so to have this reason is to know that we are in a certain phenomenological state. But to know that one is in a certain phenomenological state would seem to involve the ability to identify the present state as being the same as other states of the same type, and then we are off on the slippery slope of an infinite regress. Fortunately, there is a mistake here. I have asserted that my reason for thinking that *X* and *Y* are the same is my knowing that I am in the state of being unable to distinguish between them. But this claim is ambiguous in a way that most claims about persons' epistemic states are ambiguous—it does not make clear whether my knowing that I am in that state is external or internal knowledge, i.e., whether I must know of the state in which I find myself that it is the state properly *called* "being unable to distinguish between *X* and *Y*" or whether I must simply find myself in a state which is *in fact* properly so called.[16] A bit of reflection indicates that only the latter is required. In judging that two states are the same because I cannot distinguish between them, clearly it is irrelevant whether: (1) I know what *words* describe my being in the state of being unable to distinguish between them; or (2) I recall any other cases of being in the state of being unable to distinguish between two states; or anything else of this sort. All that is important is that I am aware of being in the state which is in fact the state of being unable to distinguish, and that awareness is external knowledge. As we saw in Chapter Four, such external knowledge is incorrigible. Hence we have succeeded in anchoring our judgments of phenomenological sameness in an incorrigible foundation, and thereby have explained how our knowledge of phenomenological sameness is possible. We can encapsulate this by expanding principle 3.4 as follows:

(3.6) The external belief that I am in the simple phenomenological states *X* and *Y* and am in the state of being unable to distinguish between them is a prima facie reason

[16] For a discussion of external and internal knowledge and belief, see Chapter Four.

for thinking that X and Y are phenomenologically the same.

3.2.2 *Reidentifying phenomenological states.* So far I have talked about identifying two present states as being phenomenologically the same. We also make such judgments about states separated in time. In other words, we can reidentify one state as being the same as an earlier state.[17] What is our basis for such reidentification? Sometimes we recall a previous state, in the sense of almost literally "reliving" it, and then compare the resulting "image" with the present state. For example, in deciding whether two separated surfaces look the same color to me, I may carefully examine one, try to hold an image of it in my mind, and then turn to the other surface and compare my image with the color the other surface looks to me. The image I have is equally an image of my being presented with the colored surface, and insofar as I am comparing not just the color but also the color's being perceptually presented rather than, e.g., imagined, I am comparing the remembered phenomenological state with the present one via principle 3.6. This aspect of the reidentification proceeds just like the identification of two contemporary states. When we turn to the memory that is involved in the reidentification, we see that it is propositional memory. What we remember is that our earlier phenomenological state was the way our present image represents it. Thus we need no new principles to account for this aspect of our reidentification. It proceeds entirely in terms of the prima facie reasons enumerated in Chapter Seven.

The above sort of reidentification wherein we have a memory image of the earlier state is to some extent unusual. It is perhaps more common to simply *recognize* a present state as being the same as an earlier state. For example, upon feeling a peculiar sensation or seeing an unusual color, I may simply recognize it as being the same as a sensation I had earlier or a color I saw once before. This recognition is possible without my being able to resurrect any kind of image of the earlier state prior to my being in the present state. I may be quite unable to recall the previous state "in a vacuum". In this case the reidentification proceeds entirely in terms of memory, without having to appeal even to principle 3.6.

[17] This is reidentification of the state type, not the individual state.

Thus once again we need no new principles to account for reidentification.

The above cases of reidentification are cases in which we actually remember the earlier state rather than merely remembering that it was a state of a certain sort. But we can also reidentify on the latter basis. For example, I may recall that on a certain occasion I heard a clear tone which was C-sharp. When on a later occasion I again hear a C-sharp tone, I can judge that my state of being presented with that tone is phenomenologically the same as my earlier state, even though I do not remember the earlier state. Or to take another example, I may discover inductively that whenever I eat onions I get a characteristic queasy feeling. Then upon eating onions once more I may know inductively that my present feeling is the same as what I had last time I ate onions, even though I don't remember how I felt then. These reidentifications are essentially inductive. In learning to use the label "C-sharp", I must discover inductively that all tones so labeled are phenomenologically the same. Thus upon encountering two such tones, I can conclude on the basis of their both being C-sharp that they are phenomenologically the same. Similarly, in the second example I discover inductively that the queasy feelings I get on any two occasions of eating onions are phenomenologically the same. Thus it is possible to reidentify phenomenological states inductively as well as directly via principle 3.6 and propositional memory.

3.3 *The Projectibility of Phenomenological Sameness*

The fact that we can reidentify phenomenological states inductively is of extreme importance. It requires that the concept of phenomenological sameness be projectible, and that is all we need for the account of knowledge of other minds given in sections 1 and 2. It was argued there that our basis for ascribing P-states to others is inductive. I have maintained that most P-states are hybrids of M-states and phenomenological states, so the problem of dealing inductively with P-states is ultimately the problem of dealing inductively with phenomenological states. On this account, our basis for ascribing a phenomenological state to another person is our discovering that whenever one is in a certain M-state he is in that phenomenological state. To discover inductively that whenever one is in a certain M-state he is also in a certain (type of) phenomenological state is to discover that, on any two occasions of persons being in that M-state, the persons will also be in phenomenological states which are phenomenologically the same. All we need to make this sort of reasoning possible is for phenomenological sameness to be projectible, and we have just seen that it must be. Thus there is no obstacle to the sort of inductive reasoning about other minds that has been proposed by the defender of the argument from analogy and the modified criteriologist.

Of course, this only secures inductive reasoning for phenomenological states—not for P-states in general. In order to deal inductively with other P-states we must first see how they are to be analyzed in terms of phenomenological state and M-states, and then deal with them as we do in general with pseudoprojectible conditionals.[18] Although some of these analyses may be difficult to come by, there would seem to be no difficulty in principle here. I think we can regard the problem of other minds as solved.

4. Personal Identity

Now we come to one of the most perplexing problems regarding the concept of a person. What has come to be called "the problem of personal identity" is the problem of reidentifying persons. There have been basically two theories regarding personal identity. On the one hand there have been those philosophers who maintain that questions of personal identity are to be settled by an appeal to bodily identity. On the other hand there have been those philosophers who have sought "mentalistic" criteria of personal identity. Among the latter philosophers, the predominant candidate for a mentalistic criterion has been some form of memory criterion. In the ensuing discussion I shall come down rather weakly on the side of the memory theorists.

4.1 *First-Person Reidentification*

The problem of reidentification can be fruitfully divided into two problems: how do we reidentify other persons, and how do we reidentify ourselves? Let us begin with the latter question. How can I know that I am the person picked out by some term that makes reference to an earlier time? Sometimes I reidentify myself in the same way as I reidentify others. For example, looking at a

[18] For a discussion of pseudoprojectibility, see Chapter Eight.

newspaper picture of a crowd I may see my own face. How do I know that I am the person of whom that picture was taken? In this case I reidentify my body on the basis of appearance and then reidentify myself on the basis of the reidentification of my body. Here my reidentification is substantially the same as what I would do in reidentifying another person. But philosophers have usually wanted to maintain that we have another more direct way of reidentifying ourselves. We don't generally have to examine our body to know that we are the person who performed some action in the past, or witnessed some past event. We have some "internal" way of knowing this. Thus we are led to memory.

Locke and other modern philosophers tried to make personal identity consist of the possession of a continuous stream of consciousness. As they recognized, the only way to make sense of this notion was in terms of memory of phenomenological states. To say that a stream of consciousness is continuous is to say that at each instant one can remember some of his past phenomenological states. In attempting to make this both a necessary and sufficient condition for personal identity, these philosophers encountered insurmountable difficulties. For example, a person suffering from amnesia may remember none of his earlier phenomenological states, but he does not thereby lose his personal identity. More simply, upon awakening from sleep I may remember none of my earlier phenomenological states. Consequently, this cannot be a necessary condition for personal identity. Is it at least a sufficient condition? Not as stated. It is a mistake to suppose we cannot remember the phenomenological states of others. If I know that another person feels anger or humiliation, I can subsequently remember his anger or humiliation. But this is not truly a counterexample to what these philosophers had in mind. When they talk about remembering an earlier phenomenological state, they really mean remembering *their being in* that state. This *is* a sufficient condition for identity. If I remember that I was in a certain phenomenological state, then of course it follows that I was the person who was in that state. However, this is not terribly helpful for most cases of reidentification. Characteristically we are more interested in knowing whether, e.g., I am the person who broke the window yesterday. I do not generally come to know this by knowing anything about the phenomenological states of the person who broke the window. Rather, as Shoemaker [1963] and others have called to our attention, I may simply remember that I broke the window. Memory gives us much broader access to our past than merely to our past phenomenological states.

The way in which memory helps us to settle questions of personal identity is not entirely straightforward. Although I may remember that I broke the window, I do not thereby remember that I was *the* person who broke the window. In order to conclude the latter, I must also know that only one person broke the window. I may know this on the basis of memory, too, but that is unnecessary. This is simply an impersonal fact about the past, and I can know it in any of the ways that I acquire historical knowledge. In general, the way memory helps me to settle questions about my personal identity is by providing me with facts about my past which show that I satisfied a certain description which I know, on some grounds or other, was only satisfied by one person. What I am proposing here is not really a memory *criterion of identity* at all (except perhaps in a very attenuated sense). Rather, I am proposing that memory can give us facts about our past history, and then we can use these facts to infer that we uniquely satisfied certain descriptions.[19]

There is a common response to the above observations. It is replied that it is a trivial tautology that if I remember doing something then I did it, but that this is epistemologically irrelevant to questions of personal identity. A necessary condition of remembering something is that it be true, and so it seems that before I can know I really remember something (rather than merely recalling it) I must first know that what I purport to remember is true, and in order to know that I must first settle the question of personal identity that is involved in the memory claim.[20] Common though this argument is, it should be obvious what is wrong with it. It overlooks the existence of prima facie reasons. We have already seen that my recalling-that-*P* is a prima facie reason for me to believe-that-*P*, and for me to believe that I remember-that-*P*. If it were not, historical knowledge would be impossible. In order to know that I remember, I do not first have to establish the truth of what I claim to remember; my having the recollection auto-

[19] In effect, I am agreeing with Shoemaker [1963] that we do not employ any *criterion* in reidentifying ourselves. If there is a criterion for reidentification, it is only for third-person reidentification.

[20] For example, this argument is given by Williams [1956].

matically gives me a reason for thinking that what I recall is true. We need not concern ourselves further with this standard objection to memory criteria.

The above observations seem to indicate that we need nothing new to make it possible for us to reidentify ourselves. All that is required is propositional memory, and that has already been secured in Chapter Seven. But at this point an objection is apt to arise. This objection gets its substance by asking why we cannot reidentify others in the same way we reidentify ourselves. For example, it may seem that just as I reidentify myself by remembering facts about myself, so I can reidentify my neighbor by remembering facts about him and thus knowing that he uniquely satisfied certain descriptions. But I cannot literally remember that my present neighbor used to satisfy certain descriptions. I cannot remember this because it violates the previous-awareness condition. All I can literally remember is that certain things were true of a man of such-and-such a description. My reidentification of that man as my present neighbor is something over and above what I remember. I could not remember that those facts were true of my present neighbor, because that would require me to have known previously that the facts were then true of a certain man, and also to have known at that time that that man was going to be my neighbor at the present time.[21]

Thus third-person reidentifications cannot function in the way I have described first-person reidentifications as functioning. But isn't this a problem for first-person reidentifications too? That is, does it not also violate the previous-awareness condition for me to remember that certain facts were true of myself? It might seem so, but upon reflection this is not so obvious. The immediate-awareness condition requires that in order for me to remember that I was φ, I must have previously known that I was φ. But of course, I did know that. That is, the person who was I knew of himself that he was φ. One is tempted to suppose that there is an ambiguity here—that what the previous-awareness condition requires is that the person who was I knew of me now that I was then φ. Frankly, I find this distinction unintelligible. I see no reason to think the previous-awareness condition is not satisfied. I think the proper

[21] Of course, it is possible, although not usual, for me to have known all of this, but to know that a certain man was going to be my neighbor at this time presupposes an ability to reidentify in some other way.

conclusion to be drawn is that "I" functions quite unlike a definite description or proper name. Although "I knew of the man who is now my neighbor that he was φ" expresses a different proposition than "I knew that the man who was going to now be my neighbor was φ", no similar distinction can be made between two senses of "I knew that I was φ". To sort this out clearly would take us beyond the scope of this investigation, but we need not beg any questions here—I shall now argue that if, contrary to what I have just maintained, we were to decide that the previous-awareness condition is violated by my remembering that I was φ, this would make no difference. Rather than concluding that I cannot remember that I was φ, we would instead be forced to relax the previous-awareness condition in such a way as to allow this.

Suppose that my remembering that I was φ would violate the previous-awareness condition. Should we conclude then that one cannot literally remember such a thing? That would be a mistake. If I do not literally remember that I was φ, then my "remembering" it must be treated in the same way as my "remembering" that certain facts were true of my neighbor. That is, there must be some description such that what I literally remember is that the person of that description was φ, and then on some other grounds I reidentify myself as the person satisfying that description. The difficulty is that there is no such description. When I remember that I had cereal for breakfast, or that I just talked to an insurance agent on the telephone, I do not automatically know of any description of myself at that time. There is no way to analyze my recollection except as recollection literally and directly about myself. We must conclude that one can literally remember that he was φ, regardless of whether this violates the previous-awareness condition. If it does violate the previous-awareness condition, what this shows is that that condition was drawn too narrowly in the analysis of propositional memory, and not that we do not remember. But, as I have maintained above, I do not see any reason to think that the previous-awareness condition is violated here.

Not all cases of first-person reidentification arise in this way from my remembering facts about myself. I have already mentioned the case of recognizing my face in a picture of a crowd. Perhaps then we must augment the above account of first-person reidentification with some additional principles. The best way to get clear on this is to turn to third-person reidentification, because these other cases of reidentification seem to be essentially the same as third-person reidentifications.

4.2 *Third-Person Reidentification*

It is clear, I think, that we generally reidentify another person by reidentifying his body. Thus it is plausible to suppose that bodily identity is a logically necessary and sufficient condition for personal identity, and indeed many philosophers have supposed this.[22] Some philosophers have defended this on the grounds that a person is identical with his body.[23] But we have already seen that this is not the case. Rather, a person is composed of his body.[24] And a person's being composed of his body does not guarantee that he can be reidentified in terms of his body. It simply is not true that when one thing X is composed of another thing Y, then it must always be composed of that same thing Y, and hence X can be reidentified in terms of Y. For example, a statue is composed of a certain set of molecules. But those molecules are in a constant state of flux. Some of them are continually migrating into and out of the structure constituting the statue, and with each change the statue is composed of a different set of molecules. Thus the fact that a person is composed of his body in no way guarantees that he can be reidentified in terms of his body.

Although a person is not the same thing as his body, it might still be true for some other reason that bodily identity is a necessary and sufficient condition for personal identity. Let us turn to this question directly. There are at least three reasons why bodily identity cannot be a necessary and sufficient condition for personal identity. First, two persons can share a single body. We have already seen an example of this in discussing the problem of co-personality. Second, it is a contingent fact that persons have bodies. Ghosts and magnetic men are not logical absurdities, and although they have no bodies, we would not find it impossible to reidentify them. We would do this on the basis of their P-attributes—their memories, abilities, personalities, etc. Thus personal identity cannot be *simply* a matter of bodily identity. Finally, although persons do in fact have bodies, they need not retain the same body. This can be seen by considering the following example. Suppose that the art of medicine is in a quite different state than

[22] For example, Ayer [1964].
[23] For example, Cowley [1971].
[24] See section 4 of Chapter Six.

it is in fact. On the one hand, doctors know nothing about germs. They attribute physical ailments to gremlins in the body. On the other hand, doctors are so skilled at organ transplants that they can transplant any organ at all with total success. Their cure for a gremlin is to lop off the infested organ, and replace it with another organ taken from cold storage. They have discovered that if a gremlin-infested organ is put in cold storage for one week, that kills the gremlin and the organ can then be used for someone else, thus assuring a constant supply of organs for transplants. But there is one problem. These gremlins are wily creatures, and great care must be taken that they do not find out about an impending transplant. Otherwise they will simply move to a neighboring organ and avoid the transplant. Now let us suppose that we have two men with particularly wily gremlins. The doctors keep lopping off organs and replacing them with others from the freezer, but the gremlins keep getting away. In time, every organ of each man's body has been replaced by another from the freezer. Let us suppose that at no point in the sequence of transplants was there any apparent change in the memories, knowledge, personalities, abilities, etc., of either man. For example, while one man was having his head transplanted he was in the process of writing a letter home to his mother. As this was a relatively simple transplant, the doctors used only a local anesthetic, so he was able to continue writing throughout the operation. He described in lurid detail how it feels to have one's head cut off and a new one sewn on. At no point was the chain of thought broken. Under these circumstances, there would be no temptation to say that he is no longer the same person after the transplant. Finally, after transplanting every organ of each man's body, the doctors succeed in eliminating the gremlins. But then it is discovered that, purely by chance, each man has ended up with all of the organs that originally made up the body of the other man. In effect, each body was disassembled and then reassembled around the other man. In this way, they have come to exchange bodies. There would not be the slightest temptation to identify the men in terms of their bodies, either by the men themselves or by anyone else who was witnessing it all. Consequently, bodily identity is neither necessary nor sufficient for personal identity.

We do, of course, generally rely upon bodily identity in making third-person reidentifications. But this cannot be a conclusive reason for such reidentifications. Perhaps it is a logical reason, but only a prima facie one. But even this cannot be so. Our judgments of personal identity cannot be based ultimately on bodily identity for a very simple reason: judgments of bodily identity presuppose judgments of personal identity. This is because, even given that persons do have bodies, it is a contingent fact, to be discovered inductively, what sorts of physical objects are bodies. In order to discover that objects of a certain sort are the bodies of persons, we must discover that each of these objects encompasses all of the locatable phenomenological states (pains, proprioceptive sensations, etc.) of some person over at least a small interval of time. It is not enough that the object encompass all of the locatable phenomenological states at an instant—if it were, and if at some instant a person's only sensation was a pain in his finger, we would be led to say that his finger was his body at that instant. But in order to know that an object encompasses all of a person's locatable phenomenological states over an interval of time we must be able to reidentify that person over that interval of time. Thus, rather than forming the basis for judgments of personal identity, the concept of a body presupposes an independent ability to judge personal identity.

On the other hand, several philosophers have repeated what seems to be a very strong argument to the effect that bodily identity must be a criterion.[25] The argument is this. If bodily identity is not a criterion, then it seems that the logical basis for reidentifying a person must be "mental", i.e., must consist of our knowing that he is in certain P-states. Thus in order to reidentify another person, we must ascertain that he has certain P-attributes. But, as we have seen, this will involve observing the person's behavior. This cannot take place instantaneously. Behavior always takes time. And we must know that it is one and the same person whose behavior we are observing over the interval in which we are ascertaining what P-attributes he has. We cannot know this on the basis of his P-attributes, because they are what we are attempting to discover. It seems we must be assuming that bodily identity, at least over the period of observation, is indicative of personal identity. In other words, any mental reasons for reidentification seem to presuppose that bodily identity is a criterion.

[25] See, for example, Williams [1956], p. 336; and Shoemaker [1963], pp. 196-199.

This argument is persuasive in the abstract, but when we try to apply it to concrete cases, it is no longer plausible. For example, if a person utters a sentence, this consists of a whole sequence of sounds. By what right do we tie all of these sounds together into a single sentence which we attribute to one person? We certainly do not do this on the basis of bodily identity. We would tie the sounds together just as readily if we heard them without perceiving the body of the person who uttered them. For that matter, we would tie them together just as readily if they were uttered by a ghost. What really happens here is quite simple. We have seen that our knowledge of the P-states of others is inductive, arising ultimately from observation of our own P-states and their physical concomitants. These physical concomitants are physical events. Physical events do not, as a general rule, occur instantaneously. Most interesting physical events are complexes of instantaneous events. But we do not need anything like the presence of a single physical object (like a human body) to tie the different elements of a compound physical event together into a single complex event. *Any* events can be tied together to form a complex event. What we discover inductively is that certain complex events (such as a sequence of sounds of a certain character) are accompanied by the presence of persons in certain P-states. Nowhere in this reasoning is there any logical requirement of sameness of body. Of course, as a matter of contingent fact, the presence of a single body is often a part of the physical concomitants of a P-state, but this is something we discover inductively and is not a logical part of our reasoning.

There are good reasons why bodily identity cannot be a logical reason for judging personal identity, and there are no viable arguments to the contrary. We must conclude that any noninductive reasons for judging personal identity must be mental. However, there is a good reason why there should be no mental logical reasons either: we don't need any. We do not need *any* noninductive logical reasons, either mental or physical, in order to make third-person reidentifications. Given that we can make first-person reidentifications, we can use data acquired on that basis and make third-person reidentifications inductively. But given that it is possible to make third-person reidentifications without appealing to any mental (or physical) logical reasons, it becomes a substantive question how reliable any mental indicator of personal identity is, and such a substantive question cannot be settled by appeal to principles of logic. Thus such mental indicators can only be contingent reasons for judging personal identity. Third-person reidentification must be entirely inductive.

Apparently our knowledge of personal identity is completely analogous to our knowledge of other P-states. On the one hand, we have a special way of acquiring knowledge of our own personal identity. This arises from the fact that we can literally remember things about ourselves in a way that we cannot remember things about others. On the other hand, the concept of personal identity is projectible so we can use our knowledge of our own personal identity to acquire inductive reasons for ascribing personal identity both (1) to ourselves in cases where we do not remember enough relevant facts and (2) to others. Predominant among our inductive reasons for ascribing personal identity is bodily identity, but this is only an inductive reason and must not be supposed to have the status of a logical reason.

4.3 *Exchange of Bodies*

Now we come to what is basically a side issue, but which has been discussed so much in the literature that it has become important. This is the matter of exchange of bodies. If, as I have maintained, bodily identity is only an inductive reason for judging personal identity, then it should be possible to describe cases in which we would say that a person had exchanged bodies, acquiring a new one. I have already described one case of this sort—the example of consecutive organ transplants. But this is not the sort of example philosophers have sought. They want an example in which a person acquires a new body "in one fell swoop" rather than a piece at a time.

Most of the putative examples of this sort have the outstanding characteristic of being problematic.[26] I think that the reason they are problematic is very simple. They are described as unique occurrences set against the background of our normal inductive generalizations. Because of the strength of the inductive evidence supporting the conclusion that sameness of body guarantees personal identity, that evidence immediately weakens any single example which contravenes this. This difficulty can be avoided easily

[26] The best-known such example is probably Shoemaker's brain-exchange case in Shoemaker [1963]; but see the reply in Williams [1970].

enough by constructing examples in which we would never have been led in the first place to suppose that bodily identity is indicative of personal identity. Consider yourself a resident of the following sort of world. Suppose children are always born in pairs—fraternal twins. At intervals of ten hours twins always get an overpowering urge to run up and embrace one another. After such an embrace, they exhibit interchanged memories, personalities, etc. If they are physically prevented from embracing, both twins die on the stroke of the tenth hour. If I were a resident of such a world, I would never have concluded inductively that bodily identity is (unqualifiedly) indicative of personal identity. On the contrary, starting from my own case and reidentifying myself on the basis of my recollections, I would conclude that every ten hours I exchange bodies with my twin, and I would subsequently conclude inductively that the same thing is true of others. In this world, bodily identity over an interval of more than ten hours but less than twenty hours would never come to acquire the status of a reason for reidentification, and hence would not be an obstacle to judging that two persons had exchanged bodies.

4.4 *Borderline Cases of Personal Identity*

In a way, the problematic examples of exchange of bodies are more interesting than the clear cases. For example, suppose a man arises in the morning, looks in the mirror, and is astonished at the countenance staring back at him. He professes to be Jones, and he exhibits all of Jones's memories, personality traits, etc., and yet he is in the body of Smith. Furthermore, upon looking up Jones's body, we find a person in the reverse situation—one who professes to be Smith and exhibits all of Smith's memories and personality traits. What are we to say—that Jones and Smith have exchanged bodies, or that their P-attributes have been interchanged? I do not think we would know which to say. On the one hand we have an inductive reason for reidentifying the persons in terms of their memories and other P-attributes, but on the other hand we have an inductive reason for reidentifying them in terms of their bodies. Neither reason is notably stronger than the other. The important thing about this example is that our inability to decide the question of personal identity does not arise out of our ignorance of relevant facts. We can suppose that we know every true proposition which is relevant as evidence in this case, but we are still unable to decide who is who. Our concept of personal identity is such that *there is no way to decide.* In this case *there is no answer* to the question of personal identity. Borderline cases like this are inevitable for any concept, like personal identity, whose justification conditions arise ultimately from prima facie reasons. It is always possible to have the prima facie reasons defeated by the total set of relevant true propositions in such a way that there is in principle no way to decide whether the concept applies.

The existence of borderline cases is not surprising for most concepts. But it is astonishing in the case of personal identity. As Derek Parfit puts it, people ordinarily believe that "Whatever happens between now and any future time, either I shall still exist, or I shall not. Any future experience will either be *my* experience, or it will not."[27] It is undeniable that there are borderline cases having to do with the continued existence of a physical thing. Shoemaker [1963] gives the example of the bridge of Santa Trinità in Florence, which was destroyed during World War II and subsequently rebuilt using some of the original stones and some new stones. Is it the same bridge? We cannot decide this unequivocally. It is largely a matter of convention which we say. But it does not seem that it can be equally a matter of convention what we say about questions of personal identity. For example,[28] suppose I am Jones in the previous example prior to the exchange (leaving open whether it is an exchange of bodies or of P-states). Suppose I know that the exchange is going to take place (it is being brought about intentionally by a group of scientists), and I know that the person in one of the two bodies will then be tortured. I can now choose which body it will be. We can suppose that my only concern is that it will not be myself who is tortured. It makes a great difference to me which of the persons after the exchange is me. It seems outrageous for me to say, "Oh well, it is just a matter of convention which will be me. Torture whichever one you like." There seems to be something horribly wrong with any account of personal identity which leads to the conclusion that there can be borderline cases.

Despite the apparent absurdity of borderline cases of personal identity, I think that they are a real possibility. What makes it seem incomprehensible for there to be borderline cases is not the concept

[27] Parfit [1971]; he is concerned to argue that this belief is false.

[28] I take this line of argument from Williams [1970].

of personal identity itself but rather the peculiar concern each person has for his own future welfare. A person has a natural, unreasoned, innate concern for his own future welfare. As Shoemaker [1969*a*] argues, some such concern is essential to the very concept of welfare. If a person did not have concern for his welfare, it would not count as welfare. And to have concern for your welfare is to have concern for your future welfare, because your present state is already here and it is too late to do anything about it. This does not require that we always have a concern for our future welfare, but it does require that we ordinarily have such a concern.

The problem is that this unreasoned concern for our own welfare has no automatic focus in the problem cases. The reason we think the question of personal identity must have an answer in the problem cases (and don't think the same thing about physical objects) is that when we view the cases from a first-person point of view, we want a focus for the special concern we have for our own future welfare. We are instinctively driven to satisfy this concern, and we cannot do so without first answering the question of personal identity. Without such a focus that concern does not make sense.

But there is no reason why such a concern must make sense. By Shoemaker's argument, it follows that we must have such a concern in the normal case, but we need not always have it. And innate concerns (being "unreasoned" or "nonrational") need not always be coherent. We might imagine a species which has a special concern for the strongest of their number, coupled with disdain for other members that are almost as strong but not quite as strong as the strongest member. Such a concern might have definite survival value. But when faced with *two* strongest members, they would not know what to do, and reason could not help them. Analogously, there is no reason we should have to be able to resolve (through reason) our quandary regarding the focus of our concern in the problem cases of personal identity. Our concern could be incoherent. Given that our concern is innate, and given that the problem cases do not actually arise (although they might in the future), evolution has not led to our concern being sufficiently articulated to have a focus in the problem cases, and there is no way that rational considerations can carry out the articulation. It must be concluded that there is no logical absurdity in the possibility of borderline cases of personal identity. When actually faced with such a case, we would have an irresolvable problem.

5. The Concept of a Person

I have had a great deal to say about how we acquire knowledge of persons. What can we conclude from this about what a person is? In the history of philosophy there have been two traditional answers to this question, which we may simplistically call the *materialist* and the *Cartesian* theories. The materialist proposes that a person is simply a body of a certain sort, while the Cartesian maintains that a person is essentially nonphysical. The materialist is wrong. As we have seen, a person cannot be identified with his body. But the Cartesian is also wrong. Because a person is composed of his body, he inherits numerous physical attributes from that body. A person has size, shape, weight, location, is composed of molecules, etc. These are presumably the sort of things that are denied by saying that a person is nonphysical. It must be concluded that a person is a physical entity.

Nevertheless, although a person is a physical entity, it is only a contingent fact that he is. It is logically possible that persons might not have been composed of bodies. Consequently, although it is not true that persons are essentially nonphysical, it is true that persons are not essentially physical. We are led to a position intermediate between the materialist and Cartesian theories.

But we are still left with the question of what sort of thing a person is that he can be a physical entity but not essentially physical. What the philosopher who asks this question really wants is a reductive analysis of the concept of a person, but it is pretty obvious that no such analysis is possible. The concept of a person is "logically primitive" in the same sense as is the concept of a physical thing. We cannot explain it by "taking persons apart" into something simpler. The best we can do is explain how we operate with the concept of a person. Let us ask, in a general way, how we come to know about persons.

We can literally perceive (i.e., see, hear, feel, etc.) persons, because the attribute of being perceived is inherited from the body. But this only gives us inductive knowledge about persons because it is only a contingent fact that persons are composed of bodies. In order for us to discover this contingent fact, it seems there must be some direct noninductive way of observing persons. What might that be? One is apt to suppose that the best (perhaps the only) way to directly observe a person is to observe oneself. But Hume complained that, no matter how hard he tried, he was never able to find himself in introspection—all he could observe were his P-states. Hume has noticed something very important. *Direct* (i.e., noninductive) observation of a person is only possible by knowing of his P-states. This is no less true of oneself than of others. Our access to persons is always "through" their P-states. There is no way to observe a person "denuded of P-states".[29] When we introspect we do not happen upon ourselves—we find our P-states. When we observe another human body we only know that it is alive (i.e., constitutes a person) by seeing that it manifests P-states.

It is noteworthy that nowhere in our account of our knowledge of persons (which is knowledge of the P-states of persons) have we made any essential use of the persons themselves. For example, although copersonality is the relation of being P-states of the same person, copersonality construed simply as a relation between P-states has been characterized without talking about the persons. In effect, persons are conceptually redundant. We could get by perfectly well just talking about P-states. This has prompted some philosophers to suppose either (1) that there is no person, there are only P-states (the "no-ownership theory"), or (2) that the person is to be identified with the set of his P-states (the "bundle theory").

The no-ownership theory is wrong. If there are P-states, there are persons. It is a matter of logic that P-states must have persons as their subjects.[30] To say that a person exists is not to add anything to saying that a P-state exists. The no-ownership theorist is guilty of a common logical fallacy. If something can be "analyzed away", or shown to be conceptually unnecessary, it does not follow that it does not exist; on the contrary, this may show that it exists automatically because for it to exist is for something seemingly quite different to be true. In the case of persons, we might say that they are the *tautological possessors* of P-states. They are the tautological

[29] One might make the similar observation that there is no way to non-inductively observe a physical thing except through its perceptual attributes. There is no way to observe a physical thing denuded of those attributes.

[30] I am guilty of a similar oversimplification here. The subjects of P-states need not be persons—other animals also possess P-states. But as it is primarily persons I am interested in, I will continue to talk as if the only living beings were persons.

possessors because to know that there is a person in a P-state we do not first have to find out that there is a person and then ascertain that he is in the P-state; all we have to do is become aware of the existence of the P-state and it follows automatically that there is a person in it. To become aware of the existence of a P-state is automatically to become aware of a person. This is the substance of Hume's observation.

The no-ownership theory is wrong. What about the bundle theory? The bundle theory amounts to a category mistake. A set of P-states is an abstract entity; a person is not. This is underscored by noting that sets of P-states have attributes not defined for persons. For example, the set of a person's P-states has a cardinality, but a person does not have a cardinality. So no identification is possible here. We might say that a person is "logically correlated with" the set of his P-states but he is not the same thing as that set. Still, the bundle theory contains an important insight. Although a person cannot be identified with the set of his P-states, there is a sense in which he is nothing over and above that set either. If we know all of a person's P-states (for all time), we know everything there is to know about him. Or more precisely, the only additional facts we need ever know are not facts directly about him. For example, if we know all of Jones's P-states, we know that he inhabits a certain body (that is a P-state). Then in order to know that Jones is standing next to Smith we need not discover anything further about Jones. All we need is information about the body which is in fact his, and about Smith. In this sense, although a person cannot be identified with the set of his P-states, he can still be regarded as a logical construct out of the set of his P-states. But he is none the worse for that—he still exists.

Our concept of a person is the concept of a possessor of P-states. Thus to analyze the concept of a person is to analyze the concept of the possession of P-states. But this is just to analyze the concept of the occurrence of a P-state, because P-states are automatically possessed—they cannot just float around free. In turn, to analyze the concept of the occurrence of a P-state is to analyze statements ascribing P-states to persons. Thus, in the end we are led to say about persons something analogous to what we said about the concept of a physical thing. To analyze the concept of a person is to analyze all of the various kinds of statements about persons.

This is not the sort of analysis the traditional philosopher was seeking, but it is the only sort of analysis that can be given. We cannot "take persons apart into their metaphysical constituents" any more than we can do that for physical things, but there is no reason why we should be able to do that either.

Chapter Ten

Truths of Reason

1. Introduction

IT HAS traditionally been supposed that there are two kinds of truths. On the one hand there are "empirical" truths that can only be known by experience of the world; but on the other hand there are "truths of reason" that can be known simply by reflection, independently of any experience of the world. For example, one could know that all bachelors are unmarried without ever having met a bachelor, or even without there ever having been any bachelors. Such knowledge has traditionally been called *a priori knowledge*. Knowledge that is not a priori is called *empirical*.

There is a whole network of concepts connected with the a priori/empirical distinction. In contemporary philosophy, it is generally claimed that a priori truths are "true by virtue of meaning". Such truths are called *analytic*, so it is claimed that a priori truths are analytic. "Necessary truths" or "logical truths" are truths that are somehow "logically precluded from being false"; they are "true in all possible worlds". It is generally supposed that the a priori truths are the same as the necessary truths.

Connected with the notion of a priori truth is that of logical implication. We say that *P implies Q* just in case it is possible to construct an argument leading from *P* to *Q* which can be certified, on a priori grounds, to be valid. Although the terms "implies" and "entails" are generally used interchangeably, let us make a distinction and define "entails" so that it is related to necessary truth in roughly the same way as "implies" is related to a priori truth. So construed, *P* entails *Q* iff it is necessarily true that, if *P* were true, *Q* would be true. Then if the a priori truths are the same as the necessary truths, it will turn out that implication is the same thing as entailment.

1. Introduction

It has generally been supposed that a priori truth is definable in terms of implication via the "law of noncontradiction". According to this proposal, P is true a priori iff $\sim P$ implies a contradiction. Analogously, it is supposed that P is necessarily true iff $\sim P$ entails a contradiction.

The problem with which we are now faced is to make all of these notions clearer, explore their interrelations, and explain how we can have knowledge of a priori truths, necessary truths, etc. We will concentrate on the notion of a priori truth. It will turn out that, if we can clarify that notion, the other concepts can then be clarified in terms of it. The definition of "a priori knowledge" with which we began this chapter is obviously inadequate. It must be asked in what sense a priori knowledge is independent of experience. This cannot mean simply that one could have this knowledge without having had any experience of the world, because it might be false that any knowledge has this characteristic. We cannot have knowledge without first acquiring the requisite concepts, and it might be true that we cannot acquire any concepts until we have some experience of the world. What must be meant by saying that this knowledge is independent of experience of the world is that experience does not provide us with reasons or grounds upon which this knowledge is based. For example, our reason for thinking that all bachelors are unmarried is not based upon our having conducted a poll of bachelors.

However, it is too strong a requirement that a priori knowledge be independent of *all* experience in this way. For example, many philosophers have wanted to say that the source of a priori knowledge is some kind of intuition of relations between universals. This intuition, if it exists, is a kind of experience, but clearly it is not the kind of experience of which a priori knowledge is supposed to be independent. Presumably, however we ultimately explain the possibility of a priori knowledge, it will involve our having *some* sort of experience, but this must not be taken to mean that this knowledge is not really a priori. The kinds of experience that philosophers have traditionally wanted to require this knowledge to be independent of are sense perception, memory, interoceptive sensations, etc. But it is extremely difficult to give a list of all the sorts of experience that must be ruled out. It is not even clear, for certain kinds of experience, whether they should be ruled out. For example, what about introspection? Most introspection should be ruled out, but some philosophers have urged that a certain kind of introspection provides us with the characteristic grounds for a priori knowledge. For example, Hume suggested that a priori knowledge is based upon our determining introspectively whether we can imagine a certain kind of state of affairs.

It will be seen below that it is much easier to say upon what kinds of experience a priori knowledge is dependent than to say of what kinds it is independent. To begin, we must work with only a rather rough list of the kinds of knowledge we want to call "a priori". We cannot begin by giving any precise definition of this kind of knowledge. We have a rather vague understanding of what kind of thing it is that we are talking about, but the clarification of the concept must wait until later. It will turn out that the clarification of the concept will come simultaneously with an explanation of how a priori knowledge is possible.

2. Logical Skepticism

In connection with a priori knowledge we find what is perhaps the only contemporary example of a widely accepted skepticism. A surprising number of good philosophers profess to disbelieve in a priori knowledge. The popularity of this logical skepticism is probably due to the brilliant writings of its most able defender—W. V. Quine.[1] Quine has argued very persuasively, and in great detail, that no truth condition analysis of the concept of a priori truth can be given. He has concluded from this that there is no such concept—the pronouncements of other philosophers regarding purported a priori truths do not even make sense according to Quine. Thus what Quine is defending is not quite a traditional skepticism. He is not maintaining merely that we cannot know which truths are a priori. He goes further and maintains that there is not even such a concept. This is a rather natural variation on traditional skepticism, and was suggested by Hume in connection with skepticism regarding other forms of knowledge. If it can be shown that knowledge of some subject matter is impossible, it seems reasonable to conclude that the concepts involved do not really make sense.[2]

[1] See Quine [1953] and [1960], and especially [1951].

[2] This is an awkward way of talking. It would be better to say that the

Despite the brilliance of Quine's defense, sober reflection would seem to indicate that logical skepticism is just as preposterous as any other form of skepticism. As Grice and Strawson [1956] noted in their famous reply to Quine, that there is *some* distinction marked by the philosopher's terms "a priori" and "empirical" can hardly be denied. I should think that this is patently obvious, but if it is not it is at least indicated by the fact that there is such a large measure of agreement among philosophers (and nonphilosophers too!) concerning what propositions are clearly a priori, what propositions are clearly empirical, and what propositions are of problematic status. This agreement extends not just to propositions that have been discussed in the philosophical literature but to new examples not previously considered. It is also remarkable how easy it is to teach the concept of a priori knowledge to college students. The presentation of a few examples is generally all that is required to enable a student to go on and make the same judgments a professional philosopher would make regarding what propositions are a priori. In the face of this I cannot but feel that the antiskeptical argument given in Chapter One applies to logical skepticism with a vengeance: any argument whose conclusion is logical skepticism is best regarded as a reductio ad absurdum of its premises. No set of premises which entails logical skepticism can be as clearly true as logical skepticism is clearly false. In the case of the admittedly skeletal argument I attributed to Quine,[3] it seems obvious which premise to reject. I agree with Quine that no truth condition analysis of a priori truth can be given. But Quine assumes (implicitly) that it follows from this that there is no concept of a priori truth. Perhaps this implicit premise is initially plausible (I personally do not find it so), but once it is seen to lead to the preposterous conclusion of logical skepticism, surely one must reject this premise rather than accept logical skepticism. This premise represents just one more instance of the traditional assumption that the meaning of a concept must arise from its truth conditions, and hence that reductive analyses are always possible.

Despite the absurdity of logical skepticism, Quine is onto some-

---

concepts do not exist rather than that they do not make sense. The notion of a senseless concept would seem to be self-contradictory.

[3] Quine has given other arguments too, but this objection seems to apply just as readily to them.

thing important. Although we cannot reasonably deny the existence of the concept of a priori knowledge, we certainly can question whether it has all the convenient attributes traditional philosophers have supposed it to have. To a large extent, what Quine and his followers have argued is not that no distinction is marked by the philosopher's use of the terms "a priori" and "empirical" but that there is no concept which has all the nice properties traditionally attributed to a priori truth. I have considerable sympathy with this position, so perhaps my disagreement with the logical skeptics is not so great as our verbal pronouncements would make it seem. But if this is really their point, they have stated their position in a misleading way. Be that as it may, what should be in question is not the existence of the concept of a priori knowledge but its significance. How does it connect up with other concepts? What can we legitimately say about it to clarify it, and once we have clarified it what can we do with it? These are the questions that I will investigate, in a preliminary way, in this final chapter.

It should be clear that I am in very substantial agreement with one of the most significant points made by the logical skeptics.[4] This is that, whatever the nature of the concept of a priori truth, philosophers have grossly overused it. They have been much too quick to propose myriad propositions as a priori truths. This overuse is part and parcel of the entire reductionist philosophy that has been my principal target throughout this book. However, my rejection of reductionism does not extend to the point of shunning the concept of a priori truth completely in philosophical analysis. Although I believe that truth condition analyses can rarely be given, the logical tools with which I have replaced such analyses (prima facie and conclusive reasons) were themselves introduced by giving truth condition analyses of them.

3. Two Theories of A Priori Knowledge

3.1 *Logical Intuitionism*

There are essentially two kinds of theories that have been held concerning a priori knowledge. The first, and historically oldest, might be called "logical intuitionism". According to logical intui-

[4] This point is made most clearly by Hilary Putnam [1966], who is perhaps only peripherally a logical skeptic.

tionism we have some sort of direct intellectual apprehension of a priori truths. Some a priori truths are "self-evident" in that one can simply "see" that they are true, and then other a priori truths are derived from these basic self-evident truths by giving proofs each step of which is self-evident. This basic position of logical intuitionism can be embroidered in a number of ways. Hume attempted to explain this power of intuition as a kind of introspective knowledge of what it is possible for us to imagine. According to Hume a self-evident truth is just one such that we cannot imagine what it would be like for it to be false. On the other hand, Bertrand Russell [1912] described these intuitions as arising from our being directly acquainted with universals and relations between universals (although it is questionable whether this has any explanatory value).

Logical intuitionism is subject to a number of immediate difficulties. First, this faculty of intuition seems very mysterious, and without further elaboration it does not seem to explain anything. To say that we know a priori truths intuitively seems to amount to nothing more than saying that we know them but do not know how we know them, which is no explanation. Second, and perhaps even more serious, is the fact that different people's intuitions, or judgments of self-evidence, do not always agree. What is self-evident to an eminent mathematician may be anything but self-evident to a college freshman. This would seem to make a priori truth relative to the individual. What is a priori true for one person may not be a priori true for another, and might even be a priori false for another. But surely what is true cannot vary from person to person. Thus this cannot be a correct account of a priori truth. These and similar difficulties have served to make logical intuitionism no longer respectable in the eyes of most contemporary philosophers. Nevertheless, we will return to this position later, and it will be argued that these difficulties are merely superficial and that logical intuitionism is after all the correct account of a priori knowledge.

3.2 *Reductionism*

The alternative to logical intuitionism is some form of reductionism according to which there is no special intellectual faculty involved in a priori knowledge, but instead putative a priori knowledge is really a disguised form of empirical knowledge. The least plausible kind of reductionism is Mill's inductivism. According to John Stuart Mill, purportedly a priori truths were really just very general inductive generalizations about the world, differing from ordinary scientific generalizations only in their generality. This view is obviously false. It simply does not accord with the way in which we actually acquire a priori knowledge. For example, according to Mill, we learn that $5 + 7 = 12$ by discovering inductively that whenever we put five things together with seven things we end up with twelve things. If we really did have to learn this inductively, we would not accept it at all, because it frequently happens that when we put five things together with seven things the result is not twelve things. For example, if we put five pieces of uranium together with seven pieces of uranium, where each piece is one eighth of a critical mass (the mass necessary to lead to a nuclear explosion), the result will most certainly not be twelve pieces of uranium, but no one would regard this as relevant to the question of whether $5 + 7 = 12$. It must be concluded that laws of addition have nothing whatever to do with processes of physical combination. Empirical truths of this sort are not relevant in learning that a particular a priori truth is true.

A second kind of reductionism is Frege's logicism. According to this theory, a priori truths reduce to truths of logic when definitions are supplied for some of the concepts involved in them. For example, "All bachelors are unmarried" reduces to "All unmarried men are unmarried" when the definition is supplied for "bachelor", and "All unmarried men are unmarried" is a truth of logic. On this view, a priori knowledge reduces to knowledge of truths of logic together with knowledge of definitions. This is Frege's explanation of a priori truth, and it has been quite popular in contemporary philosophy. Unfortunately, it is subject to a number of immediate difficulties.

The first difficulty that arises for logicism concerns whether all a priori truths do in fact arise from definitions in the manner suggested. For example, "Nothing can be both red and green all over" is an a priori truth, but it does not seem to be possible to give definitions of "red" and "green" which, when substituted into this statement, yield anything recognizable as a truth of logic. The same thing seems to be true of "All mountains are material objects", and "No lemons are rivers".

Even supposing that the above difficulty can be circumvented, logicism really explains nothing until it is filled out further. First, we must ask what sort of thing it is that we are defining. When we define "bachelor", are we defining the *word* "bachelor", or are we providing a definition for a nonlinguistic or only partly linguistic entity—the *concept* of being a bachelor? Which answer we seize upon makes a great difference. Consider the answer that we are defining concepts rather than words. This answer does not advance our understanding of a priori knowledge. If we are to explain a priori knowledge in terms of knowledge of the definitions of concepts, then this latter knowledge must itself be clear. But knowledge of the definition of a concept would seem to be nothing but another example of a priori knowledge. For example, to know that the concept of being a bachelor is the same as the concept of being an unmarried man, if this is not construed as a report on how words are used, would seem to be the same thing as knowing a priori that a person is a bachelor if, and only if, he is an unmarried man.

Let us turn then to the other answer—that it is words that we are defining. This answer attempts to reduce a priori knowledge to knowledge of the definitions of words and knowledge of truths of logic. Supposing for the moment that there is nothing problematic about how we know the definitions of words, let us turn to knowledge of truths of logic. The first difficulty that arises here concerns what is to count as "all of logic". What is included in logic—the propositional calculus, the predicate calculus, the predicate calculus with identity, second order logic, higher order logic, set theory, modal logic, deontic logic, epistemic logic, or what? There does not seem to be any sharp dividing line between truths of logic and other a priori truths. I would suggest that *any* a priori truth could be considered a truth of logic provided it is contained in a systematic treatment of a number of related a priori truths. But if this is so, then truths of logic will be the same thing as a priori truths, and not a restricted subclass of them. This makes it fruitless to try to explain a priori truth in terms of truths of logic.

An equally serious difficulty concerns how one knows truths of logic. If a priori knowledge is to be explained in terms of knowledge of truths of logic, then the latter must be clearer than the former. But unfortunately, it seems to be no easier to understand how knowledge of truths of logic is possible than it is to understand how a priori knowledge in general is possible. I would say that it is the same problem in both cases. Certainly one's initial reaction is to say that knowledge of truths of logic is just another example of a priori knowledge, and thus nothing is achieved by attempting to reduce the latter to the former.

3.3 *Conventionalism*

The attempt has been made to reduce a priori knowledge to knowledge of certain features of language—the definitions of words—together with knowledge of truths of logic, but the latter knowledge seems to be no easier to understand than a priori knowledge in general. This leads naturally to the suggestion that perhaps logic can be left out of the picture altogether and a priori knowledge explained entirely in terms of knowledge of language. The suggestion is that a priori truths somehow simply reflect the rules of our language, and as such a priori knowledge can be explained entirely in terms of knowledge of the rules of language. This is *conventionalism.* Conventionalism is by far the most popular contemporary view of a priori knowledge, although I think that it is wrong. However, it is much more difficult to refute conventionalism than the other forms of reductionism.

The general position of conventionalism is that a priori truths express rules of language. A priori truths are *made* true by the linguistic community's adopting certain rules of language; a priori truths are created by people rather than being discoveries about a mysterious independently existing realm of concepts and propositions; there are no a priori truths until there is language.

Conventionalism has the effect of reducing purportedly a priori knowledge to empirical knowledge. Because language only contingently has the structure that it does, a priori truths are not necessary truths—they would not have been true had language had a different structure than it in fact has. Presumably, according to conventionalism, there are no necessary truths. Of course, we do discover a priori truths just by reflecting—we do not have to undertake an empirical investigation of language—but this is only because we speak the language fluently and so come to the situation already knowing a great deal about the language. Insofar as our knowledge of language is largely *practical* knowledge rather than *theoretical* knowledge (that is, we know how to behave linguistically, but we are not generally able to describe what factors lead to our deciding how to act in any given case), we may have to reflect to decide whether something is true a priori. But our reflection is not a process of examining some mysterious Platonic entities—our reflection consists of our deciding what we would say in certain circumstances, thus deciding whether something is a rule of language. Consequently, although our purportedly a priori knowledge *seems* to be independent of all experience, it is not really. It is based on an introspective examination of our own willingness, as speakers of the language, to say certain things. Although this knowledge is empirical, it is not based on the sort of inquiry that would be undertaken by a linguist studying some previously untranslated language. This is the reason it seems to be nonempirical, and this is the reason we may be initially reluctant to say that our a priori knowledge is merely knowledge of rules of language.

The rules of language must consist of more than just definitions of words. Of course, there are also syntactical rules, but more important for present purposes, there must also be rules relating words to the world—rules telling us *how to use* certain words. For example, we must have a rule telling us how to (under what circumstances we can) justifiably assert "That is red". We cannot teach the use of "red" simply by relating it to other words. The use of the word "red" must be taught ostensively rather than verbally. This rule can of course be expressed verbally, but only trivially, viz., by saying that "x is red" is true iff x is red. These are rules of practice, or perhaps better, pragmatic rules. Thus we have at least three kinds of rules—syntactical rules, semantical rules relating words to words, and pragmatic rules relating words to the world. Of course, in a broader sense the pragmatic rules are also semantical, giving, as they do, part of the meaning of the word.

Pragmatic rules are important for the conventionalist explanation of a priori truth. There is an undeniable phenomenological difference between those a priori truths that are somehow "self-evident", that we can just "see" without giving proofs, and those that must be proven. Conventionalism must be able to explain this difference. It seems that it can do so in terms of pragmatic rules. Our linguistic behavior is psychologically conditioned to proceed in terms of certain rules. But given that we behave *in terms of* certain rules, it follows logically that we behave *in accordance with* infinitely many other "derivative" rules. Those semantical rules that we behave in terms of provide us with self-evident truths—we can ascertain that these truths are true simply by reflecting on what we would be willing to say under certain circumstances. But those a priori truths that reflect derivative linguistic rules may not be at all obvious to us. We can only determine their truth by seeing that they are logical consequences of self-evident a priori truths. If this were taken to mean that we must have not only linguistic knowledge but also independent knowledge of the truths of logic, then we would be back in the position of the Fregean logicist and would find ourselves unable to explain a priori knowledge. However, the inferences that we must make in proving non-self-evident a priori truths on the basis of self-evident ones can be explained in terms of another kind of linguistic knowledge—knowledge of *how to make inferences*, which knowledge is provided by our being conditioned to follow certain pragmatic rules. For example, consider the meaning of "if . . . then". The rules giving the meaning of "if . . . then" cannot be simply semantical rules. For example, part of the meaning of "if . . . then" is contained in the rule which tells us that from *P* and "if *P* then *Q*" we can infer *Q*. This latter rule cannot be a semantical rule. Such a semantical rule would say simply that "if *P* and, if *P* then *Q*, then *Q*" is true, but this rule would be no help because the expression of this rule uses "if . . . then" in an essential way and consequently we could not understand the rule unless we already understood "if . . . then". Instead we must have a pragmatic rule telling us *to do* something—to infer *Q* from "*P* and if *P* then *Q*". Thus, whereas semantical rules provide us with self-evident truths, some pragmatic rules provide us with "obvious" rules of inference. Combining the two kinds of rules, we can arrive at a priori truths that are not self-evident.

The picture of a priori knowledge provided by conventionalism is very seductive. It seems to explain something quite mysterious—a priori knowledge—in terms of something not at all mysterious—our knowledge of the rules of the language we speak. Unfortunately, popular though this position is, it is subject to several insurmountable difficulties. The simplest objection to conventionalism is that a priori truth resides, not in linguistic expressions, but rather in what they express. According to conventionalism, what is true a priori is a sentence of the language. But this is just a mistake. We must distinguish between, for example, knowing that all bachelors are unmarried and knowing that the sentence "All bachelors are unmarried" is true (or better, expresses a true proposition). One could know that all bachelors are unmarried without speaking English or ever having heard of the English language.

What is known a priori is that all bachelors are unmarried, not that the sentence "All bachelors are unmarried" expresses a truth in English. If we were to change the meaning of the word "bachelor", this would in no way affect the truth of what we *now* mean by "All bachelors are unmarried". It would remain true that all bachelors are unmarried even if we could not express this in our language, or even if we had no language. This truth is not created by our adopting rules of language; it is true independently of any facts about language. What is true is not a sentence of the language but what is expressed by the sentence, and this is what philosophers have traditionally termed a "proposition". Of course, at this stage propositions seem like rather mysterious sorts of things, and a great deal should hopefully be said to clarify their nature, but it is inescapable that there are such things and that they rather than sentences are what are true a priori.

If the above objection to conventionalism is not deemed conclusive, it seems that we can nevertheless give an absolutely conclusive proof of the inadequacy of conventionalism as an explanation of a priori knowledge. We can do this by turning to mathematical knowledge, which is one of the clearest kinds of a priori knowledge. Consider that type of proof which is exemplified by ordinary working mathematicians doing mathematics who are not interested in the philosophy of mathematics and are not explicitly working within an axiom system. Let us call this "proof in the classical sense" or "classical proof". If we look closely at classical mathematical proof, it is apt to appear mysterious. The difficulty is, where does the mathematician get the basic principles from which his proofs begin? Where does he get his raw material? A proof does not begin from nothing. In any proof there are premises which are not proved in that proof and from which the proof proceeds. Of course, in any given proof most of the premises may have been proven previously by other proofs. But it can never be the case that *all* of the premises used in *all* of these proofs have been proven. The mathematician had to start somewhere, and what he started with he did not prove. Where do these basic premises come from?

The conventionalist answer to the above question is that these basic premises are axioms, laid down by stipulative conventions which give us the meaning or content of our mathematical concepts. On this view the basic premises are man-made—mathematicians themselves (or perhaps the linguistic community as a whole) "decided" what to take as axioms. The axioms are established by convention, and then mathematical proof can be viewed as the mechanical development of these axioms.[5]

If the conventionalist picture of mathematical proofs as the formal derivation of consequences from stipulative axioms is to explain classical mathematical proof, we must also be able to mechanize the methods by which we develop the consequences of the axioms. In other words, we must be able to work within a particular system of formal logic whose axioms and rules of inference reflect rules of language. If we could not do this, then the proof that something is a consequence of the axioms would involve what is essentially a classical mathematical proof. Combining the mathematical axioms with the axioms and rules of inference of the system of formal logic, we get a formal axiomatic theory. Then the proposal is that classical mathematical proofs are just somewhat sloppy versions of formal proofs which are part of the purely mechanical development of this formal axiomatic theory. Let us call this theory of mathematical proof the *Conventionalist Thesis.*

Now let us look at the precise content of the Conventionalist Thesis and see how it must be stated if it is to constitute a satisfactory explanation of mathematical proof. First, there may well be different axiomatic theories in different areas of mathematics. For example, there may be one for number theory, another for set theory, another for the theory of complex variables, and so on. But we can combine the axioms of all of these theories into one set of axioms yielding a single axiomatic theory which, if the Conventionalist Thesis is true, is adequate for the whole of extant mathematics. To extend this theory would be to extend extant mathematics. So let us suppose there is such an axiomatic theory *T* within which we can do all of extant mathematics. What can we require of *T* if it is to make Conventionalist Thesis true?

The first thing that comes to mind is that if proof within *T* ("*T*-proof" for short) is to constitute an explanation of classical proof, then we must be able to recognize a *T*-proof without having to rely upon a classical proof to determine that something is a *T*-proof. If we can tell that a *T*-proof is a *T*-proof without having to *prove* that it is, then we must be able to tell that it is just by looking at it. This means in particular that we must be able to tell

[5] See, for example, Hempel [1945*a*].

by inspection that a line of the proof which purports to be an axiom really is an axiom. The only properties that a sentence can be seen to have simply by inspection are its formal or syntactical properties. Thus what makes a sentence an axiom must be some purely formal or syntactical feature of it. And as we can only check the sentence for finitely many syntactical features, there must be a finite list of syntactical features adequate to characterize all of the axioms of T. Otherwise, we could not tell by inspection whether a sentence is an axiom. The axioms of T are supposed to be the result of stipulative conventions concerning what we are going to take as axioms. Thus the axioms must be given to us by a finite set of conventions, each of which tells us that all sentences satisfying some particular syntactical condition are axioms. Note also that, as we must always be able to determine that an axiom is an axiom, given any axiom we must in principle be able to determine that it satisfies these syntactical conditions. If we now form the disjunction of the syntactical conditions specified by the conventions, we can say that the axioms of T are characterized as the set of all sentences satisfying this particular (disjunctive) syntactical condition, and this condition must be such that if a sentence satisfies it then we can in principle determine that it does.[6]

Similarly, if any given line of a proposed T-proof is correctly inferable from the previous lines of the proof using any given rule of inference of T, then we must be able to tell that it is simply by inspection. Otherwise we would again have to resort to a classical proof to determine that something is a T-proof. We can think of a rule of inference as telling us that if a given sequence Σ of sentences is already a T-proof, and the sentence φ bears a certain relation $R(\Sigma, \varphi)$ to Σ, then the sequence Σ^* which results from appending φ to Σ is also a T-proof. This is the most general form of a rule of inference. As we must be able to tell by inspection that φ can be correctly inferred from Σ by a single application of this rule, $R(\Sigma, \varphi)$ must be a purely syntactical relation, and furthermore it must be one such that if it holds between a given sentence φ and a given sequence Σ, we can in principle determine that it does.

[6] Note that any recursive or recursively enumerable set of axioms satisfies this weak restriction. But by stating it in this way rather than by requiring that our axioms constitute a recursively enumerable set, which is the customary procedure, we avoid having to assume Church's Thesis.

Furthermore, as we must be able to tell just by looking at a T-proof that it is a T-proof, we must be able to tell by inspection that *there is* a rule of inference which allows us to introduce any given line of the proof. We can only check finitely many syntactical conditions R, so there must be only finitely many rules of inference in T.

Thus both the axioms and the rules of inference of T can be characterized purely syntactically. From this it follows that the notion of a T-proof can itself be defined in purely syntactical terms—a finite sequence of sentences is a T-proof iff each sentence in the sequence either is an axiom or else can be appended to the sequence of its predecessors using one of the rules of inference of T. And as we can always tell by inspection that an axiom is an axiom and that a sentence which can be correctly inferred at any given stage using the rules of inference can be so inferred, we can always tell by inspection that a T-proof is a T-proof.

This means also that theoremhood in T can be characterized syntactically. A sentence φ is a theorem of T iff there exists a finite sequence of sentences which satisfies the syntactical conditions necessary to make it a T-proof, and φ is the last member of the sequence. Furthermore, if a sentence is a theorem of T, then we can always establish that it is—simply by giving a T-proof of it.

The theory T is supposed to contain all of extant mathematics. This means in particular that we must be able to formulate sentences of elementary number theory (that is, all sentences of number theory that can be formulated in an applied first-order functional calculus in which the only nonlogical symbols are individual constants referring to the natural numbers and symbols for addition and multiplication) within the language of T. The theory called Peano's arithmetic is the theory that results from combining Peano's axioms for number theory with first-order logic with identity. The theorems of Peano's arithmetic are certainly among extant mathematics, so it must follow that they are all theorems of T—that T contains Peano's arithmetic.

Using Gödel's methods, we can now enumerate the expressions of the language of T, letting $\#\varphi$ be the Gödel number of an expression φ,[7] and then for any syntactical predicate **F** of expressions

[7] There do exist "languages" whose expressions cannot be Gödel numbered, and so it might be supposed that this provides a way of avoiding the consequences of this argument—perhaps the language of T is such a lan-

of the language of T, we can construct within elementary number theory (and hence within the language of T) a corresponding predicate F of natural numbers such that we can prove classically that, for any expression φ, $\mathrm{F}(\varphi)$ is true iff $F(\#\varphi)$ is true. In particular, remembering that theoremhood in T can be characterized syntactically, we can construct a number-theoretic predicate $P(x)$ within the language of T such that we can prove classically that

(1) for any sentence φ of the language of T, $P(\#\varphi)$ is true iff φ is a theorem of T.

Provability within T is supposed to correspond to classical provability, so we must have:

(2) For any sentence φ of the language of T, φ is provable classically iff φ is a theorem of T.

We saw that if a sentence φ is a theorem of T, we can always establish that it is simply by constructing a T-proof of it. Then using 1 we can prove classically that $P(\#\varphi)$. Hence by 2, this must be a theorem of T:

(3) For any sentence φ of the language of T, if φ is a theorem of T, then $P(\#\varphi)$ is also a theorem of T.

Presumably classical provability is consistent. If it weren't the entire enterprise of trying to explain a priori knowledge would collapse. On this supposition, it follows from 2 that T is also con-

---

guage. But this does not provide a way out. There are only two ways in which a language may fail to be Gödel numberable: (1) it may have nondenumerably many primitive symbols (e.g., a primitive individual constant for each real number); (2) the syntax may be so irregular that the sentences of the language are not generated by any regular rules. But I think that both of these alternatives are precluded by the supposed conventional origin of the language of T. First, there must be conventions which generate the sentences of the language in some mechanical manner, thus making the second alternative false. And second, those conventions must start from a finite set of primitive symbols—no language that people could actually use could have infinitely many distinct primitive symbols (although it could of course have infinitely many expressions that are generated by concatenating the primitive symbols). For example, English starts with the twenty-six letters of the alphabet and a few punctuation symbols, and then everything else is generated from these primitive symbols.

sistent. Thus the Conventionalist Thesis commits one to the following proposition:

(CT) There is a consistent theory T and a number-theoretic predicate $P(x)$ such that:
(*a*) it is provable classically that, for any φ, φ is a theorem of T iff $P(\#_\varphi)$;
(*b*) for any φ, φ is provable classically iff φ is a theorem of T;
(*c*) for any φ, if φ is a theorem of T then $P(\#_\varphi)$ is a theorem of T;
(*d*) T contains Peano's arithmetic.

I shall now prove that CT is false:

(3.1) *Theorem*: There is no theory T and predicate $P(x)$ satisfying CT.

Proof: Suppose otherwise. Using familiar Gödelian constructions, we can find a sentence θ such that $[\theta \equiv \sim P(\#_\theta)]$ is a theorem of Peano's arithmetic, and hence of T. So

(4) $[\theta \equiv \sim P(\#_\theta)]$ is a theorem of T.

Suppose θ is a theorem of T. Then by *c*, $P(\#_\theta)$ is a theorem of T. Then by 4, $\sim \theta$ is a theorem of T, which is impossible as T is consisent. Thus:

(5) θ is not a theorem of T.

This is something we have proven classically. Thus by *a*, it is provable classically that $\sim P(\#_\theta)$. From *b* we can conclude that $\sim P(\#_\theta)$ is a theorem of T. Then by 4,

(6) θ is a theorem of T.

This contradicts 5. Thus there can be no such theory T.

It follows that classical provability cannot be explicated as provability within a formal axiomatic theory, and hence that conventionalism does not provide a correct account of a priori knowledge.

A common response to this argument has been that it confuses provability in the object language with provability in the metalanguage, so let us see why this does not help. It is indeed true that the technique used in the theorem to construct a classical proof of $\sim P(\#_\theta)$ is such that, reconstructed formally, it would take place in the metalanguage. However, this makes no difference to its classical provability. Regardless of how we did it, we would have established that $\sim P(\#_\theta)$ was true a priori. Now the response is that if we allow such proofs as this, of course theoremhood within T does not correspond to classical provability; but if we add theoremhood within the metalanguage of T, and the metametalanguage of T, etc., then this will correspond to classical provability. This may well be, but it misses the whole point of conventionalism. The conventionalist does not have at his disposal this infinite hierarchy of metatheories. According to the conventionalist, what we can here and now prove classically corresponds to what can be generated from the conventions that we have here and now adopted. These conventions constitute a theory T which may be the metatheory of another theory, and this second theory may be the metatheory of another theory, etc. But as T constitutes the totality of what can be proven from the conventions so far adopted, those conventions are not adequate for the metatheory of T itself. To go on to the metatheory of T must necessarily involve the adoption of new conventions. It is quite true that the classical proof given above which cannot be carried out within T can be carried out within the metatheory of T,[8] but in order for the *conventionalist* to do this he must adopt *new* conventions which allow him to establish the new metatheory. It is simply not true that the conventions he already has are adequate for the proof of everything we can already prove. Consequently, a priori truth cannot be explained in terms of conventions that we have adopted.

4. Logical Intuitionism

4.1 *Platonism*

Conventionalism fails because we are not limited, at any one time, to a restricted set of concepts. At any time, in proving something, we can use all the concepts there are without having to lay down any new stipulations. Thus in proving $\sim P(\#_\theta)$ in

[8] This is only obviously true, however, for the *classical* metatheory of T. This indicates that we cannot just choose any old conventions; we must choose the *correct* conventions. Thus our "conventions" are not really conventions.

theorem 3.1, we were free to make use of the metalinguistic notion of provability for sentences of *T*. That we are free to use new concepts without adopting new linguistic conventions (except, perhaps, introducing new words to express the new concepts) indicates that the concepts cannot be identified with words or other linguistic entities. The concepts are there first, and the words are introduced later to express them. It is inescapable that concepts are Platonic entities, in some sense of this term. Concepts are not "made" by men any more than a priori truths are man-made. We *discover* a priori truths, and that amounts to discovering relations between concepts.

For the same reason that concepts are essentially nonlinguistic, so are the truths that report relations between concepts. These relations hold prior to their being expressible in language, and hence the a priori truths that we discover in discovering these relations between concepts cannot be identified with sentences. These truths are *propositions*, in some sense of this admittedly problematic term.

Although I proclaim that concepts and propositions are Platonic entities, I do not profess to be able to say what that means. I know what propositions and concepts are *not*, viz., sentences and words, but I do not know what they are. I use the term "Platonic entity" largely for shock value. I am primarily concerned to prize a priori truth apart from language. I do not want to go on and say anything metaphysical about what propositions and concepts are.

4.2 *Logical Intuitions*

I have argued that a priori truths report relations between concepts, but we are still left with the question of how we discover these relations. Of course, we establish many of them by giving proofs. But we have to begin our proofs with relations that we know to hold without proof. These are relations that are in some sense "self-evident". We just "see" that they hold. The conventionalist attempted to explain this intellectual seeing as linguistic knowledge, but he failed. This seeing cannot be reduced to anything else. It apprises us of relations between concepts, and as we have seen, these concepts are abstract entities. None of our other kinds of knowledge gives us access to abstract entities. In order to get at these Platonic entities we need a new mode of intuition distinct from any we have so far discussed. This mode of intuition must consist simply of this intellectual seeing which gives us knowledge of self-evident truths. This seeing must be taken seriously in its own right rather than analyzed away. There are truths that are self-evident, that we simply "see" without proof, and these form the basis for a priori knowledge. This is the position of logical intuitionism. To say that we can simply "see" these truths is to say that we know them as a result of logical or mathematical intuition.

At this point it should be emphasized that the dispute between the logical intuitionist and other philosophers is not over the existence of mathematical intuitions but rather over their logical status. Everyone must agree that there is a distinction of some sort between those mathematical truths we can just "see" without proof and those we only come to know by giving a proof. For example, suppose you are asked whether it is true that if all *A*'s are *B*'s and all *B*'s are *C*'s then all *A*'s are *C*'s. Upon reflection you will no doubt agree that this is true. How did you arrive at this conclusion? You might have reasoned it out from something else, but more likely you did not. Once you got clear on what the principle means, you just "saw" that it was true. This is an example of your logical intuition at work. The controversy between the intuitionist and the conventionalist cannot be about whether there are such things as logical and mathematical intuitions, but rather must be about their epistemological status. The intuitionist maintains that these intuitions constitute logical reasons for judging that statements are true, while the conventionalist maintains that they only constitute contingent reasons for judging that statements express rules of language. As we have seen, the conventionalist is wrong, and it seems to follow that the intuitionist, holding the only theory that is left, is correct.

The thought that mathematical and logical proof is based ultimately on intuition seems to be repugnant to many philosophers. And yet, I think that the conclusion is inescapable. We do in fact rely upon such intuitions in choosing our basic premises, and such intuitions cannot be explained away in terms of some other kind of knowledge (e.g., linguistic knowledge). There is a characteristic phenomenological state which consists of "seeing" self-evident truths, and this is what we are calling "intuition". There is no reason to think that these intuitions are in any way mysterious. We must have some sort of mental faculty that allows us to intuit these things, and this mental faculty is presumably just as capable of physiological explanation as is our faculty of sight or hearing. Even the conventionalist must agree to this. The only room for disagreement is over whether these intuitions provide logical reasons for a priori judgments. Given that conventionalism is false, it seems to follow that they must.

An objection that has frequently been raised to intuitionistic ethics will no doubt be raised here. What happens when different people's intuitions disagree? This cannot mean that the proposition in question is "true for one person" and "false for another". Truth and falsity are not relative in this way. One of the two people must be mistaken. How is it possible to decide who is right? But I think that this question is quite easily answered. Our logical intuitions can profitably be compared with our faculty of sight. Logical intuitions do not provide us with conclusive reasons for a priori judgments, any more than our sight provides us with conclusive reasons for judging the colors of things. If something looks red to us, then we have a prima facie, but not conclusive, reason for thinking that it is red. And similarly, if our logical intuitions tell us that something is true, we have a prima facie, but not conclusive, reason for thinking that it is true. We can perfectly well recognize a logical intuition to be incorrect, just as we can recognize that something is not the color it looks to us. This is done by relying upon other logical intuitions and using them to prove the falsity of what we thought we intuited to be true. A particularly clear case of this is the Axiom of Comprehension in set theory. Almost everyone's intuitions seem to be in agreement that, given any predicate $\varphi(x)$, there exists a set of all objects satisfying this predicate. But this principle leads to the set-theoretic antinomies, which are contradictions, and thus the principle is false. The proof that the principle entails a contradiction can itself be viewed as grounded on intuitions, so we are using intuitions against intuitions to show that certain intuitions are incorrect. In precisely the same manner, we use facts discovered by relying upon our sight to show that certain things are not the way they look to us. We may judge that something that looks red to us is not really red but just looks that way because there are red lights shining on it, but in order to discover the connection between the apparent color of something and its illumination by colored lights we had to rely upon our sight elsewhere. Thus our logical intuitions, like our sight, provide us with prima facie reasons for a priori judgments, but these prima facie reasons can be overriden in a particular case by using other mathematical intuitions *against* a particular intuition.

An important objection to intuitionism was raised in section 3. It was objected that "this faculty of intuition seems very mysterious, and without further elaboration it does not seem to explain anything. To say that we know a priori truths intuitively seems to amount to nothing more than saying that we know them but do not know how we know them, which is no explanation." However, this objection misconstrues the nature of our logical intuitions. They are mysterious in one respect—unlike sight, hearing, and most other modes of intuition (but in common with memory), we do not now have even a rough physiological or neurological account of the mechanism underlying these logical intuitions. However, this must not be interpreted as casting doubt upon their existence. Logically intuiting something is a phenomenologically unique experience which, although it may not be analyzable into other more familiar kinds of experience, is nevertheless a kind of experience a person can be quickly taught to recognize and label. No one can deny that there is a difference between those truths that are in some sense self-evident and those that must be proven. As such, intuitionism does not amount simply to saying that we know a priori truths but we do not know how we know them. Intuitionism tells us how we know a priori truths—in terms of our logical intuitions.

4.3 *The Phenomenology of Our Logical Intuitions*

I have argued that our a priori knowledge is based upon our logical intuitions. We are going to want to say precisely how it is based upon them, but before we can do that we must become aware of certain phenomenological features of those intuitions. As we shall see, there is more than one kind of logical intuition, and different kinds of intuitions function differently in a priori knowledge.

Some truths are self-evident. We intuit that $2 + 2 = 4$, that either it is raining or it is not raining, that it is not the case that Socrates was both bald and not bald at the same time, etc. Here we have *intuitions of truth*. But intuitions of truth are not the only kind of logical intuition. For example, we also intuit that being a bachelor requires being unmarried, or that there being ten chairs in this room requires there to be more than six chairs in the room. These are *intuitions of implication.* There is no obvious way to reduce intuitions of implication to intuitions of truth. It would be natural to suppose that we intuit the implication $(P \rightarrow Q)$ whenever we intuit the truth of $(P \supset Q)$.[9] But this fails for the simple reason that we can intuit the truth of $(P \supset Q)$ simply by intuiting either the truth of $\sim P$ or the truth of Q, and that is not enough to guarantee that we intuit an implication. The intuition of an implication takes the form of "seeing" a connection between concepts wherein one concept is "included in" another. This is phenomenologically distinct from intuiting truths.

There is a third kind of logical intuition which is particularly interesting because it has been generally overlooked. This is the *intuition of possibility.* In philosophy, when we give a counterexample to a philosophical thesis, we describe a situation that is logically possible. The situation need not be actual, because we are merely trying to show that the philosophical thesis, which claims that something is necessary, is false. But how do we know that a situation is logically possible? We know this by, in some sense, being able to conceive of the situation's actually occurring. This is a kind of logical intuition. If we did not have these intuitions, it would be inexplicable how we could ever know that something which is not true is nevertheless logically possible. Such intuitions are not involved in mathematics and so have been largely overlooked by philosophers, but paradoxically enough, they are essential to the philosopher's own discipline. It is also of interest to note that they create another dire problem for the conventionalist. There is no way that the conventionalist could explain how we can know that something is logically possible, because there is no way that these intuitions of possibility could, even with initial plausibility, be identified with knowledge of any kind of rules of language.

We have seen that there are three kinds of logical intuitions—those of truth, implication, and possibility. There is also another division of logical intuitions which cuts across this first one. A mathematician does not regard all intuitions as bases for constructing proofs. A good mathematician can often see intuitively that very complicated theorems hold, but he does not rest content with such an intuition. Rather, he uses the intuition to guide him

[9] Having made the distinction between implication and entailment, I will use "$\rightarrow$" to symbolize implication.

in proving the theorem, and if he is unable to prove the theorem, he comes to doubt the intuition. Such intuitions are psychological starting points for investigations, but they are not logical grounds for belief. On the other hand, there are intuitions that do provide starting points for proofs. The mathematician would never dream of trying to *prove* that for any two natural numbers n and m, $n + m = m + n$.[10] This he takes to be self-evident, and he will happily use it in constructing proofs of new theorems.

There is a phenomenological difference between those intuitions that provide the initial premises of proofs and those that merely guide the mathematician in trying to construct proofs. The latter involve seeing that something is true by seeing *why* it is true, whereas the former just involve seeing *that* it is true. The "why" can often be pretty vague and unarticulated; a great mathematician, upon seeing that something is true, may still have a large job ahead of him to construct a proof of it. These "why" intuitions seem to involve the mind's ability to put many steps of reasoning together at one time and leap great conceptual distances. Then it is up to the mathematician to work painfully over his leap and make the individual steps all precise.

The "why" intuitions are really intuitions to the effect that something can be proven in a certain way and are not logical intuitions in the same sense as are those that provide self-evident starting points for proofs. They are more akin to grasping how to perform some complicated physical task, and although they are psychologically important for a priori knowledge, they are not epistemologically important. The only epistemologically important intuitions are those that consist of simply seeing *that* something is true. Only these intuitions can provide us with logical reasons for a priori judgments. Let us call those intuitions that do provide us with logical reasons *simple intuitions*. Simple intuitions can never be of the "intuiting why" variety.

In light of the distinction between simple and nonsimple intuitions, let us consider once more the three kinds of intuitions: intuitions of truth, of implication, and of possibility. Are there both simple and nonsimple intuitions of each of these kinds?

Simple intuitions of implication are what are involved in con-

[10] Unless, of course, he is trying to show that it follows from the axioms of some axiomatic theory, and then he is not trying to prove that it is true (he already knew that) but rather that it follows from the axioms.

clusive reasons. Conclusive reasons are those implications that are self-evident, so in order for P to be a conclusive reason for Q, it must be possible to intuit that $(P \rightarrow Q)$. And whenever we intuit such an implication, the antecedent can provide us with a logical reason for believing the consequent.[11] It is apparent, then, that there are both simple and nonsimple intuitions of implication. The simple ones are required by conclusive reasons, and by stringing them together the mind often generates nonsimple intuitions.

Next consider intuitions of possibility. There is no way these intuitions can be reduced to intuitions either of truth or of implication. That something is possible is roughly the opposite of saying that something is necessary or that an implication holds. Thus intuitions of possibility are not replaceable by intuitions of truth or implication. It follows that there must be simple intuitions of possibility. And given that we can prove some things to be possible if we are given that other things are possible,[12] it also follows that there can be nonsimple intuitions of possibility.

But when we turn to intuitions of truth, the situation changes. There are several reasons why there can be no simple intuitions of truth. It will be argued that all intuitions of truth (except, of course, intuitions of the truth of propositions asserting implications and possibilities) are nonsimple intuitions arising out of simple intuitions of implication. The first reason there can be no simple intuitions of truth concerns how such intuitions could arise. By definition, a simple intuition is one that provides a prima facie reason for an a priori judgment. If there were simple intuitions of truth, they would provide prima facie reasons for believing the propositions intuited. The only way prima facie reasons (of any sort) can arise is as part of the justification conditions of ostensive concepts or ostensive statements. Thus there can be no simple

[11] It would be a mistake, however, to suppose that before we can take P to be a conclusive reason to believe Q, we must *come to know* that $(P \rightarrow Q)$ on the basis of our logical intuitions. If we have to know that something is a reason before we can use it as a reason, we would have an infinite regress, because knowing that something is a reason requires us to have reasons for thinking it is a reason. In order to be justified in taking P to be a conclusive reason for believing Q, it is enough if we have the intuition that $(P \rightarrow Q)$ and we have no defeaters. We need not go on and make the judgment that P does imply Q.

[12] For example, using "$\diamond$" to symbolize logical possibility, such proofs can proceed by the principle that if $\diamond P$ and $(P \rightarrow Q)$, then $\diamond Q$.

intuitions of truth for nonostensive statements. But surely if an intuition of the truth of one statement is a prima facie reason for believing it, then the intuition of the truth of any other statement must be a reason for believing it, and this cannot turn on whether the statement is ostensive. Simply put, the intuition of the truth of a statement could provide a prima facie reason for believing a statement only if this were built into the justification conditions of all statements, and it cannot be built into the justification conditions of all statements because not all statements are ostensive.

A similar problem does not arise for intuitions of implication and possibility. Intuitions of implication provide prima facie reasons only for statements of the form "$P \rightarrow Q$", and hence these prima facie reasons can be regarded as being built into the justification conditions of the concept of implication, which is an ostensive concept. Similarly, intuitions of possibility provide prima facie reasons only for statements of the form "$\Diamond P$", and so can be regarded as being built into the justification conditions of the concept of logical possibility.

A related reason why the intuitions of the truth of a statement cannot provide a prima facie reason for believing the statement is that this would lead to logical connections between distinct modes of intuition. For example, suppose one intuited the truth of "I am appeared to redly".[13] Then that intuition would give him a prima facie reason for believing that he is appeared to redly. But having this intuition and being appeared to redly are two distinct modes of intuition, and a logical connection between distinct modes of intuition is impossible. Any correlation there may be between distinct modes of intuition can only be discovered inductively—there can never be any kind of logical presumption for such a correlation.

I have argued that intuitions of truth are always nonsimple. Now I want to argue that they are of the "intuiting why" variety and arise from stringing together simple intuitions of implication. For example, consider why (P v $\sim P$) is self-evident. We do not just see *that* it is true; we see *why* it is true—because if either disjunct were false, the other would be true. And we see the latter

[13] That no one ever has such a logical intuition makes no difference to the argument. The intuition is at least a logical possibility. It could arise, presumably, through some malfunction of the nervous system.

by intuiting the implications $(\sim P \rightarrow \sim P)$ and $(\sim \sim P \rightarrow P)$. That either of these implications is in turn a reason for believing the disjunction is built into the concept of disjunction: in general, "$\sim P \rightarrow Q$" is a conclusive reason for believing "$P \vee Q$".

Similarly, consider why $\sim (P \& \sim P)$ is self-evident. Again, we see why it is true—because the first conjunct of $(P \& \sim P)$ implies the negation of the second, and this is a conclusive reason for denying a conjunction.

In general, I think that all intuitions of truth are of this character. They are intuitions of why a statement is true, and they proceed by stringing together intuitions of implication which, properly combined, yield conclusive reasons for believing the statements whose truth is intuited. If this is true, then all a priori truth can be regarded as arising ultimately out of the conclusive reasons that are built into various concepts, and hence can be regarded as arising from the meanings of concepts. In the next section I will try to say a bit more precisely just how the notion of a priori truth arises out of the notion of implication.

Before leaving the discussion of the phenomenological character of our logical intuitions, it must be noted that there is a connection between our intuitions of implication and our intuitions of possibility. Our concepts of implication and logical possibility are strongly connected. Both concepts are ostensive, and our logical intuitions provide the prima facie reasons around which their justification conditions are built. But each concept provides the defeaters for the prima facie reason involved in the other concept. For example, a logical type I defeater for an intuition that $(P \rightarrow Q)$ is the statement $\Diamond (P \& \sim Q)$. And similarly, a defeater for an intuition that $\Diamond (P \& Q)$ is the statement $(P \rightarrow \sim Q)$. For this reason, the modes of intuition involved in intuiting implication and possibility cannot be unrelated. If they were, we would have one mode of intuition logically related to another distinct mode of intuition. Our logical intuitions must be such that having an intuition of $(P \rightarrow Q)$ automatically precludes having an intuition of $\Diamond (P \& \sim Q)$, and having an intuition of $\Diamond (P \& Q)$ automatically precludes having an intuition of $(P \rightarrow \sim Q)$. We can see that this is correct if we try to say a bit more about the character of our logical intuitions.

A natural way to express the intuition involved in intuiting $\Diamond P$ is to say that it consists of "conceiving of its being the case that P".

This should not be regarded as a description of the intuition in terms of something we already understand, because the conceiving in question is a special kind of logical conceiving. For example, it is not the same thing as imagining. We can conceive of many things we cannot imagine. However, although this does nothing to clarify the concept of logical possibility, it seems to be an apt way of expressing our intuitions of possibility.

Now consider the intuition of $(P \rightarrow Q)$. This is related to the intuition of possibility. To intuit $(P \rightarrow Q)$ is to observe that conceiving of its being the case that P contains as part of it the conceiving of its being the case that Q; or more simply, *in* conceiving of its being the case that P, we conceive of its being the case that Q. For example, in conceiving of its being the case that John is a bachelor, we conceive of its being the case that John is unmarried. The "part of" relation here is the same as that in observing that raising one's arm contains as part of it raising one's forearm. We observe by introspection that one phenomenological state (the state of conceiving of its being the case that Q) is literally part of a second phenomenological state.

This account of our intuitions of implication and possibility shows that there is a connection between them. If we intuit $(P \rightarrow Q)$, we cannot simultaneously conceive of its being the case that $(P \,\&\, \sim Q)$, because in conceiving of its being the case that P we automatically conceive of its being the case that Q. There is no room for a conflict between intuitions of implication and intuitions of possibility.

5. A Priori Truth and Implication

I have given a rough account of how we discover a priori truths. We begin with our logical intuitions which provide us with prima facie reasons for "self-evident" a priori judgments. These basic judgments are judgments of implication and logical possibility. By combining these we construct proofs of new a priori truths. This is the basic picture of how we acquire a priori knowledge. Now we want to make this more precise. What we want is a complete account of the justification conditions of the concepts of implication and possibility, and then a definition of a priori truth in terms of these concepts. In what follows, we will symbolize "P is true a priori" as "$\mathfrak{R}P$" ("$\mathfrak{R}$" for "truth of reason").

5.1 *Implication*

What it means to say that $(P \rightarrow Q)$ is that Q can be validly inferred from P, possibly as a result of a long argument. The basic steps of such an argument are provided by those implications that we can simply intuit. Let us define the notions of *immediate implication* and *immediate equivalence* to represent these basic steps:

(5.1) $(P \rightarrow^* Q)$ iff P is a conclusive reason for Q.
$(P \longleftrightarrow^* Q)$ iff $(P \rightarrow^* Q)$ and $(Q \rightarrow^* P)$.

Thus immediate implications are those implications attested to by our logical intuitions. We cannot hope to give a complete list or axiomatization of all the immediate implications there are, because they arise piecemeal from all our various concepts one at a time. Thus the best we can do in characterizing implication is (1) explain how we can know immediate implications (characterize the concept in terms of its justification conditions), and (2) give a characterization of implication in terms of immediate implication.

5.1.1 *Immediate implication.*

It is rather easy to describe the justification conditions for the concept of immediate implication. To begin with:

(5.2) "S logically intuits that $(P \rightarrow Q)$" is a prima facie reason for S to think that $(P \rightarrow^* Q)$.

A type I defeater for this prima facie reason is $\diamond(P \;\&\; \sim Q)$. Furthermore, this seems to be the only type I defeater. All those cases in which we regard ourselves as having shown that an implication does not hold seem to be explicable in terms of this one reason. For example, we may reject a putative implication $(P \rightarrow Q)$ on the grounds that it has a true antecedent and false consequent. But $(P \;\&\; \sim Q)$ is a conclusive reason for thinking that $\diamond(P \;\&\; \sim Q)$, and so the implication is defeated by the possibility statement. Thus we have:

(5.3) $\diamond(P \;\&\; \sim Q)$ is a conclusive reason for judging that $\sim(P \rightarrow Q)$,

and

(5.4) $(P \rightarrow^* Q)$ is a conclusive reason for $(P \rightarrow Q)$.

By 5.3, knowing $\Diamond (P \,\&\, \sim Q)$ justifies us in judging $\sim (P \rightarrow Q)$, which by 5.4 justifies us in judging $\sim (P \rightarrow^* Q)$.

Type II defeaters for the prima facie reason formulated in 5.2 seem to be exclusively inductive. They include such things as being hypnotized, being drugged, etc.

Are there any other reasons one may have for believing that $(P \rightarrow^* Q)$? It seems that one can have an inductive reason for believing this. First, there are general theoretical reasons why this must be the case. In order for it to be possible to have inductive type II defeaters, the concept of immediate implication must be projectible. But if it is projectible, we can also determine the existence of immediate implications inductively. Second, we can describe concrete cases in which this is obviously what we are doing. For example, if one fails to have the logical intuition that $(P \rightarrow Q)$, but everyone else expresses amazement at this and professes to find it self-evident that $(P \rightarrow Q)$, one will generally give in and reluctantly agree that $(P \rightarrow^* Q)$ even though he just does not see it. Certainly he is proceeding inductively here. He has learned inductively that other people can generally be trusted regarding their reports of immediate implications, and so he takes their reports as evidence for the existence of such immediate implications even when he does not share their intuitions. This implies that failure to have the intuition that $(P \rightarrow Q)$ is not a conclusive reason for thinking that $\sim (P \rightarrow^* Q)$ but only a prima facie reason:

(5.5) "*S* does not intuit that $(P \rightarrow Q)$" is a prima facie reason for *S* to think that $\sim (P \rightarrow^* Q)$.

The defeaters for 5.5 appear to be entirely inductive.

5.1.2 *Implication.* Now consider how implications are generated by combining immediate implications. By virtue of 5.4, the immediate implications themselves give us a basic stock of implications. Then various combinations of implications constitute conclusive reasons for (i.e., immediately imply) other implications. A few obvious examples are:

(5.6) $(P \rightarrow Q) \,\&\, (Q \rightarrow R). \rightarrow^* (P \rightarrow R).$

(5.7) $(P \rightarrow Q) \,\&\, (P \rightarrow R). \rightarrow^* (P \rightarrow .Q \,\&\, R).$

(5.8) $(P \& Q. \rightarrow R) \& \Re Q. \rightarrow^* (P \rightarrow R)$.

(5.9) $(P \rightarrow Q) \rightarrow^* (\sim Q \rightarrow \sim P)$.

In assessing these principles, one must keep in mind what the meaning of implication is. To say that *P* implies *Q* is to say that *Q* can be derived from *P* by some valid argument. For example, what 5.8 tells us is that once we have established that *Q* is true a priori we can introduce it into any argument without having to count it as a premise.

Principles 5.6–5.9 are merely examples of conclusive reasons that go into making up the justification conditions of the concept of implication. No claim is made that they constitute a complete list of such reasons. We would like to be able to give such a list, but that is not something that can even be attempted here. However, we can give a less informative account of the way implication grows out of immediate implication. All principles like 5.6–5.9 have the form

$$[(P_1 \rightarrow Q_1) \& \ldots \& (P_n \rightarrow Q_n)] \rightarrow^* (P \rightarrow Q).$$[14]

Thus we can regard implication as being the closure of immediate implication under immediate implication itself. Formally:

(5.10) $(P \rightarrow \mathrm{Q})$ iff there is a sequence of ordered pairs $\langle P_1, Q_1\rangle, \ldots, \langle P_n, Q_n\rangle$ such that $P = P_n$ and $Q = Q_n$ and for each i, either $P_i \rightarrow^* Q_i$, or there are ordered pairs $\langle R_1, S_1\rangle, \ldots, \langle R_k, S_k\rangle$ preceding $\langle P_i, Q_i\rangle$ in the sequence such that $[(R_1 \rightarrow S_1) \& \ldots \& (R_k \rightarrow S_k)] \rightarrow^* (P_i \rightarrow Q_i)$.

Thus we define implication in terms of immediate implication, and characterize immediate implication in terms of its justification conditions. However, the characterization of the justification conditions of immediate implication used the notion of logical possibility, so before our account is complete we must also discuss that concept.

[14] At first, principle 5.8 seems to be a counterexample to this claim. However, we will see in section 5.4 that "$\Re Q$" can be defined as either "$\sim Q \rightarrow Q$" or "$\sim Q \rightarrow (R \& \sim R)$". Thus 5.8 can also be regarded as having this form.

5.2 *Logical Possibility*

As in the case of implication, our ultimate access to logical possibilities is through our logical intuitions. Those possibilities that are attested to directly by our intuitions of possibility can be called *immediately possible*, and symbolized as "$\Diamond *P$". This is analogous to immediate implication. Then we have:

(5.11) "S intuits that $\Diamond P$" is a prima facie reason for S to believe that $\Diamond *P$.

A logical type I defeater for this prima facie reason is a proof that P is false, i.e., $\mathfrak{R} \sim P$:

(5.12) $\mathfrak{R} \sim P \rightarrow^* \sim \Diamond *P$.

I think that this is the only noninductive type I defeater. However, there are inductive type I defeaters, just as there were for immediate implication. There are also inductive type II defeaters.

As in the case of immediate implication, not intuiting that P is a prima facie reason for thinking that P is not immediately possible:

(5.13) "S does not intuit that P" is a prima facie reason for S to believe that $\sim \Diamond *P$.

The defeaters for this prima facie reason appear to be exclusively inductive.

Our knowledge of possibilities that are not immediate possibilities arises out of our knowledge of immediate possibilities and implication. Whatever is implied by something that is possible is itself possible:

(5.14) $\Diamond P \,\&\, (P \rightarrow Q) . \rightarrow^* \Diamond Q$.

This seems to be the only way one can reason from possibilities to possibilities. No other logical laws hold which allow us to infer possibilities from possibilities. There is, however, one other way to discover that something is possible. Whatever is true is possible:

(5.15) $P \rightarrow^* \Diamond P$.

The question that now arises is how we are to define possibility. Two avenues are open to us. The standard procedure is to define

"$\Diamond P$" to mean "$\sim \mathfrak{R} \sim P$". Then we would have to prove that principles 5.14 and 5.15 hold. The other alternative is to define possibility in terms of the way we actually discover what is possible, i.e., in terms of immediate possibility and principles 5.14 and 5.15. There are three ways we can discover that P is possible. P might be true, or P might be immediately possible, or P might be implied by something Q we already know to be possible. If Q is possible because it is true, then P is true. If Q is possible because it is implied by something R which is immediately possible, then P is also implied by R. Thus this leads to a very simple definition of possibility:

$$(5.16) \quad \Diamond P \longleftrightarrow^* [P \vee (\exists Q)(\Diamond^* Q \,\&\, (Q \rightarrow P))].$$

So defined, it is an open question whether $\Diamond P$ is equivalent to $\sim \mathfrak{R} \sim P$. We will discuss this question more thoroughly in sections 5.4 and 5.6. It might be that we simply have two possibility concepts here. Possibility, as defined by 5.16, includes all those propositions which can be known a priori to be possible, and hence includes all those that are relevant as defeaters for implication. But as we shall see, there may be more propositions that are possible in the sense of not being a priori false.

We have characterized the concept of logical possibility in terms of its justification conditions. We used the concept of logical possibility in characterizing the justification conditions of implication, so this also contributes to the characterization of implication. In our characterization of logical possibility, we also used the concept of a priori truth, so we must analyze that concept before our characterization will be complete. That is our next task. At the risk of belaboring the obvious, let me point out that although implication, immediate implication, possibility, immediate possibility, and a priori truth are each characterized in terms of the others, our account is not circular. What we have here are interconnected justification conditions for ostensive concepts.

5.3 *A Priori Truth*

A priori truths are truths that can be established on the basis of our logical intuitions. Two sorts of truths that can be so established are truths saying that one statement immediately implies another, and truths saying that it is immediately possible for a statement to be true. This gives us:

(5.17) $(P \rightarrow^* Q) \supset \mathfrak{R}(P \rightarrow^* Q)$.

(5.18) $\diamond^* P \supset \mathfrak{R} \diamond^* P$.

These are our basic a priori truths. Let us call them the *self-evident* truths, and symbolize them as "$\mathfrak{R}^*P$". A priori truths that are not self-evident are derived from the self-evident ones. In what way are they derived from them? Quite simply, by being implied by them. We use the principle:

(5.19) $\mathfrak{R}P_1 \& \ldots \& \mathfrak{R}P_n \& [(P_1 \& \ldots \& P_n) \rightarrow Q]. \supset \mathfrak{R}Q$.

In this way we start with the self-evident truths, then obtain those implied by the self-evident ones, and then truths implied by these new a priori truths, and so on. However, as implication is transitive (principle 5.6) and adjunctive (principle 5.7), anything implied by propositions implied by self-evident truths is itself implied by the self-evident truths. So we can define a priori truth very simply:

(5.20) $\mathfrak{R}P \longleftrightarrow^* (\exists Q_1) \ldots (\exists Q_n)[\mathfrak{R}^*Q_1 \& \ldots \& \mathfrak{R}^*Q_n \& (Q_1 \& \ldots \& Q_{n\cdot} \rightarrow P)]$.

This, finally, completes our characterization of a priori truth, implication, and logical possibility.

5.4 *Some Formal Results*

Although our principal concern here is not with modal logic, it is illuminating to establish a few formal results regarding our concepts of a priori truth and implication. I will omit most of the proofs.

Principles 5.17 and 5.19 formulate conclusive reasons for judging that propositions are true a priori. Thus we have:

(5.21) $(P \rightarrow^* Q) \rightarrow^* \mathfrak{R}(P \rightarrow^* Q)$.

(5.22) $\mathfrak{R}P_1 \& \ldots \& \mathfrak{R}P_n \& [(P_1 \& \ldots \& P_n) \rightarrow Q]. \rightarrow^* \mathfrak{R}Q$.

It is a simple matter to list immediate implications related to the various truth functions of the propositional calculus so that we obtain the result:

(5.23) If P truth-functionally implies Q, then $P \rightarrow Q$.

Because immediate implications are conclusive reasons, we have:

(5.24) $(P \rightarrow^* Q) \supset (P \supset Q)$.

Then from 5.24 and the definition of implication (5.10) we get:

(5.25) $(P \rightarrow Q) \supset (P \supset Q)$.

We can also prove the stronger result:

(5.26) $(P \rightarrow Q) \rightarrow (P \supset Q)$.
Proof: By 5.15, $(P \mathbin{\&} \sim Q) \rightarrow \Diamond(P \mathbin{\&} \sim Q)$, and by 5.3, $\Diamond(P \mathbin{\&} \sim Q) \rightarrow \sim (P \rightarrow Q)$. So by 5.9, $(P \rightarrow Q) \rightarrow (P \supset Q)$.

From 5.10 and the transitivity of implication we obtain:

(5.27) $(P \rightarrow Q) \longleftrightarrow (\exists P_1) \ldots (\exists P_n)(\exists Q_1) \ldots (\exists Q_n)$ $\{(P_1 \rightarrow^* Q_1) \mathbin{\&} \ldots \mathbin{\&} (P_n \rightarrow^* Q_n) \mathbin{\&} [(P_1 \rightarrow^* Q_1) \mathbin{\&} \ldots \mathbin{\&}$ $(P_n \rightarrow^* Q_n) . \rightarrow (P \rightarrow Q)]\}$.

From 5.27, 5.21, and 5.22 we obtain:

(5.28) $(P \rightarrow Q) \supset \mathfrak{R}(P \rightarrow Q)$.

We derived 5.28 from immediate implications, so:

(5.29) $\mathfrak{R}[(P \rightarrow Q) \supset \mathfrak{R}(P \rightarrow Q)]$.

A theorem that will be unwelcome to many philosophers is:

(5.30) $\mathfrak{R}(P \supset Q) \supset (P \rightarrow Q)$.
Proof: By 5.22 and 5.8, $\mathfrak{R}(P \supset Q) \mathbin{\&} [R \mathbin{\&} (P \supset Q) . \rightarrow Q] . \supset (P \rightarrow Q)$. By 5.23, $[P \mathbin{\&} (P \supset Q)] \rightarrow Q$, so $\mathfrak{R}(P \supset Q) \supset (P \rightarrow Q)$.

Theorem 5.30 commits us to the infamous "paradoxes of strict implication". I do not find this bothersome, because I do not find those paradoxes paradoxical. I have argued elsewhere that the paradoxes of strict implication are just somewhat surprising theorems about implication, but are in no way paradoxical and should not be regarded as impugning the truth of principles that lead to them.[15]

From 5.29 and 5.30:

[15] See Pollock [1966]. See also Bennett [1969].

(5.31) $(P \rightarrow Q) \rightarrow \mathfrak{R}(P \rightarrow Q)$.

(5.32) $(P \rightarrow Q) \rightarrow (\mathfrak{R}P \rightarrow \mathfrak{R}Q)$.

(5.33) $(P \rightarrow Q) \longleftrightarrow \mathfrak{R}(P \supset Q)$.

Proof: By 5.26, $(P \rightarrow Q) \rightarrow (P \supset Q)$. Thus by 5.32, $\mathfrak{R}(P \rightarrow Q) \rightarrow \mathfrak{R}(P \supset Q)$. By 5.31, $(P \rightarrow Q) \rightarrow \mathfrak{R}(P \rightarrow Q)$, so by 5.6, $(P \rightarrow Q) \rightarrow \mathfrak{R}(P \supset Q)$. Conversely, by 5.32, $P \,\&\, (P \supset Q). \rightarrow Q$, so by 5.31, $\mathfrak{R}[P \,\&\, (P \supset Q). \rightarrow Q]$. By 5.8, $[P \,\&\, (P \supset Q). \rightarrow Q] \,\&\, \mathfrak{R}(P \supset Q). \rightarrow (P \rightarrow Q)$, so by 5.8, $\mathfrak{R}(P \supset Q) \rightarrow (P \rightarrow Q)$.

(5.34) $(P. \,\&\, Q. \rightarrow R) \rightarrow (P \rightarrow .Q \supset R)$.

Two traditional definitions of a priori truth are that P is true a priori iff its denial implies a contradiction, and iff it is implied by its own denial. The following two theorems justify these alternative definitions:

(5.35) $\mathfrak{R}P \longleftrightarrow (\sim P \rightarrow .Q \,\&\, \sim Q)$.

Proof: $(\sim P \rightarrow .Q \,\&\, \sim Q) \rightarrow (\sim P \supset .Q \,\&\, \sim Q)$, and $(\sim P \supset .Q \,\&\, \sim Q) \rightarrow P$. So $(\sim P \rightarrow .Q \,\&\, \sim Q) \rightarrow P$. Hencc by 5.32, $\mathfrak{R}(\sim P \rightarrow .Q \,\&\, \sim Q) \rightarrow \mathfrak{R}P$. Then by 5.31 and 5.6, $(\sim P \rightarrow .Q \,\&\, \sim Q) \rightarrow \mathfrak{R}P$. Conversely, $(P \,\&\, \sim P) \rightarrow (Q \,\&\, \sim Q)$, so by 5.34, $P \rightarrow (\sim P \supset .Q \,\&\, \sim Q)$. Then by 5.32, $\mathfrak{R}P \rightarrow \mathfrak{R}(\sim P \supset .Q \,\&\, \sim Q)$, and hence by 5.33, $\mathfrak{R}P \rightarrow (\sim P \rightarrow .Q \,\&\, \sim Q)$.

(5.36) $\mathfrak{R}P \longleftrightarrow (\sim P \rightarrow P)$.

(5.37) $\mathfrak{R}P \supset P$.

We also obtain an interesting result concerning iterated modalities:

(5.38) $\mathfrak{R}P \rightarrow \mathfrak{R}\mathfrak{R}P$.

Proof: $\mathfrak{R}P \rightarrow (\sim P \rightarrow P)$, and $(\sim P \rightarrow P) \rightarrow \mathfrak{R}(\sim P \rightarrow P)$. $(\sim P \rightarrow P) \rightarrow \mathfrak{R}P$, so $\mathfrak{R}(\sim P \rightarrow P) \rightarrow \mathfrak{R}\mathfrak{R}P$. Hence $\mathfrak{R}P \rightarrow \mathfrak{R}\mathfrak{R}P$.

By virtue of 5.38 and the other principles we have proven, the logic of implication and a priori truth satisfies all of the axioms of

Lewis's modal logic S4.[16] One naturally wonders whether it also satisfies the axioms of S5. In order to have S5 we must have the principle $(\sim \mathfrak{R}P \supset \mathfrak{R} \sim \mathfrak{R}P)$. What this principle requires is that whenever a proposition is not true a priori, we can establish a priori that it is not a priori true. This is not obvious. For example, it might happen that there are propositions which are true but unprovable, and which we can never prove to be unprovable. An example might be Fermat's conjecture. For all we know at this time, Fermat's conjecture might be true but unprovable, and furthermore it might be impossible to prove that it is unprovable; thus we would be doomed forever to look in vain for a proof or a disproof.

6. Logical Necessity and Entailment

The rather surprising observation that the principle $\sim \mathfrak{R}P \supset \mathfrak{R} \sim \mathfrak{R}P$ is problematic indicates that, although the terms "a priori true" and "necessarily true" are generally used interchangeably, it is reasonable to make a distinction between them, and correspondingly a distinction between implication and entailment. For example, consider Fermat's conjecture once more. This is the principle that for all positive integers x, y, z and for all $n > 2$, $x^n + y^n \neq z^n$. This has been proven for many particular values of n, but no one has been able to prove it for all values of n. Suppose it should happen that this principle is provable separately for each individual value of n, but there is no way to prove simultaneously that it holds for all values of n. Then each particular instance of this principle is true a priori, but the general principle is not. Still, we would want to say that the general principle is necessarily true. If each instance of it is true a priori, and hence necessarily true, then the general principle must certainly be necessary.

When a formal axiomatization of arithmetic has the characteristic that there is some predicate F such that $F(n)$ is provable for each n, but $(x)F(x)$ is not provable, the axiomatic theory is said to be *ω-incomplete*. I am raising the possibility that a priori truth may be ω-incomplete. This can be generalized to subject matters other than arithmetic. For example, in set theory we might be able to prove of each set X that $F(X)$, but be unable to prove that for

[16] See Lewis and Langford [1932].

all sets X, $F(X)$. Let us call this general phenomenon *Q-incompleteness* ("quantifier-incompleteness"). This is the only way I can see that our notion of necessary truth might diverge from our notion of a priori truth. This suggests that we can define the notion of necessary truth as the result of closing a priori truth under Q-completeness.

To make this precise we must first give a precise definition of Q-completeness. This can be done as follows. To say that necessary truth is Q-complete is to say that given any set Γ of necessarily true propositions, and any proposition P, if it is necessarily true that if every proposition in Γ is true then P is true, then P is necessarily true. Thus I suggest that we can give a recursive definition of necessary truth as follows:

(6.1) (1) If $\mathfrak{R}P$ then $\Box P$;
(2) if there is a set Γ of propositions such that (Q) $(Q \varepsilon \Gamma \supset \Box Q)$ and $\Box$(if all propositions in Γ are true then P is true), then $\Box P$.

A proposition is necessarily true iff its being necessarily true results from clauses 1 and 2 of 6.1.[17]

Of course, it is still an open question whether there is any difference between necessary truth and a priori truth. It could turn out that a priori truth is Q-complete. But at this time I can see no good reason to think that it is.

If there are necessary truths that are not true a priori, how could we ever find out that they are true? The only way this could conceivably be done is by induction. No other method presents itself. This sounds very peculiar. Most mathematicians would be horrified at the thought that one could discover the necessary truth of a proposition inductively. Should we conclude then that induction is not applicable here (i.e., necessary truth is not projectible), and hence necessary truths that are not a priori true are simply

[17] It can be shown that the modal logic resulting from this definition of necessity is precisely S5. The proof is too complicated to give here, but the idea is the following. We define validity as in Pollock [1967*a*] by requiring that every substitution instance of a valid formula be necessary. It is then verified that the axioms for S5 given in Lemmon [1957] are valid. The proofs are generally by mathematical induction, using definition 6.1, and make heavy use of Q-completeness. The completeness of S5 follows from the results of Pollock [1967*b*].

unknowable? I think not. A bit of reflection indicates that it must be possible to discover necessary truth inductively. First, a priori truth is definitely projectible. For example, if I read a textbook in mathematics and this textbook asserts that a certain proposition is provable, but that the proof is too complicated to be given at this time and so the proposition will be assumed without proof, surely I am justified in believing the author when he says that the proposition is provable. The only justification that could possibly be given for my accepting what I find in the textbook is an inductive justification. We are inductively justified in believing claims that are made in accepted mathematical textbooks. Thus it is possible to be inductively justified in believing that a certain proposition is true a priori. But then there should be no obstacle to becoming inductively justified in believing that every proposition in a set Γ is true a priori. For example, we might become inductively justified in believing that the answer to the four-color problem is affirmative. That is, upon seeing that a truly vast number of maps can be colored with four colors, we could become justified in believing that this is true of all maps. I would suggest that this is the situation we are really in with respect to the four-color problem. Although we cannot (now) prove that all maps can be colored with four colors, I think we are inductively justified in believing that they can. Consequently, we are inductively justified in believing that this is a necessary truth.

Obviously, an inductive justification of a necessary truth is not as good as a proof of it. This is the reason a mathematician would disdain such a justification. But there is one area quite close to home in which the inductive justification of necessary truths may be very important. I admit that this is almost pure speculation, but this may be what philosophers do when they defend a philosophical thesis by looking at numerous examples. When a philosopher is trying to establish some general principle about concepts, he often proceeds by looking at many specific cases and showing that the principle holds in each of them. His judgments about the specific cases would seem to be a priori. But when he then concludes that the principle holds in general in all cases, it is at least plausible to suppose that he is proceeding inductively. As I say, this is pure speculation, but it at least suggests that the inductive discovery of necessary truths may be of some importance.

7. Conclusions

We have given characterizations of the concepts of a priori truth, implication, possibility, necessary truth, and entailment. What can we conclude about the traditional views concerning these concepts? First, consider the question of analyticity. Traditionally, an analytic truth has been characterized as one that is true by virtue of meaning. This is ambiguous at best. It might be taken as meaning that analytic truths are those truths that one can discover by reflecting upon meaning. So defined, analytic truths must be true a priori. Hence necessary truths, insofar as they are not true a priori, would not be analytic. However, by principles 5.35 and 5.36, it follows that all a priori truths are analytic. By those principles, a priori truth can be defined in terms of implication, and implications can all be discovered a priori by combining immediate implications. As immediate implications are conclusive reasons, they all arise out of the meanings of propositions. Thus a priori truths are discoverable by reflection upon meaning.

However, the definition of analyticity might be taken instead to mean that a truth is analytic if what makes it true is relations of meaning. This is admittedly vague, but it can be construed to imply that all necessary truths are analytic. Necessary truths all result, ultimately, from immediate implications, and so result from relations of meaning.

A common definition of either a priori truth or necessity is in terms of the law of noncontradiction. It is often proposed that a proposition is either true a priori, or necessary, if its denial contains a contradiction. This can be made a correct definition of either a priori truth or necessary truth depending upon whether we interpret "contains" in terms of implication or entailment. A proposition is true a priori iff its denial implies a contradiction, and a proposition is necessarily true iff its denial entails a contradiction.

The most important characterization of a priori truth is in terms of our logical intuitions. This is the characterization that explains how a priori knowledge is possible. Numerous philosophers have criticized Hume, Kant, and others for giving both a "psychologistic criterion" of a priori truth and a "purely logical one" in terms of the law of noncontradiction.[18] But as Quine observed, the definition

[18] For example, see Ayer [1946], p. 78.

in terms of implication and the law of noncontradiction is essentially circular, failing, as it does, to break out of the circle of logical concepts like a priori truth, implication, possibility, etc., all of which stand in equal need of clarification. It is only the characterization of a priori truth in terms of our logical intuitions that succeeds in clarifying this concept to such an extent that we can begin to assess some of the traditional views regarding it.

References

Armstrong, David M.

1963 Is introspective knowledge incorrigible? *The Philosophical Review* 72: 417-432.

Austin, John L.

1962 *Sense and sensibilia.* Oxford: Oxford University Press.

Ayer, Alfred J.

1946 *Language, truth, and logic*, 2nd ed. New York: Dover.

1953 One's knowledge of other minds. In *Philosophical Essays.* London: Macmillan.

1956 *The problem of knowledge.* Oxford: Oxford University Press.

1964 The concept of a person. In *The concept of a person, and other essays.* London: Macmillan.

Benjamin, B. S.

1956 Remembering. *Mind* 65: 312-335. Reprinted in Gustafson [1964], pp. 171-194.

Bennett, Jonathan

1969 Entailment. *The Philosophical Review* 78: 197-236.

Blanshard, Brand

1939 *The nature of thought.* London: Allen and Unwin.

Campbell, Norman R.

1920 *Physics: The elements.* Cambridge: Cambridge University Press.

1957 *Foundations of science.* New York: Dover.

References

Care, Norman S., and Grimm, Robert H., eds.

1969 *Perception and personal identity*. Cleveland: Case Western Reserve.

Carnap, Rudolph

1950 *The logical foundations of probability*. Chicago: University of Chicago Press.

1956 The methodological character of theoretical concepts. In *Minnesota studies in the philosophy of science*, vol. 1, ed. H. Feigl et al. Minneapolis: University of Minnesota Press.

Castañeda, Hector-Neri

1966 Consciousness and behavior: Their basic connections. In *Intentionality, minds, and behavior*, ed. Castañeda. Detroit: Wayne State University Press.

Chisholm, Roderick

1957 *Perceiving*. Ithaca: Cornell University Press.

1966 *Theory of knowledge*. Englewood Cliffs: Prentice-Hall.

1969 The loose and popular and the strict and philosophical senses of identity. In Care and Grimm [1969].

Cowley, Frazer

1971 The identity of a person and his body. *The Journal of Philosophy* 68: 678-683.

Davidson, Donald

1966 Emeroses by other names. *The Journal of Philosophy* 63: 778-780.

Deutscher, Max, and Martin, C. B.

1966 Remembering. *The Philosophical Review* 75: 161-196.

Donnellan, Keith

1966 Reference and definite descriptions. *The Philosophical Review* 75: 281-304.

Geach, Peter T.

1962 *Reference and generality*. Ithaca: Cornell University Press.

1967 Identity. *The Review of Metaphysics* 21: 3-12.

Gettier, Edmund

1963 Is justified true belief knowledge? *Analysis* 23: 121-123.

Goodman, Nelson
1955 *Fact, fiction, and forecast.* Cambridge: Harvard University Press.

Gozzaniga, Michael S.
1967 The split brain in man. *Scientific American,* August 1967, pp. 24-29.

Grice, H. P., and Strawson, Peter F.
1956 In defense of dogma. *The Philosophical Review* 65: 141-158.

Grimm, Robert H., and Care, Norman S., eds.
1969 *Perception and personal identity.* Cleveland: Case Western Reserve.

Gustafson, Donald F., ed.
1964 *Essays in philosophical psychology.* Garden City: Doubleday.

Hempel, Carl G.
1943 A purely syntactic definition of confirmation. *The Journal of Symbolic Logic* 8: 122-143.
1945 Studies in the logic of confirmation. *Mind* 54: 1-26, 97-121.
1945*a* On the nature of mathematical proof. *American Mathematical Monthly* 52: 543-556.
1958 The theoretician's dilemma. In *Minnesota studies in the philosophy of science,* vol. 2, ed. H. Feigl et al. Minneapolis: University of Minnesota Press.

Henze, Donald F., and Saunders, John Turk
1967 *The private language problem.* New York: Random House.

Langford, C. H., and Lewis, Clarence Irving
1932 *Symbolic logic.* New York: Appleton-Century.

Lemmon, E. J.
1957 New foundations for Lewis modal systems. *The Journal of Symbolic Logic* 22: 176-185.

Lewis, Clarence Irving
1946 *An analysis of knowledge and valuation.* LaSalle: Open Court.

Lewis, Clarence Irving, and Langford, C. H.
1932 *Symbolic logic*. New York: Appleton-Century.

Malcolm, Norman
1958 Knowledge of other minds. *The Journal of Philosophy* 60: 969-978.
1963 *Knowledge and certainty*. Englewood Cliffs: Prentice-Hall.

Martin, C. B., and Deutscher, Max
1966 Remembering. *The Philosophical Review* 75: 161-196.

Meehl, Paul E.
1966 The complete autocerebroscopist: A thought-experiment on Professor Feigl's mind-body identity thesis. In *Mind, matter, and method*, ed. P. F. Feyerabend and G. Maxwell. Minneapolis: University of Minnesota Press.

Nagel, Ernest
1961 *The structure of science*. New York: Harcourt, Brace, and World.

Parfit, Derek
1971 Personal identity. *The Philosophical Review* 80: 3-27.

Pollock, John L.
1966 The paradoxes of strict implication. *Logique et analyse* 34: 180-196.
1967 Criteria and our knowledge of the material world. *The Philosophical Review* 76: 28-62.
1967*a* Logical validity in modal logic. *The Monist* 51: 128-135.
1967*b* Basic modal logic. *The Journal of Symbolic Logic* 32: 355-365.
1967*c* Mathematical proof. *American Philosophical Quarterly* 4: 238-244.
1968 What is an epistemological problem? *American Philosophical Quarterly* 5: 183-190.
1970 The structure of epistemic justification. *American Philosophical Quarterly*, monograph series 4, pp. 62-78.
1972 The logic of projectibility. *Philosophy of Science* 39: 302-314.
1973 Laying the raven to rest. *Journal of Philosophy* 70: 747-754.

Putnam, Hilary
1966 The analytic and the synthetic. In *Minnesota studies in the philosophy of science*, vol. 3, ed. H. Feigl and G. Maxwell. Minneapolis: University of Minnesota Press.

Quine, Willard Van Orman
1951 Two dogmas of empiricism. *The Philosophical Review* 60: 20-43. Reprinted in Quine [1953].
1953 *From a logical point of view*. Cambridge: Harvard University Press.
1960 *Word and object*. New York: MIT Press and Wiley.

Quinton, Anthony M.
1955 The problem of perception. *Mind* 64: 28-51.
1973 *The nature of things*. London: Routledge and Kegan Paul.

Russell, Bertrand
1912 *The problems of philosophy*. Oxford: Oxford University Press.
1914 On the nature of acquaintance. *The Monist* 24: 1-16, 161-187, 435-453, 582-593.
1921 *The analysis of mind*. London: Macmillan.
1948 *Human knowledge: Its scope and limits*. New York: Simon and Schuster.

Saunders, John Turk, and Henze, Donald F.
1967 *The private language problem*. New York: Random House.

Sellars, Wilfrid
1963 *Science, perception, and reality*. London: Routledge and Kegan Paul.

Shoemaker, Sydney
1963 *Self-knowledge and self-identity*. Ithaca: Cornell University Press.
1969 Time without change. *The Journal of Philosophy* 66: 363-381.
1969*a* Comments on Chisholm [1969]. In Care and Grimm [1969].

Squires, Robert
1969 Memory unchained. *The Philosophical Review* 77: 178-197.

Strawson, Peter F.
1952 *Introduction to logical theory*. London: Methuen.
1959 *Individuals*. London: Methuen.

Strawson, Peter F., and Grice, H. P.
1956 In defense of dogma. *The Philosophical Review* 65: 141-158.

Thomson, Judith Jarvis
1965 Reasons and reasoning. In *Philosophy in America*, ed. Max Black. Ithaca: Cornell University Press.

Williams, Bernard
1956 Personal identity and individuation. *Proceedings of the Aristotelian Society* 57: 229-252. Reprinted in Gustafson [1964].
1970 The self and the future. *The Philosophical Review* 79: 161-180.

Wittgenstein, Ludwig
1953 *Philosophical investigations*. Translated by G.E.M. Anscombe. New York: Macmillan.

Index

Index

Library of Congress Cataloging in Publication Data

Pollock, John L
Knowledge and justification.

Bibliography: p.
Includes index.
1. Knowledge, Theory of. 2. Concepts. 3. Analysis (Philosophy). 4. Perception. I. Title.
BD161.P725 1975 121 74-2974
ISBN 0-691-07203-5